T0192631

Beginning Visual Studio for Mac

Build Cross-Platform Apps with Xamarin and .NET Core

Alessandro Del Sole

Apress®

Beginning Visual Studio for Mac

Alessandro Del Sole
Cremona, Italy

ISBN-13 (pbk): 978-1-4842-3032-9   ISBN-13 (electronic): 978-1-4842-3033-6
https://doi.org/10.1007/978-1-4842-3033-6

Library of Congress Control Number: 2017957992

Cover image by Freepik (www.freepik.com).

Managing Director: Welmoed Spahr
Editorial Director: Todd Green
Acquisitions Editor: Joan Murray
Development Editor: Laura Berendson
Technical Reviewer: Jordan Matthiesen and Mathieu Clerici
Coordinating Editor: Jill Balzano
Copy Editor: Kim Wimpsett

Distributed to the book trade worldwide by Springer Science+Business Media New York, 233 Spring Street, 6th Floor, New York, NY 10013. Phone 1-800-SPRINGER, fax (201) 348-4505, e-mail orders-ny@springer-sbm.com, or visit www.springeronline.com. Apress Media, LLC is a California LLC and the sole member (owner) is Springer Science + Business Media Finance Inc (SSBM Finance Inc). SSBM Finance Inc is a **Delaware** corporation.

For information on translations, please e-mail rights@apress.com, or visit www.apress.com/rights-permissions.

Apress titles may be purchased in bulk for academic, corporate, or promotional use. eBook versions and licenses are also available for most titles. For more information, reference our Print and eBook Bulk Sales web page at www.apress.com/bulk-sales.

Any source code or other supplementary material referenced by the author in this book is available to readers on GitHub via the book's product page, located at www.apress.com/9781484230329. For more detailed information, please visit www.apress.com/source-code.

Printed on acid-free paper

To my father, the brave, strong man I always hope to be like.
To Angelica, who brings the sunshine into my life every day.
To my mother, I can feel you're still around.

Contents at a Glance

Contents

About the Author

Alessandro Del Sole has been a Microsoft Most Valuable Professional (MVP) since 2008, and he is a Xamarin Certified Mobile Developer and Microsoft Certified Professional. Awarded MVP of the Year in 2009, 2010, 2011, 2012, and 2014, he is internationally considered a Visual Studio expert and a .NET authority. He has authored many books on programming with Visual Studio, Xamarin, and .NET, and he has blogged and written numerous technical articles about Microsoft developer topics in Italian and English for many developer sites, including MSDN Magazine and the Visual Basic Developer Center from Microsoft. He is a frequent speaker at Microsoft technical conferences, and his Twitter alias is @progalex.

About the Technical Reviewers

Jordan Matthiesen is a motivated and personable technology leader with nearly 14 years of experience successfully delivering technology solutions for product companies, marketing teams, and governments. He is an expert in web solutions architecture and development, using tools and techniques such as Microsoft .NET, HTML5, JavaScript, Ajax, high-performance web site design, test-driven development, unit testing, and Microsoft SQL Server. Jordan's specialties include solutions architecture, Microsoft .NET, team leadership, project management, and software development.

Mathieu Clerici is the CEO and lead Xamarin architect at Los Xamarinos, a Xamarin consultancy company. He has been a .NET developer since 2009 and has been focused on Xamarin development since 2013. He frequently gives speeches at monthly .NET mobile meetups in Guadalajara about Xamarin technology and contributes to open source Xamarin plug-ins in his spare time.

Acknowledgments

Writing books is hard work, not only for the author but also for all the people involved in the reviews and in the production process.

Therefore, I would like to thank Joan Murray, Jill Balzano, Laura Berendson, and everyone at Apress who contributed to publishing this book and made the process much more pleasant.

A very special thanks to Jordan Matthiesen and the people on the Visual Studio for Mac team at Microsoft who have tech-edited this book. These folks did an incredible job walking through every single sentence and every single line of code, and their contributions were invaluable to the creation of this book.

I would also like to thank the Technical Evangelism team of the Italian subsidiary of Microsoft and my Microsoft MVP lead, Cristina G. Herrero, for their continuous support and encouragement for my activities.

As the community leader of the Italian Visual Studio Tips & Tricks community (`www.visualstudiotips.net`), I want to say "thank you!" to the other team members (Laura La Manna, Renato Marzaro, Antonio Catucci, and Igor Damiani) and to our followers for keeping strong our passion for sharing knowledge and helping people solve problems in their daily work.

Thanks to my everyday friends, who are always ready to encourage me even if they are not developers.

Finally, special thanks to my girlfriend, Angelica, who knows how strong my passion for technology is and who never complains about the time I spend writing.

Introduction

In recent years, the world of software development has changed a lot and for many reasons. Among others, the large diffusion of mobile devices with different operating systems and of cloud platforms and services has had a huge impact on the way developers write code and what they write code for. If you think about how software development was just a few years ago, you will recognize some even bigger changes.

In fact, in the past, if you wanted (or needed) to build applications for different operating systems, platforms, or devices, you had to use proprietary development tools and native frameworks on each specific platform. For example, Microsoft Visual Studio has always been the development environment of choice if you wanted to build Windows and web applications based on the .NET Framework with C#, F#, Visual Basic, and C++. If you are like me and you have a lot of experience with .NET on Windows, you know how powerful the .NET technology is. However, the limitation is that it runs only on Windows, which means it requires you to publish your .NET web apps and services only to Windows Server systems, while many companies actually want Linux as the host. Additionally, developers working on the Apple stack do not have a framework available that allows for building web apps and services at all. As another example, building mobile apps for Android, iOS, and Windows 10 requires knowledge of native frameworks, development tools, and languages, such as Java and Google Android Studio for Android, Apple Xcode and Swift or Objective-C for iOS, and Microsoft Visual Studio and C# (or Visual Basic) for Windows 10. As an implication, the effort your company might need to make to publish an app on all the major stores can be huge and might involve hiring several specialized developers to reduce the development time, which will mean higher costs. Or this might mean waiting for the current developers to acquire the skills and experience they need to build apps for different systems, which might save some money but requires much more time. And you know that time is money. The list of examples might be longer and involve other technologies, such as cloud platforms and containers, but these two are enough to give you an idea of what software development was at a certain point in time. Concurrently, the demand for applications and services to be available on multiple platforms has increased in the market. In summary, many companies have been in a situation in which they needed to be on multiple platforms but with either limited resources or a very big effort.

Microsoft was aware of all the aforementioned problems, and in the last years the company has significantly changed its vision and strategy, opening up to other platforms, embracing open source, and focusing even more on cloud services. In fact, Microsoft has been making huge investments in bringing technologies, platforms, developer tools, frameworks, and services to other operating systems such as Linux and macOS and to typically non-Microsoft audiences by focusing on services much more than in the past. In this strategy, cross-platform development is of primary importance and relies on two major technologies (apart from cloud services and platforms).

- .NET Core, a modular, open source, cross-platform subset of the .NET Framework that enables developers to write applications and services that run on Windows, Linux, and Mac in C# and F#

- Xamarin, a technology that allows developers to write mobile applications that run on Android, iOS, and Windows with C# and F#

In this vision, there is one important pillar: using .NET languages such as C# and F# to write code for any platform. The most important thing is that developers can reuse their .NET skills on Linux and macOS, not just Windows. But to make this possible, developers need professional tools they can use to create the next generation of application. Those working on Windows have Visual Studio 2017, the most powerful version ever of the premiere development environment from Microsoft, which now supports a variety of non-Microsoft technologies. For other systems, Microsoft released Visual Studio Code (http://code. visualstudio.com), an open source, cross-platform tool that provides an enhanced coding experience. However, Visual Studio Code has no built-in designer tools, has no support for Xamarin (at least currently), and does not provide specialized tools that developers might need, for example, integrated publishing tools or profiling instruments. After all, its focus is on providing an evolved editing experience. With its history and tradition of delivering the best developer tools in the world and because you need a Mac to build, sign, and distribute apps for iOS and macOS, Microsoft finally released Visual Studio 2017 for Mac (in May 2017), an integrated development environment that can be used on macOS to build apps that run on any platform and any device in C# and F# and that perfectly fits into this mobile-first, cloud-first vision. Visual Studio 2017 for Mac is neither a simple porting of Visual Studio on Windows nor is it an evolution of Visual Studio Code. Instead, it is a professional development environment specifically built for the Mac, with native user interface and tools tailored for macOS and for cross-platform development.

This book provides a comprehensive guide to Visual Studio 2017 for Mac, paying particular attention to the integrated development environment, the workspace, and all the integrated tools you can leverage to build high-quality, professional applications for mobile devices and the Web, using C# as the programming language of choice. A basic knowledge of C# is strongly recommended to get the most out of the book because it is not possible to concurrently teach the language and the Visual Studio for Mac environment in one book. Therefore, I will assume you are familiar with the syntax and with the most common constructs. You will also find an introduction to the Xamarin and .NET Core technologies so that you will learn the necessary foundations to get started. Then you will be able to separately deep-dive into both technologies. Actually, with Visual Studio for Mac, you can also develop games based on Unity (http://unity3d.com). Game development with Unity will not be covered in this book, but it is worth mentioning that Visual Studio for Mac already includes the tools for Unity out of the box, and you only have to install the Unity engine separately.

Visual Studio 2017 for Mac is available in three different editions: Community, Professional, and Enterprise. If you do not have an MSDN subscription and you are an individual developer, you can install the Community edition for free from http://bit.ly/2tsuJvR. This edition can also be used under strict licensing terms in both enterprise and nonenterprise organizations. Microsoft has a specific page that describes the license for Visual Studio 2017 for Mac Community, available at www.visualstudio.com/license-terms/mlt553321.

Unless expressly specified, all the topics described in this book are available in all three editions. Regarding system requirements, you will need a Mac with at least 4GB RAM, an 1.8GHz processor, and 1GB of disk space. El Capitan 10.11 is the minimum version of macOS that supports Visual Studio for Mac. Of course, the recommended configuration is with macOS Sierra 10.12 and with 8GB RAM. Just to give you an idea, the machine I used to write this book is a Mac Mini 2014 with 8GB RAM.

After this short introduction, it is time to get started. But before you can put your hands on Visual Studio for Mac, you need to set up and configure your Mac machine for development. That is what Chapter 1 is going to explain.

PART I

Preparing for Development

CHAPTER 1

■ ■ ■

Configuring the Mac Development Machine

Visual Studio 2017 for Mac is a full-stack and *mobile-first, cloud-first* integrated development environment (IDE) that allows you to build a variety of mobile and web applications using the most powerful technologies from Microsoft, such as Xamarin for iOS and Android development and .NET Core for web development, using C# and F# as the programming languages.

To fully leverage all the powerful features that Visual Studio 2017 for Mac offers, you first need to enable some Apple services, and you need to install and configure Apple's software development kits (SDKs) on the development machine. In this chapter, you will learn how to configure your Mac development machine from start to end. If you already have experience in building applications with the Apple developer tools on a Mac, the first part of this chapter is just a recap. If you instead come from the Microsoft Windows world, the entire chapter provides guidance to properly set up your Mac for the first time, explaining a number of concepts that you might not be familiar with. By completing this chapter, you will be ready to start building mobile and web apps with Visual Studio for Mac. Going forward, I will refer to Visual Studio 2017 for Mac also as Visual Studio for Mac, Visual Studio, or VS for Mac interchangeably.

Getting an Apple ID

An Apple ID is a valid e-mail address that is linked to a number of Apple's services and is required to set up a developer account. If you own an iPhone or an iPad, you probably already have one because it is required to download apps from the Apple Store, to access iTunes, and to set up your profile.

An Apple ID can be any valid e-mail address with any e-mail provider, so it is not necessary to create a new alias for development. Instead, you can easily associate an existing e-mail address as an Apple ID. Whether you create a new e-mail address or use an existing e-mail address, you can create your Apple ID at `http://appleid.apple.com/account`.

■ **Note**   When you buy a Mac computer and you turn it on for the first time, during the first configuration macOS will ask you to enter your Apple ID. Though this is not mandatory, it is strongly recommended that you supply your Apple ID at this point so that the operating system can set up your user profile. For this reason, it is important that you get your Apple ID before you do anything else on your Mac.

© Alessandro Del Sole 2017
A. Del Sole, *Beginning Visual Studio for Mac*, https://doi.org/10.1007/978-1-4842-3033-6_1

The Apple ID's management page will ask you to enter your basic personal information, including your e-mail address, and ask you to specify your security questions and the list of news you want to receive in your inbox (optional). As you will see, this is a simple step.

Upgrading macOS

The Apple SDKs and developer tools typically require the latest version of the operating system. At this writing, the most recent version of macOS is 10.12.3 (also known as Sierra). Having that said, open the App Store, select Updates, and make sure you install any updates available for macOS before going on.

Creating a Developer Account

With macOS, you can build applications using Xcode, the proprietary development environment from Apple, or with third-party development tools such as Microsoft Visual Studio.

When compiling an application for iOS or macOS, third-party development tools will invoke Xcode and the Apple SDKs behind the scenes to produce the binaries. Regardless of the tool you use, Xcode needs to know and recognize who is going to build applications on the Mac. For this reason, every developer needs a so-called developer account. A developer account is required to set up the proper development certificates on the Mac and to test and debug an application on a physical device. Actually, a developer account is also required to publish apps to the Apple Store. Apple provides the following options to get a developer account:

- *Free developer account*: This is the most basic account and can be easily enabled with your Apple ID.

- *Apple Developer Program*: This is a paid account and provides everything developers need to build, test, debug, and publish apps to the App Store. This account includes cloud-based analytics and allows for distributing private builds to testers.

- *Apple Developer Enterprise Program*: This is a paid account and provides specific options for signing and distributing in-house apps within the organization.

- *MFi program*: This is a special program that allows developers to get all the components, tools, and documentation required to build electronic accessories that connect to the iPhone, the iPad, and the iPod.

In this book, I will use the free developer account for your convenience. However, the free account has the following limitations that you should keep in mind once you get more experienced in building apps for iOS with Visual Studio and Xamarin:

- You can deploy apps to only one physical device. This must be your own device.

- You cannot publish apps to the App Store.

- You cannot distribute an app to testers with the Test Flight service, and you cannot compile your code using the ad hoc or in-house configurations.

- You cannot leverage tools and services such as iCloud, push notifications, in-app purchases, the Game Center, and the wallet.

- Your Apple ID must not be already associated to other Apple Developer programs.

You can find more information about the aforementioned account options and pricing at http://developer.apple.com/programs. In the next sections, I will explain how to set up the free developer account in Xcode.

Installing and Configuring Xcode

The Apple SDKs and development tools are the foundation for building apps on a Mac machine. Actually, you do not need Xcode if you only want to build .NET Core applications with Visual Studio for Mac, but because this book also explains how to create iOS apps with Xamarin, Xcode is a requirement. This section explains how to install and configure Xcode before moving on to installing Visual Studio for Mac.

Installing Xcode

Xcode is the integrated development environment from Apple. You use Xcode to build native apps for macOS, iOS, and tvOS.

Of course, this is not the topic of this book, but Visual Studio for Mac invokes Xcode to compile your Xamarin projects for iOS and macOS, so you need to install it before you do anything else. Open the App Store and search for *Xcode*. If you click the Xcode icon, you will see all the information about the latest available release. Figure 1-1 shows how Xcode appears in the App Store.

Figure 1-1. *Installing Xcode from the App Store*

On your machine, you will see Install instead of Open. The current version of Xcode is 9.0 and requires at least version 10.12.6 of macOS. The download size of Xcode is 5.39GB, so it will take some time to download and install. The App Store takes care of installing Xcode the proper way, so you just need to wait. The installation also includes all the necessary Apple SDKs and the iOS simulator, which will be useful when testing and debugging apps for the iPhone and the iPad.

Configuring the Developer Profile

After the installation has completed, the next step is configuring the developer profile inside Xcode. This involves creating a blank project and configuring the developer account so that Xcode can generate signing identities and team provisioning profiles.

■ **Note** Signing identities and team provisioning profiles are required by Apple to sign and distribute your applications for iOS devices. A team provisioning profile contains an app identifier, one or more certificates that identify the developer (or developers), and a list of registered devices. A device such as an iPad or iPhone is registered when you connect it to the Mac; this is required by Xcode to generate the provisioning profile when building apps for iOS. If you are building applications for macOS, Xcode registers the current Mac machine.

To accomplish this, start Xcode and select "Create new Xcode project." You can select any of the available project templates, but for the sake of simplicity, select Single View Application (see Figure 1-2) and then click Next.

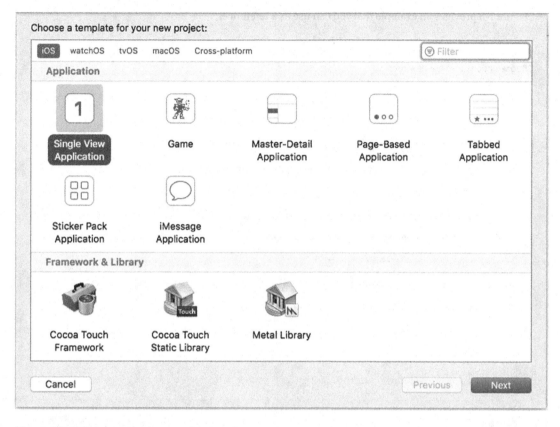

Figure 1-2. *Selecting a project template*

The next screen is of crucial importance. In fact, here you must specify some settings that will be used later in Visual Studio for Mac. Because you will not actually need to write code, it makes no difference at all what programming language (Swift or Objective C) or supported devices you specify here. The fields you must fill in are the following:

- Product Name, which defines the application name. The product name you supply here will also be used in Visual Studio for Mac because of the association between the tools and your developer profile.

- Team, which allows you to associate one or more developer accounts to the application. Click Add Account, enter your Apple ID, and then click "Sign in." From the drop-down box, you will be able to select your Apple ID that will be recognized as Personal Team.

- Organization Name, which contains your name or your organization's name.

- Organization Identifier, which represents a unique identifier for your organization. By convention, the organization identifier includes the *com.* prefix.

- Bundle Identifier, which is actually a read-only, autogenerated field, but it is of particular importance. The bundle identifier uniquely identifies an application against the App Store and the Apple services. Xcode concatenates the organization identifier with the product name to generate the bundle identifier. Take note of the bundle identifier, as it will be used in Visual Studio for Mac when building apps for iOS with Xamarin.

Figure 1-3 provides an example that you can use as a reference.

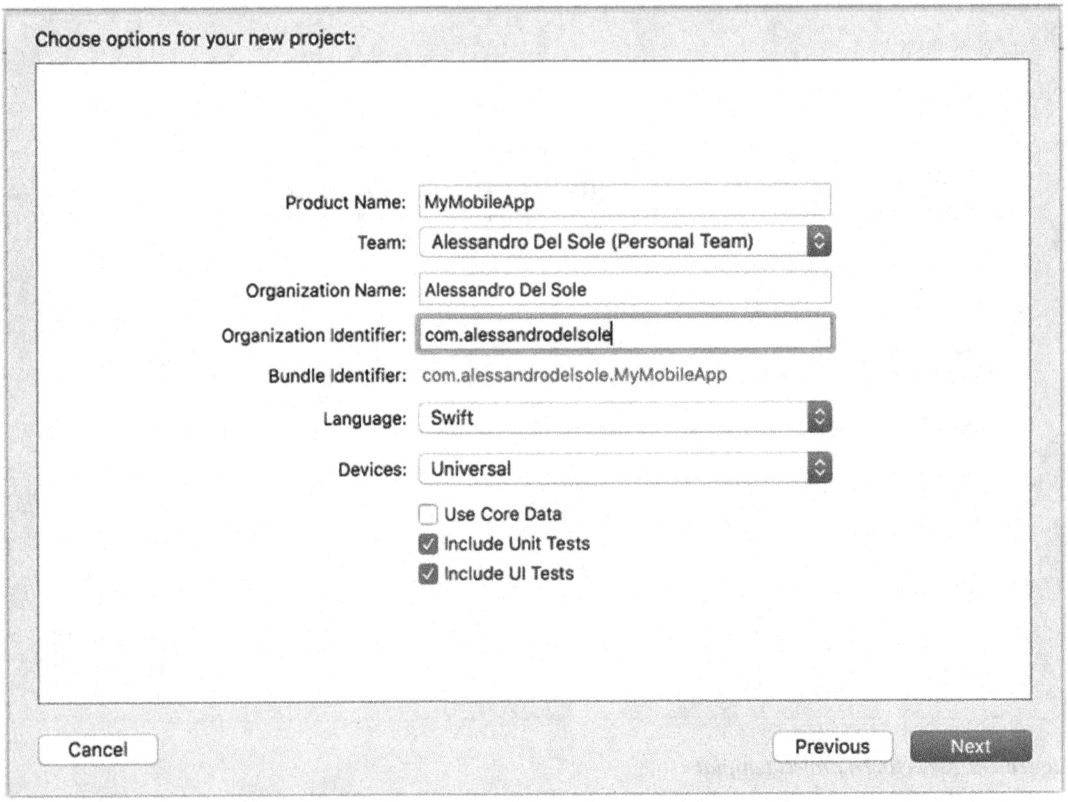

Figure 1-3. *Configuring the project properties*

When you click Next, Xcode will ask you to specify a target folder for the new project. Select any location, for example, the Desktop. After a few seconds, Xcode completes generating the certificates and provisioning profiles for the current developer account, and it shows the project properties. Figure 1-4 shows the Identity and Signing tabs, where you can see the application information and the provisioning profile information, respectively.

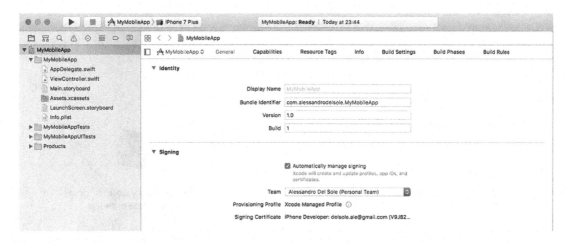

Figure 1-4. *Identity and signing information for the current project*

Now that the developer account has been configured and the provisioning profile has been generated, it is time to enable the developer mode for the current Mac machine. To accomplish this, select one of the available configurations for the iOS simulator (if you use Figure 1-4 as a reference, you can click where you see iPhone 7 Plus) and then start the sample app by pressing Command+R. Xcode will show a pop-up requesting your permission to enable the developer mode. Click Enable and wait for the application to be started in the simulator. You do not really need to work with the app at this point, so you can just break the application and quit the simulator.

Installing and Configuring Visual Studio for Mac

The final step in configuring your Mac is installing Microsoft Visual Studio for Mac. You can download the tool from `http://visualstudio.com/vs/visual-studio-mac`. When the download is completed, you will find the proper `.dmg` installer in the Downloads folder, so just click it to start the installation.

When the installer starts, you will need to click the Install Visual Studio for Mac button. You will then be prompted with the license agreement, which you must accept to proceed. After accepting the license, the installer will show the list of available components, as shown in Figure 1-5.

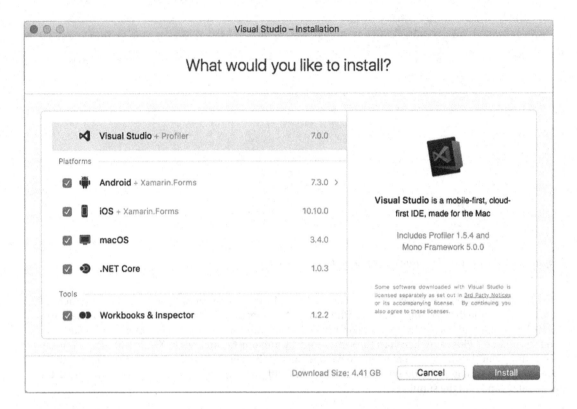

Figure 1-5. Selecting components to be installed

As you can see, you can only select both Xamarin and .NET Core components. For the sake of consistency with this book, make sure that all the components are selected and click Continue. Components' names are really self-explanatory: Android is required to build Android apps; iOS and macOS are required to build apps for iOS and macOS, respectively; and Workbooks & Inspector provides instrumentation for Xamarin to analyze an application's behavior. On the next screen, you will be invited to read and accept individual license agreements for the various SDKs that will be installed on your machine. Once you have accepted the license agreements, the installer will start downloading the required components, as shown in Figure 1-6 where you can see the operation in progress.

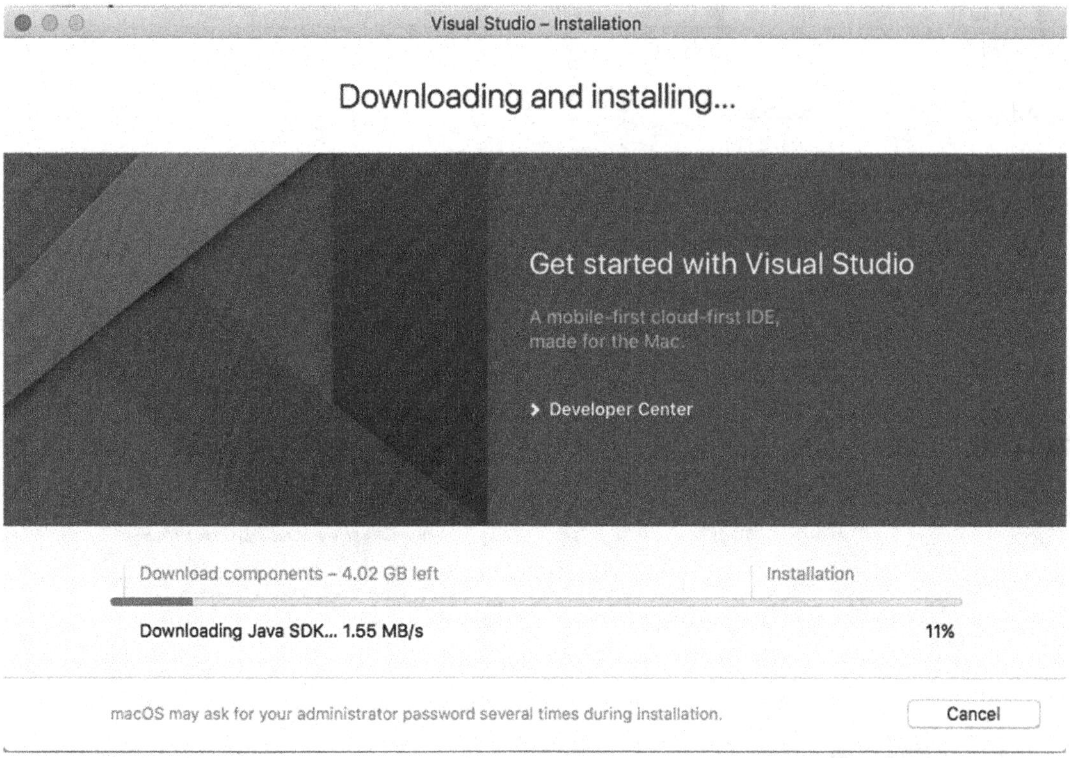

Figure 1-6. *The installation progress*

The installation process can take some time, because the download size can be up to 4.5GB depending on the selected components. At the end, you will find the Visual Studio icon in the Applications folder that you can easily open with the Finder tool. Double-click the icon to launch Visual Studio. When first started, the IDE will look similar to Figure 1-7 (your news items will vary).

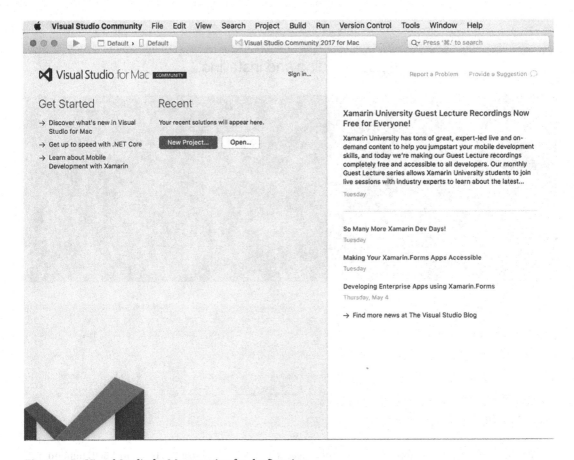

Figure 1-7. *Visual Studio for Mac running for the first time*

By default, when you install Visual Studio, you get the Community license. To unlock all the available features and services or in order to enable a different license if you downloaded Visual Studio from an MSDN subscription, it is strongly recommended that you log into Visual Studio for Mac with a Microsoft account, which is normally an e-mail address based on an Outlook, Hotmail, or Live provider. To accomplish this, simply click Sign In. A dialog will ask you to enter your credentials and will offer a shortcut to a web page where you can create a Microsoft account if you do not already have one. Once you have successfully signed in, you will see your username appearing instead of the Sign In shortcut. In the sign-in dialog, you will also be able to add multiple Microsoft accounts. This can be useful if you have different accounts for work and home or for development and testing. At this point, you have completed all the necessary steps to get your Mac computer ready for development with Visual Studio for Mac. Starting in the next chapter, you will learn how to use this powerful environment to build the next generation of applications based on the Microsoft stack.

Summary

To build applications with Visual Studio for Mac, you first need to configure the Mac for development. You need an Apple ID that is associated to the Apple services and that can be used as a developer account.

You can opt for a free developer account, which is perfect for development and debugging, or for a paid subscription. Whatever developer account you get, you need to install and configure Xcode and the Apple SDKs. Xcode is Apple's proprietary development environment that ships with the Apple SDKs that Visual Studio for Mac invokes behind the scenes to compile Xamarin projects for iOS. The last step in configuring the development machine is, of course, installing Visual Studio for Mac, which you can install through a simple step-by-step installer. In the next chapter, you will start working with Visual Studio for Mac, and you will learn everything you need to know to be productive with the integrated development environment.

CHAPTER 2

■ ■ ■

Getting Started with the IDE and with Projects

As a developer, you will spend most of your time working with Visual Studio for Mac. This provides an integrated development environment (IDE) that includes not only a rich code editor but also a large number of integrated tools and features that make developers extremely productive.

Because Visual Studio for Mac is the tool you are going to use for your daily work, you need to know in detail most of the features and tools it offers, from the code editor to productivity features to how it handles file management. In this chapter, you will learn everything you need to know to get the most out of the IDE and out of the code editor, and you will get familiar with all the features that you will typically use in your developer life.

This is probably the most important chapter in the book, so I recommend you to read it carefully to get familiar both with the IDE and with the concepts that will be used throughout the rest of the book, especially in chapters where I explain how to build Xamarin and .NET applications. As a final note, keep in mind that there are keyboard shortcuts for every tool I describe in this chapter. I will not use keyboard shortcuts very often because I prefer you to learn where to find commands within menus, and there you will be able to see keyboard shortcuts.

■ **Note** Visual Studio for Mac also allows working with the F# programming language against some specific project types. However, F# will not be used in this book because it is tailored to functional programming. C# is more popular, it is a general-purpose language, and it is fully supported by all of the available Xamarin and .NET Core projects you can create with VS for Mac.

Taking a Step Back in History: Xamarin Studio

When Xamarin was a stand-alone company and started to offer the Xamarin development platform, it also provided its own integrated development environment, called Xamarin Studio.

This IDE, which is still popular in the developer community, has some important points of strength: it runs on Windows and macOS; it has adopted the Microsoft Visual Studio format for solutions and projects, which also allows a Xamarin project to be opened in Visual Studio 2015 and 2017; and it allows working in the same way regardless of the operating system. Microsoft immediately realized the potential of Xamarin Studio and of how it could fit into the *mobile-first, cloud-first* strategy. For this reason, when Microsoft

© Alessandro Del Sole 2017
A. Del Sole, *Beginning Visual Studio for Mac*, https://doi.org/10.1007/978-1-4842-3033-6_2

acquired Xamarin, Microsoft decided to evolve Xamarin Studio and introduce two important additions: empowering the IDE with the .NET Compiler Platform (also known as Project Roslyn) for rich code editing and live code analysis experience, and adding support for .NET Core and cross-platform web development. As you can imagine, Visual Studio for Mac is the result of the evolution of Xamarin Studio, and this book explains how to get the most out of it.

Looking at the Welcome Page

When Visual Studio starts, the first thing you see is the welcome page. This contains a number of shortcuts and links that simplify common tasks. Figure 2-1 shows how the welcome page looks.

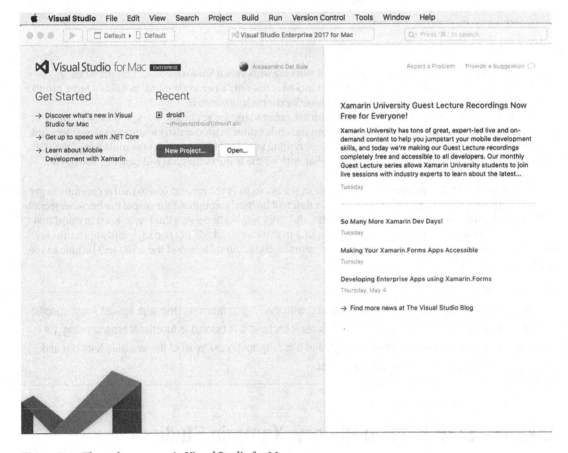

Figure 2-1. *The welcome page in Visual Studio for Mac*

You can visit the welcome page at any time by selecting Window ➤ Welcome Page. In the next subsections, you learn more about the various areas and shortcuts.

The Get Started Area

On the left side of the welcome page, you find the Get Started area. Here you find links to official online resources that you can read to get further information about Visual Studio for Mac, .NET Core, and Xamarin. Each link will open your web browser pointing to the appropriate learning resource.

The Recent Area

The Recent area displays the list of most recently used projects and is located on the right of the Get Started area. If this is the first time you are starting Visual Studio, the Recent area will be empty. In Figure 2-1 you can see a list of most the recently used projects as it appears on my machine.

Simply click a project name to open it. You can also filter the list by typing in the Filter text box. When you hover your mouse over a project name, you will also see an icon with the *x* symbol, which allows you to remove projects from the list. Notice that this action does not delete the project from disk; it just removes the project from the list of most recently used ones.

The News Area

The News area is located at the right side of the welcome page and aggregates news and updates from the Visual Studio team's blog and other Microsoft online resources.

Simply click a hyperlink to open your web browser and read the full article or blog post online. This is a convenient way to receive updates from Microsoft official sources and learn about new features and releases of Visual Studio for Mac.

Reporting Problems and Providing Suggestions

At the top of the News area, you will also see two shortcuts called Report a Problem and Provide a Suggestion. The first shortcut allows you to report any problems found in Visual Studio directly to Microsoft.

Visual Studio opens a page on the Developer Community web site (`http://developercommunity.visualstudio.com`), where developers can report problems and monitor them for responses from the product team. The second shortcut, Provide a Suggestion, will open the User Voice web site in your browser. User Voice is the place where users can send their suggestions or feature requests about a particular Microsoft product.

Understanding Runtimes and SDKs

Like any other development tool, Visual Studio for Mac relies on specific runtimes and software development kits. These are necessary because both Visual Studio and the applications you build with Visual Studio require them to work.

Visual Studio for Mac relies on the following four main platforms:

- *The Mono framework*: This is the popular cross-platform and open source porting of the .NET Framework to operating systems such as macOS and Linux. Mono is required by Visual Studio for Mac because it's the engine that empowers mobile applications that you create with Xamarin. Additionally, as you will discover later, Mono allows you to build ASP.NET web applications and services for macOS exactly as you would on Windows with .NET and Visual Studio 2017.

- *The Java SDK*: This is required to build Android apps using Xamarin in Visual Studio for Mac.

- *The .NET Core platform*: This is the new cross-platform, open source, and modular runtime for the next generation of web applications that run on macOS, Windows, and Linux.

- *The Apple SDKs*: Visual Studio for Mac needs these to compile Xamarin projects for iOS and macOS.

Except for the Apple SDKs and for .NET Core that you installed when reading Chapter 1, the runtime platforms are installed by the Visual Studio for Mac installer. You will get more detailed information about Mono and .NET Core in Chapters 4 and 9, respectively, but this minimum knowledge is necessary for a better understanding of the project types that you can create with VS for Mac.

Working with Projects

■ **Note** If you have experience creating projects with C# in Microsoft Visual Studio for Windows, many concepts in this section will be familiar to you and will still be valid with Visual Studio for Mac.

Each time you want to develop an application, you create a *project*. A project is a collection of source code files, resources, metadata, references and all the other files you need to build (or *make* in other systems) an application or a library. In the Visual Studio family, a C# project is represented by a `.csproj` file, whose structure is based on the Extensible Markup Language (XML) and which contains all the information required by the IDE to fully represent a project.

An application or a library can be built from multiple projects linked together at compile time. For this reason, Visual Studio has the concept of *solution*. A solution can be thought of as a container of projects, and each can contain an infinite number of projects of different kinds, written in different programming languages and with different targets. For example, a solution can contain a Xamarin project, a .NET Core library, and an ASP.NET Web API service. Solutions are represented by `.sln` files, whose structure is based on XML. A solution file stores the information required by the IDE to manage all the projects a solution contains. It is important to mention that solution and project files are standard across operating systems; this means that Visual Studio for Mac can open a solution created with Visual Studio 2017 on Windows, and vice versa. Of course, Visual Studio for Mac will only be able to open solutions that contain supported projects, such as Xamarin and .NET Core projects. For a better understanding of why this is so important, think of team collaboration: both Visual Studio 2017 and Visual Studio for Mac support Git as a source control engine. As a consequence, people on a team can share their work on the source code, and they will be able to collaborate on the same solution regardless of the operating system and IDE. This makes particular sense with Xamarin, where it is common to have some people working on Mac computers and other people working on Windows PCs. In the next subsections, you will learn the fundamentals about creating, running, and managing projects in Visual Studio for Mac. Then, you will get more detailed information about specialized project templates starting from Chapter 4.

Creating Projects

Creating projects in Visual Studio for Mac is a simple task. You click the New Project button on the welcome page or select File ➤ New Solution. Both actions open the New Project dialog, where you can see the full list of available project templates. Figure 2-2 shows an excerpt of the full list, which you can see by scrolling the list on the left side of the dialog.

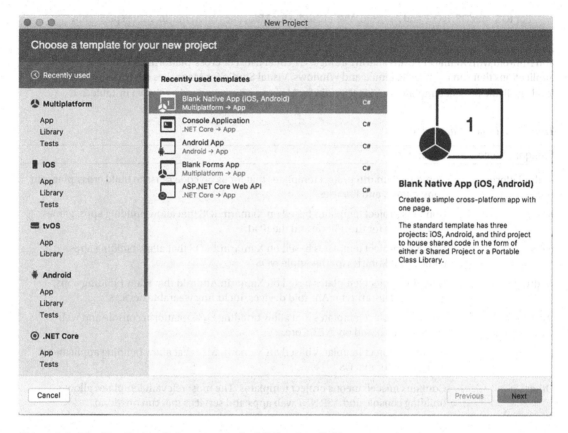

Figure 2-2. *The New Project dialog presents the full list of available supported project types*

In the next subsection, you will get a full explanation of the available project templates. Then in Chapters 4 to 11 you will learn how to use most of them in detail. As a tip, remember that you can simply click a project template to see a description on the right side of the dialog. For example, in Figure 2-2 you can see a description of the Blank Native App (iOS, Android) project template. In this case, the description explains how this project template generates a solution made of three projects: an iOS project, an Android project, and a project to share reusable code. You will get a similar description when clicking the other project templates.

■ **Note**   The New Project dialog also presents a tab called "Recently used," where you will see a list of the most recently used project templates.

Understanding Available Project Types

Visual Studio for Mac allows for building applications for iOS, macOS, tvOS, Android and Android Wear, and Windows.

For iOS, macOS, tvOS, and Android, Visual Studio for Mac relies on Xamarin. More specifically, you create apps for iOS and tvOS with the Xamarin.iOS libraries; apps for macOS with the Xamarin.Mac libraries; apps for Android with the Xamarin.Android libraries; and cross-platform mobile apps for iOS and Android with Xamarin.Forms sharing a single C# codebase. For cross-platform console and web applications that run on macOS, Linux, and Windows, Visual Studio for Mac relies on .NET Core. At a higher level, available project templates in Visual Studio for Mac can be categorized as shown in Table 2-1.

Table 2-1. *Project Categories*

Category Name	Description
Multiplatform	Contains Xamarin project templates that focus on code reuse to build cross-platform apps, games, and libraries.
iOS	Contains project templates based on Xamarin.iOS that allow building apps, games, and libraries for the iPhone and the iPad.
tvOS	Contains project templates based on Xamarin.TVOS that allow building apps, games, and libraries for the Apple tvOS.
Android	Contains project templates based on Xamarin.Android that allow building apps, games, and libraries for Android devices, including wearable devices.
.NET Core	Contains project templates that allow building cross-platform console and web applications based on .NET Core.
Mac	Contains project templates based on Xamarin.Mac that allow building applications and games for macOS.
Other	Contains miscellaneous project templates. The most relevant templates allow building console and ASP.NET web apps and services that run on Mono.

I will now provide a complete explanation for each available template. Some of them will be used in the book to demonstrate how to build mobile and web applications using Xamarin and .NET Core, respectively.

Multiplatform Templates

The Multiplatform category offers project templates that aim to maximize code reuse. In this category, you find templates that allow sharing code by platform, such as Xamarin.Forms, or by project kind, such as Shared Projects and Portable Class Libraries, all explained very shortly.

The Multiplatform category is divided into three subcategories: App, Libraries, and Tests. The subcategory names are self-explanatory: App contains project templates that allow creating an app, Libraries contains project templates that allow producing reusable libraries, and Tests contains project templates that allow creating projects for UI test automation. You will find the same subcategories in the iOS and Android template categories. Table 2-2 summarizes the project templates in the App category.

Table 2-2. *Project Templates in the App Category*

Platform	Template Name	Description
Xamarin.Forms	Forms App	Generates a solution that contains a cross-platform Xamarin.Forms project and an ASP.NET Web API back end based on .NET Core and optimized for publication to Microsoft Azure. The Xamarin.Forms project contains sample data and sample views to simulate a to-do list app, including CRUD operations and authentication.
Xamarin.Forms	Blank Forms App	Generates a solution that contains a blank Xamarin.Forms project.
Native (iOS, Android)	Native App (iOS, Android)	Generates a solution that contains a Xamarin.iOS project, a Xamarin.Android project, and a project to share code between the two Xamarin projects. This can be either a shared project or a portable class library. Xamarin projects include an ASP.NET Web API back end based on .NET Core and sample data and views to simulate a to-do list app, including CRUD operations and authentication. The back-end project is optimized for distribution to Microsoft Azure.
Native (iOS, Android)	Blank Native App (iOS, Android)	Generates a solution that contains blank Xamarin.iOS and Xamarin.Android projects, plus a project to share code between the two, which can be either a shared project or a portable class library.
Games (iOS, Mac)	SpriteKit Game	Generates a solution that contains a Xamarin.iOS project that allows creating 2D games based on the SpriteKit framework from Apple.
Games (iOS, Mac)	SceneKit Game	Generates a solution that contains a Xamarin.iOS project that allows creating 3D games based on the SceneKit framework from Apple.

The Library subcategory contains instead project templates that allow creating reusable libraries or shared projects. Table 2-3 summarizes the available project templates in this subcategory.

Table 2-3. *Project Templates in the Library Category*

Platform	Template Name	Description
General	Shared Project	Generates a solution that contains a so-called Shared Project, which allows sharing loose assortments of files between projects.
General	Portable Class Library	Generates a solution that contains a portable class library (PCL), which can be consumed in Windows, Mac, Windows Phone, Xamarin.iOS, and Xamarin.Android.
General	Multiplatform Library	Generates a solution that contains a PCL and a corresponding NuGet package that can be compiled and distributed to the NuGet gallery. If you are new to NuGet, the "Adding and Managing Dependencies" section later in this chapter provides a detailed explanation about it.
General	.NET Standard Library	Generates a solution that contains a C# library based on the .NET Standard specifications. At this writing, Visual Studio for Mac supports version 2.0 of .NET Standard.
Xamarin.Forms	Class Library	Generates a solution that contains a PCL that can be consumed by Xamarin.Forms projects.

While all the project templates in Table 2-3 have the goal of maximizing code reuse and of sharing code between projects, you might be confused by the three main types of Shared Project, Portable Class Library, and .NET Standard Library, so I will provide some clarifications.

The Shared Project type can be thought of as a loose assortment of files, such as code files, images, and XAML files. It does not produce a DLL library, and it can be just referenced from the projects in the solution it belongs to. With cross-platform Xamarin projects, such as Xamarin.Forms, it allows using preprocessor C# directives to invoke platform-specific code easily. For instance, using the Shared Project type, you could write something like the following:

```
#if __ANDROID__
    // Write code invoking the Android APIs
#elseif __IOS__
    // Write code invoking the iOS APIs
#else
    //Write code invoking the Windows APIs
#endif
```

The Portable Class Library type is a special kind of library that will run on all the platforms and operating systems you specify. Thus, it offers a common set of APIs that varies and is restricted based on your selection. It does generate a compiled library that can be reused in other solutions and that can be distributed to other developers. It does not allow using preprocessor C# directives to invoke platform-specific code, so in platforms such as Xamarin.Forms, you have to use different patterns like the dependency service pattern.

The .NET Standard Library type provides a set of specifications for APIs that all the .NET development platforms, such as .NET Framework, .NET Core, and Mono must implement. This allows for unifying .NET platforms and avoids future fragmentation. By creating a .NET Standard Library project, you will be sure your code will run on any .NET platform without the need of selecting any targets. Microsoft has recently released version 2.0 of .NET Standard, which provides full unification for the .NET Framework, .NET Core, and Mono, and Visual Studio for Mac supports .NET Standard up to version 2.0. Microsoft has a well-done blog post about .NET Standard and its goals and implementations that you can find at https://blogs.msdn.microsoft.com/dotnet/2016/09/26/introducing-net-standard/.

The last subcategory is called Tests and contains only one template called UI Test App. This project template generates a solution with a project that allows automating tests against the user interface both locally and on Xamarin Test Cloud, the platform that provides a cloud-based environment with dozens of devices that you can use to test the behavior of your apps.

iOS Templates and tvOS Templates

The iOS category is still divided into three subcategories called App, Library, and Test. In general, the iOS category contains project templates that allow generating Xamarin.iOS projects that you can use to build native iOS apps with C#.

Table 2-4 offers a detailed description of the iOS category.

Table 2-4. *Project Templates in the App Category*

Platform	Template Name	Description
General	Single View App	Generates a solution that contains a Xamarin.iOS project for a single-page app with a Storyboard object that contains a View, a View Controller, and a C# class.
General	Master-Detail App	Generates a solution that contains a Xamarin.iOS project based on a Master-Detail view and that displays a list of sample items. It is optimized for different screen form factors, including a Navigation Controller for the iPhone and a Split View on the iPad.
General	Tabbed App	Generates a solution that contains a Xamarin.iOS project based on multiple pages contained in tabs. It includes a Tab Bar Controller and a View Controller for each tab bar item.
General	Page-Based App	Generates a solution that contains a Xamarin.iOS project that shows how to implement navigation between multiple pages using a Page View Controller.
General	WebView App	Generates a solution that contains a Xamarin.iOS project that allows displaying HTML contents inside a WebView object, based on the Razor templating engine.
Games	SpriteKit Game	Generates a solution that contains a Xamarin.iOS project that allows creating 2D games based on the SpriteKit framework from Apple.
Games	SceneKit Game	Generates a solution that contains a Xamarin.iOS project that allows creating 3D games based on the SceneKit framework from Apple.
Games	Metal Game	Generates a solution that contains a Xamarin.iOS project that allows creating games based on Metal, a GPU-accelerated 3D framework from Apple.
Games	OpenGL Game	Generates a solution that contains a Xamarin.iOS project that allows creating 2D and 3D games based on the OpenGL framework APIs.

The Library subcategory offers two project templates: Class Library, which allows for generating C# class libraries that are tailored to Xamarin.iOS, and Bindings Library, a special project template that allows for generating C# class libraries that can consume third-party Objective-C libraries for iOS. This particular topic will not be covered in this book, but the Xamarin documentation has a specific page that you can find at https://developer.xamarin.com/guides/cross-platform/macios/binding/objective-c-libraries/.

The Tests subcategory offers two project templates called UI Test App and Unit Test App. The first project template is similar to its corresponding template in the Multiplatform category, but it is tailored to Xamarin.iOS and allows for automating tests against the user interface both locally and on Xamarin Test Cloud. The second template creates a test project for Xamarin.iOS apps and libraries where you can write unit tests based on the Touch.Unit framework.

Regarding tvOS, Visual Studio for Mac offers project templates that generate Xamarin.iOS projects optimized for this kind of device. Supported project templates are Single View App, Tabbed App, SceneKit Game, SpriteKit Game, and Metal Game. The description for each project template is the same as provided in Table 2-4.

Android Templates

The Android category is divided into three subcategories called App, Library, and Test. In general, the Android category contains project templates that allow generating Xamarin.Android projects that you can use to build native Android apps with C#. Table 2-5 offers a detailed description of the Android category.

Table 2-5. *Project Templates in the App Category*

Platform	Template Name	Description
General	Android App	Generates a solution that contains a Xamarin.Android project with a single sample screen (Activity) with a button and a label.
General	Wear App	Generates a solution that contains a Xamarin.Android project that targets the Android Wear operating system.
General	Blank Android App	Generates a solution that contains a Xamarin.Android project with a single sample screen (Activity) and empty user interface.
General	WebView App	Generates a solution that contains a Xamarin.Android project that allows displaying HTML contents inside a WebView object, based on the Razor templating engine.
Games	OpenGL Game	Generates a solution that contains a Xamarin.Android project that allows creating 2D and 3D games based on the OpenGL framework APIs.
Games	OpenGL ES 2.0 Game	Generates a solution that contains a Xamarin.Android project that allows creating 2D and 3D games based on the OpenGL ES 2.0 APIs. ES stands for Embedded Systems.
Games	OpenGL ES 3.0 Game	Generates a solution that contains a Xamarin.Android project that allows creating 2D and 3D games based on the OpenGL ES 3.0 APIs. This is a most recent version with new features and is backward compatible with 2.0.

The Library subcategory offers two project templates: Class Library, which allows for generating C# class libraries that are tailored to Xamarin.Android, and Bindings Library, a project template that allows for generating C# class libraries that can consume third-party Java libraries for Android. This particular topic will not be covered in this book, but the Xamarin documentation has a specific page that you can find at https://developer.xamarin.com/guides/android/advanced_topics/binding-a-java-library/.

The Tests subcategory offers two project templates called UI Test App and Unit Test App. Similarly to the iOS templates, the first project template is similar to its corresponding template in the Multiplatform category, but it is tailored to Xamarin.Android and allows for automating tests against the user interface both locally and on Xamarin Test Cloud. The second template creates a test project for Xamarin.Android apps and libraries where you can write unit tests.

.NET Core Templates

The .NET Core project templates are extremely important in Visual Studio for Mac because they represent one of the most evident points of evolution when comparing this IDE with Xamarin Studio. As you will learn in more detail in Chapter 9, .NET Core is an open source, modular, cross-platform runtime that allows building apps that run on Windows, Linux, and macOS with C#.

To build .NET Core apps, Visual Studio for Mac offers a number of specific project templates available in the .NET Core category. This is divided into the App and Tests subcategories. Table 2-6 describes project templates in the App subcategory.

Table 2-6. *Project Templates in the App Category*

Platform	Template Name	Description
General	Console Application	Generates a solution that contains a C# project for a stand-alone, empty console application
ASP.NET	ASP.NET Core Empty	Generates a solution that contains an empty ASP.NET Core web project
ASP.NET	ASP.NET Core Web App	Generates a solution that contains an ASP.NET Core project that scaffolds a web application based on the MVC framework
ASP.NET	ASP.NET Core Web PI	Generates a solution that contains an ASP.NET Core project that scaffolds a RESTful service based on the Web API framework

The Tests subcategory contains only one project template called xUnit Test Project that allows creating unit tests based on the xUnit test framework.

Mac Templates

The Mac category is also interesting because it provides project templates that allow building applications, games, and libraries for the macOS operating system using Xamarin.Mac with C#. This category is divided into the App and Library subcategories, and Table 2-7 describes the App one in more detail.

Table 2-7. *Project Templates in the App Category*

Platform	Template Name	Description
General	Cocoa App	Generates a solution that contains a Xamarin.Mac project with a Storyboard for a stand-alone Mac application based on the Cocoa framework from Apple
Games	SpriteKit Game	Generates a solution that contains a Xamarin.Mac project that allows creating 2D games based on the SpriteKit framework from Apple
Games	SceneKit Game	Generates a solution that contains a Xamarin.Mac project that allows creating 3D games based on the SceneKit framework from Apple
Games	Metal Game	Generates a solution that contains a Xamarin.Mac project that allows creating games based on Metal, a GPU-accelerated 3D framework from Apple

The Library subcategory contains the Class Library and Bindings Library project templates. Their purpose is the same as described for their counterparts in Xamarin.iOS, with an important clarification for the Class Library template: this one relies on the so-called Unified APIs, which means that code in this library can be shared between Xamarin.Mac and Xamarin.iOS on both 32-bit and 64-bit systems.

Other Templates

Not limited to Xamarin and .NET Core projects, Visual Studio for Mac allows working with a number of additional project types. Among the others, the most important thing to highlight at this point is that the IDE supports several classic .NET projects such as Console, ASP.NET MVC, and ASP.NET Web Forms projects.

This is possible because of the Mono runtime, which allows running these kinds of applications even on a Mac. The miscellaneous supported project types are available in the Other category, which is divided into the .NET, ASP.NET, and Miscellaneous subcategories. Except for where any differences are expressly stated, here .NET means the .NET Framework, not .NET Core.

■ **Note**　The project templates described in this subsection will not be used in this book, whose goal is to demonstrate how to use VS for Mac with a *mobile-first*, *cloud-first* strategy. Still, it is important that you know they exist and that you can use them to work on a variety of .NET projects even on a Mac. It is also worth mentioning that most of these projects not only support C# and F# but also Visual Basic as a programming language.

Table 2-8 describes the project templates in the .NET subcategory.

Table 2-8. *Project Templates in the .NET Category*

Template Name	Description
Console Project	Generates a solution that contains an empty console project
Empty Project	Generates a solution that contains an empty C# project with only the basic references
Gtk# 2.0 Project	Generates a solution that contains a project based on Gtk#, a cross-platform framework for creating user interfaces
Library	Generates a solution that contains an empty C# class library project for .NET
F# Tutorial	Generates a solution that contains an F# project with a single file that contains a variety of code examples
NUnit Library Project	Generates a solution that contains a library project for unit tests based on the NUnit framework
NuGet Package	Generates a solution that contains a project that allows for building a NuGet package from files and libraries

As I said before, VS for Mac also supports some classic ASP.NET project types, such as MVC and Web Forms. Supported projects are included in the ASP.NET subcategory, and they are described in Table 2-9. Regarding ASP.NET on Mono, it is worth mentioning that Mono is not supported for running web applications in production, whereas .NET Core is.

Table 2-9. *Project Templates in the ASP.NET Category*

Template Name	Description
Empty ASP.NET Project	Generates a solution that contains an empty ASP.NET web project with its basic infrastructure
ASP.NET MVC Project	Generates a solution that scaffolds an ASP.NET MVC web project using Razor views
ASP.NET Web Forms Project	Generates a solution that scaffolds an ASP.NET project based on the Web Forms technology

The projects described in Table 2-9 give Visual Studio for Mac great flexibility and allow you to work with your existing codebases even on a Mac. The last subcategory is called Miscellaneous and provides the project templates summarized in Table 2-10.

Table 2-10. *Project Templates in the Miscellaneous Category*

Template Name	Description
Blank Solution	Generates an empty solution that you can populate with any of the project types described so far.
Workspace	Generates a new workspace, which might be thought of as a container of solutions. Notice that workspaces are not supported in Visual Studio 2017 on Windows.
Empty Project	Generates a solution that contains a completely empty C# project.

After the detailed description of each project type, you should have a clearer idea of what kind of applications you can build with Visual Studio for Mac.

Opening Existing Solutions

You have different options to open existing solutions from disk. You can select a solution by clicking the Open button on the welcome page, or you can select File ➤ Open. Notice that Visual Studio for Mac is not limited to open solution files; it also allows opening individual project (`.csproj`) files, and then it will generate a root solution for the project.

Additionally, you can open solutions from the list of most recently used ones that is available on the welcome page, or you can do this by selecting File ➤ Recent Solutions and then select the solution you need from the submenu that appears. This submenu also provides a command called Clear that deletes the list of most recently used solutions.

Creating Your First C# Project

In this section, you will learn how to create your first C# project in Visual Studio for Mac. Though it might seem an easy step, and actually it is, you will also learn a number of concepts and features you will reuse with whatever project template you choose to work with. For the sake of simplicity, you will start with a C# console application based on .NET Core.

In fact, the focus of this chapter is not explaining how the various development platforms work; rather, the focus is on getting to know the most common and important features in the IDE that you need to know when working with any kind of project. Thus, the Console project template is perfect because it's the simplest template possible. Having that said, click New Project on the welcome page or select File ➤ New Solution. When the New Project dialog appears, select the Console Application template in the .NET Core category and then click Next. If multiple versions of the .NET Core runtime are installed on your machine, VS for Mac will ask you to select one. Select either 1.1 or 2.0 and click Next. At this point, the New Project dialog asks you to specify a project name and a solution name, which is common to all the supported project templates. The Solution Name text box is automatically populated as you type the project name, but you can certainly provide a different solution name (which is not uncommon). Because everything starts with a Hello World example, type **HelloWorld** as the project name. Figure 2-3 shows how the New Project dialog appears at this point.

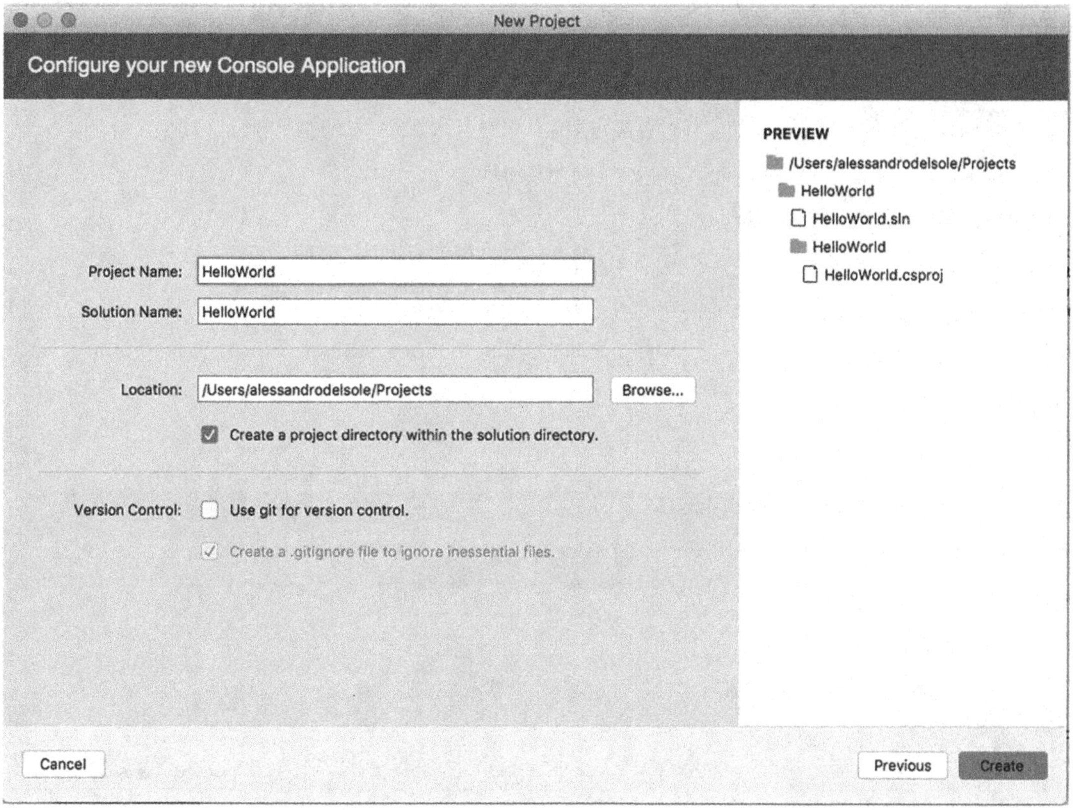

Figure 2-3. Creating a new project

The Location text box allows you to specify a folder for your new solution. By default, Visual Studio for Mac creates a Projects folder under the Home directory of your Mac. You can click Browse to select a different folder, or you can simply type a new folder name, and you can also change the default folder in the IDE options, as you will learn in Chapter 13. I recommend you leave the check box called "Create a project directory within the solution directory" selected. This option ensures that a root folder is created for the solution and that a subfolder in the solution folder is created for the new project. This helps keep the solution's structure well organized, especially if you plan to add new or existing projects to the solution later. The New Project dialog provides a visual representation of the solution's folder structure on the right side, under Preview. You will see how this preview changes depending on selecting or deselecting the directory check box. You also have an option to enable Git version control for the solution, but this will be discussed in more detail in Chapter 12, so let's leave this out for now. Click Create when ready. After a few seconds, your new project will be ready. If you have never made customizations to the IDE before, by default you will see the Solution pad on the left side of the workspace and the code editor on the right side. You might also see additional pads, such as Errors. If you do not see the code editor, expand the project view in the Solution pad and double-click the Program.cs file. At this point, your workspace should look like Figure 2-4.

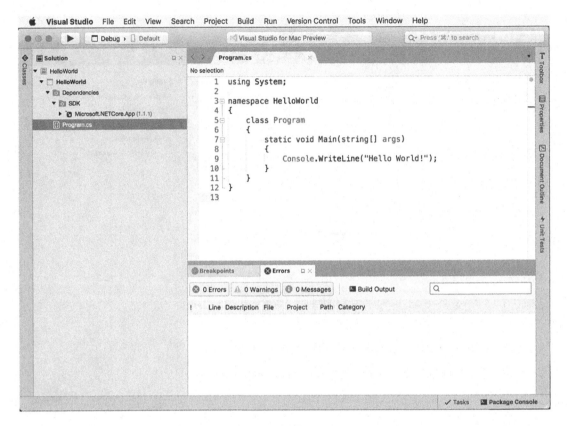

Figure 2-4. *The workspace after the project has been created*

When you create a new project or open an existing solution, Visual Studio for Mac will automatically attempt to refresh any references to external libraries, such as NuGet packages. This might take a few seconds, and you will see the progress of the restore operation in the upper status bar (where you can normally see the Visual Studio icon and product name). This is important to remember because you might have projects that have dependencies, and you might see some error squiggles in the code editor until the process of restoring libraries is completed. The Solution pad is an important tool, and you will work with it all the time. It basically provides a hierarchical view of your solution, and it allows you to browse for files and folders.

■ **Note** Generally speaking, a *pad* is a pane that can be rearranged on the screen or hidden and that can either contain some kind of specific information or allow for executing contextualized actions. Visual Studio for Mac provides many pads that the section "Working with Pads" in this chapter will discuss intensively.

In the Solution pad, you can also right-click the solution name and then select Add ➤ New Project or Add ➤ Existing Project to add new or existing projects, respectively, which is common. You can also add individual files and folders (referred to as *solution items*) that will not be part of the build output but that you might need for several purposes, such as documents or images you might want to include for your team.

For each project in the solution, the Solution pad not only shows files but also dependencies your project has on specific SDKs (such as .NET Core in the current example) or on external libraries. Dependencies will also be covered in more detail in this chapter. Notice how the code editor provides syntax colorization for any of the supported languages, as you might certainly expect. While developing, you will need to test and debug an application many times, so you need to understand how to start an application for debugging and the concepts related to this task.

Building and Running an Application

Compiling code and running the resulting application in Visual Studio for Mac is certainly easy, but it requires you to be familiar with two concepts: assemblies and build configuration. This section explains both concepts, and then you learn how to start an application with or without the debugging tools attached.

Understanding the Concept of Assemblies

In .NET terminology, a very important word is *assembly*. Put succinctly, an assembly is the final compiled output that results from building a .NET or .NET Core project and can refer both to an executable and to a .dll library. Assemblies are self-describing units made of metadata and Intermediate Language (IL) code. Metadata describes the name, the version number, the icon, and the types and members defined in the assembly. The Intermediate Language is what compilers actually produce. Then when you start a .NET application, the IL in the assembly is compiled on the fly by the just-in-time compiler into machine language.

Discussing in more detail assemblies, how they are made, and how .NET manages assemblies is out of the scope of this chapter. Some more details and concepts will be provided in Chapter 9, while full documentation is available in the MSDN documentation at https://msdn.microsoft.com/en-us/library/8wxf689z(v=vs.110).aspx. For the purposes of this book, when you encounter the word *assembly*, remember it can refer to both an executable and a reusable .NET library.

Understanding Configurations

Build configurations, or simply configurations, influence the way your code is compiled into an assembly or app package. A configuration determines whether the compilation output should include debug symbols and which architecture your application should target, such as x86, x64, or both.

By default, Visual Studio for Mac offers two built-in configurations: Debug and Release. As its name implies, the Debug configuration is used when you want to test and debug an application at development time; it is optimized for debugging scenarios because it generates debug symbols that are included in the compilation output and attaches an instance of the debugger to the application. On the contrary, the Release configuration does not include debug symbols and does not attach an instance of the debugger to the application, so you will use this one when you want to release your app or library. The easiest way to select the build configuration is from the appropriate drop-down box in the toolbar, as shown in Figure 2-5.

Figure 2-5. *Selecting a build configuration*

You can also create custom configurations, as discussed in the "Configuring Build Options" section later in this chapter. Now that you have knowledge of configurations, you can compile and run your first project.

Compiling and Building Projects

Before you can run, test, and debug an application, you need to build your solution. Building a solution means generating an assembly or app package by compiling the source code from all the projects into intermediate objects that are then linked to the appropriate libraries.

As for Visual Studio 2017 on Windows, in Visual Studio for Mac, solutions might be made of multiple projects of different kinds. This means that the various projects in a solution must be built individually and then linked to one another, and to the necessary libraries, into the final executable. Luckily enough, Visual Studio for Mac leverages the popular MSBuild engine that handles the entire build process for you from start to end, taking care of compiling projects in the appropriate order, invoking external tools when necessary, and then generating the complete build output. In Visual Studio for Mac, you build a solution (or individual projects) with commands from the Build menu or with same-named shortcuts available if you right-click the solution or project name in the Solution pad. More specifically, you have the following commands that target an entire solution:

- *Build All*: This command builds a solution and generates the proper output, such as an executable, a library, and an app package.

- *Rebuild All*: This command is similar to Build All, with an important difference: Build All performs a full build only the first time; the next time, it only updates the build output by compiling updated code. Rebuild All, instead, performs a full build of the solution every time.

- *Clean All*: This command cleans the build output and is useful when you want to refresh the build process.

■ **Note**   Saying that building a solution produces an executable, a library, or an app package must be further clarified. In fact, there are situations in which building a solution generates more than one output. For instance, in a single solution you might have different project types, such as a Xamarin project and an ASP.NET Core back-end project. In such situations, Visual Studio does not produce a single app package or application; instead, it generates multiple build outputs, an app package, and an ASP.NET Core web application. Situations like this are extremely common, especially with solutions that contain many library projects and a project for an executable or app package.

The Build menu also offers Build, Rebuild, and Clean commands against individual projects in the solution. These can be useful when you make edits to a particular project and you want to see if it is compiled correctly. When you build a solution or an individual project, the IDE's status bar shows the operation progress, and it offers a red Stop button that you can click to cancel the build operation. Remember that the time for the build process varies depending on the number of projects in the solution and on their complexity.

The build output, and thus one or more assemblies generated by the compiler, will be available by default in the Bin\Debug or Bin\Release project subfolders, depending on the active build configuration. Later in the section called "Configuring Build Options," I will explain how to change these paths. Once you have built your solution, you can run it for testing and debugging.

Running Applications with and Without a Debugger

You can run your solutions with the Start button in the toolbar and with two commands from the Run menu: Start Debugging and Start Without Debugging.

In the first case, you select the Debug configuration, and then you invoke the command. This will launch the application from within the IDE, with an instance of the debugger attached, and will enable the powerful debugging tools in Visual Studio that you will learn to leverage in the next chapter. In the second case, you can select the Release configuration, and the application will start without an instance of the debugger and detached from the IDE. You can certainly leave the Debug configuration selected when running the application without debugging, but the generated debug symbols will be ignored. Once you have selected the configuration, you can start the application; besides the two commands in the Run menu, the easiest way to do this is by clicking the Start button, which you can see in Figure 2-5. When you start the application, Visual Studio first performs a Build All operation if it detects some changes from the last build or if you have never built the solution before. It does not perform a Build All operation if you already called Build All or Rebuild All before starting the application. Figure 2-6 shows the sample console application running in Terminal.

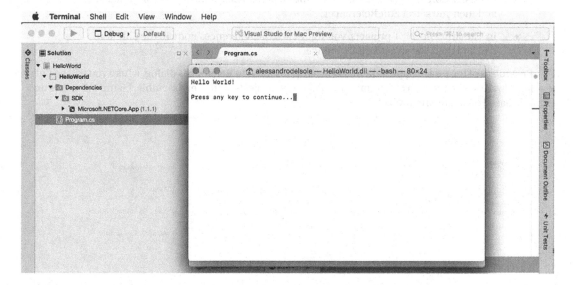

Figure 2-6. *Running an application*

In this case, the application has been started with the Debug configuration enabled; thus, an instance of the debugger is attached. All the steps you have seen so far apply to all the supported project types, and the only difference will be the application host, which can be a Terminal window, a web server, a device simulator, or a physical device depending on the project type.

Adding and Managing Dependencies

Any application needs core runtime platforms or libraries to work. These are known as *dependencies*. For example, the .NET Core SDK is a dependency for any .NET Core application. The Mono runtime is a dependency for any Xamarin project.

Regarding core dependencies, Visual Studio for Mac takes care of adding the proper references based on the type of project you create. More often than not, your applications will need to use third-party libraries, or libraries you developed, that expose APIs and objects that the core libraries do not provide out of the box. When this happens, you are introducing additional dependencies. In VS for Mac you have two main ways to add and consume dependencies in your applications: adding references to libraries on disk and downloading NuGet packages. This section walks through both scenarios.

■ **Note** Remember that references are per project, not per solution.

Adding References to Libraries

If you need to consume a library that is on disk, either third-party or developed by you, in the Solution pad you can add a reference to the library. The way you add a reference to a project changes a bit depending on the project type.

- In a .NET Core project, you right-click the Dependencies node in the Solution pad and then you select Edit References.

- In Xamarin and .NET projects, you right-click the References node in the Solution pad and then you select Edit References.

Regardless of the project type, Edit References opens the Edit References dialog, where you will be able to select libraries with the help of four tabs: All, Packages, Projects, and .Net Assembly. Figure 2-7 shows an example based on a Xamarin project.

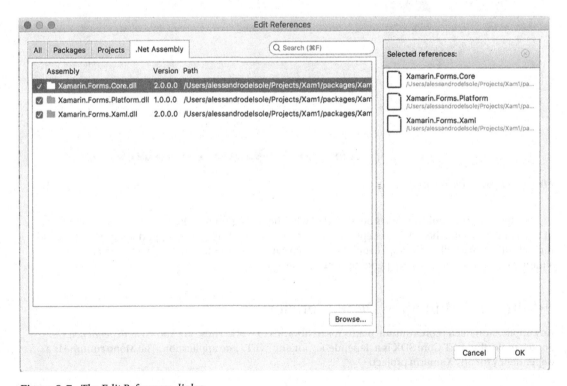

Figure 2-7. *The Edit References dialog*

The Packages tab lists installed libraries that Visual Studio is able to detect as available for the current project. The Projects tab allows adding a reference to other projects in the solution, which is common when you have class library projects that expose custom objects or APIs. The .Net Assembly tab shows a list of .NET assemblies that are currently referenced by the project. For instance, you could simply double-click a library listed on the Packages tab to immediately add a reference. If the library you need is not listed but available on disk, you can click Browse, locate the library, and select it to add a reference. At this point, you will be able to consume the objects exposed by the library in your code. This approach for adding dependencies has three important limitations.

- It requires you to have the library on your disk.

- It does not automatically resolve any additional dependencies that the library you are referencing might rely on, so this is something you must take care of manually.

- It makes it difficult to manage different versions of the library and its dependencies once new versions are available. For instance, if a new version of a library is available and it also relies on an updated version of a dependency, you must take care of both manually. The same concept applies if you want to downgrade to a less recent version.

NuGet solves all these problems, and it is discussed thoroughly in the next subsection.

Working with NuGet Packages

NuGet is an integrated package manager that has been very popular among developers using Microsoft Visual Studio on Windows and Xamarin Studio since the beginning. Through a convenient, integrated user interface, the NuGet Package Manager allows you to download and reference a huge number of popular libraries, and it also automatically resolves any further dependencies that a library might need.

Not limited to this, NuGet makes it extremely easy to manage different versions of a library and of its dependencies. Libraries are bundled into so-called NuGet packages, which are files with the .nupkg extension and that contain the library, metadata that helps developers identify a library, and information about dependencies that a library needs to be consumed properly. NuGet packages are hosted on (and can be published to) an online repository available at NuGet.org. If you visit this web site, you will be able to browse the gallery outside of Visual Studio and see what's available.

I recommend you spend some time getting familiar with NuGet because it is becoming the *de facto* standard for managing dependencies both in Visual Studio for Mac and in Visual Studio on Windows. As a general rule, in the Solution pad you right-click the Dependencies node for .NET Core projects and the References node for Xamarin and .NET projects and then you select Add Packages. This will open the Add Packages dialog, which you can see in Figure 2-8.

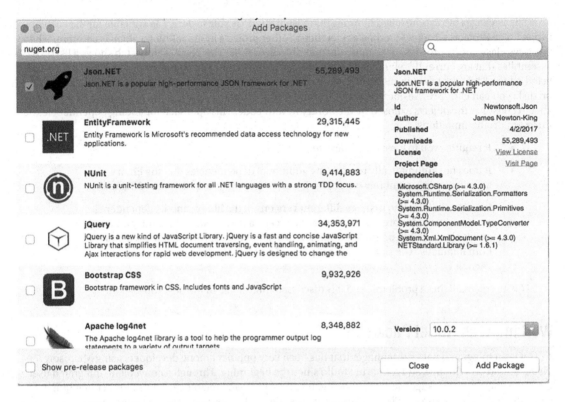

Figure 2-8. *Adding NuGet packages*

The Add Packages dialog shows the list of available packages from NuGet.org.

■ **Note**   Because NuGet packages contain libraries, talking about references to NuGet packages and to libraries has basically the same meaning.

You can also create custom repositories, as I will discuss in Chapter 13. As you can see in Figure 2-8, for each package you can see the description, the author, the publication date, the number of downloads, and, very important, the license agreement and the additional dependencies the package requires. By default, only stable releases are displayed, but you can select the "Show pre-release packages" check box to show also prerelease versions. In the Version drop-down box, you see the latest version available by default, but you can pick a different one. You can select multiple packages, but for now simply select the Json.NET package, the most popular library for .NET that makes it dramatically easy to serialize and deserialize to and from JSON markup. You will not actually use the library in code in this chapter; it is just the package I'll be using for demonstration purposes. At this point, Visual Studio will show a dialog that contains a list of all the libraries that will be installed and a link to the license agreement for each. When ready, click Accept to accept the license agreement for all the libraries. While Visual Studio downloads and installs the NuGet package with its dependencies, you will see the operation progress in the status bar. When finished, you will be able to see the Json.NET library just installed in the Solution pad, but the location changes based on the project type. For .NET Core 2.0 projects, installed NuGet packages are located under the Dependencies node; for .NET Core 1.*x* projects, installed NuGet packages are located under the NuGet node; for Xamarin projects, installed NuGet packages are located under the Packages node. Packages can be also expanded to see the list of dependencies they rely on. Figure 2-9 shows an example based on the Json.NET library and a .NET Core 1.1 project.

Figure 2-9. *References added via NuGet and their dependencies*

When a NuGet package and its dependencies are installed, Visual Studio for Mac automatically adds a reference so that you can consume libraries in your code. If you want to install a different version of an already installed package, you have two options. The first option is automatically updating NuGet packages to the latest stable release available, which you do by right-clicking the solution name in the Solution pad and then selecting Update NuGet Packages or by selecting Project ➤ Update NuGet Packages. The second option instead allows you to select a specific version of a NuGet package: simply right-click the NuGet node and then select again Add Packages. Select the package you want to upgrade (or downgrade), select the version number in the Version drop-down box, and finally click Add Package. Figure 2-10 demonstrates this.

Figure 2-10. *Selecting a different NuGet package's version number*

Whenever Visual Studio for Mac performs any operations related to NuGet packages, it displays the output in the Package Console pad, which you enable with View ➤ Pads ➤ Package Console. Figure 2-11 shows an example.

Figure 2-11. *The Package Console pad shows output from NuGet*

The Package Console pad is particularly useful when installing NuGet package fails because it provides detailed messages. A common reason for failure is selecting a NuGet package that is not compatible with the current project or a dependency of the selected NuGet package that is not compatible with the current project.

The way NuGet packages are managed is a little bit different depending on the development platform you are working on. For .NET Core, the list of required NuGet packages is stored inside the .csproj project file. Additionally, when NuGet packages are downloaded, they are stored inside a local cache for easy reuse.

For other project types, such as Xamarin and the full .NET, NuGet packages are downloaded into a project subfolder called Packages, and Visual Studio stores the list of required packages inside a file called Packages.config. In both cases, Visual Studio for Mac always knows what NuGet packages a solution needs. This is important because, if a library is missing, Visual Studio can easily restore it. For example, if a solution is under source control, it's not uncommon that libraries are not sent to the server. So, when you download a solution from the Git source control repository of your choice for the first time, VS for Mac will check if all the NuGet packages are available locally. If not, it will perform a restore operation. Another example of when restoring NuGet packages is required is when you share a solution with other people, such as in the form of a .zip archive or on a web site. Because your solution might rely on a large number of packages, you can exclude them from the archive to save a lot of space. This is typically the case with Xamarin or full .NET projects, where you can completely delete the content of the Packages subfolder. When other people open the solution on their machine, Visual Studio checks if the required libraries are available; if not, it reads the content of Packages.config, and then it performs a restore operation. Usually, restoring NuGet packages occurs automatically when you open a solution, but you can restore packages manually by right-clicking the solution name in the Solution pad and then selecting Restore NuGet Packages or by selecting Project ➤ Restore NuGet Packages.

■ **Note**   The official NuGet repository is hosted on a web site, so you should typically have an Internet connection when working with NuGet packages. However, Visual Studio for Mac manages a local cache of all the NuGet packages that are minimally required to create new projects. This is the case with Xamarin and full .NET projects. Regarding .NET Core, a local cache is also available and is managed by the platform directly. Put succinctly, you will always be able to create any of the supported projects even when offline. Then, if you need to download or update NuGet packages, you will need an Internet connection. Luckily enough, you can even create a local NuGet repository so that you will be able to reference the NuGet packages you use the most even if an Internet connection is not available.

Configuring Project Options

Visual Studio for Mac provides you with deep control over a project. In fact, you can edit a number of project properties and options so that you can provide additional information and also influence the build process. This section describes options that are commonly available to all the supported project types in VS for Mac; the project options that are specific to .NET Core and Xamarin solutions will be detailed in the appropriate chapters.

You access the project options with Project ➤ {ProjectName} Options or by right-clicking the project name in the Solution pad and then selecting Options. The Project Options window appears at this point (see Figure 2-12).

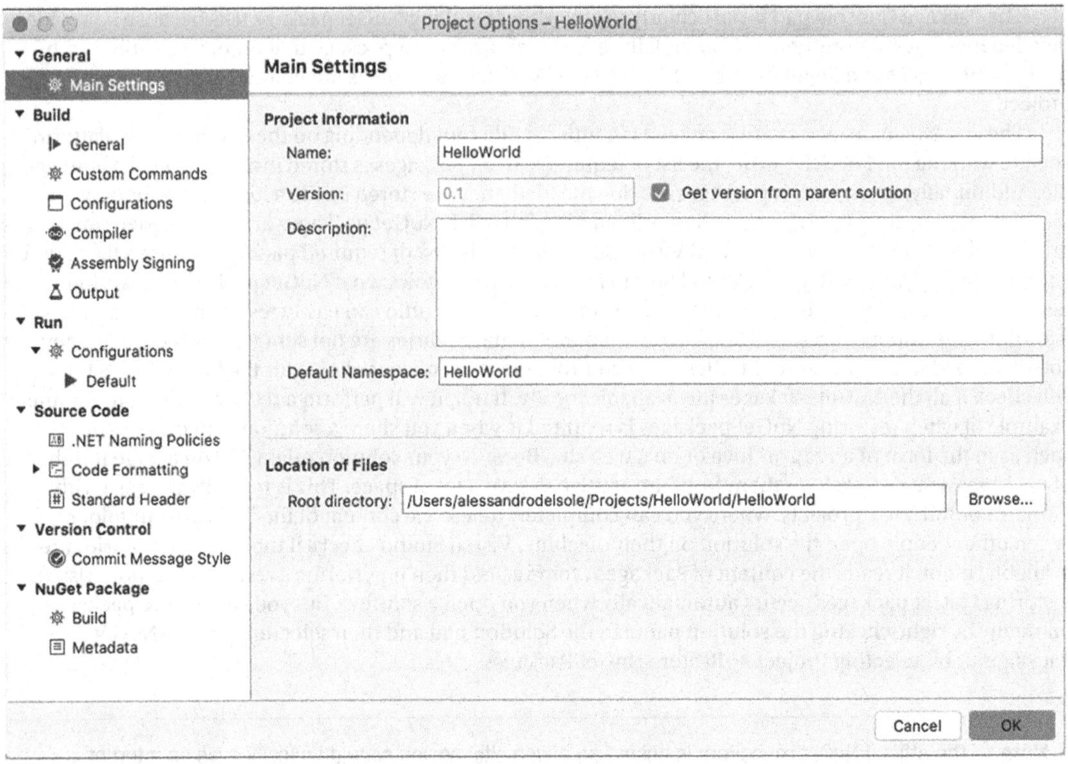

Figure 2-12. *The Project Options window*

In the General node, you find Main Settings, which is the same for all the supported project types. Here you can specify a different project name, a specific version number, an optional description, and the root C# namespace, and you can change the root directory where the project files are stored. By default, the project version is inherited from the solution version, but you can deselect the "Get version from parent solution" check box and provide a new version. The other settings are generated based on the information you supplied when you created the project, and unless you have specific requirements, I recommend you leave them unchanged.

■ **Note** Some options can be configured at the solution level by right-clicking the solution name in the Solution pad and then selecting Options. Common options you might set are those that projects inherit, such as the version number, the author information, and the output folder for binaries. I recommend you work with the project options rather than with solution options because every project has its own specific settings and requirements.

Configuring Build Options

In the Build node of the Project Options dialog, the General tab allows you to change the target framework. For .NET Core projects, the target framework is by default the latest runtime version available. With Android projects, the target framework is the version of the Android APIs used for the build process. With iOS projects, the target framework represents the SDK that should be used depending on the target device (iOS or WatchOS). Figure 2-13 provides an example based on a .NET Core application.

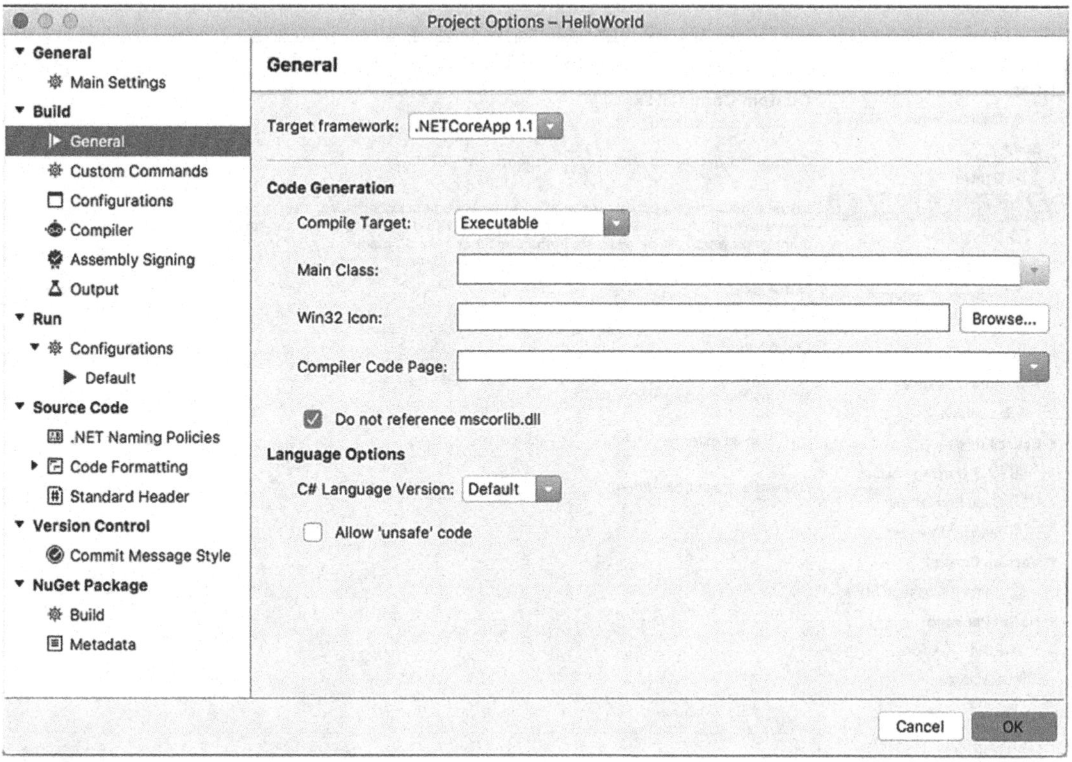

Figure 2-13. *The General options*

In the Code Generation group, you can change the compile target (Executable, Library, Executable with GUI, Module), the startup C# class in the Main Class box, the icon file in the Win32 Icon box, and the encoding code page for source files in the Compiler Code Page box. I recommend you not change the default options, including the "Do not reference mscorlib.dll" check box value, because the defaults are already optimized for your project. Changing these options makes sense in full .NET projects, not .NET Core.

Additionally, you can specify the C# version the compiler should use in the C# Language Version box. The Default setting ensures the compiler uses the latest version of the language available. The "Allow 'unsafe' code" check box should be left unselected in a .NET Core project, as you will not typically invoke native code.

The Custom Commands Tab

The Custom Commands tab allows you to specify any actions that should be executed before, during, or after a build or clean process. Actions are per configuration, so you can specify different actions for different configurations. By default, the Configuration drop-down box shows the active build configuration, but you can choose a different one and provide any actions. You specify one or more actions with the Select Project Operation drop-down box. Supported actions are Before Build, Build, After Build, Before Clean, Clean, After Clean, and Custom Command. Figure 2-14 shows an example based on the After Build action.

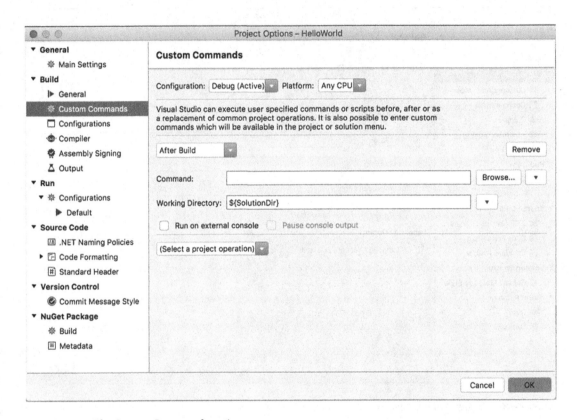

Figure 2-14. *The Custom Commands options*

You can specify the action that must be executed by supplying an application name in the Command text box (or you can click Browse instead of manually typing the name). Commands could need to receive parameters, for example, the solution or project name. Because VS for Mac identifies such parameters with special constants, you can select the appropriate constant by clicking the button with the arrow icon and selecting one of the self-explanatory values from the drop-down. The same applies to the Working Directory check box, where you can specify the directory in which the command should be executed. In Figure 2-14 you can see the $(SolutionDir) constant that represents the solution directory and that is listed as Solution Directory in the constants drop-down box.

The Configurations Tab

The Configurations tab allows you to manage build configurations. By default, it shows the Debug and Release configurations, as you can see in Figure 2-15.

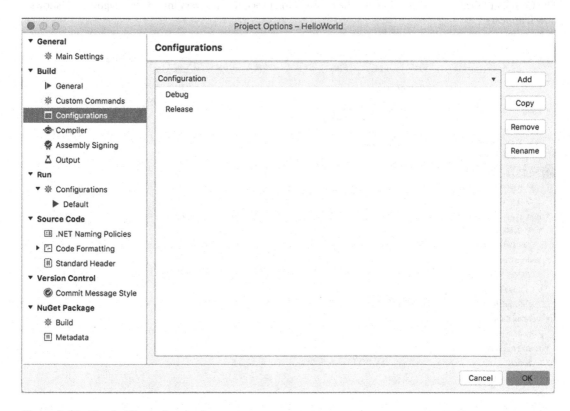

Figure 2-15. *The Configurations options*

Here you can manage configurations by adding, copying, removing, and renaming configurations with the appropriate buttons. The reason why creating a new configuration could be useful will be clearer when discussing the next tab, Compiler. For now, you can create a new configuration by clicking Add and then entering the configuration name in the New Configuration dialog, as shown in Figure 2-16.

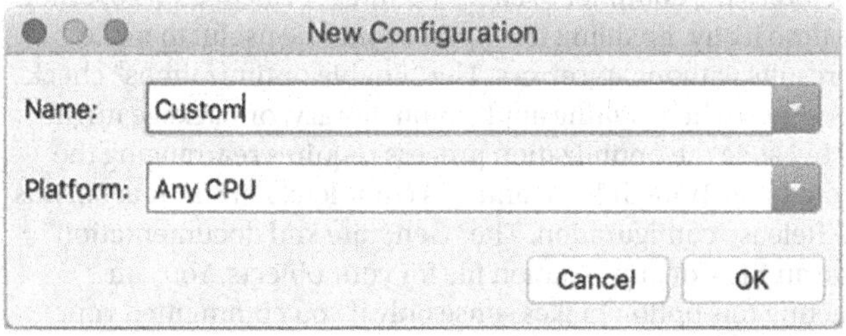

Figure 2-16. *Creating a new configuration*

When you click OK, the new configuration will be listed in the Configuration tab.

The Compiler Tab

The Compiler tab allows you to influence the compilation process and is very interesting. Figure 2-17 shows how it appears.

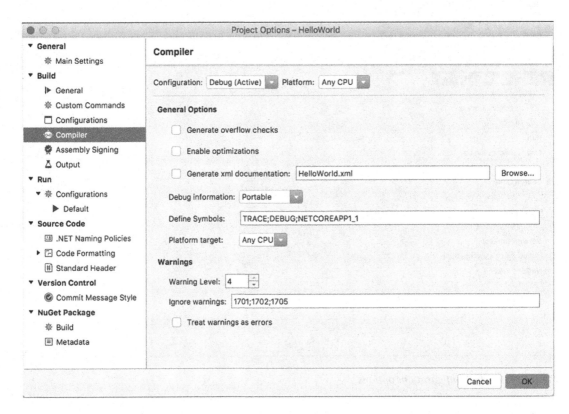

Figure 2-17. *The Compiler options*

Compiler options are per configuration, and the default is the active build configuration, but you can select a different configuration in the Configuration drop-down box. In this way, changes you make on this tab will be applied when you build your solution using the specified configuration. In the General Options area, the "Generate overflow checks" check box forces the compiler to check for integer calculations overflow and to throw an OverflowException at compile time if any. Enabling this option could be useful to make integer calculations faster and to avoid storing results without any errors. The "Enable optimizations" check box forces the compiler to optimize the build output so the resulting application, library, or package might be smaller, faster, and more efficient. However, because the optimization process requires rearranging the code in many ways, the debugging experience could be more difficult and less complete. For this reason, this check box is automatically enabled only for the Release configuration. The "Generate xml documentation" check box makes Visual Studio for Mac generate an XML documentation file for your objects. You can specify an output file name in the text box. Selecting this option makes sense only if you commented your source code with XML comments, which is explained in the "Introducing XML Comments" section later in this chapter.

The "Debug information" drop-down box allows specifying the level of accuracy for the debug symbols that the compiler will generate. Technically speaking, the compiler generates a program database (.pdb) file that contains all the information and symbols that a debugger needs to instrument an application. Table 2-11 summarizes all the available options and their descriptions.

Table 2-11. *Possible Values for the Debug Information Box*

Value	Description
Full	Generates full debugging information and PDB files for a complete debugging experience. Not recommended with .NET Core.
Symbols only	Generates PDB files that only contain symbol information.
Portable	Generates a portable, cross-platform PDB file that is optimized for .NET Core apps and .NET Standard libraries.
Embedded	Embeds debugging information into the build output.
None	No debugging information is generated.

The default value for the Debug configuration in .NET Core is Portable, while for the Release configuration it's None. It is worth mentioning that the Portable option is quite new for the C# compiler, as it has been introduced together with .NET Core to allow for cross-platform .pdb files. When Portable is enabled, the compiler only includes .NET symbols and excludes everything that has to do with native code. This makes .pdb certainly smaller and simpler, but the debugger cannot perform operations such as Edit and Continue. Portable is definitely recommended with .NET Core projects. The Define Symbols text box allows specifying environment variables that you can use to detect whether your code is running under a specific build configuration. If you look at Figure 2-16, you can see that the TRACE, DEBUG, and NETCOREAPP1_1 symbols are defined. For example, you could write the following check if you wanted to execute some code only if the active configuration for the application is Debug:

```
#if DEBUG
// Code inside this block will run only if the active configuration is Debug
#endif
```

Debug symbols are treated as constant variables, and they also are available per configuration, so if you select another configuration such as Release, you will see different variables. Having an option to customize the debug symbols is one of the most important reasons you might want to create custom configurations. You can certainly extend existing build configurations with new symbols, but if you want them to be available only in some cases, a custom configuration is the proper place. "Platform target" allows you to specify the processor architecture that the compiler should target, and the default is Any CPU. Possible other values are x86, x64, and Itanium. In the Warnings group, you can control how the compiler should handle some warning messages. In C#, warnings represent potential problems that the developer should not ignore but that do not prevent the compiler from building the project. In the Warning Level box, you can specify a value from 0 to 4 (the latter is the default), whose description is available in Table 2-12.

Table 2-12. *Warning Level Values*

Value	Description
0	The compiler does not report any warning messages.
1	The compiler reports severe warning messages.
2	The compiler reports warnings as in level 1, plus less severe warnings (e.g., hiding class members).
3	The compiler reports warnings as in level 2, plus less severe warnings (e.g., expressions that always evaluate to `true` or to `false`).
4	The compiler reports all warnings as per level 3, plus informational warnings.

Warning messages, as well as blocking errors, are represented by a unique identifier. In the "Ignore warnings" box, you can control which warnings must be ignored, given their identifier. Actually, in C# the full error or warning identifier is preceded by the *CS* literal. In VS for Mac, the default ignored warnings are related to problems that can occur with references to assemblies with the same name and can be left unchanged. Later in this chapter, in the section called "Browsing Help and Documentation," I will explain how to find documentation about error and warning codes. If you are impatient, you can jump to that section, have a look, and then come back here. You can also prevent the compiler from building a project by selecting the "Treat warnings as errors" check box. Unless you have specific requirements, my suggestion is that you leave the default selections so that you can also distinguish well between warnings and errors. The Errors pad, described shortly, will help you get more details about warnings and errors.

The Assembly Signing Tab

The next tab is Assembly Signing, and it allows you to sign an assembly with a digital signature, also referred to as a *strong name* (see Figure 2-18). Supported files are `.snk` and `.pfx` files.

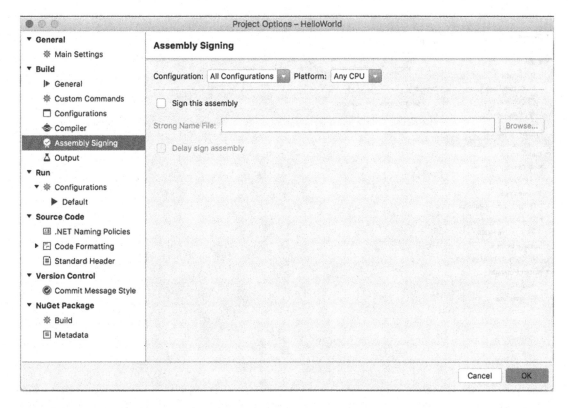

Figure 2-18. *The Assembly Signing options*

The .pfx format also allows for specifying a password, so it should be preferred. To specify a digital signature, enable the "Sign this assembly" check box and then click Browse to select your .snk or .pfx file from disk.

The "Delay sign assembly" check box allows you to save some space in the assembly for the digital signature, which will be provided at a later stage.

The Output Tab

The last tab in the Build node is called Output (see Figure 2-19). Here you can specify the assembly name and the directory for the build output.

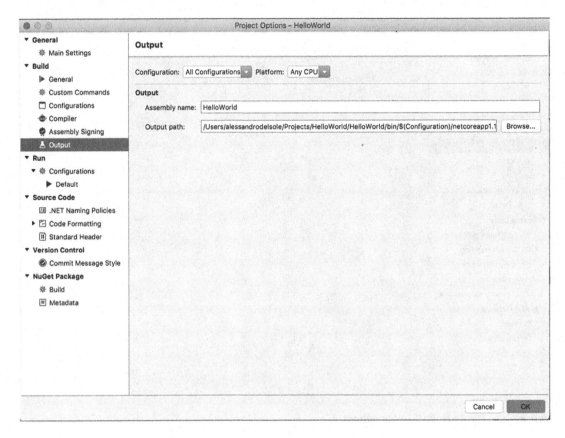

Figure 2-19. *The Output options*

Of course, Visual Studio for Mac provides some default values based on the information supplied when you created the project, but these can be changed if required.

For .NET Core projects, an additional subfolder representing the current runtime version is also generated, and it actually contains the build output. In the Run node, you can specify what action Visual Studio must take when starting the project with or without debugging. More specifically, in the Default node under Configurations, you can decide what Visual Studio for Mac must do when you start a project (see Figure 2-20).

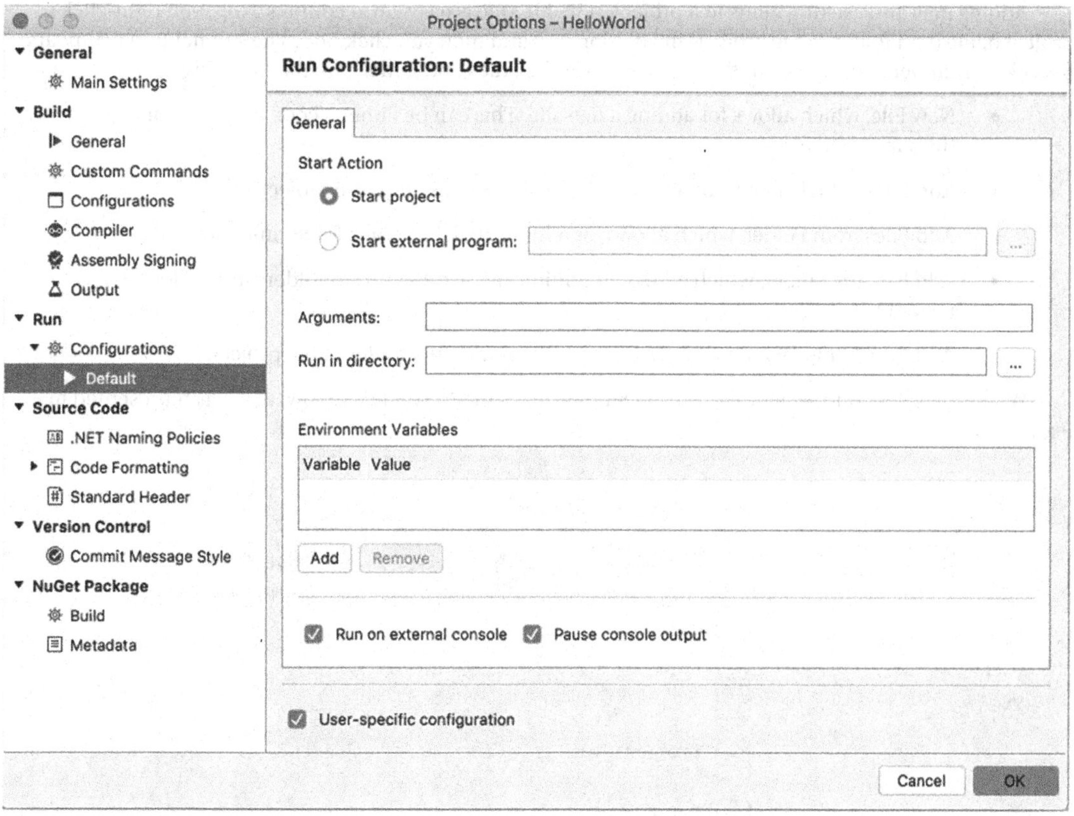

Figure 2-20. *The Default options for starting a project*

The default option is "Start project," which is fine for most of the times. You can select "Start external program" if you instead want to run an external program against the current project, for example, a third-party debugger, and you can supply the arguments for the external program. You can specify the working directory and any environment variables the external program might need. In the case of console applications, the default option is that they run inside an instance of the Terminal's console, but you can deselect the "Run on external console" check box to redirect the application's output to the Output pad. The other options are self-explanatory. In the Project Options dialog, you can also see other nodes such as Source Code, Version Control, and NuGet Package. Though these options are also available per project, they can actually be set at the IDE level in the Visual Studio options, so I will discuss them in more detail in Chapter 13 together with other interesting features. This is also because you first need to know more about source control support, which is discussed in Chapter 12. It is now time to walk through project options for Xamarin.

Adding, Removing, and Renaming Items

More often than not, you will need to add new or existing files or folders to a project, for example, when you need additional code files or resources such as images and other assets.

49

Adding new and existing items to a project in VS for Mac is easy. To accomplish this, you right-click a project name (or a folder in the project) in Solution pad and then you click Add. The submenu that appears provides a number of options, but those related to adding files and folders are the following:

- New File, which allows for adding a new file. This can be either a code file or any of the supported files.

- Add Files, which allows for adding existing files on disk into the project.

- Add Files from Folder, which allows for adding all the files in a folder into the project.

- Add Existing Folder, which allows for adding all the files and subfolders in a folder recursively.

- Add New Folder, which allows for creating a new empty folder in the project.

When you select Add ➤ New File, Visual Studio shows the New File window, which is represented in Figure 2-21.

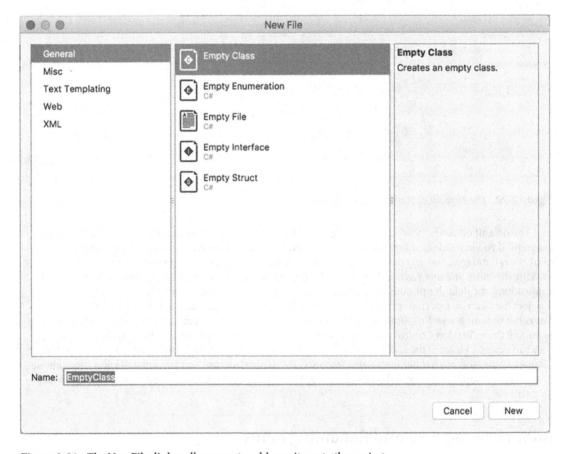

Figure 2-21. *The New File dialog allows you to add new items to the project*

The list of available items is divided into several categories and may vary depending on the project type you are working with. You can browse items in each category, and you can simply click an item to see a description on the right side of the dialog. When ready, simply type a name for the new item and click New.

As a best practice, it is recommended that you group files that are common to a specific area or task into subfolders. This helps you keep your code and project items well organized. For example, if you build a line-of-business application, you might want to group files such as `Customer.cs`, `Order.cs`, or `Supplier.cs` into a folder called Model or DataModel.

Visual Studio for Mac also allows adding items to solutions. The most common scenario is when you want to add a new or existing project to the current solution. To accomplish this, in the Solution pad right-click the solution name and then select Add ➤ Add New Project or Add ➤ Add Existing Project. You can also add individual files to a solution by selecting Add ➤ Add Files. Additionally, you can group files into folders by selecting Add Solution Folder and then adding files to the new folder. Solution folders and individual files are useful when you want to include items such as documents, text files, and images that you want to always be part of the solution but that you do not want to be included in the build output.

You can remove items from a project by right-clicking and selecting Remove. The command is instead called Delete if you want to remove a project from a solution. Make sure you remove items you really no longer need because an improper deletion might compromise the build process.

Renaming a code file can be accomplished by right-clicking the file name in the Solution pad and then selecting Rename. The cursor will appear on the selected file, and you will be able to enter a new name. If you come from Visual Studio on Windows, you might expect that renaming a file that contains a type will also rename the type. This is not supported in Visual Studio for Mac, and you will need to rename types manually, using the technique described in the "Renaming Identifiers In-line" subsection later in the chapter.

Working with Pads

Pads are floating tool windows that are responsible for various tasks. Pads in Visual Studio for Mac can be compared to tool windows in Visual Studio on Windows and to pads in Apple's Xcode. Pads can be docked and arranged in the workspace according to your preferences so that you can customize the development environment in the best way for you.

In the previous sections, you have worked with the Solution pad, which allows you to browse and manage projects and code files in a solution. In this section, you will learn about the other most important and common pads in Visual Studio for Mac. Some other specific pads will be instead discussed where appropriate. As a general rule, pads can be enabled by selecting View ➤ Pads.

■ **Note** This section does not discuss debugging pads, which are instead presented in the next chapter.

Docking, Hiding, and Rearranging Pads

When you open a pad, it is automatically docked and positioned in a specific place in the IDE, but you can rearrange pads as you like. You can also undock a pad and treat it as a stand-alone window. Pads can also autohide so that you can show them only when necessary and maximize the editor area, by simply clicking their label. To undock a pad, you click its title, drag it by keeping the mouse left button pressed, and then release when you see that its height is not constrained into other areas of the workspace. Figure 2-22 shows how to undock the Solution pad.

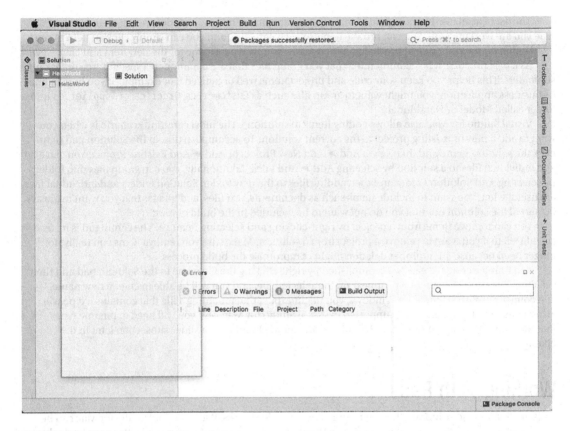

Figure 2-22. *Undocking a pad*

In the undocked state, a pad works like a stand-alone window; therefore, it has the classic three buttons to close, minimize, and maximize it. You can dock a floating pad by simply clicking the Dock button on its toolbar. Visual Studio will automatically dock the pad in the position it was docked previously. In the docked state, the Dock button changes to Auto-Hide, which you can click to completely hide the pad except for its label, which you can click to open the pad. Then it will be autohidden again once you click outside of it. In Figure 2-28, you can see a number of pads in a hidden state and with only their labels visible, such as Classes, Toolbox, Properties, Document Outline, and Unit Tests. You can also completely close a pad by clicking the Close button on its toolbar, but then you will need to select View ➤ Pads to open it again. To rearrange a pad in the workspace, you click the pad's title and then move it to the desired position, as demonstrated in Figure 2-23.

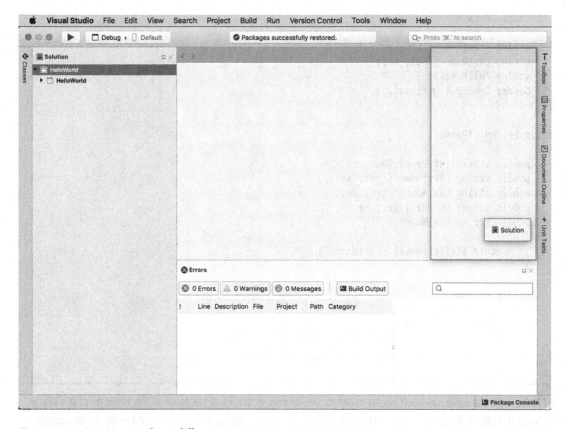

Figure 2-23. *Moving a pad to a different position*

When moving a pad, the IDE draws rectangles that represent a place in which it's possible to dock the pad. When you are satisfied with the position, just release the mouse button, and the pad will be moved to the new place. Notice that the pad will still be visible in the original place until you release the mouse button. After this explanation on how to arrange pads in the workspace, it's time to get to know the most important of them.

The Classes Pad

The Classes pad provides a hierarchical view of all the types and their members defined within the projects in a solution. For a better understanding of how it works, inside the root namespace of the Program.cs file, add the following code:

```
public enum Gender
{
    Female,
    Male
}
```

```
interface IPerson
{
    string FirstName { get; set; }
    string LastName { get; set; }
    string FullName();
    Gender Gender { get; set; }
}

class Person: IPerson
{
    public static int PeopleCounter;
    public string FirstName { get; set; }
    public string LastName { get; set; }
    public Gender Gender { get; set; }
    public string FullName()
    {
        return $"{FirstName} {LastName}";
    }

    public Person()
    {
        PeopleCounter += 1;
    }
}
```

■ **Note** All the code has been added to the same file only to demonstrate some of the features of the Visual Studio IDE both in this section and in other sections later in the chapter, but in real-world projects you should create appropriate files for better organization and separation.

The code defines an interface called IPerson, which a class called Person implements. Among others, the code defines a Gender enum that is used as the type for the same-named property. The FullName method returns the concatenation of FirstName and LastName, while the PeopleCounter static field acts as a counter for all the instances of the Person class. At this point, the Classes pad appears like in Figure 2-24.

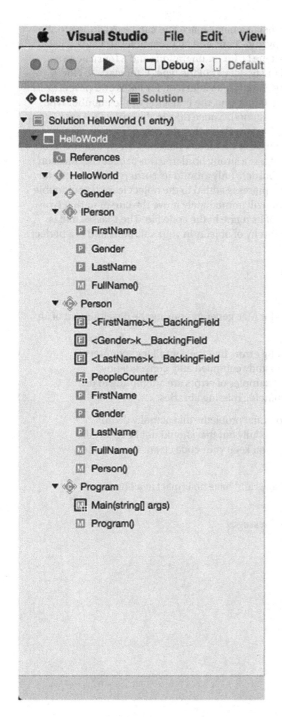

Figure 2-24. *The hierarchical view of types and members in the Classes pad*

As you can see, Classes shows all the types defined inside a namespace and can be expanded to show the members they define. Namespaces are represented by gray icons and an open bracket. Value types are represented by a green icon and the first letter of the type (*E* for enumerations and *S* for structures). Reference types are represented by light blue icons and the first letter of the type (*C* for classes, *I* for interfaces, and *D* for delegates). Type members are represented by a violet icon for fields and properties, by a light blue icon for methods, and by a red icon for constants, plus the first letter of the member type (*F* for fields, *P* for properties, *M* for methods, and *C* for constants). Notice that, in the case of C# auto-implemented properties, the Classes pad also shows the backing fields that the compiler generates behind the scenes. Icons also help with understanding a type or member's visibility: if a type or member is public, the icon has no border; if it is private, the icon has a strong border; if it is protected, the icon has a thin border; and if it is internal, the icon has thin borders only around its corners. Notice how, for static members, an overlay icon representing four black squares is added to the object icon. If you double-click a type or member in the Classes pad, the code editor will immediately move the cursor to that type or member, and it will also highlight all the occurrences of its name in the code file. The Classes pad is extremely useful to get a visual representation of the hierarchy of objects in your solutions and is a perfect companion for the Solution pad.

The Errors Pad

The Errors pad shows all the messages that Visual Studio for Mac generates during the development of an application. Messages can be of three kinds.

- *Errors*: These include any problems or blocking errors that the compiler encounters and that prevent your code from being successfully compiled and, consequently, that prevent your application from running. Examples of errors are attempting to use an undefined object, syntax errors, and referencing missing libraries.

- *Warnings*: These include messages about potential problems that actually do not prevent your code from being compiled successfully but that should not be ignored. The compiler also reports warnings that help you keep your code clean, for example, with unused declared variables.

- *Messages*: These are just informational messages and have no impact at all on the build process.

Figure 2-25 shows how the Errors pad displays error messages.

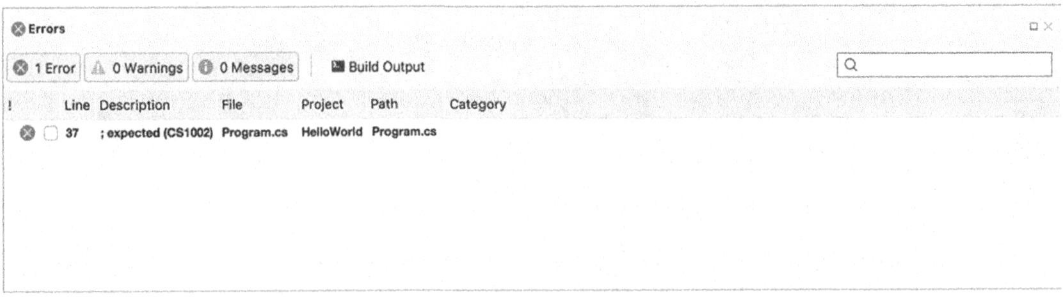

Figure 2-25. *The Errors pad showing error messages*

For each error, warning, or message, the Errors pad shows the line number in the code file (Line column), the error description (Description column), the code file where the problem was detected (File column), in which project (Project column), and the path (Path column). Optionally, the Errors pad might show a category based on the .NET coding rules. Messages can be filtered excluding errors, warning, and messages by simply clicking the corresponding button or by typing key words in the search box. If you double-click a message, the code editor will move the cursor to the code file and line number where the problem was detected. Additionally, you can right-click a message and select Show Error Reference to find information about the error code on the Internet.

Actually, the Errors pad is not the only way for Visual Studio to report errors and warnings. In fact, the code editor also plays a key role in this by underlining errors and warnings with the so-called squiggles, in other words, wavy lines that appear under code issues and that are red for errors and green for warnings. This topic will be discussed in the next section, but it is important to mention that the Errors pad shows errors and warnings as you type. This is possible because of the background C# compiler that performs live static code analysis. The Errors pad takes the messages sent by the compiler, displaying them in the list you saw in Figure 2-25. Not limited to errors and warnings, the Errors pad can also show messages that the compiler raises during the build process. This is extremely useful to understand where and why a build process failed and is also useful for finding possible solutions. To accomplish this, you simply click the Build Output button in the Errors pad and then build your project or solution. Figure 2-26 shows an example of output messages when a build fails.

Figure 2-26. *Build Output displays messages the compiler raises during the build process*

As you can see, the compiler reports detailed information about the build process, and it also raises error messages that explain where and why a build failed. The Build Output tools is very useful because some errors that are not related to your code can be detected only at compile time. If the build succeeds, then in Build Output you will see a success message. Notice that the Build Output tool can be resized as if it were a column, and it can completely hide the error columns.

The Properties Pad

In Visual Studio terminology, everything has *properties*. A property is a characteristic of a particular item, where the item can be a file, a class, a window, a layout in a visual app, and so on. For example, the height and width are properties of a window. The filename is instead a property of a file.

Because you often need to set properties for your .NET objects, layouts, and files, Visual Studio for Mac provides a convenient tool to set properties called the Properties pad. The appearance of the Properties pad is different according to the item you need to set properties for, but it generally appears as a two-column table, in which the left column displays the property name and the right column shows or sets the property value. Figure 2-27 shows an example of the Properties pad for a C# code file.

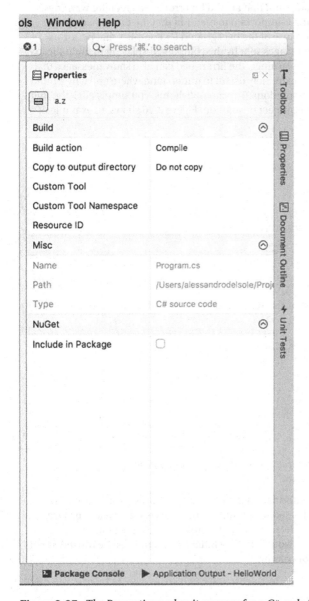

Figure 2-27. *The Properties pad as it appears for a C# code file*

You will use the Properties pad often in this book, so additional explanations will be provided where appropriate. The Properties pad is particularly useful when working with user interface elements in a web or Xamarin projects because it allows you to set object properties with a visual tool instead of setting all the properties manually in the code.

The Tasks Pad

Keeping the focus on your productivity, Visual Studio for Mac provides an integrated tool that allows you to create and manage task lists that can help you in the application development life cycle. This tool is the Tasks pad.

The Tasks pad can show a list of tasks based either on specific tokens you insert in your comments in the code or on user tasks. For example, consider Figure 2-28 where you can see the Tasks pad showing two items.

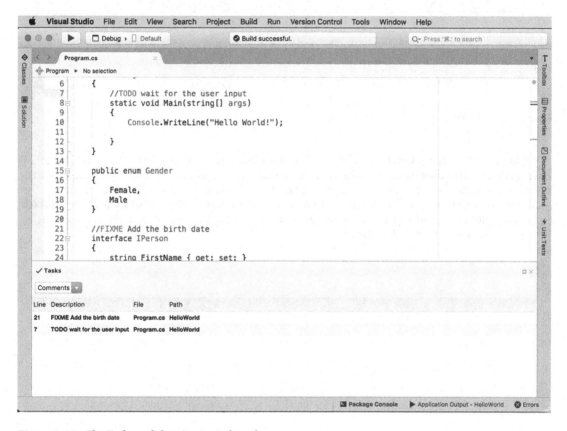

Figure 2-28. *The Tasks pad showing items based on comments*

Now if you take a look at the code editor, you will see two special tokens in the comments called TODO and FIXME. When Visual Studio encounters these tokens, it understands they represent tasks that must be done and displays them in the Tasks pad. As an enforcement, you can see how tokens have different colors in the code editor. Supported tokens are FIXME, TODO, HACK, and UNDONE. Double-click an item, and the code editor will move the cursor to the comment that contains the selected token. To mark a task as completed, you can either remove the comment or right-click the task and then select Delete. Additionally, you can create user-level tasks. In the Tasks drop-down box, select User Tasks. You will see that the Tasks pad's layout will change, and you will have buttons and fields to enter your tasks, providing a description and the task's priority (see Figure 2-29).

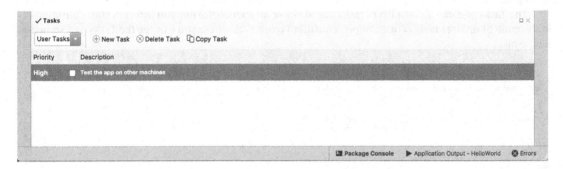

Figure 2-29. *The Tasks pad showing user tasks*

While tasks based on tokens in the source code comments are per project, user tasks are available to you regardless of the project you are working on. You can mark a user task as completed by simply selecting the check box at the left of the task description. You can also add custom tokens, and you can customize colors based on the task priority. To accomplish this, select Visual Studio ➤ Preferences, and in the Tasks tab (see Figure 2-30) you can add tokens, edit existing tokens, and customize the color that will be used in the Tasks pad to display items, based on their priority.

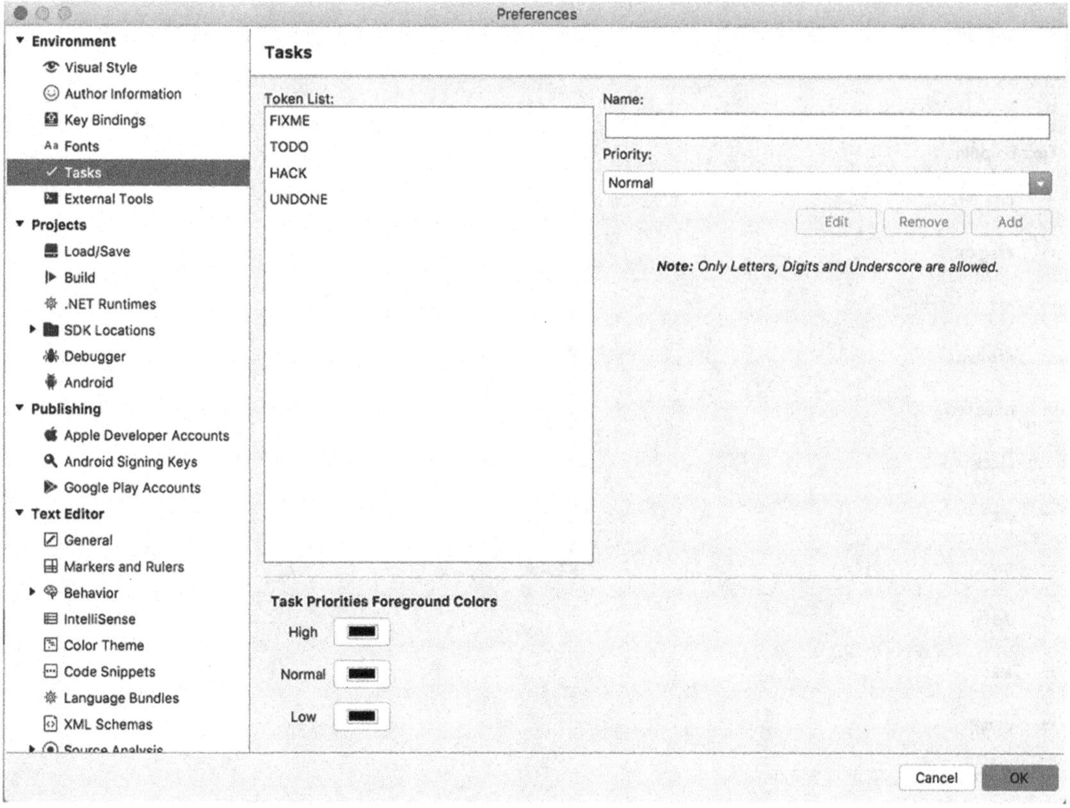

Figure 2-30. *Customizing tasks*

The Toolbox Pad

The Toolbox pad makes it easy to add items to your code or to elements of the user interface. Instead of manually writing code snippets or writing the code that defines a piece of user interface at design time, you can drag items from the Toolbox pad onto the code editor or the designer surface.

The Toolbox pad will be used many times in the next chapters, but for now you can take a look at Figure 2-31, which shows the Toolbox as it is available over a C# code file, presenting a list of available code snippets.

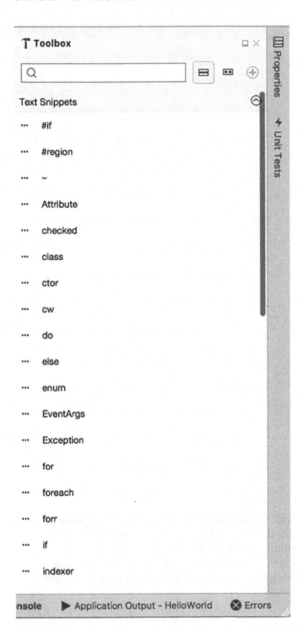

Figure 2-31. *The Toolbox pad for a C# code file*

In this case, the Toolbox pad contains a list of code snippets that you can drag onto the code editor to insert a ready-to-use code block.

The Package Console Pad

The Package Console pad displays the output from the NuGet Package Manager. It is useful to understand the process of downloading, installing, and restoring NuGet packages. You already saw this pad in action in the "Working with NuGet Packages" subsection earlier, and Figure 2-11 shows an example.

Working with the Code Editor

The code editor in Visual Studio for Mac is the place where you will spend most of the time in your developer life, and therefore it deserves a thorough explanation. In this section, you will learn how to get the most out of the features that empower the code editor in order to boost your productivity, and you will see how most of the tools work directly in the active editor window so that you will never lose the focus on your code.

As a general rule, Visual Studio will open a new editor window every time you double-click a code file in the Solution pad. Each code file lives in a separate editor window that is represented by a tab. Visual Studio can handle infinite editor windows (and tabs). By default, the code editor shows the full view of a code file, but you can split a single editor window into two columns with View ➤ Editor Columns ➤ Two Columns. This is useful when you need to work on different places in the same code file concurrently. Use View ➤ Editor Columns ➤ One Column to restore the original view.

Using Syntax Colorization

As you would expect, Visual Studio for Mac's code editor provides syntax colorization for all of the supported code file types, such as C#, F#, XML, XAML, HTML, JavaScript, JSON, and Visual Basic. In all the other cases, the code editor will treat files as plain-text documents.

Using the Edit Menu

The Edit menu offers common commands for editing source text, such as Copy, Paste, Cut, Undo, Redo, and Select All. It also provides the Format submenu, which includes commands to fix spaces such as Format Document, Indent, and Unindent.

You can also quickly convert a line, string, or identifier to uppercase and lowercase with the same-named commands. With Join Lines, you can bring a number of selected lines of code to a single line. With Toggle Line Comments, you can quickly comment or uncomment one or more lines.

For each command, the Edit menu also shows the proper keyboard shortcuts. The most common are certainly Command+C (Copy), Command+V (Paste), Command+X (Cut), and Command+Z (Undo).

Zooming the Code Editor

You can zoom the content of the active editor by pressing Option and then moving the mouse wheel up (zoom out) and down (zoom in).

Fast Coding with IntelliSense

IntelliSense has always been one of the biggest points of strength in Microsoft Visual Studio on Windows, and now this technology is also available in VS for Mac. IntelliSense is an advanced word completion engine, which provides suggestions based on the context, and it offers help and tips on how to use a type or member.

IntelliSense shows up when you start typing in the code editor. Figure 2-32 shows a first example in which the developer starts writing a type name.

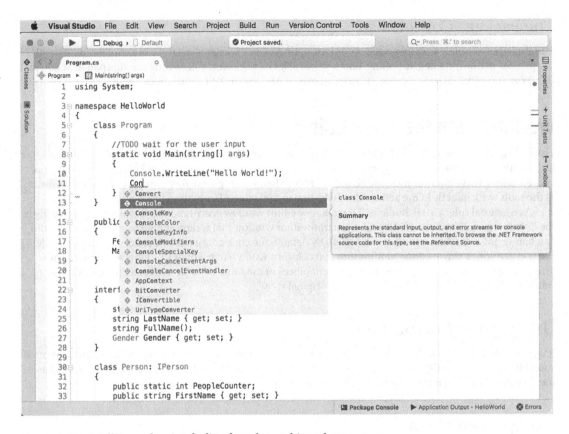

Figure 2-32. *IntelliSense showing the list of words matching what you type*

IntelliSense automatically filters the list of available words for completion as you type. When you scroll the list and select an item, a tooltip appears and shows documentation about that item.

■ **Note** IntelliSense is able to show documentation only if this has been provided via XML comments, which is certainly the case with .NET libraries, but it is something you must remember if you want IntelliSense to work the same way against types and members you code.

You can press the spacebar or Tab to insert the selected word. Notice how items in the list have the same icons with the same colors you saw previously with the Classes pad. It is worth mentioning that IntelliSense here is showing only what it thinks it is suitable in the current context, so it does not show reserved words or other objects that should not be in a method body. If you insert a word and then press the dot, IntelliSense will show objects available for the inserted item. Figure 2-33 shows an example based on a method.

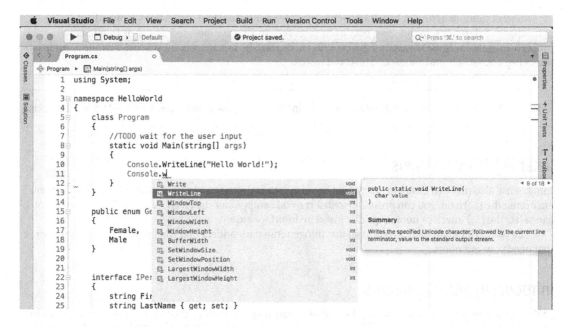

Figure 2-33. *IntelliSense showing the list of members of a type*

Notice how the icons and their colors match the Classes pad. Also, when you scroll the list of members, you will see a tooltip with the member signature and the documentation. In the case of methods, if you press the left and right cursor keys, you will be able to scroll the list of method overloads. Additionally, when you insert methods, IntelliSense will show contextualized documentation for method parameters when you open the left parenthesis, as shown in Figure 2-34.

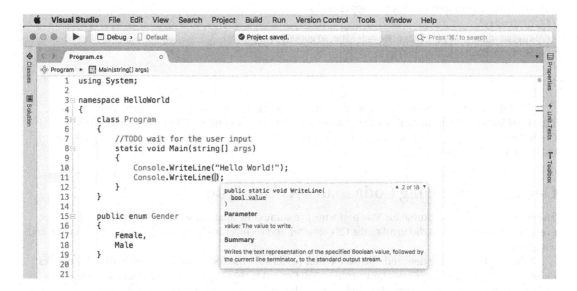

Figure 2-34. *IntelliSense showing detailed documentation for method parameters*

Another demonstration of how IntelliSense provides contextualized suggestions is outside of namespace declarations. In this case, only a few reserved words are supported, and thus IntelliSense properly suggests only the words that the compiler accepts to be outside a namespace declaration, such as the using, unchecked, and namespace reserved words.

■ **Note**   You can customize the IntelliSense behavior in Visual Studio ➤ Preferences ➤ Text Editor ➤ IntelliSense.

Inserting Code Snippets

IntelliSense also makes it easier to insert ready-to-use code snippets via the so-called templates. When you encounter the (...) icon, you can press Tab to insert a code snippet for the given template. For instance, you can select the (...) interface item to quickly insert an interface stub.

The code editor will then highlight all the autogenerated identifiers that you might want to rename or that need your attention.

Introducing XML Comments

At the beginning of this section, you saw how IntelliSense displays tooltips containing summary information about types and members and details about parameters (see Figures 2-40, 2-41, and 2-42). This kind of documentation is available for all types and members that have been commented with the so-called XML comments.

Most of .NET and Mono built-in types include these comments, but you can add XML comments to your code as well so that IntelliSense will display informational tooltips for your types and members. XML comments can be added by typing three / symbols like in the following code and then specifying the required information:

```
/// <summary>
/// The main entry point of your application
/// </summary>
/// <param name="args">The command-line arguments.</param>
static void Main(string[] args)
{
}
```

The full documentation for XML comments is available at https://msdn.microsoft.com/en-us/library/b2s063f7.aspx. Remember that you must select the Generate XML Comments option in the Compiler tab of the project options, as explained in the "The Compiler Tab" subsection earlier in this chapter (shown in Figure 2-17).

Detecting and Fixing Code Issues As You Type

The code editor in Visual Studio for Mac performs live static code analysis as you type. This means that, at every key stroke, Visual Studio invokes the C# compiler and receives back any code issues such as errors and warnings.

When code issues are detected, the code editor underlines the code that has issues with red squiggles for errors and with green squiggles for warnings. Not limited to this, the code editor places an in-line message, which contains the error description, near the code issue. Figure 2-35 shows an example based on a class that should implement the IDisposable interface but that actually does not.

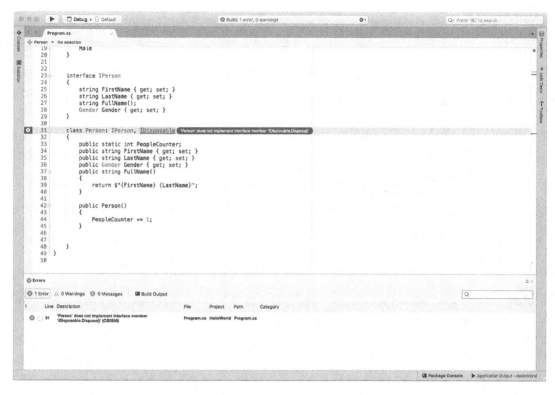

Figure 2-35. *The code editor highlights code issues*

■ **Note** You can control inline messages with View ➤ Inline messages. The default setting is Errors and Warnings. Other available options are None and Errors.

With most of errors and warnings raised by the compiler, Visual Studio is also able to offer a proper fix. For example, if you right-click a code issue and then select Quick Fix, the code editor will offer one or more possible code fixes for that context, with a live preview of how the code will look after the fix. In the current example, the code editor offers four alternatives to implement the IDisposable interface, with a live preview for each (see Figure 2-36). As an alternative, you can click the word that is underlined with a squiggle and wait for a little overlay line that appears over the word, which you can click to enable the quick fix actions. Also, you can press Option+Enter to bring up the quick fix list at any time so that you do not have to move your fingers from the keyboard.

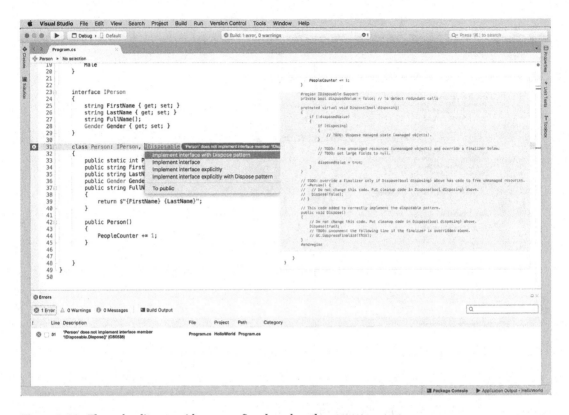

Figure 2-36. *The code editor provides proper fixes based on the current context*

The preview shows new lines of code in green, and it will highlight in red any lines of code that will be removed by applying the fix. Listing and describing all the available code fixes for all the errors and warnings the compiler can detect is not possible here, but just keep in mind that one or more fix is available for code issues that occur when using the C# language and libraries from Microsoft.

Live analysis and code fixes dramatically improve your coding experience, as they provide a convenient way to fix code issues within the active editor window, always keeping your focus on the code.

■ **Note**   As a tip, you can see the list of available analysis rules and of quick fix actions in the Visual Studio preferences. To accomplish this, select Visual Studio ➤ Preferences ➤ Text Editor ➤ Source Analysis ➤ C#. The dialog will be divided in two tabs, one containing the list of code issues and one containing the list of actions. You can also disable and enable both via the corresponding check boxes.

Quickly Adding Using Directives

It is common for developers to write a type name that is not recognized because the namespace that defines that type has not been imported with a proper using directive or because the type name is not fully qualified (that is, does not include the namespace); therefore, the type name is underlined with a red squiggle, and an error message says that the type or namespace could not be found.

In this situation, instead of manually adding the using directive (which also implies you remember the namespace name), you can right-click the type name, select Quick Fix, and then the pop-up menu will offer to add the proper using directive or to fully qualify the type name by including the containing namespace.

Behind the Scenes of Code Issues and Quick Fixes: Roslyn

The .NET Compiler Platform, also known as Project Roslyn (http://github.com/dotnet/roslyn), is the engine behind the live static analysis, code issue detection, quick fixes, and refactorings. Roslyn provides open source, cross-platform C# and Visual Basic compilers with rich code analysis APIs.

Put succinctly, before Roslyn, an IDE had to implement its own code analysis rules to detect issues in the source code. This is what Microsoft had always offered with Visual Studio up to version 2013. With Roslyn, compilers expose APIs that any tool can invoke. With these APIs, you can invoke a snapshot of the compiler, analyze source code, retrieve any code issues, and, most important, plug in your custom analysis rules. What you get with Visual Studio for Mac is a number of analysis rules coded at Microsoft, but these can be extended with your analysis rules and with custom refactorings. For instance, if you produce and sell libraries, you could also offer code analyzers that detect an improper usage of your types. Of course, discussing Roslyn in more detail and extending the coding experience with your own rules (as well as other topics such as code generation) is out of the scope of this book, but it is important that you know that the analysis engine comes from the compiler and is independent from any IDE. More information can be found at http://github.com/dotnet/Roslyn and, if you also work with Visual Studio on Windows, in my e-book *Roslyn Succinctly*, which is available for free at https://www.syncfusion.com/resources/techportal/details/ebooks/roslyn.

Refactoring Your Code

Refactoring is the process of rewriting a piece of code in a better way, without changing its original behavior. By leveraging the C# compiler's APIs, the code editor in Visual Studio for Mac offers a large number of built-in code refactorings. In this section, you will learn about the most common code refactorings.

As a general rule, you can select a piece of code, right-click, and then select either Refactor or Quick Fix to see whether a code refactoring is available. Additionally, Visual Studio automatically detects the availability of a code refactoring for a specific code block, so it underlines a keyword or block with an overlay icon that you can recognize by three small dots and that you can click to discover potential refactorings. Keep these options in mind because only the most common refactorings will be discussed here. You can select a single identifier or type name, you can select a line of code, and you can even select a code block, as refactorings are available at different levels.

■ **Note**   As for quick fix, a live preview of the code is also available for the Refactor command.

Detecting and Removing Redundant Code

After spending a lot of time writing code, it is not uncommon to have redundant code such as unused variables and unnecessary using directives. Redundant code does not block your builds, but it makes your code unnecessarily more complex. Visual Studio for Mac automatically detects redundant code, which you can recognize by a lighter color.

For example, names of unused variables or namespaces are colored in gray instead of black, and keywords referring to redundant code are colored in light blue. When you see redundant code, you can hover over with the mouse, and the code editor will show a descriptive tooltip of the full message; then you can right-click the redundant code, select Quick Fix, and choose the proper fix. Figure 2-37 shows an example based on redundant using directives, where you can also see a live preview in which red code represents the lines that will be removed.

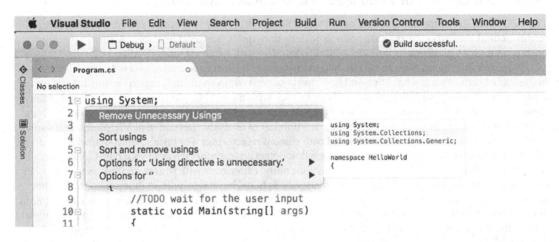

Figure 2-37. *Removing redundant code*

With specific regard to using directives, you can always right-click them, select Quick Fix, and decide to sort directives or to both sort and remove unnecessary directives.

Extracting Code Blocks

Another common refactoring technique is dividing long code blocks into smaller code blocks. For example, you can create a method from a set of lines of code inside another method.

To accomplish this, select the code block you want to extract, right-click and select Quick Fix, and then select Extract Method. Once the method has been created, you will be provided with an option to enter a new method name. Another useful refactoring allows extracting an interface from a class. To accomplish this, right-click a class name, select Quick Fix, and then select Extract Interface.

Renaming Identifiers In-line

The code editor in VS for Mac allows you to easily rename identifiers directly in-line, without modal dialogs. For example, you can right-click a variable name and then select Refactor ➤ Rename.

At this point, the identifier will be highlighted (see Figure 2-38). Just type the new name, and you will see how all the occurrences of the identifier will be renamed as you type. Also, the code editor highlights the line numbers for lines where an occurrence of the identifier is being renamed.

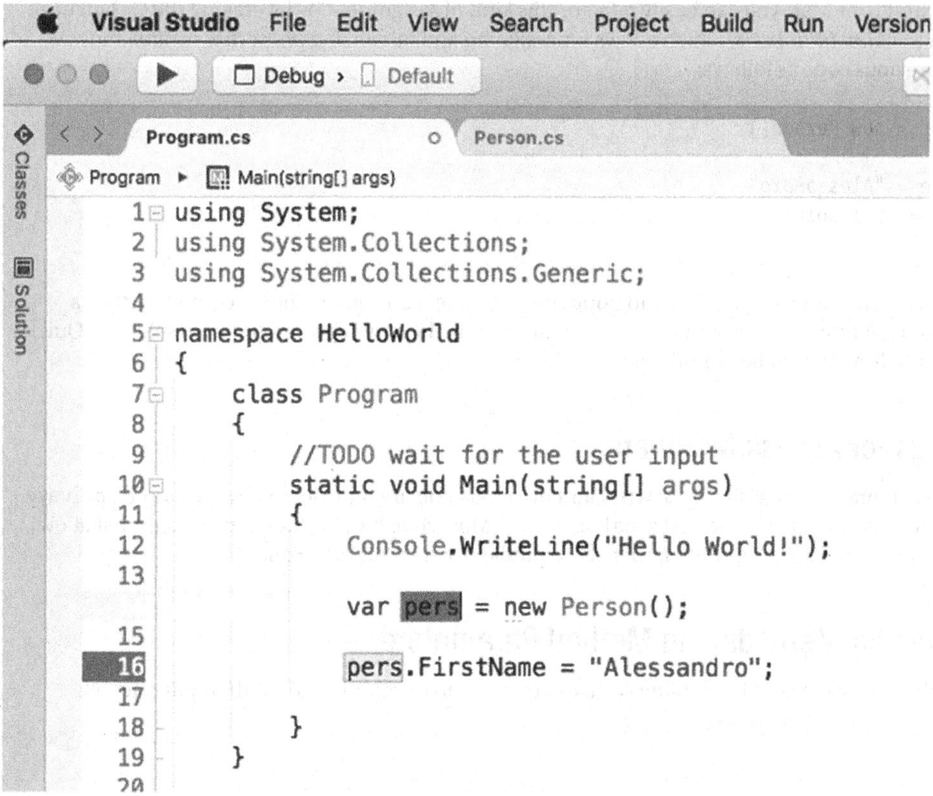

Figure 2-38. *In-line renaming identifiers*

Moving Type Definitions to Files

In some cases, such as in the example of the Person class I provided when I discussed the Classes pad, you might have multiple type definitions inside the same code file. This is not best practice, and Visual Studio for Mac has a solution for that.

In fact, you can right-click a type name (such as a class name or structure name), select Quick Fix, and then select Move To (followed by an autogenerated file name). Visual Studio for Mac will create a new C# code file and will move the type definition into the new file that you will see in the Solution pad.

Improving Object Initialization Expressions

A common programming task is declaring an instance of an object and assigning object properties like in the following snippet:

```
Person person = new Person();
person.FirstName = "Alessandro";
person.LastName = "Del Sole";
```

In Visual Studio for Mac, you can easily refactor this kind of assignment by leveraging the C# language feature known as *object initializers*, which allows for assigning and initializing properties in-line, thus rewriting the previous code as follows:

```
Person person = new Person()
{
    FirstName = "Alessandro",
    LastName = "Del Sole"
};
```

As you can see, this way of declaring and populating an object is cleaner. The C# compiler offers a specific refactoring for this that you can enable by right-clicking the new keyword and then selecting Quick Fix ➤ Object Initialization Can Be Simplified.

Refactorings for Access Modifiers

Access modifiers represent the visibility of types and members and are represented by the public, private, internal, protected, and protected internal keywords. Most code blocks share refactorings that allow you to quickly change the access modifier, such as To public, To private, and so on.

Refactorings for Methods and Method Parameters

The C# compiler provides some interesting code refactorings for methods and method parameters. Table 2-13 provides a quick summary.

Table 2-13. *Refactorings for Methods and Method Parameters*

Name	Scope	Description
Change signature	Method	Allows you to quickly change the signature of a method
To...	Method	Allows you to quickly change the access modifier of a method
Create Overload Without parameter	Method	Offers to create a method overload without parameters, if one does not already exist
Add null check for parameter	Parameter	Introduces a code snippet that checks whether a parameter value is null (only with reference types)
Add contract requiring parameter must not be null	Parameter	Introduces a code snippet based on the Code Contracts library that ensures the parameter value is not null

Don't forget the tip to right-click an object in the code editor and then to select either Quick Fix or Refactor to see what code refactorings are available.

Suppressing Warning Messages

Sometimes the compiler might report warnings that you are aware of or that you cannot simply avoid because of how your code is architected. In such situations, you might want to suppress warning messages for one or more analysis rules.

To accomplish this, you can write a #pragma warning disable directive manually, or you can simply leverage a specific code refactoring that does the work for you. In the code editor, right-click the code that raises a warning, then right-click, select Quick Fix ➤ Options for {warning name}, and select Suppress {rule code}, where {warning name} is the name of the warning as raised by the compiler at that point in the code and {rule code} is the identifier for the analysis rule. Figure 2-39 shows an example.

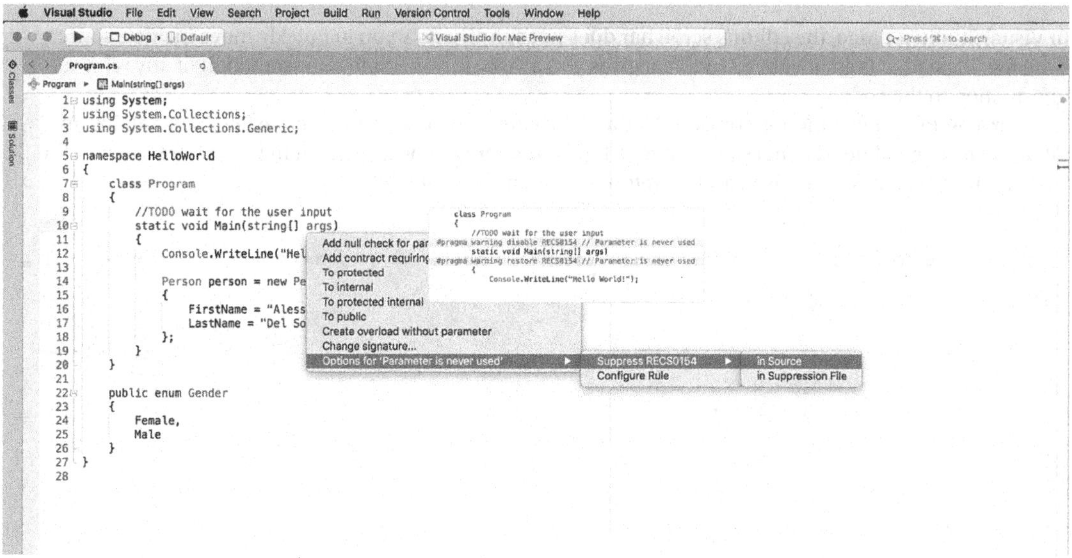

Figure 2-39. *Suppressing warnings*

If you choose "in Source" as the option, the code editor will surround your code with the #pragma warning disable and #pragma warning restore directives. If you instead choose the "in Suppression File" option, the IDE will generate a file called GlobalSuppression.cs where it will store a directive that disables the warning for all the projects.

Navigating Your Code

Visual Studio for Mac offers a number of features to browse your source code quickly and to move between files, types, and members easily. This section explains these features, and you will learn how to additionally increase your productivity in the editing experience.

For a better understanding of the available features, I will use the sample code provided in the section "The Classes Pad" earlier in this chapter. A useful edit that can be done to the code is using the Move To refactoring described in the "Moving Type Definitions to Files" subsection to move the Person class definition to a separate Person.cs code file.

Navigating Between Files

Instead of moving to a different file using the Solution pad, you can press Control+Tab. Visual Studio will show a pop-up containing the list of files that can be opened with an editor window; then you can simply keep pressing Control and press Tab to select a different file. Just release both keys when you have made your choice.

As an alternative, you can open the Window menu and select the file you want to open in the editor, or you can select Window ➤ Next Document and Window ➤ Previous Document to quickly move in the sequence of open files.

The Scroll Bar

In Visual Studio for Mac, the editor's scroll bar does not simply allow you to quickly move inside a source code file. Instead, it is an advanced tool that gives you a visual, immediate representation of any relevant information in the code.

For a better understanding, consider Figure 2-40, where you can see a C# code file that contains an intentional error at line 12 (a missing ;), plus a TODO comment and warnings on the args parameter of the Main method, which is never used and therefore considered redundant.

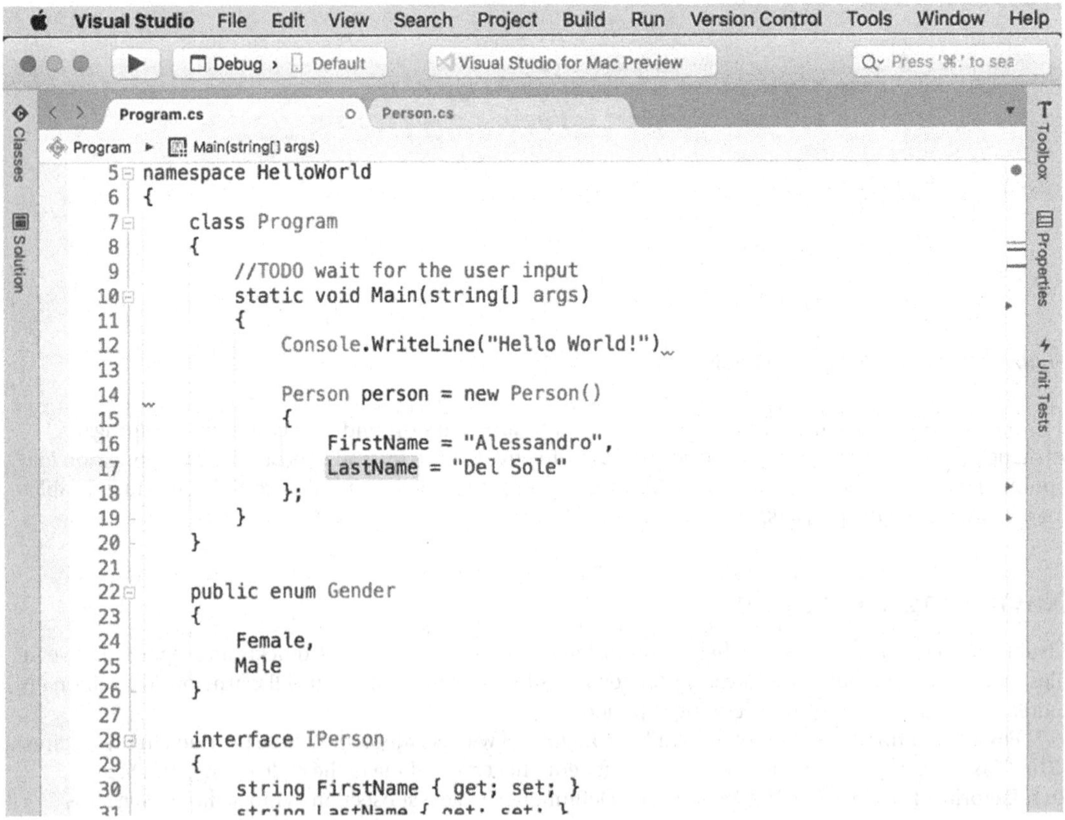

Figure 2-40. The scroll bar showing information about the code

As you can see, the scroll bar shows a number of symbols that make it easier for you to understand where errors, warnings, comments, and the cursor are. Generally speaking, you can hover over a symbol and see a tooltip that describes the related message; then you can click the symbol, and the code editor will move the cursor to the line that is affected by the information. More specifically:

- Errors are represented with a red line, whereas warnings are represented with a blue line.

- Tasks within comments are represented with a green line.

- The current position of the cursor is represented with a light blue glyph. If the cursor is currently on an identifier, the scroll bar will show a red glyph for each occurrence of the identifier in the code.

If the code contains any errors or warnings, the scroll bar will show a small colored circle at the top. This circle will be yellow if the code contains only warnings or red if it contains at least one error. You can hover over the circle to see a detailed message, and you can click it to quickly go to the next error or warning.

The Minimap Mode

You can right-click the scroll bar and select Show Minimap to enable a small code preview on the scrollbar, as shown in Figure 2-41. You can scroll the map or click the code map to quickly move to a different portion in your code file.

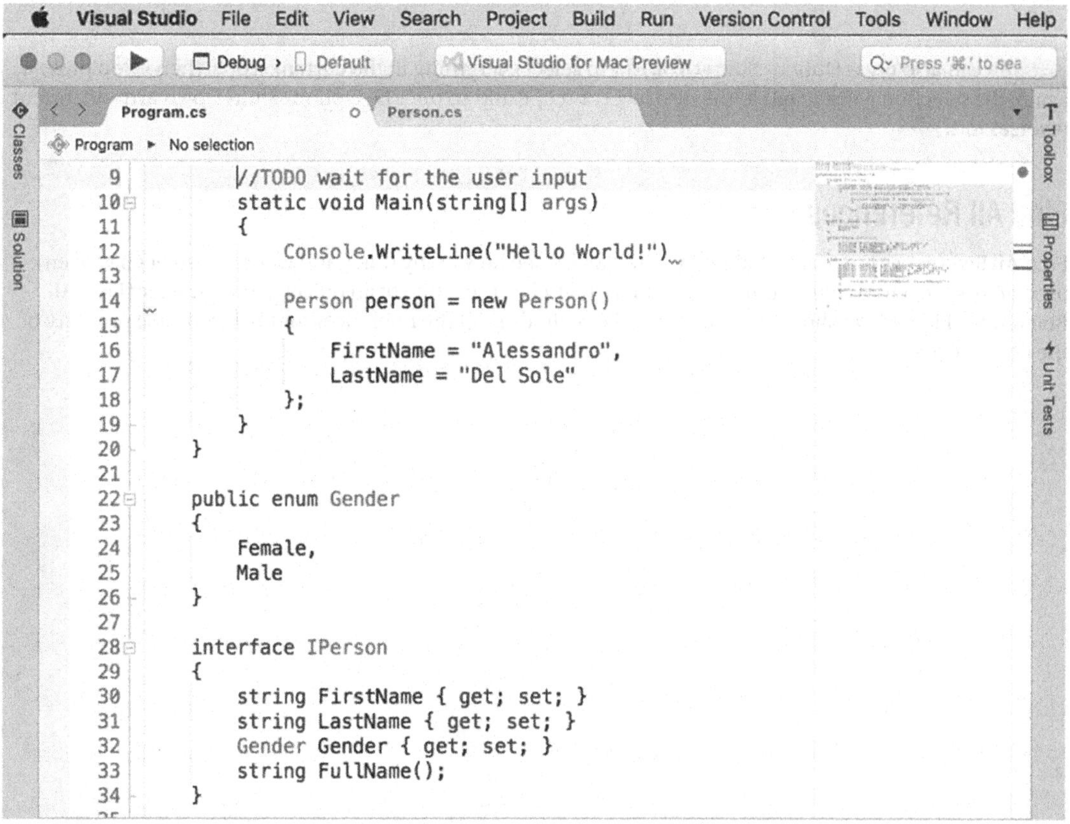

Figure 2-41. *The scroll bar showing the code map*

You can disable minimap mode by right-clicking the scroll bar and then selecting Show tasks. The code map is useful with long code files and continues to show icons and glyphs on its right side.

Block Delimiter Selection

With complex, long, and nested code snippets, it might be difficult to understand the enclosing blocks. When you click the opening or closing tag for a given code block, VS for Mac automatically highlights both enclosing tags, such as brackets or parentheses, as shown in Figure 2-42.

```
Console.WriteLine("Hello World!");

Person person = new Person()
{
    FirstName = "Alessandro",
    LastName = "Del Sole"
};
    }
}
```

Figure 2-42. *Enclosing brackets are automatically highlighted for code blocks*

You can also press Option+Shift+Up arrow to select everything in the current scope; then if you press it again, the selection will expand to the next level of scope and so on. The Option+Shift+Down arrow shortcut reverses this.

Find All References

Find All References is a tool that allows you to quickly see how many times and where an object has been used across the entire solution. To use this tool, right-click the name of an object and then select Find All References. Figure 2-43 shows an example based on finding all the references for the FirstName property of the Person class.

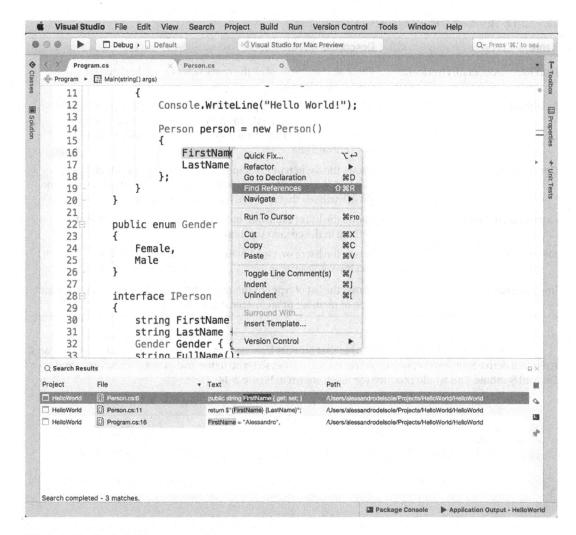

Figure 2-43. *Finding all references of a type or member*

The list of references appears in the Search Results pad. At the bottom of the pad you see the number of results. The Project column shows the name of the project in which the reference was found. The File column contains both the name and the line of the code file in which the reference was found. The Text column is useful because it shows a preview of the code that contains the reference with syntax colorization. The Path column shows the folder path for the code file. You can double-click a reference to move to the related code in the editor, and Visual Studio will open a new editor window on the file if it is not the same of the active editor window. The reference will be automatically highlighted in the code.

The Navigate Tool

The Navigate tool works similarly to Find All References, but it provides more advanced capabilities for specific scenarios. Navigate can be enabled by right-clicking an item in your code and then selecting Navigate. The submenu that appears offers the navigation commands summarized in Table 2-14 and whose results are shown in the Search Results pad like for Find All References.

Table 2-14. *Available Commands in the Navigate Tools*

Name	Description
Find References of All Overloads	Finds all references of all the overloads of a method that have been used in the solution.
Base Symbols	Shows the list of base types and interfaces that the type on which you invoked Navigate inherits from or implements. If you invoked Navigate on a method, it shows the list of methods that the current one is overriding.
Derived Symbols	Shows the list of types that inherit from the type on which you invoked Navigate. If you invoked Navigate on a method, it shows the list of methods that are overriding the current one.
Extension Methods	Shows the list of extension methods for the selected type that are defined in the current solution.
Member Overloads	Shows the list of overload definitions for the type member on which you invoked Navigate.
Implementing Members	Shows the list of types or members that are implementing an abstract type or member or an interface or its members.

For example, if you had a class Employee that inherits from Person and then you wanted to see the list of types that derive from Person, you could right-click the Person type name and then select Navigate and then Derived Symbols. This would produce the result shown in Figure 2-44.

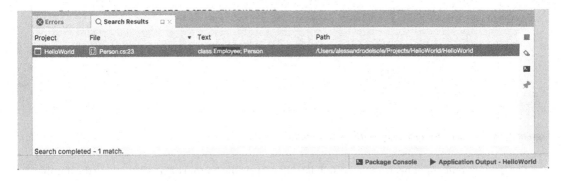

Figure 2-44. *Finding the list of derived symbols*

Browsing Objects Within a Code File

Visual Studio for Mac provides a visual way to quickly browse types and members within a code file. Each code editor window has tabs that you can click to show the list of types defined in the active code file. When you select a type, then you will be able to see the list of its members.

Figure 2-45 shows an example. If you click a member name, then the code editor will move the cursor to that member's definition.

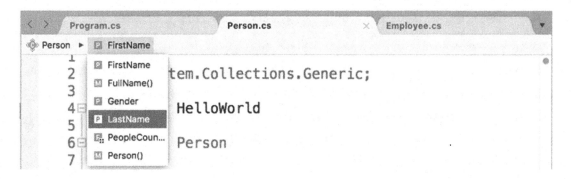

Figure 2-45. *Browsing types and members within a code file*

You fill find this feature useful, especially with long code files.

Folding Code Blocks

Code blocks can be collapsed by clicking the – symbol near the border of the code editor, and they can be expanded by clicking +. Collapsing and expanding code blocks, in Visual Studio, is called *folding*. The View menu offers a Folding submenu with the following commands:

- *Disable Folding*: With this command, code blocks can no longer be folded. You can then select Enable Folding to reenable this feature.

- *Toggle Fold*: With this command, you can collapse or expand an individual code block.

- *Toggle All Folds*: With this command, you can collapse or expand all the code blocks in your code file.

- *Toggle Definition*: This command is useful to fold all the code blocks that are nested inside a type or member definition.

Folding code blocks can be useful when you have long files and you need to focus only on a specific part of the code.

Generating Types on the Fly

As a developer, you will often realize that you need to create new types while coding. Visual Studio for Mac makes it easier to generate new types on the fly with a special kind of code refactoring. For example, suppose you declare a new variable of type Employee but that this type does not exist in your solution yet.

```
Employee empl1 = new Employee();
```

As you would expect, the editor underlines the type with a red squiggle and reports an error saying that it could not find the type. Now, if you right-click the type name and select Quick Fix, you will get a number of options that allow you to generate the new type, as shown in Figure 2-46.

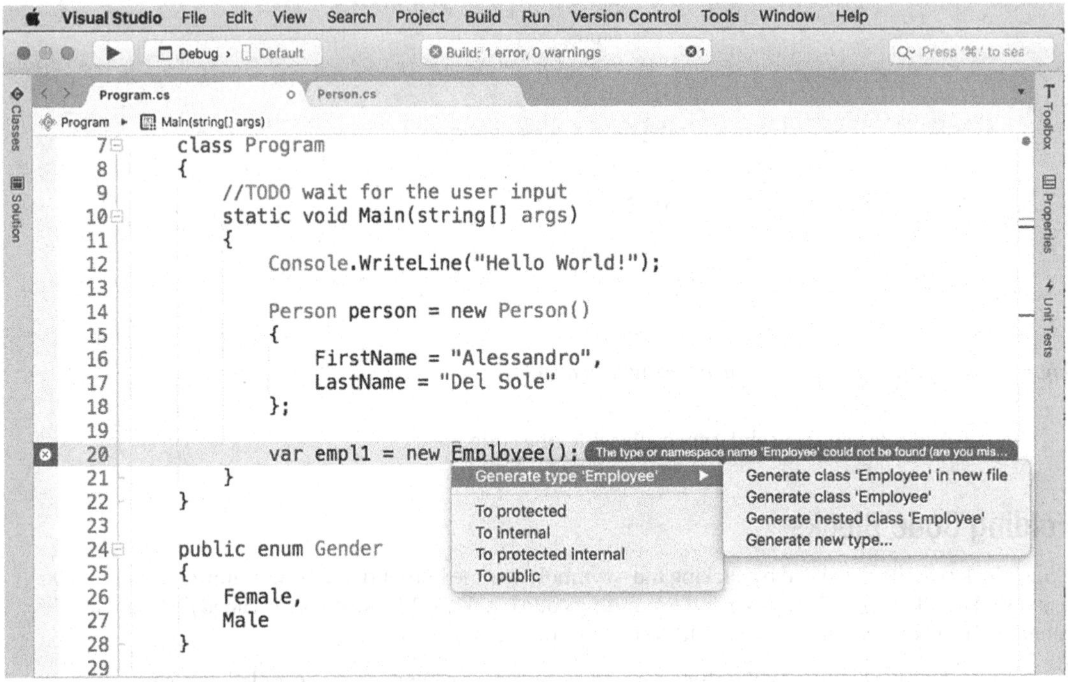

Figure 2-46. *Generating new types on the fly*

The following options are available:

- *Generate class in new file*: This option creates a new code file whose name is based on the type name and adds an empty class definition with the internal access modifier.

- *Generate class*: This option generates a new class inside the active code file, with the internal access modifier.

- *Generate nested class*: This option generates a new class, nested in the current type, with the private access modifier.

- *Generate new type*: This option shows a dialog that allows you to customize the type generation, by specifying what type you want to create (class, interface, enumeration), the access modifier, and the destination.

This quick fix is useful and allows you to keep your focus on the code while writing.

Enabling Multicursors

You can enable multiple cursors by keeping Command+Option pressed while clicking and dragging the pointer over an area or multiple lines. To understand how this can be useful, think of a class that exposes a number of internal properties that you want to change to public in batch.

You can press Command+Option while clicking and dragging to select all the internal keywords only (see Figure 2-47). Then you can start typing **public**, and the original text will be replaced on all the selected lines.

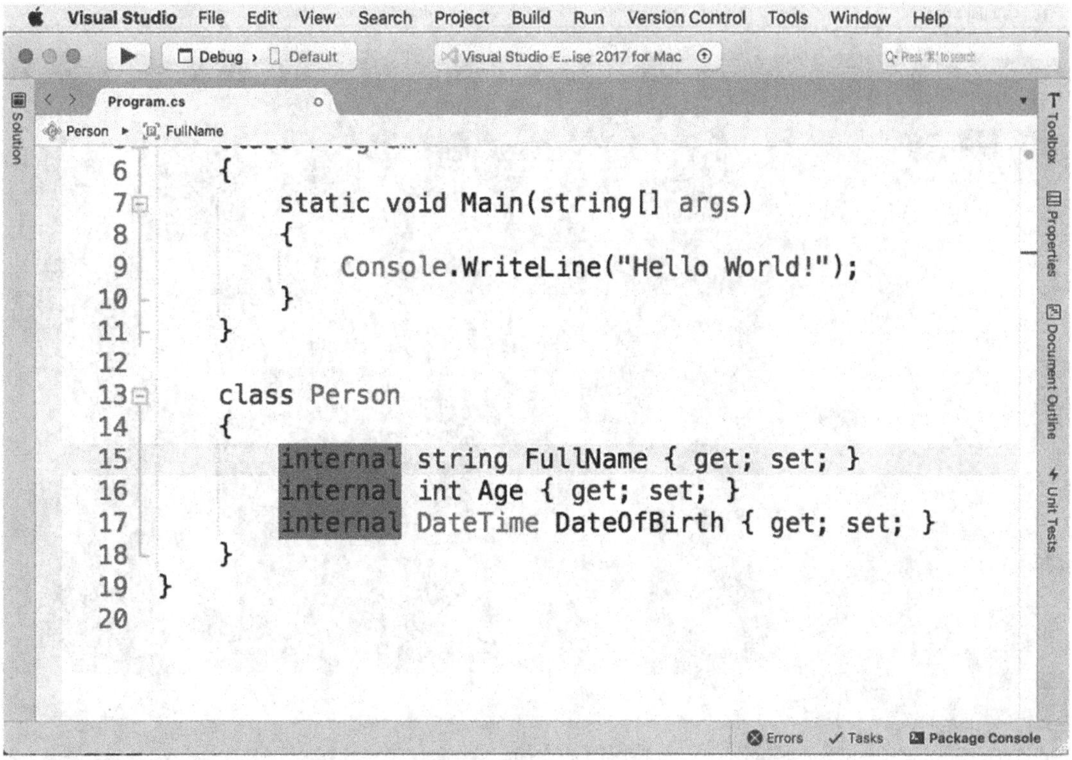

Figure 2-47. *Text selection with multicursors*

Applying Themes

You can customize the appearance of the Visual Studio IDE with themes. When you start Visual Studio for the first time, the IDE is styled with the default theme. To change the theme, select Visual Studio ➤ Preferences ➤ Visual Style.

Select one of the available themes from the User Interface Theme drop-down box. At this writing, VS for Mac offers the Light theme, which I have been using so far and which I will use across the book, and the Dark theme. Figure 2-48 shows how the IDE looks with the Dark theme.

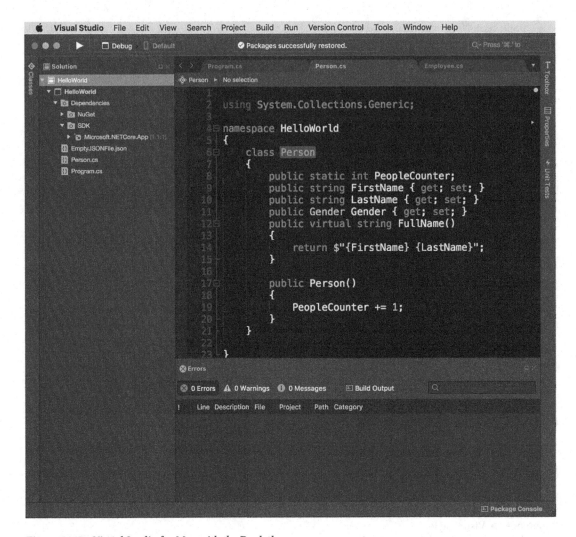

Figure 2-48. *Visual Studio for Mac with the Dark theme*

Changing the theme affects the IDE user interface, the code editor, and how syntax highlighting for source code appears.

■ **Note**   You could also apply a different theme only to the code editor, leaving the user interface unchanged. To accomplish this, select Visual Studio ➤ Preferences ➤ Text Editor ➤ Color Theme and either select one of the available built-in themes or provide a custom theme based on the supported formats listed in the dialog.

Using the Navigate To Tool

Sometimes you need to invoke a tool or command in Visual Studio but you do not remember the exact name or you do not remember from which menu it can be invoked. In other situations, you might have a solution with thousands of files and you do not exactly remember where a file you need is.

Visual Studio for Mac makes your life easier by providing a search box called Navigate To, located at the upper-right corner of the IDE, where you can type the name, or just part of it, of the tool or file you need. Visual Studio will show a contextual list of matching results, as shown in Figure 2-49. If you come from Visual Studio on Windows, this is the counterpart of the Quick Launch tool.

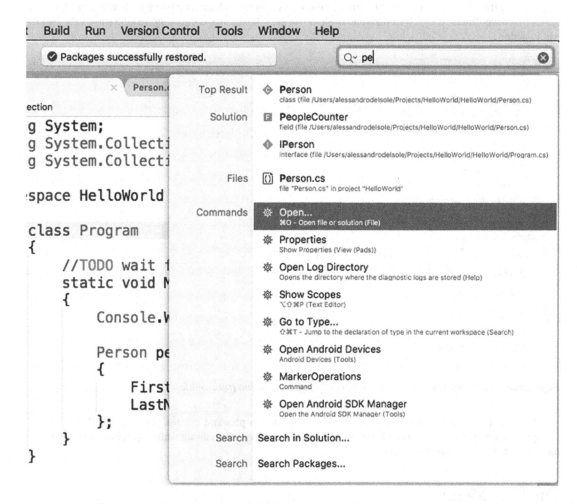

Figure 2-49. *The Navigate To tool showing results for commands, files, and types*

The list is filtered as you type and shows names of types, code files, and commands that match the search criterion. Not limited to this, if you click Search Packages, Visual Studio will open the Add Package dialog and search for any NuGet packages that match your search criterion. You can also click the arrow near the magnifier icon in the search box to filter search results by file, type, and member.

Browsing Help and Documentation

Visual Studio for Mac ships with rich documentation that covers a lot of topics and most of the needs that you might have as a developer. The documentation is available through different tools that are explained in this section.

The Help Pad

You can select View ➤ Pads ➤ Help to display the Help pad. At this writing, the Help pad shows the full reference for the Mono framework only, and therefore it is specific to Xamarin; however, it also includes topics that cover the C# programming language and the .NET base class library. Figure 2-50 shows the Help pad in action.

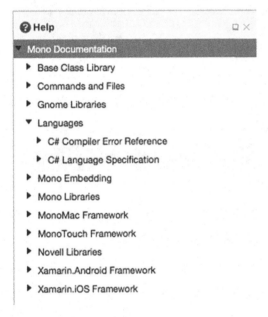

Figure 2-50. *The Help pad shows the documentation for the Mono framework*

Each node can be expanded so that you can see the list of topics and articles. For example, the C# Compiler Error Reference node can be expanded to see documentation about warning and error codes and messages that the C# compiler reports.

The Help Menu

The Help menu is the other place where you can find all the shortcuts and links to the documentation you need about Visual Studio, Xamarin, .NET, and the C# language.

The Search text box allows you to search for help topics and commands. In the case of commands, it automatically shows where they are located, displaying an arrow for easy identification, as shown in Figure 2-51. Search results include commands in the IDE and topics from the Apple documentation for macOS.

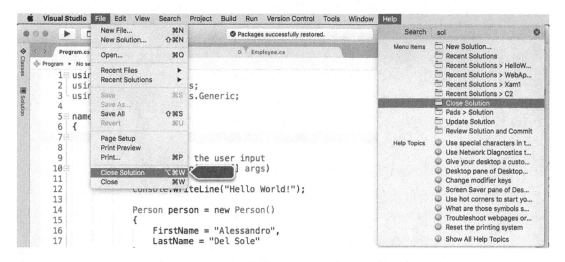

Figure 2-51. *Searching for commands and help topics with the Help menu*

The API Documentation command opens an instance of the MonoDoc application, which basically shows the same documentation available in the Help pad. Then you have four shortcuts: Microsoft Developer Network, .NET Documentation, Xamarin Developer Center, and Xamarin University. These shortcuts will open the web browser pointing to the corresponding documentation portals. Report a Problem and Provide a Suggestion allow you to report a problem and send suggestions about Visual Studio for Mac, and both match the same-named shortcuts you saw in the welcome page. In the first case, you will report a problem via the Developer Community web site; in the second case, you will be redirected to the User Voice web site (http://visualstudio.uservoice.com). The Open Log Directory command will open an instance of the Finder application, pointing to the directory where Visual Studio collects log information from Android and iOS apps while debugging. The Release Notes submenu will display the release notes in the web browser for each of the listed products. The Diagnostics submenu contains diagnostic tools that will not be covered in this chapter.

Summary

Visual Studio for Mac, as an integrated development environment, is the place where you spend most of the time in your developer life. This rich chapter has provided guidance about many topics that you need to be familiar with to be productive with the development environment.

You saw how the welcome page provides shortcuts to common tasks such as creating and opening solutions. Then you saw how to work with projects and solutions, walking through the available project types, especially for Xamarin and .NET Core, and you saw how to build, run, and configure projects, including adding references to external libraries such as NuGet packages. You then discovered pads and how they allow you to perform a number of tasks though keeping your workspace well organized. In the second part of the chapter, you were introduced to the code editor and to the many productivity features it offers, such as IntelliSense, live code issue detection and code fixes for errors and warnings, code refactorings, and code navigation. In the last part of the chapter, you saw how to customize the appearance of the IDE with themes and how to search for help topics with the Help pad and the Help menu. In the next chapter, you will discover additional, important, and powerful features in Visual Studio for Mac, specific for debugging any kind of application.

CHAPTER 3

■ ■ ■

Debugging Applications

Debugging is the task of analyzing the application's execution flow and investigating it for errors. Therefore, debugging is one of the most important tasks in your developer life.

Debugging can be a painful experience if a development platform does not offer powerful analysis tools. Luckily, both Xamarin and .NET Core provide powerful debuggers, and Visual Studio for Mac ships with unified visual tools that dramatically simplify the way you debug your code and focus on productivity. If you are familiar with Xamarin Studio or Visual Studio on Windows, you will feel at home with what Visual Studio for Mac has to offer. If you instead come from Xcode, you will be surprised about how amazing the debugging experience is with Visual Studio.

Meeting the Debuggers

Visual Studio for Mac leverages debuggers that ship with the two major frameworks it relies on.

For .NET Core, Visual Studio relies on the Microsoft .NET Core Debugger, which is included in the .NET Core SDK you installed in Chapter 1. This is the same debugger used by environments such as Visual Studio Code and Visual Studio on Windows for .NET Core apps. For Xamarin, Visual Studio leverages the Mono Soft Debugger (`http://bit.ly/2p4MwHc`), a specific debugger for Mono whose main characteristic is that it is a cooperative debugger built into the Mono framework, which is different from most debuggers that are stand-alone processes.

The goal of this chapter is not explaining what happens behind the scenes of the debuggers; rather, I will explain the powerful, unified tools that the IDE provides to debug applications regardless of the backing debugger. Obviously, Android and iOS are two different systems, and therefore the Mono Soft Debugger will send different kinds of messages depending on the current platform. The same concept applies to the Microsoft .NET Core Debugger, whose behavior is totally different from the Mono Soft Debugger; it will show its own messages, and it has its own characteristics.

Preparing an Example

For a better understanding of all the available debugging tools, a good idea is to prepare an example that contains intentional errors. So, following the lessons learned in the previous chapter, create a new .NET Core console project and assign a name of your choice.

© Alessandro Del Sole 2017
A. Del Sole, *Beginning Visual Studio for Mac*, https://doi.org/10.1007/978-1-4842-3033-6_3

When ready, edit the `Main` method as follows:

```csharp
static void Main(string[] args)
{
    // Show a welcome message. This is stored in a variable
    // to demonstrate how to use some debugging tools
    string welcomeMessage = "Reading a file...";
    Console.WriteLine(welcomeMessage);

    string content;

    // Attempt to open a text file from disk
    FileStream fileStream = new FileStream("file.txt",
                FileMode.Open);
    using (StreamReader reader = new StreamReader(fileStream))
    {
        content = reader.ReadLine();
    }

    // Show the file content
    Console.WriteLine(content);
}
```

The sample code is simple: it shows a welcome message stored in a variable and then tries to read the content of a text file that will be shown on the screen. Notice that I've intentionally stored a message inside a variable rather than passing it directly as an argument to `Console.WriteLine`, and I missed a `try..catch` block to handle input/output (I/O) exceptions; this is required to demonstrate how to leverage some of the debugging tools in the IDE.

■ **Note**   When you start debugging an application, Visual Studio shows a number of debugging pads, all discussed in detail in this chapter. However, these are displayed a few seconds after the application starts. If you select View ➤ Debug, all the debugging pads will be displayed before you start the application and will be populated with debugger information from the app startup. You can then revert to the previous layout by selecting View ➤ Code.

Debugging an Application

As you learned in Chapter 2, you debug an application by first selecting the Debug configuration and then selecting Run ➤ Start Debugging. Depending on the current development platform, Visual Studio will attach either the Microsoft .NET Core Debugger or the Mono Soft Debugger for Xamarin.

During the whole application life cycle, Visual Studio shows any messages that the debugger sends in the Application Output pad. Figure 3-1 shows an example based on the sample code provided previously, where you can also see how the debugger captured an exception.

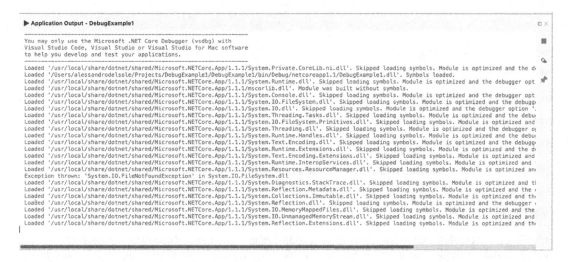

Figure 3-1. *The Application Output pad*

The Application Output pad is of crucial importance when debugging because it shows the flow of information that the debugger sends. This is particularly important in the case of runtime problems and exceptions raised by your application or errors that the system might encounter when hosting your application. Like the other pads, the Application Output pad can autohide, and it can be docked to a different position in the IDE for your convenience. You will use the Application Output pad many times in this chapter, so take the time to familiarize yourself with it.

Using Breakpoints and Data Visualizers

Breakpoints are probably the debugging tool you will use most frequently. They basically allow you to control the execution flow of your applications. A breakpoint causes an application to break its execution at the point where the breakpoint was placed.

■ **Note** Whether the application execution breaks because of a breakpoint or because of a runtime error, it enters into *break mode*.

When a breakpoint is hit and the application execution stops, you can take any necessary actions, such as investigating variable values at that point of the execution or executing the code line by line. The easiest way to add a breakpoint is to click the leftmost column in the code editor corresponding to the line of code that you want to be the point in which the application execution breaks. A breakpoint is easily recognizable because it highlights in red the line of code, as shown in Figure 3-2.

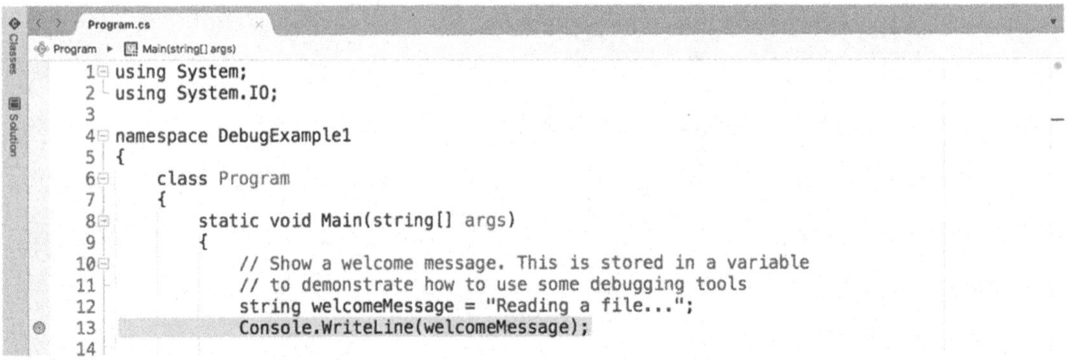

Figure 3-2. *Adding a breakpoint*

You can add multiple breakpoints in different code files to control the execution flow. Now start debugging the application to see how breakpoints work. When the application is running and the debugger encounters a breakpoint, it breaks the execution and highlights in yellow the line of code that is being debugged, before the line is executed. Figure 3-3 shows an example.

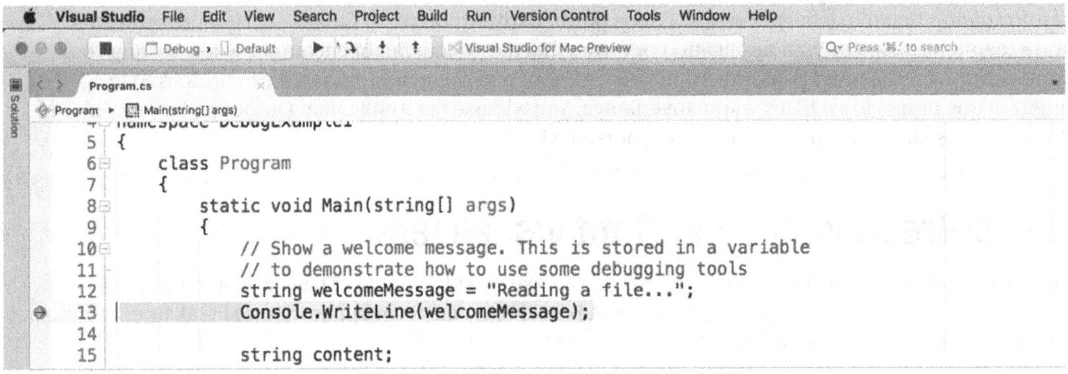

Figure 3-3. *A breakpoint being hit before the line of code is executed*

Once the breakpoint has been hit and the line of code is highlighted in yellow, you can perform many actions such as debugging in steps (discussed shortly) or investigating the content of objects and variables with the *data visualizers*. Data visualizers are small pop-ups that appear when you hover your mouse over a local variable, field, or property. For example, if you hover your mouse over the welcomeMessage variable, you will see a data visualizer that shows its value (see Figure 3-4).

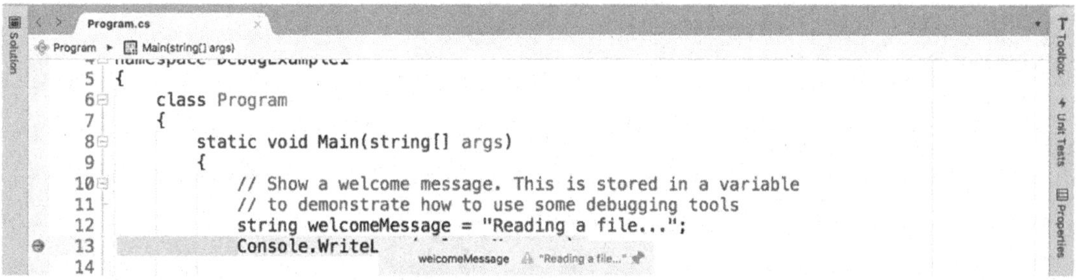

Figure 3-4. *Investigating variables with data visualizers*

In this case, the value for welcomeMessage has been supplied in code, but data visualizers are extremely useful when variables contain the result of a calculation or the evaluation of an expression, and they allow you to see whether the actual value is the expected result. If not, you can perform additional investigations to see what the problem is. You can also pin a data visualizer to the code editor by clicking the icon at its right side. Data visualizers are also available in the Locals pad, discussed shortly.

You will use data visualizers many times while debugging because they quickly help you understand if objects are populated as expected. For now, just click the Start button in the toolbar to resume the application execution. In the next section, you will learn more about executing code in steps.

Configuring Breakpoints with Settings and Actions

Breakpoints can be configured so that you can decide when and how they should condition the application execution. If you right-click the red glyph of a breakpoint and then select Edit Breakpoint, you will access the Edit Breakpoint dialog.

Here you can specify conditions and actions. *Conditions* determine when the debugger should break the application execution when it encounters a breakpoint, whereas *actions* allow special tasks to occur when a breakpoint is hit. They can work together for maximum control over the execution flow. Figure 3-5 shows the Edit Breakpoint dialog.

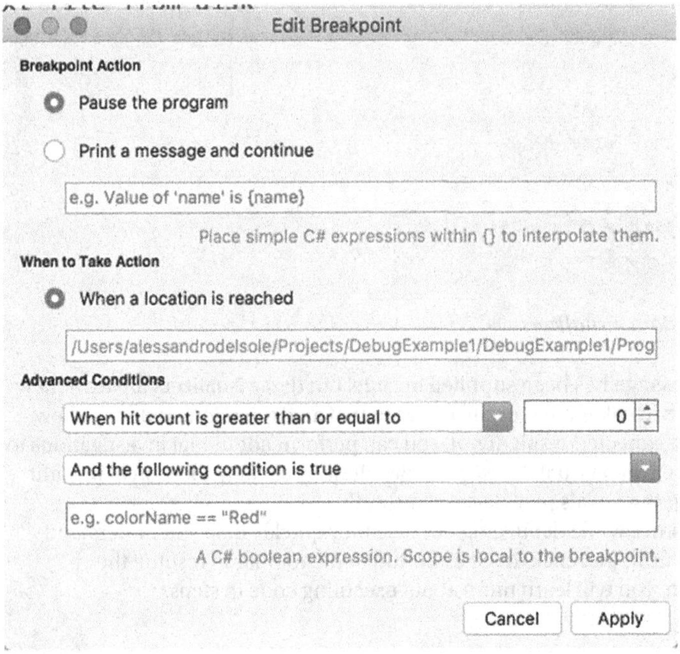

Figure 3-5. Editing action and conditions for a breakpoint

Let's start with actions. In the Breakpoint Action group, the default selection is "Pause the program," which simply causes the debugger to break the application execution when a breakpoint is hit. This is the behavior you saw when running the sample code after placing a breakpoint. As an alternative, the "Print a message and continue" option will not break the application execution. Instead, it will show a message in the Application Output pad. The interesting thing is that, in the message, you can interpolate any C# expression within curly braces, which is useful to evaluate the value of a variable or of an object's properties. In the When to Take Action group, there is only one option, called "When a location is reached." The value of this setting is the file name and line of code where the breakpoint is currently placed; this is a read-only setting, so you cannot change it.

Regarding conditions, by default the application enter breaks mode every time it encounters a breakpoint. However, sometimes you might want to place breakpoints but break the application execution only if a certain condition is true. For example, if you are iterating a collection with a foreach loop, you might want to break the application execution only after a certain number of iterations. To accomplish this, you can select one of the available conditions from the Advanced Conditions combo box (see Figure 3-5). You can see how the name of each condition starts with "When hit count is." With the "hit" word, I mean each time a breakpoint is encountered; therefore, the application execution should stop. In other words, conditions allow you to control a hit's behavior. For example, the "When hit count is greater than or equal to" condition will cause the application execution to break only after a breakpoint has been hit for a number of times that is greater than or equal to the number that you can specify with the selector on the right. Other condition names are self-explanatory, and the behavior of each condition is similar, except that the condition will be "less than" or "greater to."

You can specify additional conditions with the "And the following condition is true" and "And the following expression changes" options. The first option allows you to specify a C# expression that must be evaluated to true to break the application execution, whereas the second option allows you to decide that an application should enter break mode when the value of the supplied C# expression changes.

In summary, conditions and actions are useful when you want a breakpoint to be hit only under certain circumstances, and they allow for a better execution flow.

Adding Function Breakpoints and Exception Catchpoints

Previously, you saw how to add a breakpoint the easy way, and then you saw how to edit a breakpoint with conditions and actions. Visual Studio for Mac also allows you to specify conditions and actions, as well as other options, directly when adding a new breakpoint by right-clicking the leftmost column in the code editor and then selecting New Breakpoint.

This will open the Create a Breakpoint dialog, which looks like Figure 3-6.

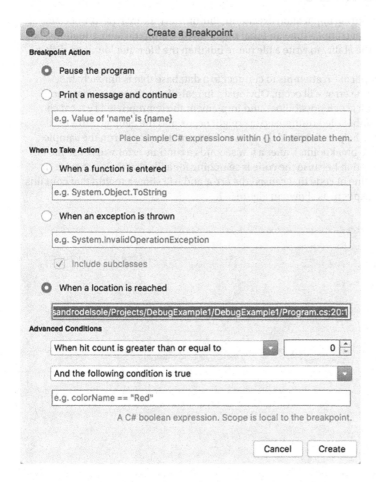

Figure 3-6. *Adding function tracepoints and exception catchpoints*

Most of the options are the same as discussed for the Edit Breakpoint dialog. Additionally, you will find the following two actions in the When to Take Action group: "When a function is entered" and "When an exception is thrown" (the default action is hitting the breakpoint when it's encountered). The first action is also referred to as a *function breakpoint*, whereas the second option is also referred to as an *exception catchpoint*. A function breakpoint will cause the debugger to break the application execution when the specified method call is invoked, regardless of its position in the code. An exception catchpoint will cause the debugger to break the application execution when the specified exception is thrown at runtime, regardless of where it happens. The interesting thing is that both options are unrelated to any line of code.

Therefore, they will act as breakpoints, but they really do not need a breakpoint in the code editor. Visual Studio keeps track of function breakpoints and exception catchpoints and allow you to control them in the Breakpoints pad, as you will discover in a moment. When ready, simply click Create, and a breakpoint will be placed on the current line of code.

Investigating Runtime Errors

A runtime error is an error that occurs during application execution. Runtime errors are typically because of programming errors that are not visible at compile time and that might involve unpredictable situations. For example, if an application gives users the ability to write a file name but then the file is not found on disk, a runtime error will occur.

As an additional example, if an application attempts to connect to a database that is unreachable for network connectivity issues, a runtime error will occur. Obviously, in real-life applications, it is your responsibility, as the developer, to predict such possibilities and implement the appropriate `try..catch` blocks. However, for various reasons, unhandled runtime errors might occur, and the debugger in Visual Studio for Mac offers the proper tools to help understand the cause of the problem. If you run the sample code provided at the beginning (with no breakpoints), after a few seconds a runtime error will cause the debugger to break the application execution because the code is searching for a file that does not exist. At this point, Visual Studio highlights the line of code that caused the error and will show a tooltip that contains the exception name and the error description, as shown in Figure 3-7.

Figure 3-7. Adding function tracepoints and exception catchpoints

In this case, the code failed because it was searching for a file that does not exist, so a `FileNotFoundException` error was thrown and was not handled by any `try..catch` block; therefore, the execution of the application was broken. So, Visual Studio shows the name of the exception that was raised and the file name that was not found (this is included in the exception message). Actually, Visual Studio allows you to investigate an exception further and retrieve all the details that the debugger was able to collect. To accomplish this, click Show Details, which opens the Exception Caught dialog (see Figure 3-8).

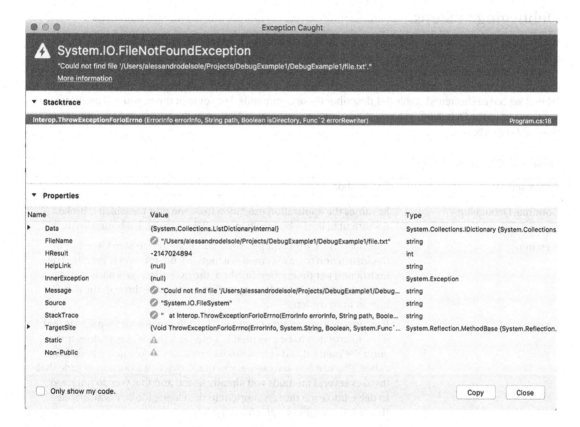

Figure 3-8. *Investigating an exception's details*

Exception Caught shows all the information about the exception, and because an exception is a .NET type that inherits from `System.Exception`, you will see the list of exception properties depending on the specialized exception type (in the case of a `FileNotFoundException`, you will see the FileName property showing the file that was not found). At the top of the dialog, the Stacktrace item shows the hierarchy of calls to classes and methods that effectively produced the error. By default, Stacktrace only shows information from your code, so if you want to see the entire call hierarchy, you need to disable the "Only show my code" option at the bottom. Also useful is the InnerException property. In our particular example, it is set to null, but it's not unusual for this item to show an exceptions tree that enables you to better understand what actually caused an error. The Exception Caught dialog also allows you to investigate property values further with data visualizers, so you can hover your mouse over a property name or its value and enable the proper visualizer, as you learned previously in the "Using Breakpoints and Data Visualizers" section.

Debugging Instrumentation

Visual Studio for Mac provides sophisticated tools for debugging code and analyzing the behavior of an application. With these tools, you can control the execution flow and retrieve detailed information about variables and object instances. They are explained in this section.

Debugging in Steps

When the application execution breaks, such as when the debugger encounters a breakpoint, you have different options to continue the execution. For instance, you can completely resume the execution or you can just execute one line of code per time or small sets of lines of code per time. To accomplish this, you use a number of commands that are available in the Run menu and in the debugging toolbar (and through the related keyboard shortcuts). Table 3-1 describes these commands. For some of them, you can use button shortcuts from the Debug toolbar, which you can see in Figure 3-7 between the configuration options and the build status bar.

Table 3-1. *Debugging in Steps*

Command	Description
Continue Debugging	Resumes the application execution from the point at which it broke. A shortcut in the Debug toolbar is available via the first button on the left.
Step Into	Executes one instruction per time. This is similar to Step Over, but if the instruction to be executed is a method, the method is executed one instruction per time; when finished, the execution goes back to the caller. A shortcut in the Debug toolbar is available through the third button from the left.
Step Over	Executes one instruction per time. The difference with Step Into is that if the instruction to be executed is a method, the debugger does not enter the method and completes its execution before going back to the caller. This can be useful when you need to debug a portion of code that invokes several methods you already tested and that you do not need to delve into each time. A shortcut in the Debug toolbar is available through the second button from the left.
Step Out	Executes all lines of a method next to the current one, until the method completes. Step Out does not work outside of methods. A shortcut in the Debug toolbar is available through the fourth button from the left.
Run To Cursor	Allows running all the code until the selected line. You call it by right-clicking a line of code and then selecting Run To Cursor.
Set Next Statement	Within a code block, allows setting the next statement to be executed when resuming the application execution after a breakpoint or stop.
Show Next Statement	Moves the cursor to the next executable statement. This can be useful if you have long code files and breakpoints are not immediately visible.
Show Current Execution Line	Moves the cursor to the current statement. This is useful when, with long code files, the cursor is in a totally different place.

Run To Cursor, Set Next Statement, Show Next Statement, and Show Current Execution Line are not available in the Debug toolbar, and you can find them in the Run menu or by right-clicking the code editor.

Stepping Into Framework Code

By default, the debugger steps into your code, not into system code. However, sometimes it would be useful to investigate further into the full code stack, which involves stepping into the code of the Mono and .NET Core libraries.

To accomplish this, you can select Visual Studio ➤ Preferences ➤ Debugger and deselect the check box called "Debug project code only; do not step into framework code." With this option disabled, Visual Studio will allow you to step into the source code of a system library by opening new editor windows where you will be able to use most of the debugging tools described in this chapter.

Debugging Pads

To make it easier to analyze an application's behavior, Visual Studio for Mac provides special pads that you can use while debugging. Visual Studio automatically shows these pads when you start debugging an application. If you decide to close one or more pads while debugging, you can always reenable them individually with View ➤ Debug Pads, and you can enable them all with View ➤ Debug.

The Breakpoints Pad

The Breakpoints pad provides a visual representation of all the breakpoints in a solution, plus a number of shortcuts that make it easier to add, edit, and remove breakpoints. Figure 3-9 shows an example where you can see a breakpoint and an exception catchpoint.

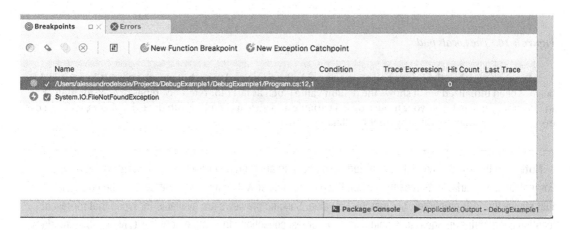

Figure 3-9. *The Breakpoints pad*

The Breakpoints pad shows the list of breakpoints, function breakpoints, and exception catchpoints, each recognizable by a specific icon. For breakpoints, it shows the code file and line number and the hit count if a condition has been specified. While debugging, the hit count will increase every time the breakpoint is encountered. You can double-click a breakpoint, and the code editor will move the cursor to the line where the breakpoint is. You can also disable one or more breakpoints using the check box at the left side. The pad's toolbar has buttons that allow you to disable, remove, edit, and add breakpoints.

The Locals Pad

The Locals pad shows the active local variables and their values while debugging. Figure 3-10 shows an example where you can see active variables for the sample code provided previously, when stepping into the Main method. For example, you can see how the value for the welcomeMessage variable is "Reading a file...". This is useful especially with local variables whose value is the result of an evaluation or of an assignment.

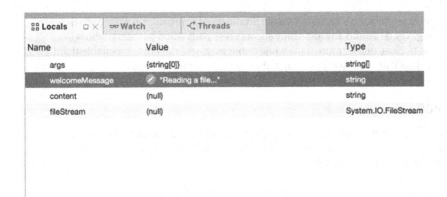

Figure 3-10. *The Locals pad*

For each variable, the Locals pad shows not only the name and value but also the type. When a variable has not been initialized yet, it shows the default value (such as null for reference types or zero for integers). In addition, you can hover your mouse over a variable and view its content with data visualizers, and you can even change a variable's value by double-clicking each one.

■ **Note**   In the Locals pad, data visualizers also show an appropriate preview based on the variable type. For instance, if a variable represents a color, the data visualizer will show a box that depicts the color and that shows the RGB properties, not just the C# value. Specific previews are available for types that represent location coordinates, images, size, points, Bezier curves, collections that implement the IEnumerable interface, and of course strings.

The Watch Pad

The Watch pad allows for monitoring object variables, methods, or expressions so that you can monitor what a variable is doing. When in break mode, you can enter the Watch pad and type in the name of a variable. Visual Studio will show the value for the variable at that specific time (see Figure 3-11).

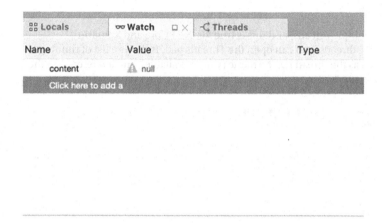

Figure 3-11. *The Watch pad*

You need to step into the code and wait for an expression to be evaluated and assigned to the variable you entered in the Watch pad. The pad will be updated every time the result of the evaluation changes.

The Call Stack Pad

The Call Stack pad allows you to view the hierarchy of method calls. By default, Call Stack shows calls in your code, but you can right-click and select Show External Code to see calls to external code such as native functions. Figure 3-12 shows an example based on the application code, with no external code.

Figure 3-12. *The Call Stack pad*

You can right-click the view and select a number of options such as Show External Code to visualize calls to native functions, or you can select Columns ➤ Language to see the programming language with which a method was written. Call Stack is particularly useful with exceptions because it helps walk you through the hierarchy of method calls so that you can understand the actual origin for the exception.

The Threads Pad

As you now, any applications can run multiple threads, and this is true for .NET Core and Xamarin applications too. To get a view of running threads, you can open the Threads pad. It shows a list of running threads with summary information such as the thread ID, the name (where available), and a reference to the code that is related to that thread (see Figure 3-13).

Figure 3-13. *The Threads pad*

This pad can be useful with multithreaded applications when you need to understand what thread a specific code block is referring to.

Debugging in Code

Both Mono and .NET Core allow interacting with their debuggers via C# code. You can verify variables and expressions in code and make the proper decisions if the application is not working as expected. To accomplish this, you use the Debug class from the System.Diagnostics namespace.

Of course, you also need to select the Debug configuration. Using the class is really simple since you invoke one of the methods it exposes, and the result of the evaluation will be shown in the Application Output pad. For example, the following code waits for the user input from the command line and then displays a formatted string that contains the text entered by the user and its length:

```
string userInput = Console.ReadLine();
Debug.WriteLine($"String {userInput} is {userInput.Length} characters long");
```

The Application Output pad will display the result shown in Figure 3-14.

```
▶ Application Output - DebugExample1    □ ×  ▦ Locals      ∞ Watch      ◁ Threads
Loaded '/Users/alessandrodelsole/Projects/DebugExample1/DebugExample1/bin/Debug/netcoreapp1.1/DebugExample1.dll'. Symbols loaded.
Loaded '/usr/local/share/dotnet/shared/Microsoft.NETCore.App/1.1.1/System.Runtime.dll'. Cannot find or open the PDB file.
Loaded '/usr/local/share/dotnet/shared/Microsoft.NETCore.App/1.1.1/mscorlib.dll'. Module was built without symbols.
Loaded '/usr/local/share/dotnet/shared/Microsoft.NETCore.App/1.1.1/System.Console.dll'. Cannot find or open the PDB file.
Loaded '/usr/local/share/dotnet/shared/Microsoft.NETCore.App/1.1.1/System.Diagnostics.Debug.dll'. Cannot find or open the PDB file.
Loaded '/usr/local/share/dotnet/shared/Microsoft.NETCore.App/1.1.1/System.IO.dll'. Cannot find or open the PDB file.
Loaded '/usr/local/share/dotnet/shared/Microsoft.NETCore.App/1.1.1/System.Threading.dll'. Cannot find or open the PDB file.
Loaded '/usr/local/share/dotnet/shared/Microsoft.NETCore.App/1.1.1/System.Text.Encoding.dll'. Cannot find or open the PDB file.
Loaded '/usr/local/share/dotnet/shared/Microsoft.NETCore.App/1.1.1/System.Runtime.Handles.dll'. Cannot find or open the PDB file.
Loaded '/usr/local/share/dotnet/shared/Microsoft.NETCore.App/1.1.1/System.Threading.Tasks.dll'. Cannot find or open the PDB file.
Loaded '/usr/local/share/dotnet/shared/Microsoft.NETCore.App/1.1.1/System.IO.FileSystem.Primitives.dll'. Cannot find or open the PDB file.
Loaded '/usr/local/share/dotnet/shared/Microsoft.NETCore.App/1.1.1/System.Runtime.Extensions.dll'. Cannot find or open the PDB file.
Loaded '/usr/local/share/dotnet/shared/Microsoft.NETCore.App/1.1.1/System.Text.Encoding.Extensions.dll'. Cannot find or open the PDB file.
Loaded '/usr/local/share/dotnet/shared/Microsoft.NETCore.App/1.1.1/System.Collections.dll'. Cannot find or open the PDB file.
Loaded '/usr/local/share/dotnet/shared/Microsoft.NETCore.App/1.1.1/System.Runtime.InteropServices.dll'. Cannot find or open the PDB file.
String I love Visual Studio for Mac is 28 characters long
```

Figure 3-14. *The output of the Debug class in the Application Output pad*

Table 3-2 summarizes the most common methods from the Debug class.

Table 3-2. *Methods Exposed by the Debug Class*

Method	Description
Assert	Checks for a condition and shows a message if the condition fails, including the stacktrace
Equals	Checks two object instances for equality and returns a Boolean value
Fail	Generates an error message
Write	Writes the specified message without a line terminator
WriteIf	Writes the specified message if a condition is true, without a line terminator
WriteLine	Same as Write but adds a line terminator
WriteLineIf	Same as WriteIf but adds a line terminator

With the Debug class, you can evaluate expressions without using breakpoints, which is useful when you want to investigate the flow of your code without breaking the application execution.

Summary

Debugging is one of the most important tasks for developers, and Visual Studio for Mac simplifies the job. This chapter explained how different debuggers exist for Mono and .NET Core and that Visual Studio for Mac provides unified tools that allow you to interact with both debuggers seamlessly.

In this chapter, you walked through important features such as breakpoints, which allow you to control the execution flow of your code, and commands, which allow you to execute your code step by step. With the help of data visualizers, you can always investigate variables' contents while debugging. Being the powerful visual tool it is, VS for Mac also ships with a number of pads that are specific for debugging, and in this chapter you saw what pads are available and what you can do with them to analyze your code and your applications' behavior. Finally, you saw how to use the System.Diagnostics.Debug class to evaluate expressions in C#, without breaking the application execution. By completing this chapter, you now have all the necessary knowledge about working with Visual Studio's IDE, and now you can finally start putting your hands on some code. Starting in the next chapter, you will learn how to create Xamarin and .NET Core projects to build applications with Visual Studio for Mac.

Building Mobile Apps with Xamarin

CHAPTER 4

■ ■ ■

Introducing Xamarin

Xamarin is, at the same time, the name of a company that Microsoft acquired in February 2016 and the name of a suite of products and services Microsoft offers to developers to build native mobile applications for Android, iOS, and the Universal Windows Platform using C# and the Microsoft developer tools.

This chapter introduces Xamarin by discussing how it fits into the *mobile-first, cloud-first* vision at Microsoft and by listing the available products and services, with a brief explanation of what you can do with each.

■ **Note**   In this chapter, I will often mention Windows 10 as one of the platforms that Xamarin supports. I will provide these mentions for the sake of completeness, but keep in mind that Visual Studio for Mac supports only Android, iOS, macOS, and tvOS. If you want to target the Universal Windows Platform in your Xamarin solutions, you must use Visual Studio 2017 on Windows.

Considerations About Cross-Platform App Development

For a better understanding of how Xamarin can solve many problems and why you should really take this technology into consideration, I will discuss the way companies build apps and the problems they face, especially with a background on the Microsoft stack.

In the past few years, we all have seen an incredible growth in the proliferation of mobile devices, not only smartphones and tablets but other kinds such as wearable devices, smart TVs, and Internet of Things (IoT) devices. All of these kinds of devices are powered by the most popular operating systems, such as iOS (Apple), Android (Google), and Windows 10 (Microsoft). With this variety of devices and operating systems, a company that wants to increase its business by offering an app to its customers should publish a version for each platform. This has a number of important implications.

- Different operating systems rely on proprietary APIs. These are completely different from one another and require completely different ways to be handled.

- The major producers (Apple, Google, and Microsoft) have their own developer tools, frameworks, and programming languages, which are completely different from one another. Apple provides Xcode with Swift and Objective-C, Google provides Android Studio based on Java, and Microsoft provides Visual Studio and C#.

- Different operating systems also have their own infrastructure, rules, and settings for the user experience and the user interface, which require knowledge of the mechanisms that are behind the scenes of the UI on each operating system.

© Alessandro Del Sole 2017
A. Del Sole, *Beginning Visual Studio for Mac*, https://doi.org/10.1007/978-1-4842-3033-6_4

As you can imagine, if a company wants to build and publish one or more apps to the Apple Store, Google Play, and the Microsoft Store, it needs a number of developers with different skills and expertise. This is certainly not uncommon for many companies, but it can be a problem if a company has always worked only with Microsoft technologies, frameworks, platforms, and languages, such as .NET and C#, when it also needs to be in the iOS and Android markets. In this situation, a company has typically two alternatives: hiring iOS and Android developers or spending the time and money to make their developers skilled and productive on the Apple and Google development platforms. In both cases, the company will have to face potentially huge costs, and only in the first case might it save some time. So, the ideal situation would be having an option to write apps for different operating systems reusing developers' existing skills on C# and .NET and sharing as much code as possible. This is where Xamarin comes in.

Understanding Xamarin and Its Objectives

Xamarin has the goal of providing developers with the tools they need to build apps for the most popular operating systems for devices (iOS, Android, Windows 10) using C#. The biggest benefit is that developers can reuse their existing skills with this language, and they can target multiple platforms by maximizing code reuse.

To make this possible, Xamarin takes advantage of the Mono framework (`www.mono-project.com`), an open source, cross-platform porting of .NET that runs on macOS, Windows, and Linux (and its various distributions) and whose development was started by two founding members of Xamarin, Nat Friedman and Miguel de Icaza. Mono supports the C# and F# programming languages and takes care of exposing platform-specific APIs in the form of .NET namespaces and types. Over the years, Mono was ported to mobile platforms as well, including iOS and Android. Put succinctly, Mono and C# are the foundations for building cross-platform, native mobile apps with Xamarin. This would not be possible without C# wrapper libraries that expose each operating system's APIs in the form of .NET types through Mono. Table 4-1 summarizes the available libraries.

Table 4-1. Xamarin Libraries

Library	Description
Xamarin.Android	A wrapper for the Java framework that allows building native Android apps in C#, including apps for wearable devices and smart TVs
Xamarin.iOS	A wrapper for Apple's frameworks that allows building native iOS apps in C# for the iPad, the iPhone, and the Apple Watch
Xamarin.Mac	A wrapper for Apple's frameworks that allow building native applications for macOS in C#
Xamarin.TVOS	A wrapper for Apple's frameworks that allow building native apps for tvOS devices in C#
Xamarin.Forms	A library that allows writing cross-platform apps in C# by sharing the user interface and all the code that is not platform-specific

As you can easily imagine, Xamarin.Android targets only Android devices, whereas Xamarin.iOS, Xamarin.Mac, and Xamarin.TVOS target iOS, macOS, and tvOS respectively. If you want to write code once and generate apps that run on Android, iOS, and Windows 10, then you can leverage Xamarin.Forms, a unified layer that allows sharing the user interface definition and code that is not platform-specific. Xamarin. Forms is described in more detail in Chapters 7 and 8. As I mentioned at the beginning of this chapter, Xamarin not only offers development tools but also includes a number of services. In the next subsection, I will provide more details on what Xamarin offers.

The Xamarin Platform

The Xamarin platform provides the development tools you use to build cross-platform apps using C#. More specifically, the Xamarin platform includes all the libraries described in Table 4-1, plus the following tools:

- Visual Studio for Mac, the integrated development environment that runs on macOS.

- Extensions for Visual Studio on Windows, which make it possible to use the premiere development environment from Microsoft to create Xamarin solutions. Both Visual Studio 2015 and Visual Studio 2017 include Xamarin extensions out of the box, and they can be installed separately on Visual Studio 2013.

- Xamarin Profiler, a new tool that allows you to analyze memory usage, CPU consumption, and where an app spends the most time. Therefore, this tool is precious to understand where and how you can improve performances.

- Xamarin Inspector, a new tool that allows for analyzing the behavior of the user interface of an app at runtime.

- Xamarin Workbooks, a playground that makes it easier to learn C# and the .NET/Mono libraries.

- Xamarin iOS Simulator for Windows, a simulator that runs locally on Windows machines but that is available only for Visual Studio 2015 and 2017 Enterprise.

With this powerful set of tools, you can quickly build cross-platform native apps reusing your existing C# skills. Hints about using the Xamarin Profiler and Xamarin Inspector will be provided in the next chapters.

The Visual Studio Mobile Center

■ **Note**   If you are already familiar with Xamarin and its services, you might know about Xamarin Test Cloud and Xamarin Insights (with HockeyApp). Both are transitioning into the Visual Studio Mobile Center, and Microsoft says the transition should be completed by the end of 2017. This is why you do not find information about them in this chapter and why I will talk only about the new portal.

The Visual Studio Mobile Center (http://mobile.azure.com) is a new portal from Microsoft that allows developers to fully manage the whole application life cycle for mobile apps. It is hosted on the Microsoft Azure platform, and it offers services that cover the application life cycle with build automation, test automation, analytics and crash reports, distribution to testers, and back-end services such as tables and authentication, based on a DevOps approach. Figure 4-1 provides a sample view of the Visual Studio Mobile Center where you can see all the available services on the left, based on an Android app written with Xamarin.

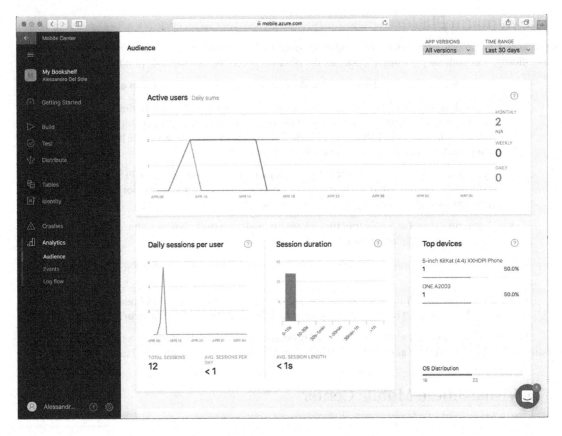

Figure 4-1. *A sample view of the Visual Studio Mobile Center*

To use cloud-based services from the Mobile Center in your Xamarin projects, you simply need to install some NuGet packages that contain portable .NET libraries that make it really easy to consume back-end services and to implement analytics. Discussing these libraries is beyond the scope of this book, but when you associate an application to the portal, the Visual Studio Mobile Center will display the list of NuGet packages you need and how to use them.

Actually, the Visual Studio Mobile Center is not limited to work with apps created with Xamarin; it also supports other proprietary languages and tools. More specifically, all of its services can be used against Android apps built with Java, iOS apps built with Objective-C and Swift, and apps built with React Native. The following paragraphs describe all the services provided by the Visual Studio Mobile Center.

Back-End Services

■ **Note**   Behind the scenes, the Visual Studio Mobile Center relies on the Azure Mobile App back-end services that you can also control from the Azure Portal (`https://portal.azure.com`).

Most mobile apps need back-end services, for example, for storing data and for authenticating users. The Visual Studio Mobile Center offers table services and identity services in the cloud. An important note is that both require you to have a Microsoft Azure subscription (trial subscriptions are also acceptable).

With tables, you can quickly set up a data store based on unrelated tables with rows and columns. With the identity service, you can quickly implement authentication based on the most popular providers, such as Microsoft, Facebook, Twitter, Google, and Azure Active Directory. You can combine the two services to restrict access to tables only to authenticated users. The biggest benefit of using the Mobile Center for back-end services is that it dramatically simplifies the way you create tables and how you implement authentication, especially when compared to how you configure both in the Azure Portal.

Analytics and Crash Analysis

With one line of C# code, you can enable analytics in your Xamarin projects and make the results available in the analytics service of the Visual Studio Mobile Center. With this service, you can review detailed information on app crashes but also on the app usage.

For instance, you can view the number of downloads; the number of sessions and of active users; countries where your app is downloaded the most; and information about the culture, language, and region of devices where your app is installed. Figure 4-1 shows an example of how the Visual Studio Mobile Center provides this information.

Build Automation

You can configure build automation for continuous integration by connecting the Visual Studio Mobile Center to any Git repository. This way, every time you commit or push changes to your source code, the service will automatically generate a new build. You can then certainly get detailed information about successful and failed builds.

It is worth mentioning that the Visual Studio Mobile Center has its own Mac agent for builds, and this potentially avoids the need of having a networked Mac when compiling Xamarin solutions for iOS. At this writing, the build automation service can connect to GitHub, Bitbucket, and Visual Studio Team Services as the hosts of Git repositories.

Test Automation

The test automation service allows you to execute automated tests against your apps, including UI tests. The Visual Studio Mobile Center allows you to execute tests on more than 2,000 devices and 400 different configurations. This service is particularly useful because it allows you to fully test your app in a variety of conditions before you ship it to customers.

Distribution to Testers

With the Visual Studio Mobile Center, you can easily send your app package to the specified testers once the automated tests pass. Testers will receive the app directly on their devices, and you will be able to view the analytics and telemetry information in the portal. This service is based on the HockeyApp engine, which Microsoft acquired.

The Xamarin University

The Xamarin University (www.xamarin.com/university) is a web site that offers training materials and courses, including live classes with instructors, where you can find everything you need to learn Xamarin and to increase your skills, expertise, and productivity.

The Xamarin University is important because it allows you to prepare yourself to get the Xamarin Certified Mobile Developer certification. This requires you to complete a number of classes and exams. Additionally, the Xamarin University occasionally publishes free webinars and online technical sessions.

Summary

In this chapter, you took a closer look at Xamarin, getting more detailed information on what it is and on how it fits into the *mobile-first, cloud-first* strategy at Microsoft.

In this chapter, you saw a number of considerations about the different approaches to building mobile applications for different OSs with proprietary technologies. Next, you saw how Xamarin solves most of the problems by providing tools that allow developers to build mobile apps with C# in a cross-platform way. In this discussion, you got information about the available libraries and development tools. Because Xamarin consists not only of developer tools, this chapter also provided a high-level overview of the complete Xamarin offerings, which includes the Xamarin platform with development tools; the Visual Studio Mobile Center, which is based on the DevOps approach and that offers services for back-end, analytics, build automation, test automation, and distribution to testers; and the Xamarin University, which is the place where you can learn and attend classes that will lead you to the official Xamarin Certified Mobile Developer certification. After this short but necessary introduction to Xamarin, in the next chapter you will start creating Xamarin projects, and the first platform you will target is Android.

CHAPTER 5

Building Android Applications

Android is one of the most popular operating systems for mobile devices such as smartphones, tablets, smart watches, and smart TVs. There are many reasons for its success, but two are probably the most relevant: it runs on an incredibly large variety of hardware configurations, which allows users to choose between high-level and cheaper devices, and it is highly customizable.

Android natively relies on the Java runtime and libraries, but with Xamarin and its Xamarin.Android flavor you can build apps for Android using C# and Visual Studio, thus reusing many of your existing .NET skills. The Xamarin tools then take care of building the Android app package, leveraging the Google and Java SDKs on your behalf. This chapter provides a high-level overview of Android app development with Visual Studio for Mac, putting the IDE and its tool at the center.

■ **Note** As you can imagine, full guidance on the Android platform, Xamarin.Android, and the Java libraries cannot be provided here because it would require an entire book. The focus of this chapter is explaining what the Visual Studio for Mac IDE offers for Android development with Xamarin, based on some code examples. By the way, here you will learn some important basic concepts about Android that will be also useful in Chapter 7. For further studies and advanced techniques, I recommend you visit the Xamarin developer resources for Android at https://developer.xamarin.com/guides/#android.

Preparing a Device for Development

With Visual Studio for Mac, as well as with other development environments that target the Android system, you can debug and test your apps on both emulators and on physical devices by simply connecting your device to an USB port on your machine. If you want to test your apps on a physical device, such as a smartphone or a tablet, you first need to enable developer mode.

To accomplish this, you open the Settings, then tap the system information item, and finally tap the operating system's build number seven times. This action will enable developer mode, and it will unlock a number of settings that are specific to development and debugging. It also will allow Visual Studio to immediately recognize your device as a target.

Creating an Android App with Xamarin

In this chapter, you will learn what the Visual Studio IDE offers for Android development with Xamarin. You will first create a sample solution, and then you will learn how to take advantage of all the powerful tools that Visual Studio provides to create Android apps.

© Alessandro Del Sole 2017
A. Del Sole, *Beginning Visual Studio for Mac*, https://doi.org/10.1007/978-1-4842-3033-6_5

The sample solution demonstrates how to capture a photo with the device camera and how to send it as an e-mail attachment. This is certainly a simple example, but it allows you to focus on the IDE rather than on complex code.

■ **Note**   The sample solution combines two examples from the official GitHub repository. The first example is about capturing a photo (`https://github.com/xamarin/recipes/tree/master/android/other_ux/camera_intent/take_a_picture_and_save_using_camera_app`), whereas the second example is about sending e-mails (`https://github.com/xamarin/recipes/tree/master/android/networking/email/send_an_email`).

To create a Xamarin.Android project, you select either New Project in the welcome page or File ➤ New Solution. In the New Project dialog (see Figure 5-1), you can select one of the available project templates under the Android group.

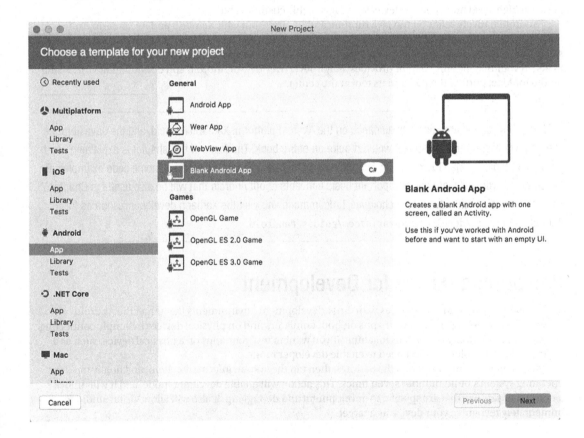

Figure 5-1. *Creating a Xamarin.Android project*

All the available project templates in the App, Library, and Test nodes were described in Chapter 2, so I will not cover them again here. In this chapter, I will use the Blank Android App project template. It differs from the Android App template in that it does not include any UI elements. Click Next when ready. On the next screen ("Configure your Android app"), you will need to specify some fundamental information about your app, such as the name, the organization identifier, the target platforms, and the theme. Figure 5-2 shows an example based on my name.

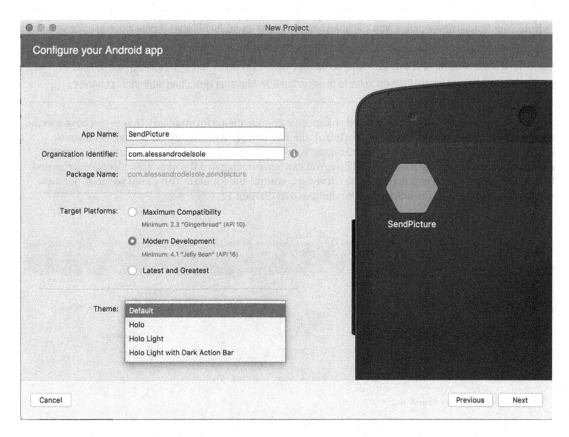

Figure 5-2. *Providing information about a new app*

In the App Name text box, enter the name for your app. This can contain blank spaces. In the Organization Identifier text box, you must supply either the organization or your identifier; this must include the *com* prefix, which is also required in the package name. If you are new to Android development, it is important that you remember that the app name and the package name are two different concepts, and the package name identifies the app package on Google Play. Visual Studio for Mac automatically generates the package name (see the Package Name box), so you do not need additional steps. In the Target Platforms group box, you can specify the minimum system that your app will run on. You have the following options:

- *Maximum Compatibility*: This option will make your app compatible with Android 2.3 and higher; as a consequence, your app will be able to leverage only APIs available to that Android version.

- *Modern Development*: This option will make your app compatible with Android 4.1 and higher and allows for leveraging a larger number of APIs.

- *Latest and Greatest*: This option allows you to leverage the most recent APIs, but your app will run only on the latest version of Android that the SDKs installed on your machine can target.

For the current example, select Modern Development. In the "Managing Emulators and SDKs" section, you will learn how to install additional API targets.

■ **Note** In Android development, you will often hear about API levels. An API level represents a specific version of the operating system and of the API it provides and is identified by a number. For example, API Level 23 identifies Android 6.0 Marshmallow, API Level 22 identifies Lollipop 5.1, API Level 21 identifies Lollipop 5.0, and so on. The best way to understand what API levels refer to is using the SDK Manager described later in this chapter.

In the Theme combo box, you can select a specific graphic theme for your app. Unless you have specific requirements, I recommend you leave the Default theme selected. When ready, click Next. On the next screen, called "Configure your new Blank Android App" (see Figure 5-3), you will need to specify a project name, a solution name, and a location on disk. You can leave unchanged the names and location proposed by Visual Studio. You can optionally enable Git version control and Xamarin Test Cloud services, but these will not be covered here (Git support will be discussed in Chapter 12).

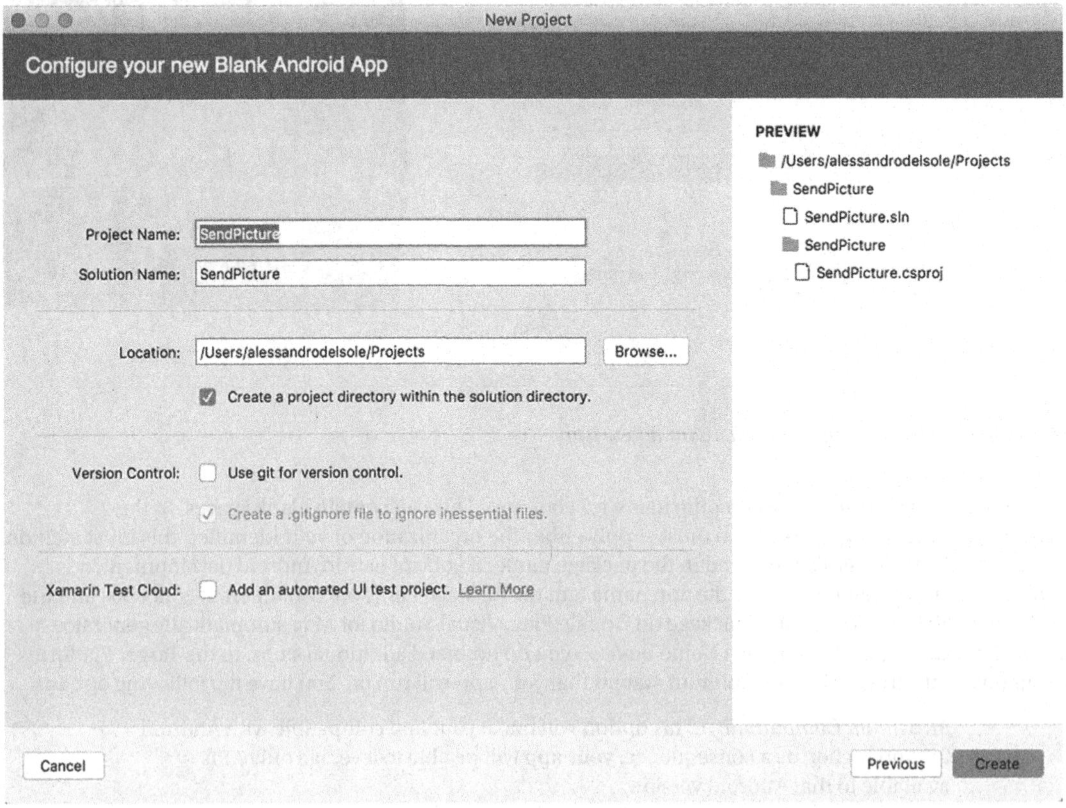

Figure 5-3. *Configuring project information*

When ready, click Create. After a few seconds, your new solution will be ready, and Visual Studio for Mac will show a Getting Started page that contains shortcuts to common tasks, such as opening the designer, adding an Azure back end, and adding a unit test project. Before writing code, it is important for you to get knowledge about the structure of Xamarin.Android solutions.

Understanding Fundamental Concepts About Xamarin.Android Solutions

The structure of a Xamarin.Android solution reflects the structure of Android projects you can create with native environments such as Android Studio and Eclipse, but of course the core difference is that you write C# code. The project system is based on MSBuild solutions (.sln files) and C# projects (.csproj files). This is important because it means you can open a solution with both Visual Studio for Mac and Visual Studio 2017 on Windows.

If you take a look at the Solution pad, you will see a number of files and folders, summarized in Table 5-1.

Table 5-1. *The Structure of a Xamarin.Android Solution*

Element	Type	Description
Assets	Folder	The place where you can add files that you want to include with your app (except for images).
Properties	Folder	The folder that contains the Android manifest and the AssemblyInfo.cs file for project properties. The manifest will be discussed later in this chapter.
Resources	Folder	The folder that contains images, string resources, localization constants, and colors.
Resources\drawable	Folder	The folder that contains images and icons at a default resolution. Files with higher resolution can be added into the folders whose name starts with *mipmap*.
Resources\layout	Folder	The folder that contains .axml files. These contain markup code that defines pages and UI elements.
Resources\values	Folder	This folder contains a file called strings.xml that defines a number of string resources. String resources will be discussed shortly.
MainActivity.cs	File	A C# file that defines the class that represents the main entry point of an Android app.

As you can see, Visual Studio generates a class that is also the main entry point for the application, called MainActivity. The concept of an activity is important in Android, so it deserves a few lines of explanation.

The Concepts of Activity and Intent

In Android, an *activity* represents an object that allows users to interact with the device via some user interface. An activity can be thought of as a page that contains a number of visual elements, whose combination allows you to execute a task. In fact, generally speaking, Android does not rely on pages; rather, it relies on activities.

Xamarin.Android exposes the `Activity` class from the `Android.App` namespace, and it is actually a wrapper for the same-named class in Java. There is also another reason for the importance of activities: the application life cycle depends on activities' life cycles. Related to activities is the concept of intent. This represents a single operation, such as sending an e-mail or making a phone call. Xamarin.Android offers the `Android.Content.Intent` class that you use to define intents and that you typically assign with two pieces of information: the action that must be executed and its data. For example, an action is sending an e-mail, and its information includes recipients and attachments. In the sample code, you will get an example of both activities and intents.

Understanding References and NuGet Packages

You can add and consume libraries in a Xamarin.Android solution by following the lessons learned in Chapter 2. The References node in the Solution pad holds a list of references to system or local libraries. If you want to consume external libraries, you can download and install NuGet packages by right-clicking the Packages node and then selecting Add Packages in the pop-up menu.

Using Components

There is actually another way to add and consume libraries in Xamarin: components. Components are not specific to Xamarin.Android and are available to all Xamarin flavors, including iOS, Mac, and Forms. Components can be libraries, user controls, themes, or SDKs, and they can be downloaded from the Xamarin's Component Store.

In the Component Store, you can find free, trial, and paid products. Therefore, if you plan to build reusable components for Xamarin, the Component Store provides you with a complete infrastructure for selling your products easily. To find and download components, you can double-click the Components node or right-click and select Edit Components to see a basic list of available components within a new tab. If you instead right-click the Components node in the Solution pad and then select Get More Components, you will access the complete component catalog. You will be required to enter your Xamarin account (if you do not have one, register for free at Xamarin.com), and then you will see the list of available components (see Figure 5-4).

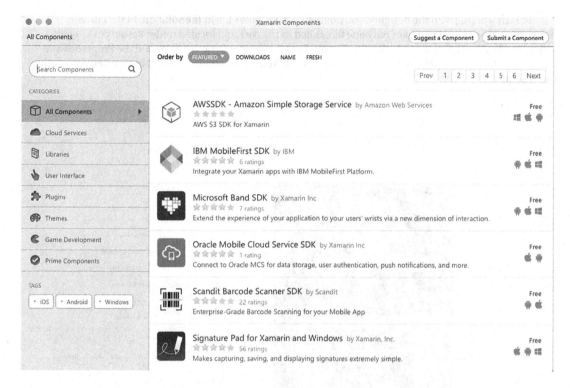

Figure 5-4. *Browsing components in the Component Store*

On the left side of the dialog, you can filter the list based on the component type. For each component, one or more icons highlight what operating system it is available for. Simply click a component name to access its details, such as full description, license information, and pricing. You will then have an option to click Add to App to download and install the selected component. Installed components will be listed under the Components node in the Solution pad. Additionally, the Components node will show any available updates so that you will be able to download a new version of a library, control, or SDK with just one click.

Designing the User Interface

In Xamarin.Android, you have two options to design the user interface: editing .axml files manually or through the Visual Studio designer. Unless you are familiar with the .axml markup, using the designer is certainly the preferred way. The designer for Android in Visual Studio for Mac is a powerful tool: it allows you to drag controls from the Toolbox onto the designer surface, and then you can arrange and resize controls and set properties in the Properties pad.

■ **Note**   In Android terminology, controls are referred to as *widgets*. From now on, I will talk about widgets rather than controls.

To start working with the designer, you double-click an `.axml` file in the solution. In the current example, at the moment you have only one file, called `Main.axml` and located under `Resources\layout`. When you double-click this file, Visual Studio will show the designer, the Toolbox, and the Properties and Document Outline pads. Figure 5-5 shows an example based on the result you will obtain when completing the example.

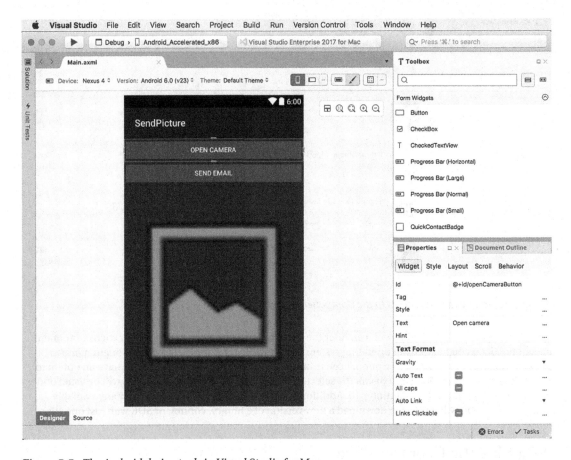

Figure 5-5. *The Android design tools in Visual Studio for Mac*

Widgets are organized into containers called *layouts*. The combination of widgets and layouts produces a *view*. In Figure 5-5, you can see two `Button` widgets and an `ImageView` widget, organized into a `LinearLayout` container. The goal of this chapter is explaining the tools available in Visual Studio for Mac to design your UI, so take a look at the official documentation (`http://developer.xamarin.com/guides/android/user_interface`) for full details about the available widgets and layouts. Having that said, from the Toolbox drag two `Button` widgets and an `ImageView` widget onto the designer surface and resize the `ImageView` to fill the available space. You can change widget properties with the Properties pad. Properties might include text, size, styles, and behaviors, and they vary depending on the widget type. For example, select the first button you dragged onto the designer. In the Properties pad, make sure the Widget tab is selected. Here you can assign the core properties for the widget. In the Text property, you can specify the button text such as "Open camera." In the Id property, you can specify the widget ID, which is particularly useful when you need to interact with a widget in C# code. The widget ID can be compared to the control name in other platforms such as Xamarin.Forms, Universal Windows Platform, and Windows Presentation Foundation, but in Android it has a fixed form. You must in fact specify the @+id/ prefix, followed by a meaningful ID for your widget, such as openCameraButton in the current example (see Figure 5-5). Every widget has an Id property, so specify @+id/sendEmailButton for the second button and @+id/photoView for the ImageView widget. For property values that represent colors, such as Foreground Tint and Background Tint, the Properties pad allows selecting colors with a picker. If you scroll the Properties pad, you will find several properties with two icons, a square with alternate filled subsquares, and a palette icon. If you click the square, you will see a color picker like in Figure 5-6, where you can also see the two icons.

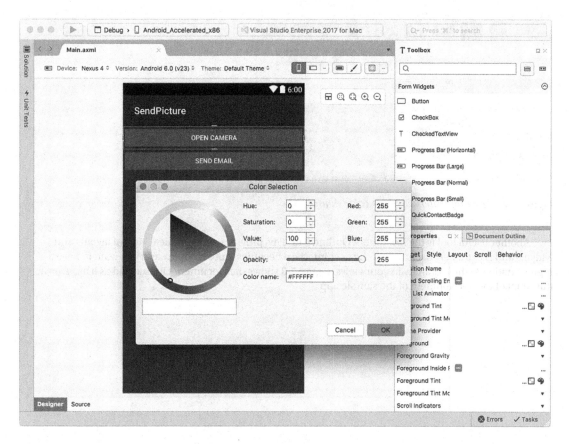

Figure 5-6. *Selecting colors with a picker*

If you instead click the palette icon, you will be able to select among possible shades for a given color based on the Material Design colors, as shown in Figure 5-7.

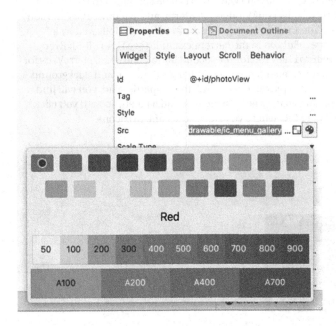

Figure 5-7. *Selecting Material Design color shades*

Another useful tool is the Document Outline pad. This provides a hierarchical view of layouts and widgets and is extremely useful when the user interface becomes more complex and you want to have a representation of the hierarchy in your views. Figure 5-8 shows the Document Outline pad as it appears at this point of the development of the sample app.

Figure 5-8. *The Document Outline pad*

You can quickly select a visual element in the designer, such as layouts and widgets, by simply clicking an item in the hierarchy. You can also right-click an item to access shortcuts such as Copy, Cut, Delete, and Properties. The latter will open the Properties pad for the selected item. There are other interesting tools in the designer that you can see in Figure 5-5. First, you can see a small toolbar with four buttons for zooming the designer in and out, to fit the window, and to highlight layout containers. In the Device combo box, you can select one of the available devices, and the designer will adapt to the form factor of the selected device so that you have a better idea of how your user interface will look. You can also select special form factors, such as wearable and smart TV devices. In the Version combo box, you will be able to select the Android version that the designer must use, and this is based on the choice you made about compatibility when creating the project. In the Theme combo box, you have an option to select a different theme so that you can see how the user interface appears with multiple themes. You can click the box, then click More Themes, and finally select a theme in the Theme Selector dialog that appears. When you select a theme, the designer will restyle the user interface based on that theme. The Portrait and Landscape buttons allow you to change the designer orientation; then with the Resource Qualifier Options button (with three dots), you can choose a different language for the UI and a different mode for the UI, such as normal, television, wearable, night mode, car dock, and many others. With the Action Bar Settings button, you can control buttons that appear in the Android's action bar, and with the Theme Editor button, you can customize a theme with pickers and system resources. The Material Design Grid buttons shows an overlay grid on the designer surface that will help you respect the Material Design guidelines (`http://material.io/guidelines`).

Declarative User Interface Definition

When you design the user interface, Xamarin.Android translates the designer's content into markup code that is stored inside .axml files. This is a tremendous benefit because the markup that Xamarin.Android generates is the same markup that Android Studio generates, so if you have existing code written with Android Studio, you could simply copy and paste the markup code into a Xamarin solution, and vice versa.

Additionally, if you are familiar with this markup, there are situations in which you might want to write the markup manually. In Visual Studio for Mac, you can access the markup code of a view just by selecting the Source tab at the bottom of the design window. This will open the .axml editor, as shown in Figure 5-9.

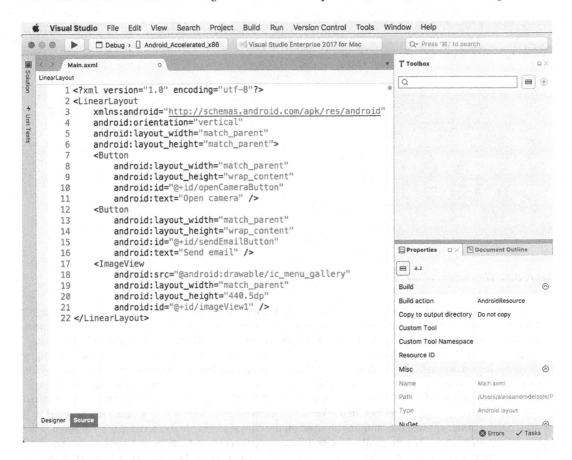

Figure 5-9. *The markup code for a view*

The markup code is based on XML and represents the visual elements of a view in a hierarchical way. This concept is not new to you if you have worked with the Extensible Application Markup Language (XAML) markup language. Put succinctly, an XML element represents a layout or widget, whereas XML attributes represent properties, and the name of each usually starts with the android: prefix. Every time you add or edit markup code, the designer in Visual Studio will automatically reflect your changes. The .axml code editor also has IntelliSense, which means you have the well-known, powerful code completion tool available. It is worth mentioning that when the Source view is enabled, the Document Outline pad shows a hierarchical representation of the XML nodes that compose the .axml file. Simply click Designer to return to the design view. After this high-level overview of the tools you have to design an Android user interface, it is time to make the UI alive by writing some C# code that accesses the Android APIs.

Accessing the Android APIs in C#

In Xamarin.Android, the user interface is defined with .axml files, whereas the imperative C# code is defined inside one or more Activity classes. For example, if you consider the current sample application, the user interface has been defined in the Main.xaml file, and the imperative code will be written in the MainActivity.cs file. For your convenience, the code will be split into multiple parts, and I will provide the proper considerations.

First, add a code file called App.cs to the project. To accomplish this, right-click the project name in the Solution pad and then select Add ➤ New File. In the New File dialog, leave unchanged the proposed selection about the Empty Class item template, provide the App.cs file name, and click New. The App class will serve as a place where to store information such as the captured image, its file name, and the camera roll folder name. The code for this class is as follows:

```
public static class App
{
    public static File _file;
    public static File _dir;
    public static Bitmap bitmap;
}
```

At this point, double-click the MainActivity.cs file so that it's open in the code editor. This class will be the place where you will add the code that takes a photo and that shares it as an e-mail attachment. Let's start with the definition of the MainActivity class and with adding some using directives that import the namespaces required to work with graphics and e-mail attachments, as shown here:

```
using System;
using System.Collections.Generic;
using System.Linq;
using Android;
using Android.App;
using Android.Content;
using Android.Content.PM;
using Android.Graphics;
using Android.OS;
using Android.Provider;
using Android.Widget;
using Java.IO;
using Environment = Android.OS.Environment;
using Uri = Android.Net.Uri;

namespace SendPicture
{
    [Activity(Label = "Send Email With Attachment", MainLauncher = true,
     Icon = "@drawable/icon")]
    public class MainActivity : Activity
    {
        private ImageView _imageView;
        Uri fileName;
```

Every Android app must have a startup activity, and the app must specify which is the startup activity. A startup activity is decorated with the `Activity` attribute with its `MainLauncher` property set as true. The `Icon` property allows you to specify the icon that will be displayed in the Android's main page (the so-called launcher), whereas `Label` indicates the activity's title. In the code there are also two fields: `_imageView` of type `ImageView` and `fileName` of type `Uri`. These will be used shortly to store a reference to the image and to its name. An activity's main entry point is a method called `OnCreate`, which sets the specified view as the current content view by invoking the `SetContentView` method. Then it executes any required initialization code. For the current example, `OnCreate` must verify the availability of apps that allow for taking photos and must create a subfolder where photos will be stored. Both checks are performed by invoking two separate methods, as shown here:

```
protected override void OnCreate(Bundle bundle)
{
    base.OnCreate(bundle);
    // Set the main layout
    SetContentView(Resource.Layout.Main);

    // Check if the app has permission to write on disk
    if (CheckSelfPermission(Manifest.Permission.WriteExternalStorage) ==
        Permission.Granted)
    {
        // Check in an app for taking pictures is available
        if (IsThereAnAppToTakePictures())
        {
            // Create a folder to store pictures
            CreateDirectoryForPictures();

            // Get a reference to widgets
            Button captureButton = FindViewById<Button>(Resource.Id.openCameraButton);
            Button sendButton = FindViewById<Button>(Resource.Id.sendEmailButton);
            _imageView = FindViewById<ImageView>(Resource.Id.photoView);

            // Set event handlers
            captureButton.Click += CaptureButton_Click;
            sendButton.Click += SendButton_Click;
        }
    }
}
```

It is worth noting how you get a reference to the widgets in the user interface, with the `FindViewById` generic method. The type parameter is the type of widget, and the name is represented by an integer constant that is mapped into the `Resource.Id` class. You can open `Resource.designer.cs` to discover how both the `Resource` and `Id` classes are defined. Also, notice how `Click` event handlers have been assigned to widgets using the well-known C# syntax. The following is instead the code of the `IsThereAnAppToTakePictures` and `CreateDirectoryForPictures` methods:

```
private void CreateDirectoryForPictures()
{
    App._dir = new File(
        Environment.GetExternalStoragePublicDirectory(
```

```
                Environment.DirectoryPictures), "CameraAppDemo");
        if (!App._dir.Exists())
        {
            App._dir.Mkdirs();
        }
}

private bool IsThereAnAppToTakePictures()
{
    Intent intent = new Intent(MediaStore.ActionImageCapture);
    IList<ResolveInfo> availableActivities =
        PackageManager.QueryIntentActivities(intent, PackageInfoFlags.MatchDefaultOnly);
    return availableActivities != null && availableActivities.Count > 0;
}
```

The first method is simple: it gets a reference to the public folder for photos (Environment. DirectoryPictures) via the EnvironmentGetExternalStoragePublicDirectory method, and it creates a subfolder (Mkdirs) with the specified name. Notice that, in Xamarin.Android, file and folder management is based on the Java.IO.File class. The second method creates an instance of the ActionImageCapture intent. Then the PackageManager.QueryIntentActivities method checks how many activities are available on the system (PackageInfoFlags.MatchDefaultOnly) to execute the requested operation and returns a Boolean value to the caller. Now that OnCreate and the methods it calls are completed, it's time to access the camera.

Using Device Features (Camera)

To enable the built-in camera, you need to write a Click event handler for the first button. The camera is activated with an intent of type ActionImageCapture, which this time is actually launched. Notice that accessing some device features, such as the camera, requires the proper permissions, which will be set in the app manifest shortly. The following is the code for the event handler:

```
private void CaptureButton_Click(object sender, EventArgs eventArgs)
{
    Intent intent = new Intent(MediaStore.ActionImageCapture);

    App._file = new File(App._dir, "SampleImg.jpg");
    this.fileName = Uri.FromFile(App._file);

    intent.PutExtra(MediaStore.ExtraOutput, this.fileName);

    StartActivityForResult(intent, 0);
}
```

As a general rule, an intent receives all the information it needs through the PutExtra method. In this case, the intent receives the file name that will be used to save an image. With this approach, an intent will receive the same information regardless of the app that the user will decide to use to take a photo. The file is represented by an object of type Android.Net.Uri, and its path is constructed by invoking the Uri.FromFile method. The intent is actually launched by the user interface of an app, that is, an activity. This means that such an activity must be started, which is accomplished by invoking the StartActivityForResult method that receives the instance of the intent that must be executed. In this particular case, the method also receives an integer that represents the result returned by the intent if the operation succeeds. Once the activity has completed, the runtime calls the OnActivityResult method, which is the place where you, as a developer, can manage and evaluate the activity result. In the current example, an intent is used to understand where the captured file should be saved (ActionMediaScannerScanFile), and then the image is displayed in the ImageView widget. The following is the code for OnActivityResult:

```
protected override void OnActivityResult(int requestCode, Result resultCode, Intent data)
{
    base.OnActivityResult(requestCode, resultCode, data);

    if (requestCode == 0 && resultCode == Result.Ok)
    {
        // Make it available in the gallery

        Intent mediaScanIntent = new Intent(Intent.ActionMediaScannerScanFile);
        Uri contentUri = Uri.FromFile(App._file);
        mediaScanIntent.SetData(contentUri);
        SendBroadcast(mediaScanIntent);

        // Display in ImageView. We will resize the bitmap to fit the display
        // Loading the full sized image will consume to much memory
        // and cause the application to crash.

        int height = Resources.DisplayMetrics.HeightPixels;
        int width = _imageView.Height;
        App.bitmap = App._file.Path.LoadAndResizeBitmap(width, height);
        if (App.bitmap != null)
        {
            _imageView.SetImageBitmap(App.bitmap);
            App.bitmap = null;
            // Dispose of the Java side bitmap.
            GC.Collect();
        }
    }
}
```

The previous code needs further considerations: it detects the display height using the `DisplayMetrics.HeightPixels` object, which is required to resize the picture; the code then invokes an extension method called `LoadAndResizeBitmap`, which will resize the captured image for a better view, and its definition will be provided shortly; and garbage collection is explicitly invoked (`GC.Collect`) to free up some memory on the Java side. The reason is that an image object represented in C# can occupy a few kilobytes, but the corresponding Java object can occupy several megabytes. `LoadAndResizeBitmap` is defined inside a separate class called `BitmapHelpers`, which you should add as a new code file to the project. When ready, write the following code (see the comments inside for a deeper understanding):

```
using Android.Graphics;

namespace SendPicture
{
    public static class BitmapHelpers
    {
        public static Bitmap LoadAndResizeBitmap(this string fileName, int width, int
        height)
        {
            // First we get the the dimensions of the file on disk
            BitmapFactory.Options options = new BitmapFactory.Options
                                        { InJustDecodeBounds = true };
            BitmapFactory.DecodeFile(fileName, options);

            // Next we calculate the ratio that we need to resize the image by
            // in order to fit the requested dimensions.
            int outHeight = options.OutHeight;
            int outWidth = options.OutWidth;
            int inSampleSize = 1;

            if (outHeight > height || outWidth > width)
            {
                inSampleSize = outWidth > outHeight
                                ? outHeight / height
                                : outWidth / width;
            }

            // Now we will load the image and have BitmapFactory resize it for us.
            options.InSampleSize = inSampleSize;
            options.InJustDecodeBounds = false;
            Bitmap resizedBitmap = BitmapFactory.DecodeFile(fileName, options);

            return resizedBitmap;
        }
    }
}
```

The code you have seen so far is what you need to launch an intent to take a picture, elaborate its result, and display the resulting image in the user interface.

Network APIs: Sending E-mails

The next step is sending the captured photo as an e-mail attachment, which involves some network APIs. Also, as you can imagine, this involves a specific intent that will be instantiated and launched in the Click event handler of the sendEmailButton widget.

The intent you use is called ActionSend, and its general purpose is initiating communications. Then you can specify that you need an e-mail by setting the ExtraEmail property and setting an array of recipients. You can also specify the e-mail subject with the ExtraSubject property and attachment with the ExtraStream property. The following code demonstrates how to send an e-mail with attachments:

```
private void SendButton_Click(object sender, EventArgs e)
{
    if (this.fileName != null)
    {
        var email = new Intent(Intent.ActionSend);

        // Check if at least one activity exists for the specified intent
        if (PackageManager.QueryIntentActivities(email,
            PackageInfoFlags.MatchAll).Any())
        {
            email.PutExtra(Intent.ExtraEmail, new[] { "someone@email.com" });
            email.PutExtra(Intent.ExtraSubject, "Sample email with attachment");
            email.PutExtra(Intent.ExtraStream, fileName);

            email.SetType("message/rfc822");

            StartActivity(Intent.CreateChooser(email, "Email"));
        }
    }
}
```

For e-mails, it is important to set the message/rfc822 MIME type with SetType. Notice how the code starts an activity that will ask the user to select the preferred app to start the intent, but only if any apps exist that support sending e-mails, and this checked (again) using the PackageManager.QueryIntentActivities method.

Setting App Properties with the Android Manifest

Before testing the application, you need to know how to set properties and permissions in the manifest. In Visual Studio for Mac, you can double-click the AndroidManifest.xml file in the Properties folder in the Solution pad. As an alternative, you can right-click the project name and select Options ➤ Android Application. This will open the manifest designer, which looks similar to Figure 5-10.

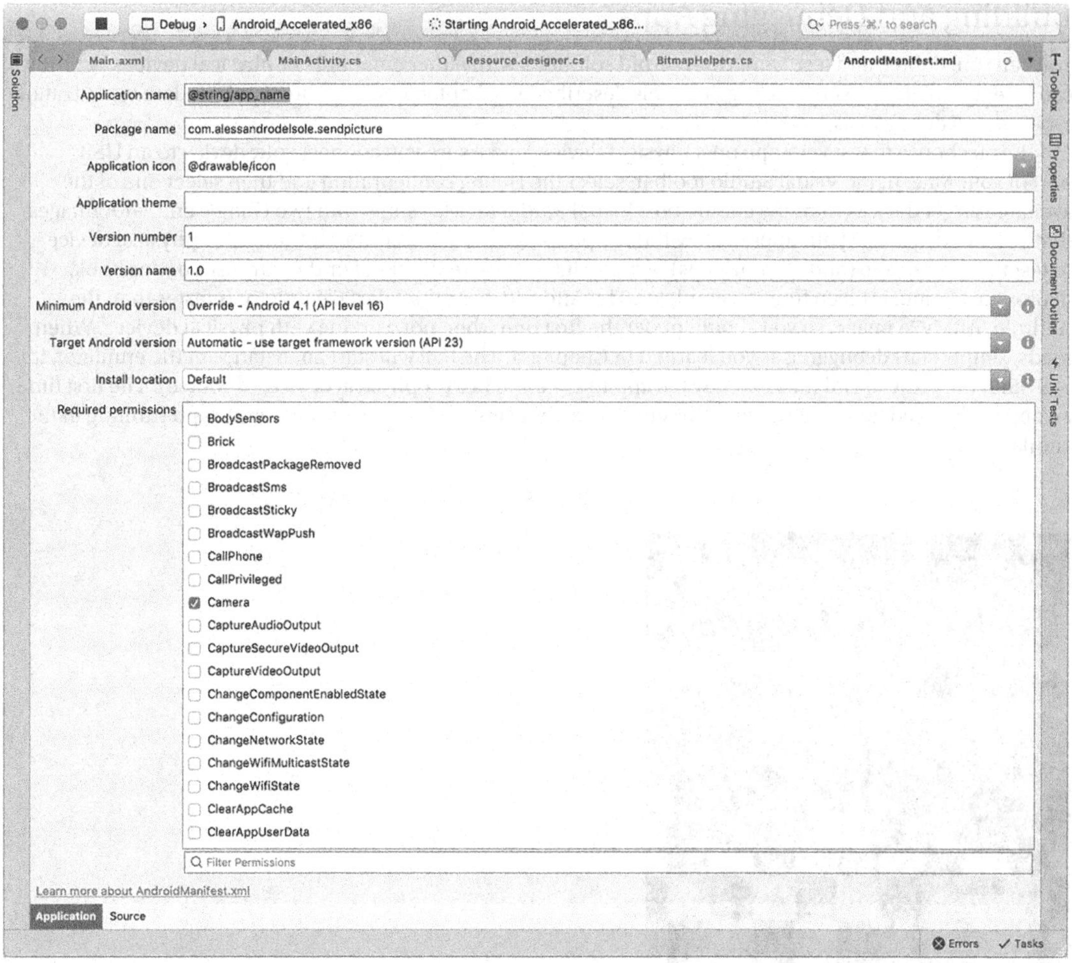

Figure 5-10. *The Android manifest*

The Android manifest reflects many choices you made when creating the project. The application name and package name should be left unchanged. The application icon must instead be provided. To accomplish this, add a file called icon.png to the drawable folder (you can certainly choose a different file name, but remember to change the file name also in the Activity attribute applied to the MainActivity class). After you add an icon to the project, you will be able to pick it up in the Application Icon combo box. You can select a different theme and change the version number and name (you will do this when archiving an app for publishing). You also have an option to select different operating system targets and to change the install location. About the latter, I recommend you leave Default as the choice because the latest Android versions no longer allow you to install an app for removable memory cards. More important is the "Required permissions" box. Here you will need to specify what permissions your app requires. For the current example, the app needs the Camera, Internet, ReadExternalStorage, and WriteExternalStorage permissions. Once you have supplied the required information, simply save your changes. Now you are ready to build and test the sample app.

Building and Debugging Apps

You can run, debug, and test Xamarin.Android solutions with either emulators or physical devices, and you can leverage all the powerful debugging tools described in Chapter 3, such as breakpoints, data visualization tooltips, and debug pads.

If you choose to test your app on a physical device, make sure you connect your device to an USB port of your Mac. In the Visual Studio toolbar, select the Debug configuration and then select one of the available target devices from the combo box. Visual Studio for Mac ships with two Google emulator images that you can use to test your apps even without a physical device. I recommend you use a physical device to test the sample app (and all your apps) because it has full capabilities. For the purposes of this book, figures are obviously taken from an emulator. The Android_accelerated_x86 emulator is faster than the Android_ARMv7a image, so you should prefer the first one when not working with physical devices. When ready, simply start debugging as you learned in Chapter 3. The IDE will start an instance of the emulator, it will build the project, and it will deploy the app to the emulator (or physical device, of course). The first time an app is deployed, the process will take some more time. Figure 5-11 shows the sample app running in the emulator.

Figure 5-11. *The sample app running in the emulator*

If you tap "Open camera" on the emulator, the camera will be emulated with an animation. In a few moments I will explain how to manage emulator settings, where you will be also able to change this behavior. Once you have taken a picture, you will be able to share it with an e-mail by tapping "Send e-mail," and of course you will see a preview of the image in the user interface. Figure 5-12 shows instead how you can leverage a number of debugging tools, including breakpoints and pads.

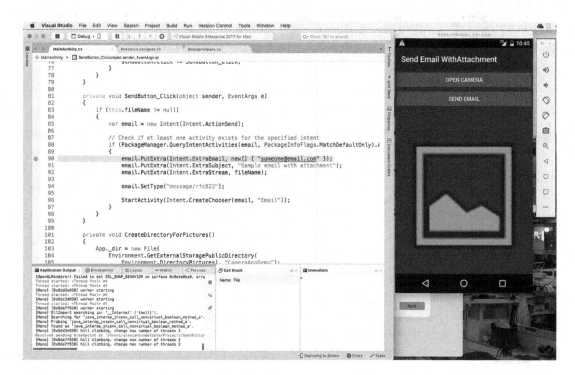

Figure 5-12. *Debugging a Xamarin.Android project*

In some cases, you will need to fine-tune the build process configuration, which is discussed in the next subsection.

Debugging with the Xamarin Live Player

You have an additional way to test and debug an Android app on a physical device, which is the Xamarin Live Player application. This app, available for both Android and iOS, can be installed from Google Play (https://play.google.com/store/apps/details?id=com.xamarin.live&hl=en) and is documented at http://xamarin.com/live.

With this app, you can pair your device to Visual Studio via a Quick Response code (QR), and then you can select the app itself as a device target when you start debugging. Debugging an app with the Xamarin Live Player makes particular sense when you are working with Visual Studio on Windows and you do not have a Mac machine in your network (though a Mac is still required for advanced development including signing iOS apps). Because with VS for Mac you are already working on a Mac and because you have fully functional Android emulators if you do not have a physical device, using the Xamarin Live Player will not be discussed further, but it is certainly an option that you must be informed about.

131

Configuring Project Options and the Build Process

In Chapter 2, you saw how to access project options that are commonly available to all the supported project types in VS for Mac. For Android projects, some additional, specific tabs and settings are available in the Project Options dialog that you can access by right-clicking the project name in the Solution pad and then selecting Options.

The Main Settings tab is identical to what you already saw in Chapter 2 and will not be covered again. The General tab presents a drop-down box called "Target framework" where you can select the version for the Android SDK that will be used to compile your app package (see Figure 5-13).

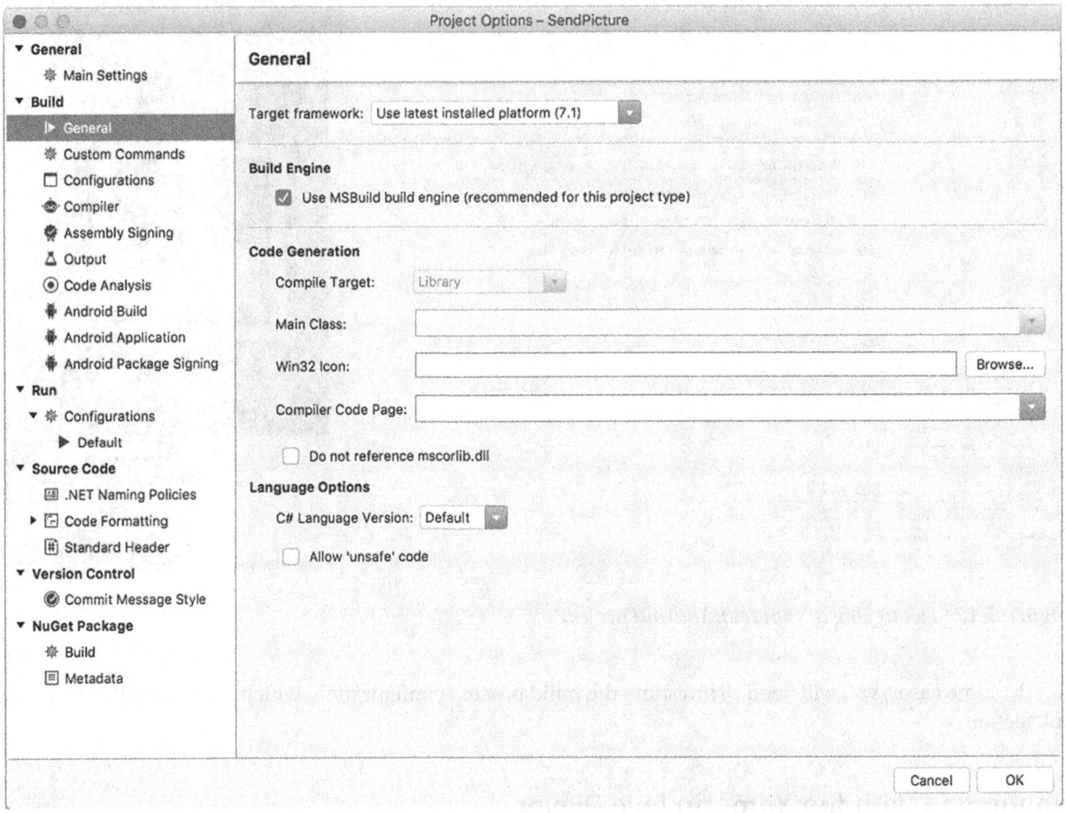

Figure 5-13. *The General tab for an Android project in Xamarin*

By default, Visual Studio lets you use the latest version of the SDK that has been detected on your system. You can select a different SDK version from the drop-down box. The next tab that you need to know about is called Android Build, where you can fine-tune the compilation process and optimize the resulting app package.

Remember that these are not Visual Studio settings; they are instead settings that are related to the Android and Google development tools required for compilation. If you right-click the project name in Solution pad and then select Options, the Android Build tab will look like Figure 5-14 (notice that you will need to stop debugging in order for the changes you make in Android Build to take effect).

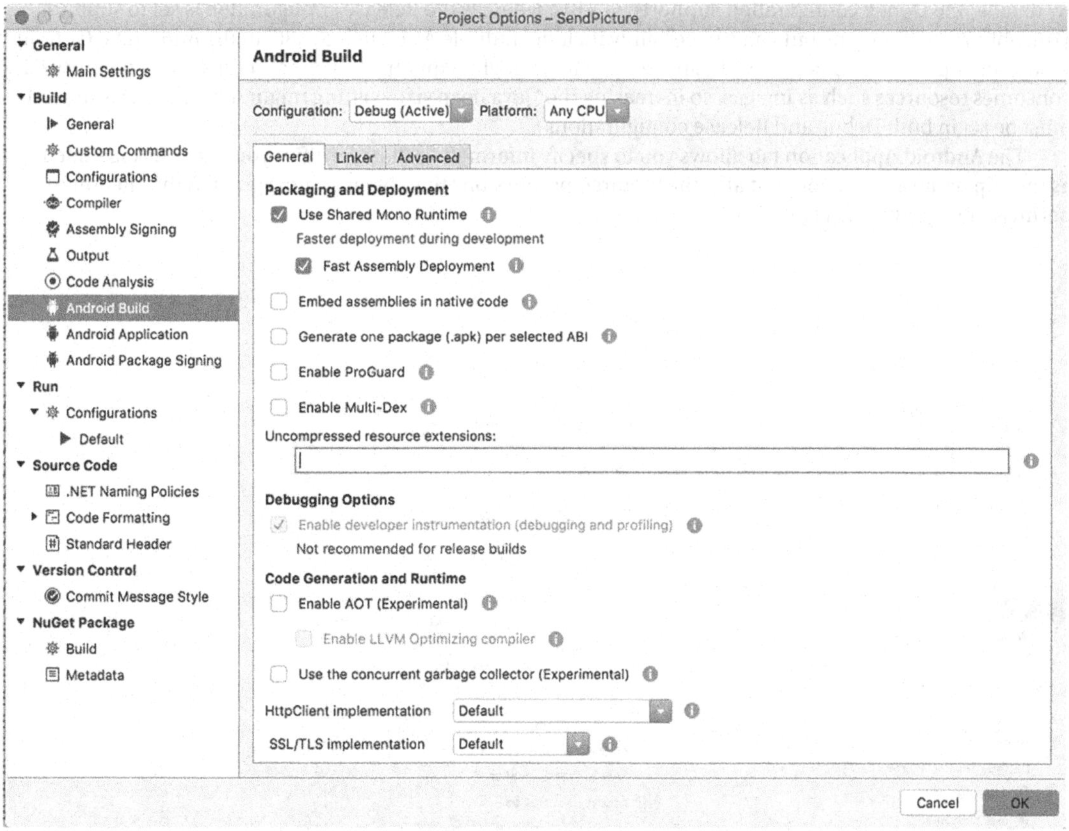

Figure 5-14. *The Android Build options*

Generally speaking, if you click the information icon, you will see a tooltip that explains what an option is about. However, I will now explain the most common options that you might need to fine-tune. Remember that options in the Android Build dialog are per configuration, which means that Debug and Release have different settings. The Use Shared Mono Runtime and Fast Assembly Deployment options are intended to be enabled only when the active configuration is Debug. The first option creates a dependency on the shared Mono runtime, which allows for faster deployment and debugging. The second option basically only updates files that have changes from the previous deployment. It can be disabled if you experience problems such as apps not starting. An interesting option is Enable ProGuard, which is recommended for the Release configuration and which allows for code obfuscation. With the Release configuration, you can also try the Enable AOT (Experimental) option, which enables Ahead of Time compilation to reduce the just-in-time (JIT) compiler overhead and therefore makes the app start up faster. This is currently an experimental feature. If you then select the Linker tab, you will see an option called Linker Behaviour. With the Debug configuration, this option is set as "Don't link," whereas with the Release configuration it is set as "Link SDK assemblies only." With this option, you can decide to remove unused code, such as types and their members, from the build output to reduce the package size. It is recommended that you leave the default settings for each configuration, especially for the Debug configuration where "Don't link" means no code will be removed from the build output, which allows for a more complete debugging experience. In the Internationalization group box, you can specify one or more optional codesets so that the linker can include the appropriate resources in the build output. On the Advanced tab, you can specify the supported Application Binary Interfaces (ABIs), which represent processor architectures.

By default, the Debug configuration supports all ABIs, whereas the Release configuration is set to support the armeabi-v7a architecture, but you can certainly include multiple ABIs such as x86. In the Additional Options group, an important option is "Java heap size." In fact, it might happen that your app runs out of memory if it consumes resources such as images, so increasing the "Java heap size" setting might help fix this issue (and must be set in both Debug and Release configurations).

The Android Application tab allows you to specify information that identifies your app package, such as the app name and version, but also the required permissions that the user must grant in the "Required permissions" group (see Figure 5-15).

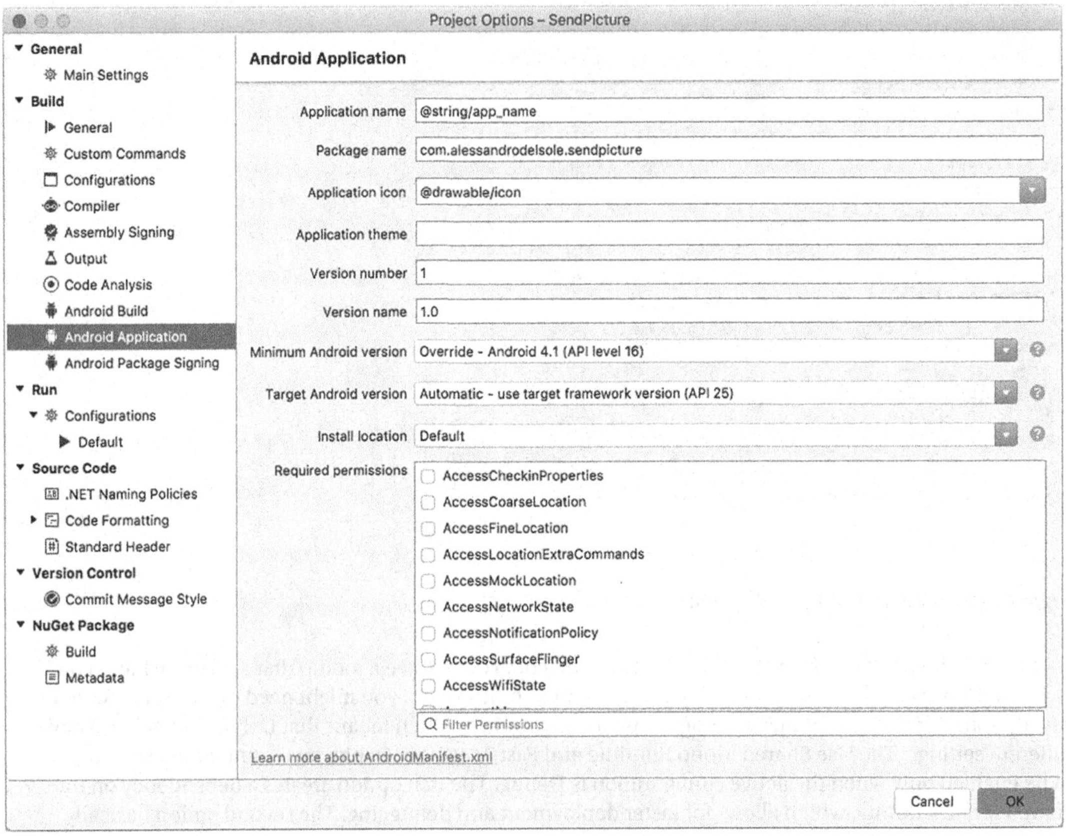

Figure 5-15. *The Android Application options*

Additionally, here you can specify the minimum Android version that your app supports. This is important because the lower the version, the fewer APIs you can use. The "Install location" option allows you to specify whether your app can also be installed on a memory card (which is no longer possible with Android 6.0 and newer). The last Android-specific tab is called Android Package Signing (see Figure 5-16), and this is where you will sign the .apk app package with a digital signature.

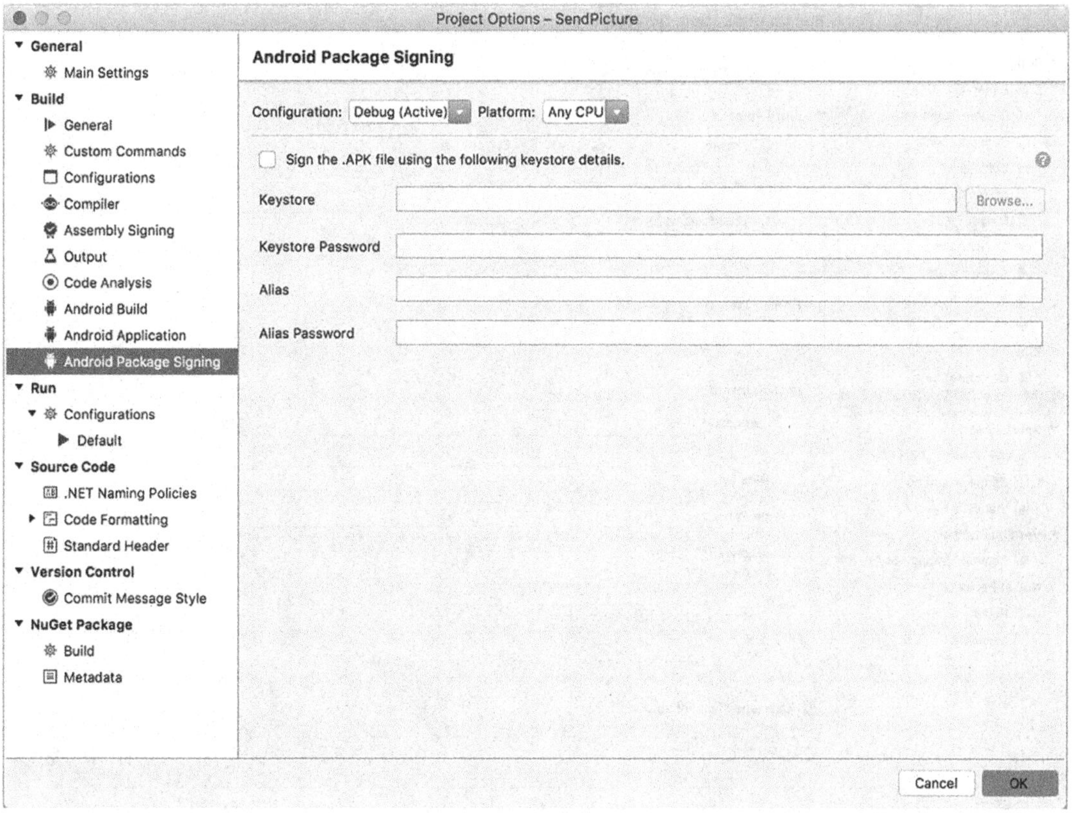

Figure 5-16. *The Android Package Signing options*

The Default tab under Run ➤ Configurations (see Figure 5-17) allows you to fine-tune an activity's behavior in the Explicit Intent and Implicit Intent options, and you can run the application as the current user or a specific user. The Intent Flags and Intent Extras tabs provide additional options that you can set to control an activity.

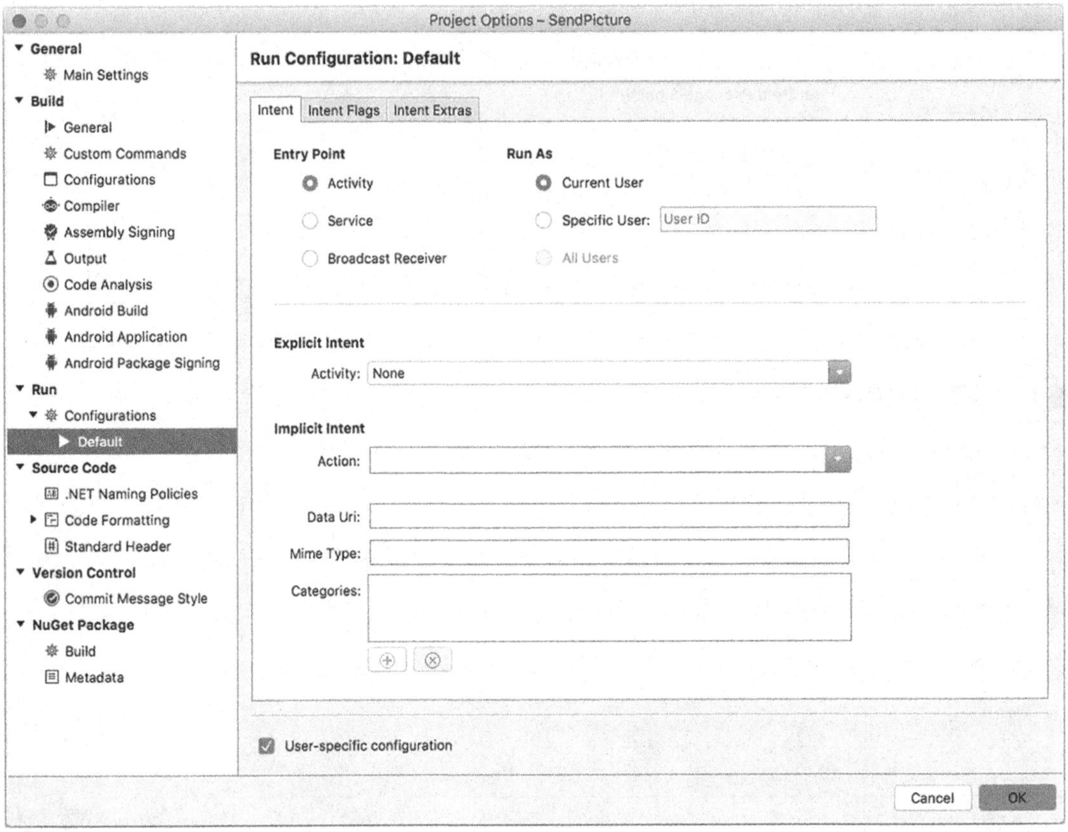

Figure 5-17. *The default settings for the startup activity*

Managing Emulators and SDKs

Visual Studio for Mac relies on the Java and Google SDKs, development tools, and emulators. As on any other platforms, including Linux and Windows, Java and Google SDKs are independent from the development environment of your choice and provide tools that make it easier for you to manage emulators and SDKs.

As a first-class development environment, Visual Studio for Mac includes shortcuts to the Google Emulator Manager and to the SDK Manager for your convenience. They are both located in the Tools menu. The Google Emulator Manager shows a list of installed emulator images and allows for editing existing emulator images and creating new ones. Figure 5-18 shows its dialog.

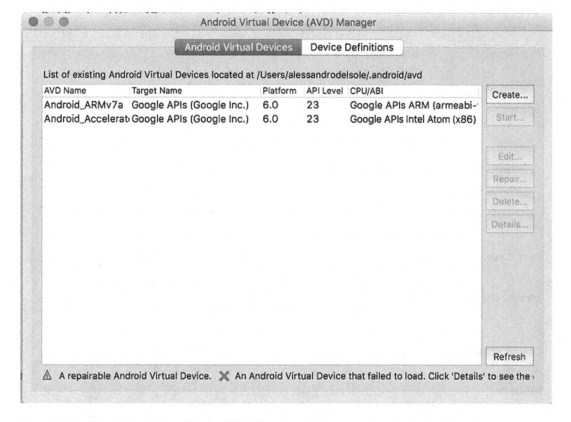

Figure 5-18. *The Android Virtual Device (AVD) Manager dialog*

You can select an existing emulator image and then click Details to see more detailed information about the emulator, such as the hardware it's emulating and the OS version. You can click Edit to change its configuration, which is something you'll need to do, for example, if the emulator's camera is not working. You will find the option called "Configure camera facing back" that must be assigned with the "emulated" value. You can also add new hardware capabilities or change existing ones. If you instead click Create, a dialog will allow you to create a custom emulator definition. Figure 5-19 shows an example based on the Nexus 5 device.

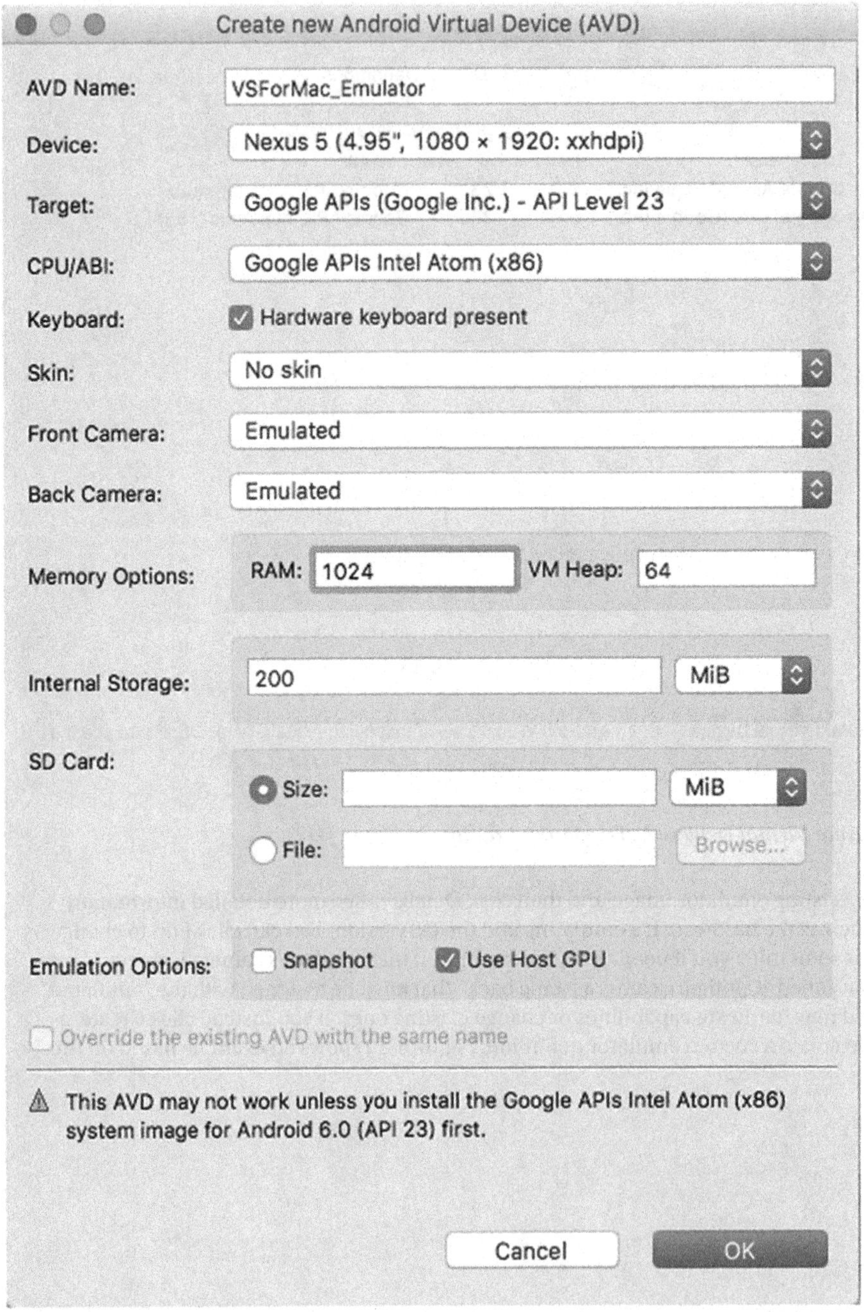

Figure 5-19. *Creating a new emulator definition*

When you click OK, details of your new image will be displayed. Then, you will find the new emulator definition in the list of target devices you can use for debugging. You can also use the SDK Manager (Tools ➤ SDK Manager) to manage and install platform tools and SDKs. This tool is extremely useful when you want to install additional SDKs to support multiple versions of the Android system. Figure 5-20 shows the Android SDKs and Tools dialog.

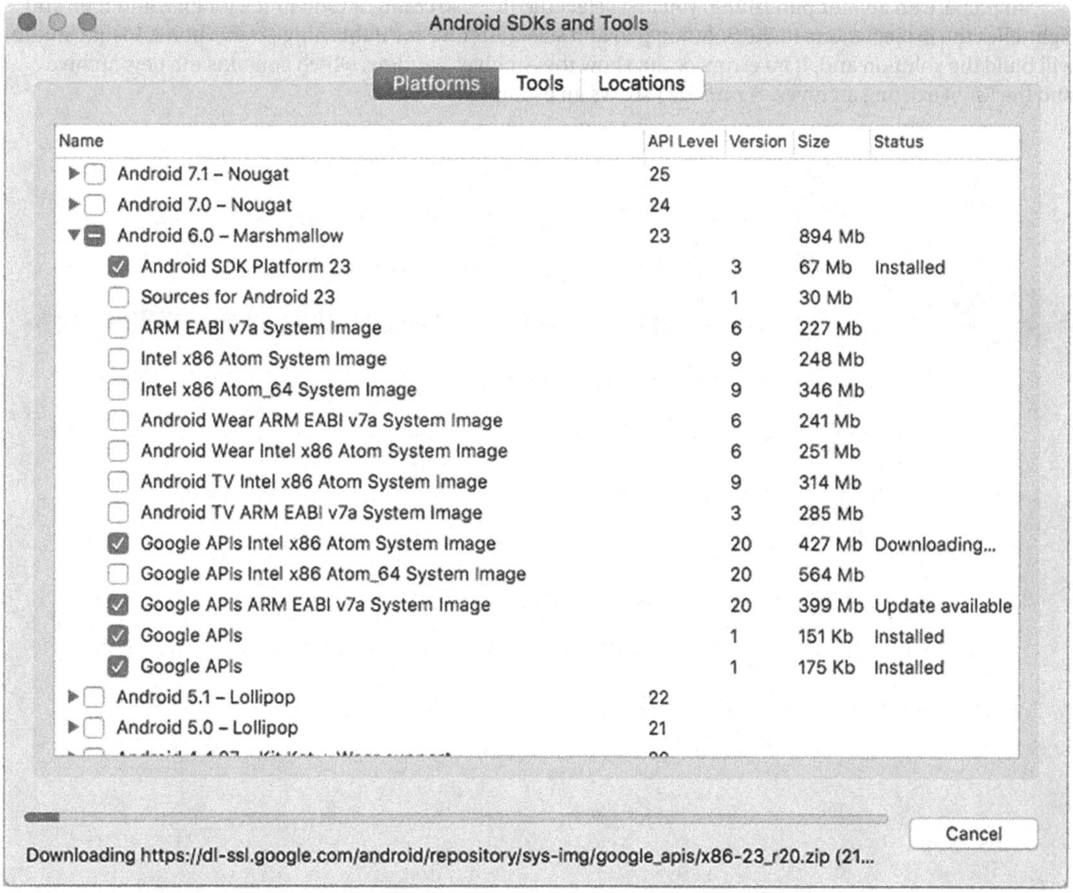

Figure 5-20. *The Android SDKs and Tools dialog allows you to manage installed tools*

It is worth noting that this is not a third-party tool; instead, it is a Visual Studio dialog. It automatically detects available updates for the installed tools and allows to download and install updates. Figure 5-20 shows the progress of an update operation. For each version of the SDK, you can select specific emulator images, such as for wearable devices and TVs. The Tools tab is specific to managing SDKs versions, whereas the Location tab allows for specifying the installation folder for the SDKs and tools. You will use this dialog to install the SDKs that target Android versions you want to support when specifying the target in the New Project dialog or in the project properties, as well as in the designer. This is not a modal dialog, which means you can use Visual Studio while an installation or update is in progress.

Preparing Apps for Publishing

Once you have finished developing an app, you typically build the app package using the Release configuration. However, additional steps are required before you can publish an app to the Google Play store, such as digitally signing your app package. Visual Studio for Mac includes all the tools you need to prepare an app for publishing and simplifies all the necessary steps.

To prepare an app for publishing, you first select the Release configuration in the toolbar, and then you right-click the project name in the Solution pad and select Archive for Publishing. At this point, Visual Studio will build the solution and, if no errors occur, show the Archives window, which contains the new archive and the list of existing archives. Figure 5-21 shows an example.

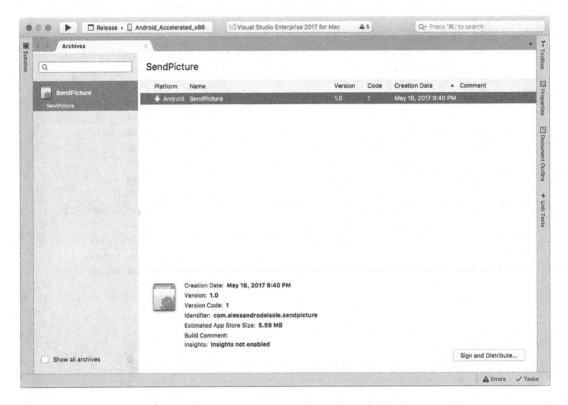

Figure 5-21. *Creating an app archive*

The version and version code identify the app package. In particular, the version code must be an incremental value with no dots, such as 1, 2, 3, and so on. Both the version number and the version code can be set in the app manifest. Notice that a malformed version number or version code is a common reason for an archive generation failure. Another common reason is that you forget to switch from the Debug to Release configuration or that the package name is not in the form of *com.companyname.appname*. Once you have an app archive, you need to digitally sign it. To accomplish this, click the Sign and Distribute button. At this point, the Sign and Distribute dialog appears, and the first choice is deciding how you want to distribute the app. Possible options are the Ad Hoc distribution and the Google Play distribution. The first option allows you to generate an .apk package that is saved to the local disk and that you will be able to upload to the Google Play store manually. The second option allows you to publish an .apk directly to the Google Play and assumes you have requested your paid account. The second option assumes you already have configured some settings in the Google Developer Console, and the first option is instead useful especially within organizations that want to upload an .apk package manually on test devices. For these reasons, only the first option is covered here, but it will not be difficult to use direct publishing if you follow the link with the instructions to make the proper configurations in Google Play. That said, select Ad Hoc and click Next. In the next screen, you can see a list of available certificates, but if this is the first time you are using VS for Mac, you will need to create one by clicking Create a New Key. In the Create New Certificate dialog, you will need to enter a friendly name for the certificate, a password, the number of years for validity, and at least one among the possible values, for example, your first name and last name or your country of residence. Figure 5-22 shows an example based on my personal data.

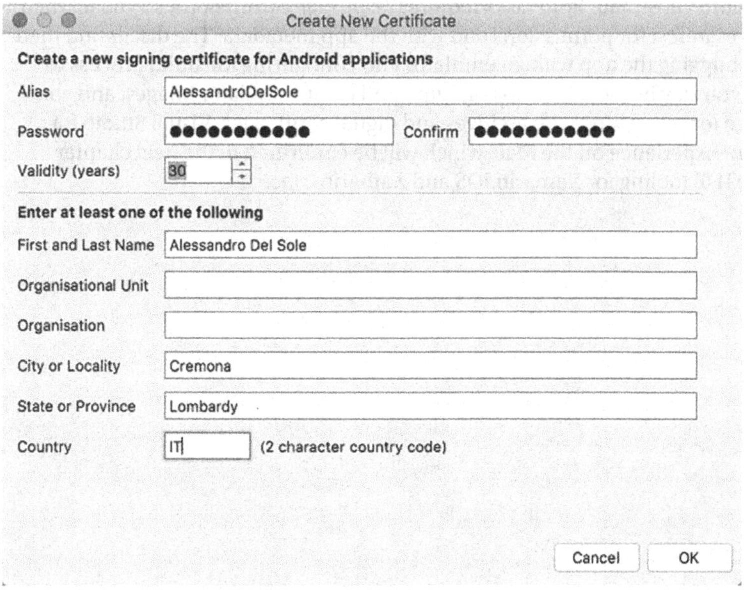

Figure 5-22. *Creating a digital certificate*

When ready, click OK. After a few seconds, your certificate will be ready and visible in the dialog. Select the certificate and then click Next. At this point, the Sign and Distribute dialog will show a summary of the collected information, and if everything is okay, you will be able to click the Publish button. You will be asked to specify the destination folder for the .apk package and the certificate password. When the app package has been generated, the Sign and Distribute dialog will offer to reveal the app package in the Finder tool. Simply click Close. Now that you have your package, you can publish your app to Google Play. Every time you update your app, remember to increment the version number and version code before you generate a new archive.

■ **Note**   Describing how to publish an Android app to the Google Play store is beyond the scope of this IDE-centric book, especially because you might just want to evaluate Android development with emulators or on your physical device before purchasing a developer account on Google Play. For this reason, publishing is not covered in this book. Once you are ready to publish your app, you can read the official Xamarin documentation that provides everything you need to know for publishing (http://bit.ly/2lqKEqf).

Summary

Building Android apps with Xamarin in C# is one of the most important development scenarios with Visual Studio for Mac, so this chapter provided an overview of what the IDE offers on this topic. First, you saw how to create and configure a Xamarin.Android project with Visual Studio. You saw how a Xamarin.Android solution is made, you learned how you can add NuGet packages and consume components, and you reviewed the concepts of activity and intent.

You also saw how Visual Studio for Mac provides powerful design tools that make it easy to create and arrange the user interface instead of editing the .axml layout files manually (though this is still possible). To demonstrate a number of other features, you saw how to write some simple C# code that uses the camera and the network APIs to share a photo via e-mail. Both tasks require the proper permissions, so you learned how to configure the Android app manifest for permissions and with the app metadata. The discussion then moved to building, testing, and debugging the app with an emulator and configuring the build process to optimize your app package. Then you saw how easy it is to configure and create emulator images, and you saw how to prepare an app package for publishing with archives and digital certificates. Visual Studio for Mac provides the best development experience on the Mac, which will be confirmed in the next chapter where you will get started with the IDE tooling for Xamarin.iOS and Xamarin.Mac.

■ ■ ■

CHAPTER 6

Building iOS Applications

With Xamarin.iOS, Xamarin.tvOS, and Xamarin.Mac, you have a set of tools and libraries that allow you to develop, build, and publish native apps for iPhone, iPad, Apple Watch, tvOS, and macOS with Visual Studio.

Xamarin allows you to fully access all the Apple frameworks, such as Cocoa, from C# code. If you have existing experience in developing apps with Xcode, you will see that object names in Xamarin and C# recall object names defined in the Apple frameworks. With Xamarin, you can build universal apps and take advantage of integrated, powerful design tools. In this chapter, you will get detailed information about what the Visual Studio IDE offers to build apps for iOS through a basic sample app. In addition, you will learn how to configure your app for publishing, which involves a number of steps that Visual Studio for Mac dramatically simplifies. I will often talk about Xamarin.iOS, but keep in mind that the same concepts apply to Xamarin.Mac and Xamarin.tvOS, except where expressly specified. Many of the concepts described in this chapter about project options and configuration will also be useful in the next chapter, where I will start covering Xamarin.Forms. At the end of the chapter, I will provide some useful hints about macOS and tvOS development.

■ **Note**   As with Android, providing a full reference and guidance about Xamarin.iOS and Xamarin.Mac is not possible in this chapter, where the focus is on the Visual Studio tooling. For a complete description about the platform and about writing code for it, you can read the official documentation at `http://developer.xamarin.com/guides/ios/`. Additionally, it is important to mention that the sample app described in this chapter is based on the combination of two sample solutions from Xamarin's GitHub repository, with a number of edits: choose a photo from the gallery (`http://bit.ly/2qel8V4`) and send an e-mail (`http://bit.ly/2qhhr06`).

Creating an iOS App with Xamarin

To understand the tools that Visual Studio offers to build iOS apps, in this chapter you will create a simple application that allows users to select an existing picture from the local library and to send the selected picture as an e-mail attachment. The steps required to create a Xamarin.iOS project are similar to what you saw for Android. In fact, you can either click New Project in the welcome page or select File ➤ New Solution. In the New Project dialog, locate the App template folder under iOS, and then you can select one of the available project templates described in Chapter 1 (see Figure 6-1). For the sake of simplicity, select the Single View App project template and then click Next.

© Alessandro Del Sole 2017
A. Del Sole, *Beginning Visual Studio for Mac*, https://doi.org/10.1007/978-1-4842-3033-6_6

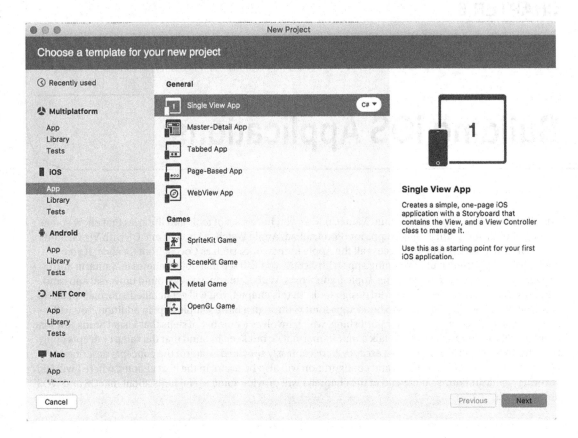

Figure 6-1. *Creating a Xamarin.iOS project*

On the next screen, you provide basic configuration settings for your project such as the app name, the organization identifier, and targets. Figure 6-2 shows an example.

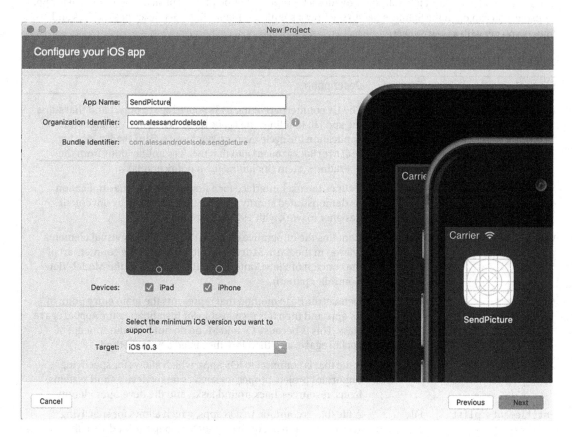

Figure 6-2. *Configuring a Xamarin.iOS project*

As the name implies, in the App Name text box you provide a name for your app. In the Organization Identifier text box, you enter your organization (or personal) identifier with the *com.* prefix. Visual Studio for Mac automatically generates the bundle identifier, which is read-only, based on the organization identifier and app name. If you want a different bundle identifier, then you must change either the app name or the organization identifier (later in the chapter you will also learn how to accomplish this in the Info.plist file). The bundle identifier is particularly important because it uniquely identifies an iOS app and will be bound to your distribution profile. By default, both the iPad and the iPhone are selected as target devices. This allows for generating universal apps, but you can certainly change this setting. In the Target combo box, you can select the minimum iOS version your app will run on. The higher the version, the most recent APIs you can take advantage of. As an implication, this will leave out all the devices that do not target that version. All these settings can be changed later in the Info.plist file and in the project options. When you click Next, you will be able to specify a different location for the project, and you will be also able to enable Git version control, exactly as you saw for Android in the previous chapter. This is not required at this point, so click Create, and after a few seconds your new Xamarin.iOS solution will be ready.

Understanding Fundamental Concepts About Xamarin.iOS Solutions

The structure of a Xamarin.iOS solution provides a C# representation of the typical elements of an iOS app. As usual, you can open the Solution pad to see how a solution is made. Table 6-1 describes the files and folders you get with a new project.

Table 6-1. *Files and Folders in a Xamarin.iOS Solution*

Element	Type	Description
AppDelegate.cs	File	The C# counterpart of the iOS's AppDelegate object and that starts the app UI. It defines the AppDelegate class that manages the application life cycle events (OnActivate, FinishedLaunching, DidEnterBackground) and that receives notifications from the operating system (including push notifications).
Main.Storyboard	File	Defines the user interface for a flow of pages in the application. As demonstrated shortly, Visual Studio provides a convenient designer to work with .storyboard files.
ViewController.cs	File	Contains the imperative code that is activated by visual elements (views) in the Main.Storyboard. It represents the counterpart of the concept of ViewController in iOS and recalls the Model-View-Controller pattern.
Main.cs	File	Defines the Main method that represents the main entry point of an app, and then it is responsible for instantiating the AppDelegate class. This is because C# and Mono do not have the concept of AppDelegate, and therefore they need a Main method.
Info.plist	File	A file that is common to iOS apps, which allows for specifying important project properties such as target devices and systems, icons, resources, background tasks, and the developer identity.
Entitlements.plist	File	A file that is common to iOS apps, which allows for specifying services the app needs to use, such as maps, iCloud, Siri, the Wallet, and others.
Assets.xcassets	File	Through a convenient window, allows for providing all the necessary icons, if different than default icons.
Resources	Folder	Contains resources the app needs, including .xib files with control libraries and visual elements.
LaunchScreen.storyboard	File	A storyboard that can be used when the app starts up instead of static images.

AppDelegate.cs can also contain initialization code for the app. If you have existing experience with Xcode, you will be familiar with most file names and their descriptions.

Understanding References and NuGet Packages

You can add and consume libraries in a Xamarin.iOS solution by following the lessons learned in Chapter 2. The References node in the Solution pad holds a list of references to system or local libraries, including the Xamarin.iOS wrapper library. If you want to consume external libraries, you can download and install NuGet packages by right-clicking the Packages node and then selecting Add Packages in the pop-up menu.

Using Components

You can use the Component Store to find libraries, user controls, themes, or SDKs, which can be downloaded from the Internet. The Component Store in Xamarin.iOS works exactly like in Xamarin.Android (see Chapter 5); therefore, you can double-click the Components item in the Solution pad to access the store, where you will get a list of free, trial, and paid products (remember you need to supply a Xamarin account).

For your convenience, Figure 6-3 shows again the Component Store. Remember that you can filter a list by operating system by clicking one or more filters in the Tags box.

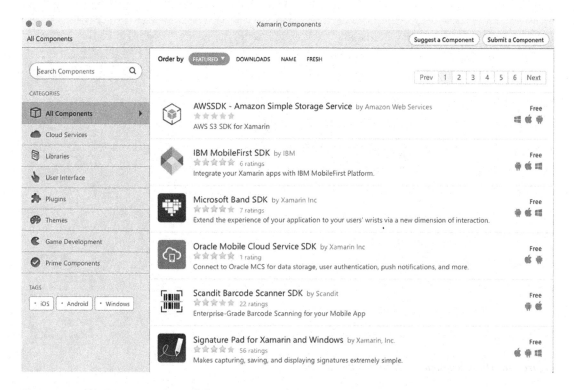

Figure 6-3. *The Component Store dialog*

Designing the User Interface

Visual Studio for Mac provides a powerful integrated designer that easily allows you to design the user interface of an iOS app. The designer is enabled every time you double-click a .storyboard file in the Solution pad. Actually, in iOS, the user interface can also be based on .xib files, which are certainly supported by Visual Studio for Mac, but .storyboard files are more modern and the most used with recent versions of the Apple SDKs and development tools.

For the sake of simplicity, in this chapter I will focus on one .storyboard file, but in real-world apps you will work with multiple .storyboard files most of the time. In the Solution pad, double-click the Main.Storyboard file. At this point, Visual Studio will show the designer and will display a list of available controllers, visual elements, and controls in the Toolbox pad. Figure 6-4 shows how the designer will appear after completing the steps described in this section, and it gives you a representation of the available tools.

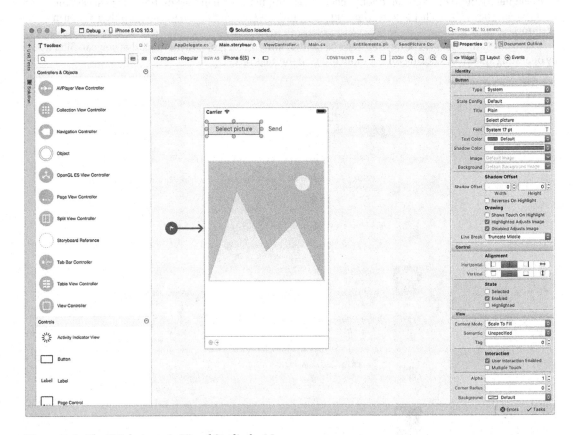

Figure 6-4. *The iOS designer in Visual Studio for Mac*

■ **Note**　The first time you create a Xamarin.iOS project in Visual Studio, the IDE will display the Toolbox pad on the right side of the workspace docked between the upper margin of the IDE and the Properties pad. For a better representation, Figure 6-4 shows the Toolbox pad docked at the left side of the IDE so that you have an extended view of both the Toolbox and Properties pads.

As you can imagine, you can drag controllers, controls, data views, gesture recognizers, and bars from the Toolbox onto the designer surface. The user interface for the sample app consists of two buttons and an image view, of type UIButton and UIImageView, respectively, that you can drag from the Toolbox and release on the designer. You can then resize and rearrange controls on the surface. In the Properties pad, you can set all the property values that a visual element supports. For example, for the two buttons, you can set the Title property to Plain in the first box, and then you can specify the text in the second box, such as Select picture and Send, respectively. In the Identity group, which is common to all visual elements, the Name property is important because here you can assign a name that you will use to interact with your controls in C# code. Assign the Name property for all three controls with SelectButton, SendButton, and ImageView, respectively. Describing all properties for each visual element is of course impossible in this chapter (the official reference at http://developer.xamarin.com/guides/ios/ provides full guidance), so now I will cover the most interesting features when working with the Toolbox. Generally speaking, you have selectors and pickers for all of those properties that accept values that you can choose from a list. Selecting colors deserves a particular mention. For instance, if you click the Text Color property value, you will see a list of default colors (see Figure 6-5).

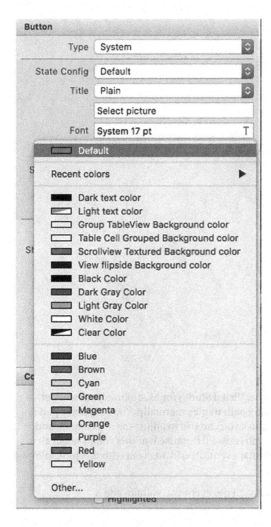

Figure 6-5. *Selecting among default colors*

If you then click Other, you can access a full color palette from which you can select a color that is not in the list, as demonstrated in Figure 6-6. You can also click the buttons at the top of the Colors title to display different palettes.

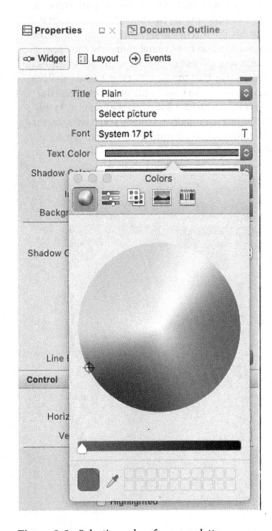

Figure 6-6. *Selecting colors from a palette*

For properties that require you to specify an image name, Visual Studio for Mac allows you to select an image from disk via the macOS file dialog instead of typing path names manually. The Properties pad has also a Layout tab, where you can find properties and values you can use to adjust the appearance and position of a visual element including margins. The Events tab is useful because it allows you to select an event handler from your C# code and associate it to a particular event. To add an event with this tool, follow these steps:

1. Place the cursor inside the text box corresponding to the event you want to add a handler for.

2. Write a name for the event handler and then press Enter.

3. When Visual Studio shows the code editor, follow the instructions in the tooltip (see Figure 6-7) and place the cursor where you want the event handler to be generated; then press Enter.

```
                                                                              AppDelegate.cs          Main.storyboard       ○  ViewController.cs       ×   Main.cs              Entitlements.plist
ViewController  ▸   Handle_FinishedPickingMedia(object sender, UIImagePickerMediaPickedEventArgs e)
 2 using CoreGraphics;
 3 using Foundation;
 4 using MessageUI;
 5 using UIKit;
 6
 7 namespace SendPicture
 8 {
 9     public partial class ViewController : UIViewController
10     {
11         UIImagePickerController imagePicker;
12         MFMailComposeViewController mailController;
13
14         public ViewController(IntPtr handle) : base(handle)
15         {
16         }
17
```

Add event handler
Use ▲ ▼ to move to another location.
Press ENTER to select the location.
Press ESC to cancel this operation.

Figure 6-7. *Adding an event handler*

When you press Enter, Visual Studio generates a method stub whose signature respects the event requirements, and its body returns a NotImplementedException that you will need to replace with your code. This way, you can generate and associate event handlers faster. Of course, you can still add event handlers with the appropriate C# syntax, but here you have a convenient alternative.

When the user interface becomes more complex, it is useful to have a visual representation of this structure. The Document Outline pad is helpful, showing the hierarchy of visual elements, as shown in Figure 6-8.

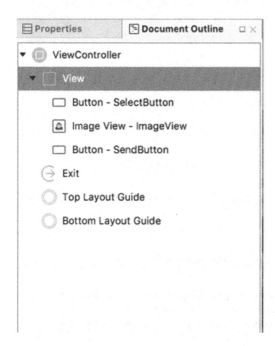

Figure 6-8. *The Document Outline shows a hierarchical view of the UI*

You can double-click a visual element and Visual Studio will select it in the designer and open the Properties pad for it. Now if you take a look back at Figure 6-4, you will notice a toolbar at the top of the designer. This toolbar provides a number of buttons that improve your productivity with the designer. The first button you encounter from left to right is called Width|Height and allows you to resize the device preview when the value of the VIEW AS combo box is Generic. From the latter, you can select one of the available form factors, and the device preview will be resized based on the selection. For instance, Figure 6-4 shows the device preview based on the iPhone 5S form factor. When a form factor is selected, changing the selection in Width|Height has no effect. Right next to the VIEW AS combo, you can find a nice button that allows you to change the orientation of the device preview by choosing between portrait (default) and landscape. Next to this, you will find the CONSTRAINTS buttons. In the iOS development, constraints allow for the so-called Auto Layout, which enables developers to create an adaptive user interface that responds appropriately to changes in screen size and device orientation. If you click the "Add recommended constraints" button (with the + icon), Visual Studio for Mac will automatically add the necessary layouts and visual elements required for Auto Layout. These new visual elements are visible not only in the designer but also in the Document Outline pad (see Figure 6-9), which makes it easier to detect changes in the UI hierarchy and to find new elements with complex layers. If you instead click the "Remove existing constraints" button, Visual Studio will be able to remove the constraints added previously.

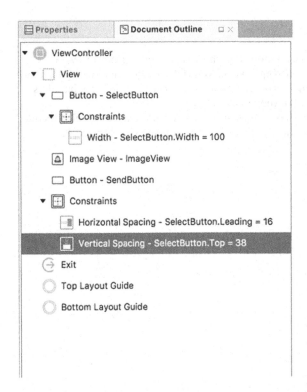

Figure 6-9. *Constraints added by Visual Studio and visible in the Document Outline pad*

You can finally click the ZOOM buttons to zoom in and out the device preview. After looking at the powerful tools available to define the user interface, it is time to see how to write C# code and leverage the iOS APIs. When the sample app is completed, you will discover other IDE amenities about project configuration and deployment.

Accessing the Apple APIs in C#

As you recall from the beginning, one of the biggest benefits of Xamarin is that it allows you to reuse your existing C# skills, and this certainly applies to iOS and Mac development too. Xamarin provides access to native libraries and frameworks, such as Cocoa, through C# namespaces, objects, and their members. In this section, you will use a couple of native APIs that include system features, such as accessing local folders and sending e-mails.

Do not forget to check out the official documentation for a complete programming reference. The core concept is that you write imperative code in a view controller, which can react to user actions in the user interface and therefore on a .storyboard file. In the Xamarin.iOS solution you created, the ViewController.cs file is the place where you will write the imperative code for the sample application. In real-world apps, you will have multiple view controllers as well as (normally) multiple .storyboard files.

Understanding Application Life Cycle Events

A view controller manages the life cycle of a storyboard through a number of events such as OnActivated, ViewDidLoad, and FinishedLaunching. ViewDidLoad is an important event, and its handler allows you to add initialization code to the view controller that will be executed after the view has been loaded. In this case, ViewDidLoad defines a couple of properties and sets up event handlers for the two buttons, as demonstrated in the following code:

```
using System;
using Foundation;
using MessageUI;
using UIKit;

namespace SendPicture
{
    public partial class ViewController : UIViewController
    {

        UIImagePickerController imagePicker;
        MFMailComposeViewController mailController;

        public ViewController(IntPtr handle) : base(handle)
        {
        }

        public override void ViewDidLoad()
        {
            base.ViewDidLoad();

            Title = "Choose Photo";
            View.BackgroundColor = UIColor.White;

            SelectButton.TouchUpInside += SelectButton_TouchUpInside;
            SendButton.TouchUpInside+= SendButton_TouchUpInside;
        }
```

Notice the following:

- The using directives import some namespaces from the Apple frameworks, such as Foundation, UIKit, and MessageUI. MessageUI exposes objects for sending e-mails, while Foundation and UIKit provide the objects that are required to access the user interface APIs.

- The class inherits from UIViewController, which is the base class for all controllers, and has an empty constructor. This might contain some startup code, but it's not necessary in this case.

- Two fields of type UIImagePickController and MFMailComposeViewController, respectively, are defined for later use.

- The ViewDidLoad event handler must call its base class's ViewDidLoad for initialization purposes, and after this invocation, it can execute initialization code. In this case, it is assigning a title to the page and a background color. More important, two event handlers are assigned to the two buttons in the UI using the typical C# syntax. The TouchUpInside event can be thought of as the counterpart of Click, Clicked, and Tapped events in other platforms.

Both event handle bodies are provided shortly.

Using System Features

The first feature that must be implemented is selecting a picture from the local library and displaying the selected picture inside the UIImageView control. This basically requires these three steps:

1. Handle the TouchUpInside event of the SelectButton control in order to display a UIImagePickerController, an iOS object that allows for selecting pictures from disk.

2. Handle the cancellation of the picture selection so that the UIImagePickerController is dismissed.

3. Handle the FinishPickingMedia event of the UIImagePickerController, which is raised once the user has selected the image and which is where the selected image is assigned to the UIImageView control.

The following is the code for the three event handlers, which includes detailed comments that explain each code snippet:

```
private void SelectButton_TouchUpInside(object sender, EventArgs e)
{
    // create a new picker controller
    imagePicker = new UIImagePickerController();

    // set our source to the photo library
    imagePicker.SourceType = UIImagePickerControllerSourceType.PhotoLibrary;

    // set what media types
    imagePicker.MediaTypes = UIImagePickerController
            .AvailableMediaTypes(UIImagePickerControllerSourceType.PhotoLibrary);
```

```
        imagePicker.FinishedPickingMedia += Handle_FinishedPickingMedia;
        imagePicker.Canceled += Handle_Canceled;

        // show the picker
        PresentModalViewController(imagePicker, true);
        //UIPopoverController picc = new UIPopoverController(imagePicker);
}

void Handle_Canceled(object sender, EventArgs e)
{
    imagePicker.DismissModalViewController(true);
}

// This is a sample method that handles the FinishedPickingMediaEvent
protected void Handle_FinishedPickingMedia(object sender,
            UIImagePickerMediaPickedEventArgs e)
{
    // determine what was selected, video or image
    bool isImage = false;
    switch (e.Info[UIImagePickerController.MediaType].ToString())
    {
        case "public.image":
            isImage = true;
            break;

        case "public.video":
            break;
    }

    // if it was an image, get the other image info
    if (isImage)
    {

        // get the original image
        UIImage originalImage = e.Info[UIImagePickerController.OriginalImage]
                            as UIImage;
        if (originalImage != null)
        {
            // do something with the image
            ImageView.Image = originalImage;
        }

        // get the edited image
        UIImage editedImage = e.Info[UIImagePickerController.EditedImage] as UIImage;
        if (editedImage != null)
        {
            // do something with the image
            ImageView.Image = editedImage;
        }
    }
}
```

```
    // if it's a video
    else
    {
        // simply return, we don't support videos
        return;
    }

    // dismiss the picker
    imagePicker.DismissModalViewController(true);
}
```

It is worth mentioning that you can invoke a controller that represents a system picker, such as the UIImagePickerController, and calls the ViewController.PresentModalViewController method, whose first argument is the controller that you want to display and the second argument is a bool value that determines whether displaying the picker should support an animation. To dismiss the picker, you instead call the DismissModalViewController method that is exposed by the instance of the object that represents the picker (in this case, UIImagePickerController).

■ **Note**　As you can imagine, an app must request permission to access the picture library. iOS 10 has changed the way you have to manage an app's privacy, and this deserves an explanation in a proper paragraph that will be provided shortly.

Sending E-mails

The next step is handling the TouchUpInside event for the SendButton button, where you will write the code required to send an e-mail with the selected picture as an attachment. Here is the code required to accomplish this, followed by a number of explanations and considerations:

```
private void SendButton_TouchUpInside(object sender, EventArgs e)
{
    if (MFMailComposeViewController.CanSendMail)
    {
        // an array of strings that represents recipients
        var to = new string[] { "someone@mail.com" };

        // MFMailComposeViewController calls the UI to send an email
        if (MFMailComposeViewController.CanSendMail)
        {
            mailController = new MFMailComposeViewController();
            mailController.SetToRecipients(to);
            mailController.SetSubject("A picture");
            mailController.SetMessageBody("Hi, I'm sending a picture from iOS", false);

            mailController.AddAttachmentData(ImageView.Image.AsJPEG(),
                        "image/jpeg", "image.jpg");
```

```
        mailController.Finished += (object s, MFComposeResultEventArgs args) =>
        {
            BeginInvokeOnMainThread(() =>
            {
                args.Controller.DismissViewController(true, null);
            });
        };
    }

    PresentViewController(mailController, true, null);
    }
}
```

The iOS APIs offer a specific controller that you can use to send e-mails, called MFMailComposeViewController, whose CanSendMail bool property allows you to understand if sending e-mails is supported on the current device.

■ **Note** On the simulator, CanSendMail always returns false. For this reason, you should test the sample app on a physical device.

MFMailComposeViewController exposes a number of methods that you can use to set up a new e-mail message, such as SetToRecipients, which receives an array of strings representing the e-mail recipients; SetSubject, which allows for specifying the e-mail subject; and SetMessageBody, which you invoke to provide the e-mail body. Of course, invoking these methods is optional since users will be able to enter the required information in the user interface of the e-mail client. Here you have to pay particular attention to the AddAttachmentData method, which takes three arguments: an object of type NSData that represents the attachment, a string that represents the MIME type for the attachment file, and the file name. The NSData class offers static methods that allow you to generate an NSData object from different data sources, but in this case things are easier because the UIImageView.Image property, which represents the image you see in the UIImageView control, exposes methods such as AsJPEG and AsPNG that return an NSData object from the image, and so they do the whole job. You still need to supply the MIME type, which is image/jpeg for JPEG images, and a file name such as image.jpg (you can certainly supply a different file name). Notice how the code handles the Finished event of MFMailComposeViewController using the lambda expressions syntax. In the lambda's body, the code calls the DismissViewController for MFMailComposeViewController, making sure this is invoked in the main UI thread via the BeginInvokeOnMainThread method. The ViewController. PresentViewController method is invoked to display the e-mail client's UI; when displaying the image picker, you called PresentModalViewController, and that made sense because the picture selection happens in-app. In this case, the app is calling another app, the e-mail client, and therefore this must not be in a modal controller. Now comes one of the most important tasks in developing for iOS (and macOS): setting app properties and permissions.

Setting App Properties and Permissions

In iOS development, as well as for macOS and tvOS, there are two files that you edit to supply the proper app settings, properties, and permissions: Info.plist and Entitlements.plist. For both files, Visual Studio for Mac provides a convenient editor based on the user interface; you can use it to avoid having to write XML markup manually. Let's start with Entitlements.plist, which is the simpler way to get started with the properties editor.

Understanding and Editing Entitlements.plist

With the `Entitlements.plist` file, you can specify a number of capabilities that your app will include and that must be explicitly specified in order to enable features such as (but not limited to) payments with the built-in Wallet feature or Siri integration. If you double-click the `Entitlements.plist` file in the Solution pad, the editor will appear and will look like Figure 6-10.

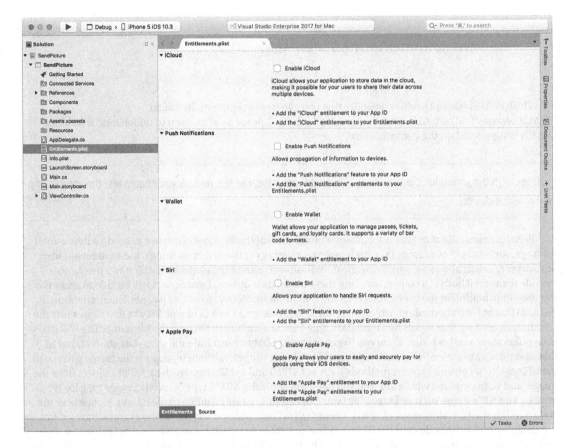

Figure 6-10. *Editing the Entitlements.plist file*

Visual Studio for Mac provides a description of each capability that you can enable by simply selecting the proper check box. Capabilities you can enable are iCloud support, push notifications, Wallet support, Siri support, Apple Pay, network access with a VPN, Keychain access, sharing audio with other apps with Inter-app Audio, associating domains to your app with associated domains, App Group interaction, HomeKit for home automation, HealthKit to access personal health information, and wireless access configuration. Notice that almost all of these capabilities require a paid developer account. Actually, you can click the Source tab at the bottom and add custom properties to include additional options. An example will be provided in the next paragraph about `Info.plist`.

Understanding and Editing Info.plist

The Info.plist file is the standard file you use to edit an app's properties and settings, meaning it is also included in Xcode projects, not only Xamarin projects. The purpose of Info.plist is providing information about identity, deployment, icons and launch images, and basic capabilities. When you double-click the Info.plist in the Solution pad, the editor will look like Figure 6-11.

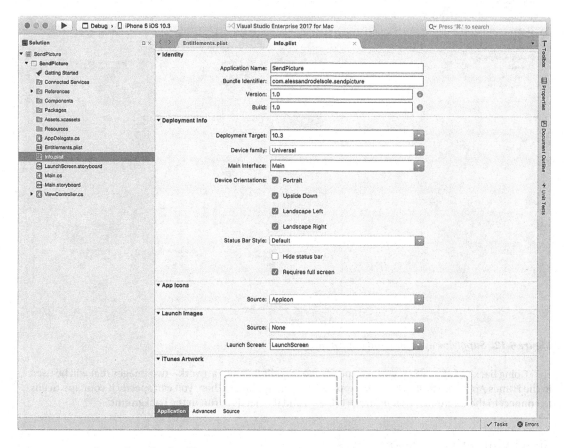

Figure 6-11. *Editing the Info.plist file*

In the Identity group, you will find the information you entered when creating the project, such as the name, bundle identifier, and version numbers. Here you can make edits; for example, you can change the version numbers when releasing app updates. In the Deployment Info group, you can specify your app targets by indicating the minimum iOS version (Deployment Target), the device family (iPhone, iPad, or Universal), the supported orientations, and the main interface, and you can control the appearance of the iOS status bar. If your app targets the iPad, you might want to select the "Requires full screen" check box. In the App Icon and Launch Images groups, you can specify the app icon and the images that will be used as splash screens. There are default settings that you can override by supplying your custom images through a specific editor, which you enable by double-clicking the Assets.xcassets folder in the Solution pad. This editor, which looks like Figure 6-12, allows you to specify icons and images for different screen factors based on the device. It shows the size for each image you need to supply and allows you to supply both app icons and launch images by clicking the desired item in the left bar.

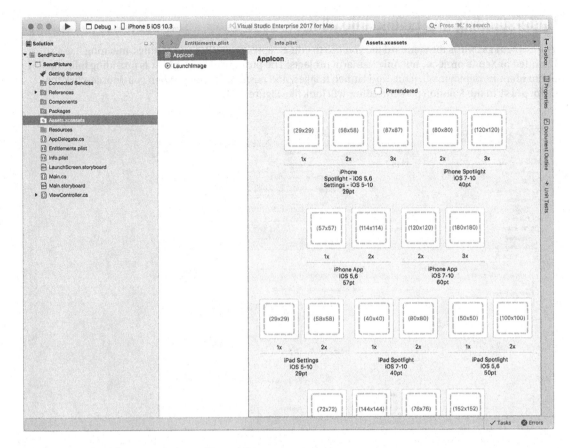

Figure 6-12. Supplying app icons and launch images

Going back to Info.plist, you can specify the so-called iTunes artwork—two images that will be used in the iTunes App Store to showcase the app. Regarding capabilities, here you can specify if your app needs to connect to the Game Center, if it supports Maps, and if it needs to run in the background.

Specifying Privacy Permissions

Info.plist is also important for another reason: it allows you to specify privacy permissions your app will request to the user, based on the device and system features it uses. For instance, the sample application needs to access the local photo library, and therefore it must request the user permission to do so. This is important, especially because of the more restrictive privacy requirements in iOS 10.

To specify a permission, first click the Source tab. Here you will see the list of properties that were already specified in the Application view of the editor, and here you can insert additional properties and options, including privacy settings. To add one, click "Add new entry." When "Custom property" appears, click the drop-down arrow at the right, and scroll the list of properties until you see those whose name starts with *Privacy*. Among these, select Privacy – Photo Library Usage Description, then specify the String type in the Type column, and finally enter a description that the app will display when requesting the user permission, as exemplified in Figure 6-13.

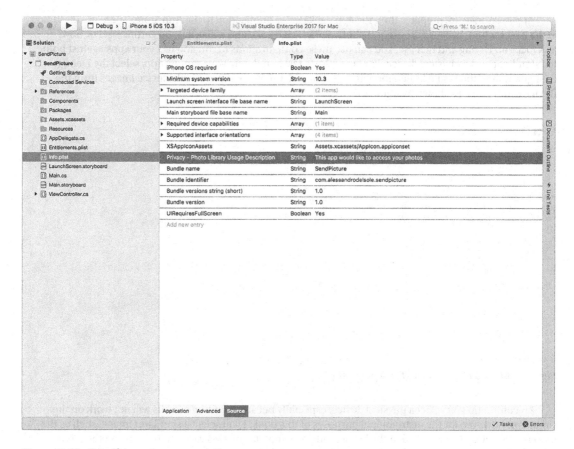

Figure 6-13. *Specifying privacy permissions*

You can specify additional privacy settings with the same steps, and the privacy items in the list are really self-explanatory. When you specify privacy items, iOS will ask the user permission to access a given resource displaying the informational message you supplied in the editor. Further information about iOS privacy permissions is available in the Xamarin official blog at `https://blog.xamarin.com/new-ios-10-privacy-permission-settings/`.

Building and Debugging Apps

When you build an iOS app, Xamarin invokes the Xcode engine and the Apple SDKs to generate an `.ipa` app package. This affects the number of available build configurations, which are the same that Xcode uses. Other than the Debug and Release configurations, here you have two additional configurations: Ad-hoc and AppStore. Ad-hoc allows you to build the app package for local usage, such as for deploying the app to your physical device or for distributing the app to the selected testers via TestFlight, HockeyApp, or the Visual Studio Mobile Center.

AppStore, instead, prepares the .ipa app package for publication to the App Store. These are discussed in the next section, because they require both a physical device and a distribution certificate. For now, let's focus on Debug and Release. You can use these configurations to run and test your apps against both the simulator and a physical device. For example, to test and debug your sample app, select the Debug configuration in the Visual Studio toolbar and then pick up one of the available device images from the Device combo box, as shown in Figure 6-14.

Figure 6-14. *Selecting a device for deployment*

I recommend you select a physical device, especially because sending e-mails will not work on the simulator; however, for the instructional purposes of this book, I will select a simulator image, such as the iPhone 7 Plus iOS 10.3. Notice that the list of available simulator images varies depending on the target version of the OS you selected in Info.plist. Once you have selected a target device, simply click the Start button. Visual Studio for Mac will build the iOS app at this point, which involves calling the Xcode engine, and therefore it might take a few minutes. It also needs to start up the simulator, which behaves like a virtual machine that needs to load the operating system. After a short wait, the sample app will be running in the simulator (or physical device), and you will be able to use all the debugging tools described in Chapter 3 (see Figure 6-15 for an example based on breakpoints and the Locals pad).

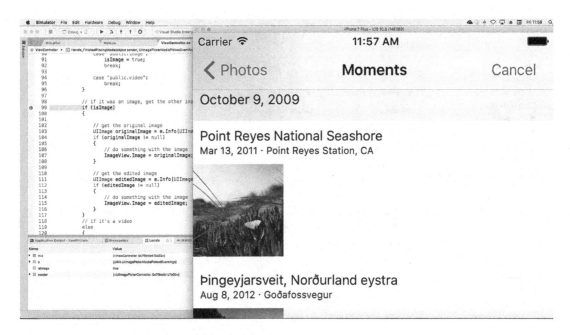

Figure 6-15. *Debugging an iOS app with the simulator*

You will instead select the Release configuration if you want to run the app without debugging.

Configuring the Build Process

In Chapter 2, you saw how to configure project options that are commonly available to all the supported project types in Visual Studio for Mac; then in Chapter 5, you saw how specific project options are available to Android projects and allow for configuring the build process. As you might expect, specific options are also available to iOS projects.

To manage these options, in the Solution pad right-click the project name and then select Options. Under the Build node of the Project Options dialog, you will find the iOS Build, iOS Debug, iOS On-Demand Resources, iOS Bundle Signing, and iOS IPA Options tabs. The iOS Build tab allows you to control the build process in a similar way to what you saw for Android in the previous chapter. For your convenience, I will summarize the most relevant options on the iOS Build tab, which is represented in Figure 6-16.

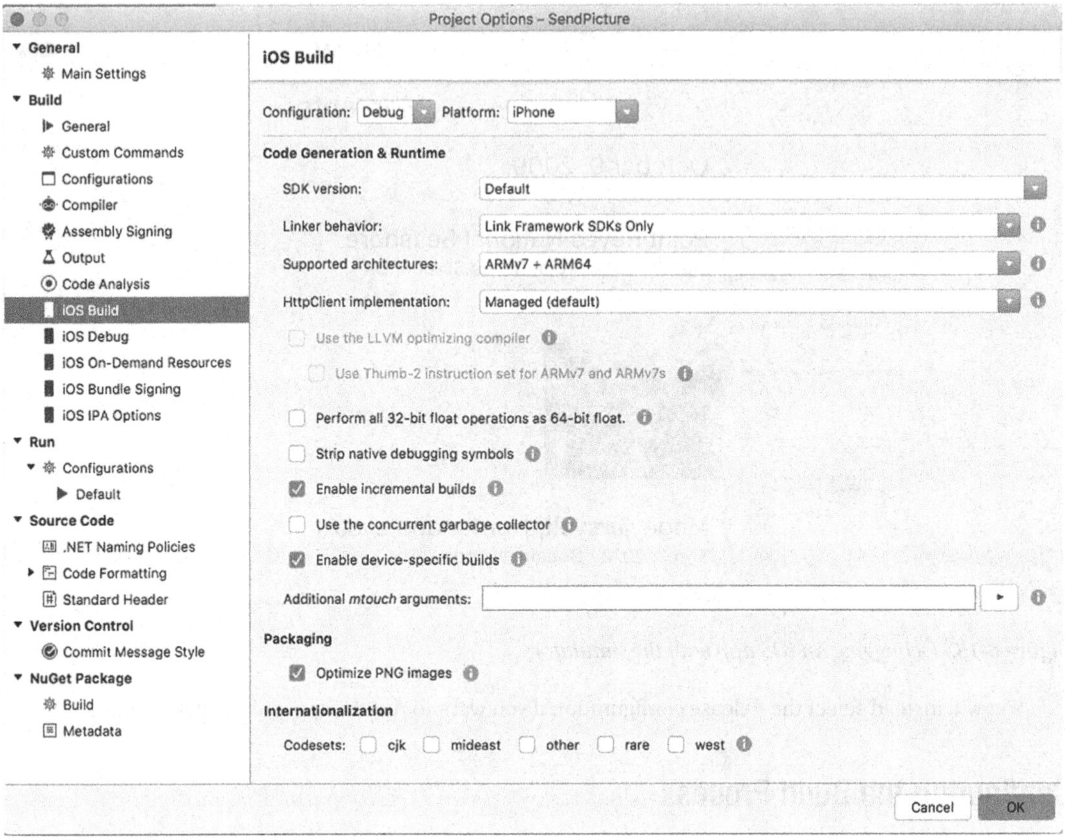

Figure 6-16. *Controlling the build options*

Like for Android, if you click the information icon, you will see a tooltip that explains what an option is about. Remember that options in the iOS Build dialog are per configuration, which means that Debug, Release, Ad-hoc, and AppStore might have different settings. Here I will cover the most relevant options. The "SDK version" option allows you to select which version of the Apple SDK must be used to build the app. I recommend you leave the Default selection so that Visual Studio knows what is the best version to use. Regarding the Linker Behavior option, you can decide to remove unused code, such as types and their members, from the build output to reduce the package size. It is recommended that you leave the default setting for each configuration, which is Link Framework SDKs Only. The "Supported architectures" box allows you to specify the supported processor architectures, and leaving the default value is the best choice. The "Enable incremental builds" and "Enable device-specific builds" options are intended to be enabled only when the active configuration is Debug. The first option only updates files that have changes from the previous build, while the second option optimizes the build for the selected target device. In the Internationalization group, you can specify one or more optional codesets so that the linker can include the appropriate resources in the build output. On the iOS Debug tab, you have options that are normally available to the Debug configuration. Among others, you can enable debugging over Wi-Fi and specify a port that the target device can use to connect. On the iOS On-Demand Resources tab, you can specify contents that are hosted on the App Store with a different bundle identifier and that your app will consume. More details are available at http://apple.co/2rHiY4i. On the iOS IPA Options tab, you can provide customizations to the information required by iTunes and that will be bundled into the .ipa app package. The iOS Bundle Signing tab contains probably the most important set of options and therefore needs a more thorough discussion. Figure 6-17 shows how this tab appears, which you can use as a reference.

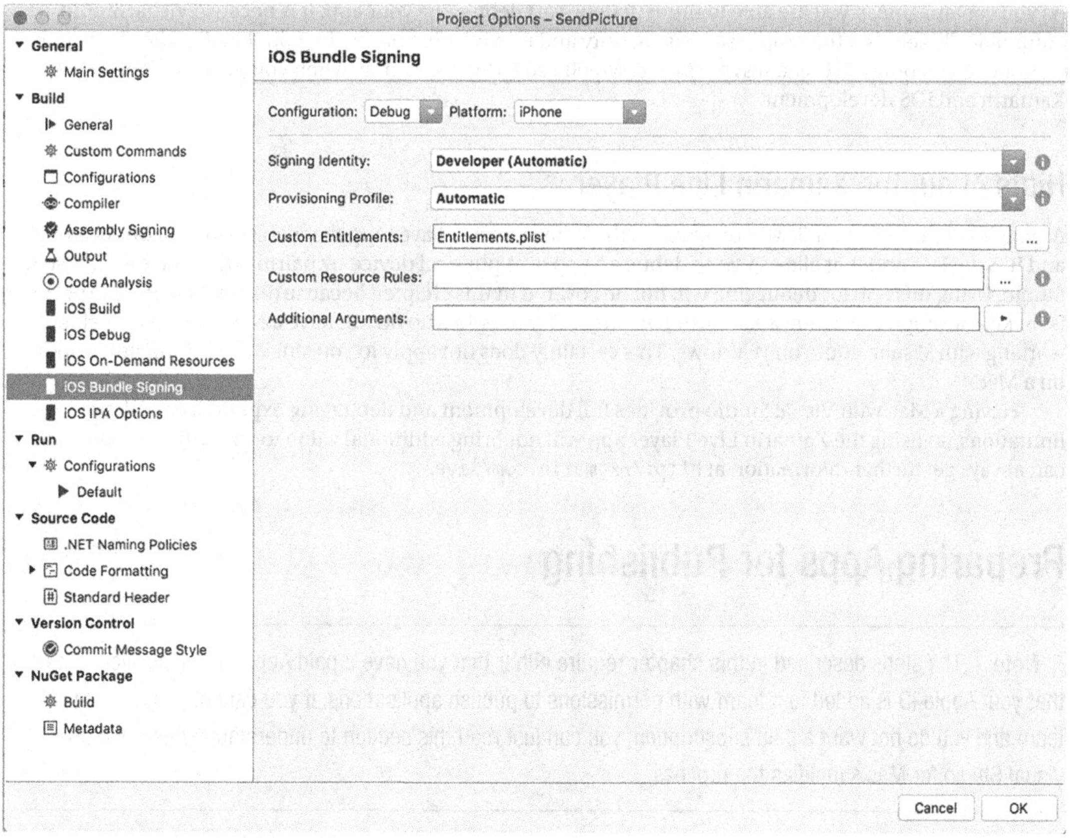

Figure 6-17. *The iOS Bundle Signing options*

The first important concept to understand is that an iOS app package must be signed not only for publishing to the App Store but also for debugging. To accomplish this, Xcode (invoked by Visual Studio for Mac) needs you to specify the so-called signing identity, which is represented by a digital certificate that can be of different types, such as Developer or Distribution. By default, your Apple ID is enabled as a free developer account, with the limitations described in Chapter 1, and Xcode generates a development certificate for it. With this certificate, you can sign an app for debugging on both the simulator and a physical device. When you purchase a developer account on the Apple's web site (http://developer.apple.com), you become eligible for removing all the restrictions on your developer account, which you can therefore use to debug and test multiple apps on a larger number of physical devices. You can also create distribution certificates that you can use to sign an app package once you are ready for publishing. This last step is explained in more detail in the next section, but it is interesting how Visual Studio for Mac can automatically detect the best signing identity based on the selected configuration. If you look at Figure 6-17, in the Signing Identity box you see Developer (Automatic). This means Visual Studio has detected that the Developer signing identity is appropriate for the selected configuration, which is Debug. Of course, you can choose a different signing identity, for example, when multiple Apple IDs are registered on the same machine. When you click the drop-down box, Visual Studio will display the list of available identities, and you will be able to understand to whom an identity belongs. Similarly, Visual Studio automatically selects the most appropriate provisioning profile based on the current configuration and signing identity. As you will see shortly, these settings will change when you want to distribute an app using the Ad-hoc and AppStore configurations.

As you can imagine, if you are able to immediately start debugging your app, it is because Visual Studio automatically selected the proper signing identity and provisioning profile for you. Finally, you can supply a different, custom `Entitlements.plist` file, which I suggest you do only when you get experienced with Xamarin and iOS development.

Hints About the Xamarin Live Player

As you learned in Chapter 5, Microsoft offers the Xamarin Live Player app that you can install on Android and iOS devices and that allows you to debug an app on a physical device by pairing the device with Visual Studio. Using this app for debugging will not be covered in this chapter, because one of the app's purposes is making it simpler to debug a Xamarin.iOS project for people who do not have a Mac, such as developers working with Visual Studio on Windows. This certainly does not apply to you since you are already working on a Mac.

Having a Mac with Visual Studio provides full development and debugging experiences with no limitations, so using the Xamarin Live Player app will not bring additional value to you with this book. You can always get further information at `http://xamarin.com/live`.

Preparing Apps for Publishing

■ **Note** The steps described in this chapter require either that you have a paid Apple developer account or that your Apple ID is added to a team with permissions to publish applications. If you cannot join an existing team and you do not want a paid subscription, you can just read this section to understand where and how Visual Studio for Mac simplifies the process.

Visual Studio for Mac dramatically simplifies the process of preparing an app package for publication with a number of built-in tools that generate the `.ipa` file in a few steps. However, before you can publish an app, you need to do a few things, such as creating an app record on Apple's developer web site and generating a distribution certificate, both necessary to see VS for Mac's tools in action. Discussing all the steps in detail is beyond the scope of this chapter, so I will provide a summary of the required steps and links to the documentation where you can find the proper information. Having that said, the following is a list of requirements you must satisfy before you can publish an app:

1. Join the Apple Developer Program (`http://developer.apple.com`) by choosing your paid subscription level. The individual account, currently $99 per year, is enough to distribute iOS apps.

2. Once your subscription has been enabled, enter the iTunes Connect portal (`http://itunesconnect.apple.com`), where you can manage your applications and distributions.

3. Create an app record by following the instructions described in the documentation at `http://apple.co/2r4NGS5`. Make sure you enter the bundle identifier you provided in your project because this will be mapped to the `.ipa` package at upload time.

4. Generating a distribution certificate for your app (see `http://apple.co/2lzClJc`).

Once you have created your subscription, created the app record, and generated your distribution certificate, you are ready to publish your app. Make sure you connect a physical device to your Mac, and then in Visual Studio select the AppStore|iPhone configuration in the toolbar. Next, in the Solution pad, right-click the project name and then select Archive for Publishing. Visual Studio will rebuild the project based on the AppStore configuration. If the build succeeds, you will see the newly generated package in the Archives window visible in Figure 6-18.

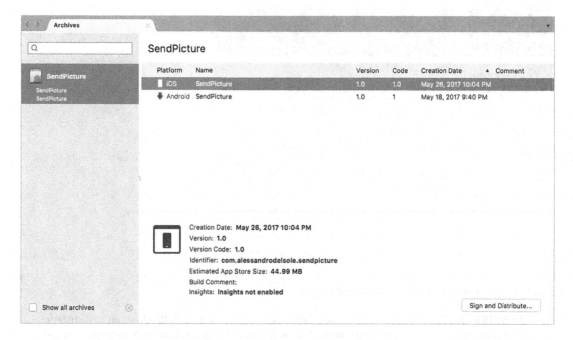

Figure 6-18. *The archive list for the app packages*

Before any other considerations, it is worth highlighting that Visual Studio for Mac shows the list of archives in the solution. Therefore, it includes Android archives, as you can see in Figure 6-18 where the archive generated in Chapter 5 is also visible. At this purpose, the Archive window reports the same kind of information regardless of the target platform both for items in the list and for the summary. If you click Sign and Distribute, you will be prompted with three options, as shown in Figure 6-19.

Figure 6-19. *Choosing the iOS distribution channel*

The Ad Hoc channel will allow you to save on disk the `.ipa` package and will allow you to distribute it via tools such as TestFlight or the Visual Studio Mobile Center. The App Store distribution channel will prepare the `.ipa` package for direct upload to the App Store via the Application Loader tool. This assumes you have created the app record on iTunes Connect and that you have registered the bundle identifier. The Enterprise distribution channel is available only to the same-name subscription level and allows for distributing app within the enterprise. By clicking Next, you will be able to upload your app package directly to the App Store, and the Application Loader tool will use the bundle identifier to correctly map your `.ipa` package to the app record you created previously. The official Apple documentation provides information about the Application Loader tool at `http://apple.co/2r6QSid`.

Hints on macOS and tvOS Development

Visual Studio for Mac allows you to create applications for macOS by leveraging the Xamarin.Mac platform and the Cocoa framework from Apple; you can also create games based on the SpriteKit, SceneKit, and Metal frameworks. When you create a new project using the Cocoa App template, you will be able to specify the minimum operating system version and options for the Dock. You will also be able to specify whether the application must rely on documents.

The structure of a Xamarin.Mac solution is similar to a Xamarin.iOS solution, which means you have .storyboard files, view controllers, Info.plist, Entitlements.plist, Assets.xcassets, and so on. This will make it simpler to write a macOS program with Visual Studio. A macOS app still relies on the bundle identifier and signing identities. At this writing, building apps for macOS is a hybrid process, meaning that editing .storyboard files cannot be done inside Visual Studio; instead, the IDE opens an instance of Xcode, and there you will be able to design storyboards and scenes. As an alternative, you can completely code your user interface in C#. Regarding tvOS development, this is really close to iOS development with Xamarin. In fact, a Xamarin.tvOS solution has the same structure as a Xamarin.iOS solution, with the same properties, requirements, and files. In Xamarin.tvOS, you can edit .storyboard files with the Visual Studio designer. Of course, tvOS has some differences in terms of screen factor and API availability, but the way you work with a tvOS solution is the same. Additionally, there is a specific Apple TV image for the simulator that you can use for debugging. So, with Visual Studio for Mac, you have everything in one place, and you can target all the Apple platforms by reusing your C# skills. Of course, you will need to know how the macOS, iOS, and tvOS operating systems work and the API they expose, but Visual Studio for Mac makes the development experience really straightforward.

Summary

Visual Studio for Mac allows you to build, debug, test, and deploy iOS, macOS, and tvOS applications using C# all in one place. In this chapter, you saw how to create a Xamarin.iOS project for the iPhone and the iPad, and you walked through important concepts such as the structure of a solution, adding NuGet packages and components, and designing the user interface with the built-in, integrated designer for .storyboard files.

Then you saw how to invoke the iOS APIs from the view controller in C# code to access the local photo library and to send an e-mail with an attachment. Actually, in iOS development there is much more than writing code, such as configuring project properties and metadata the proper way, so you saw how to use the .plist editor to customize the Info.plist and Entitlements.plist files. Info.plist is also the place where you add privacy permissions, and VS for Mac dramatically simplifies the way you do it. When it comes to debugging and testing an app, Visual Studio for Mac reveals all of its power, offering all the debugging tools you saw in Chapter 3. Additionally, the IDE makes it simple to control the build process with the Options dialog and the iOS tabs. If you have experience with other development environments, you will certainly appreciate how Visual Studio for Mac also makes it extremely simple to prepare an app for publication: you simply select the Archive for Publishing command, and the IDE will select the proper signing identities, generate the app package, and let you choose among three possible distribution options, including direct publication to the App Store with the Application Loader tool. In Chapter 5 and in this chapter, you saw platform-specific flavors of Xamarin: Xamarin.Android and Xamarin.iOS. Though all allow you to write C#, there is so much difference in terms of APIs between the two platforms, and you have to create two different solutions and two different packages and write code twice. In the next chapter, you will start working with Xamarin.Forms, the abstraction layer that makes it possible to write C# code once and generate cross-platform user interfaces.

CHAPTER 7

■ ■ ■

Building Cross-Platform Apps with Xamarin.Forms

In Chapters 5 and 6, you saw how to create native apps for Android and iOS using the Xamarin.Android and Xamarin.iOS flavors with C# and Visual Studio for Mac. In both cases, you create solutions that rely on platform-specific ways to design the user interface and that provide full access to the operating system's APIs through their libraries, which are certainly different from one another.

Though both Xamarin.Android and Xamarin.iOS are powerful, there are situations where your apps do not leverage platform-specific APIs (or at least very few), so you might want to write code once and create an app for both systems. The biggest limitation of that is that you need to create two different solutions with C# code that uses different libraries, and, most important, you need to redesign the user interface. Xamarin.Forms wants to solve a number of problems, providing Microsoft's solution to cross-platform development by sharing the user interface and maximizing code reuse. In other words, with Xamarin.Forms, you code once, and your app runs on all the supported platforms. For the sake of completeness, it is worth mentioning that Xamarin.Foms also supports the Universal Windows Platform (UWP), but this is available only on Windows PCs. In fact, if you open a Xamarin.Forms solution created with Visual Studio on Windows, you will see that Visual Studio for Mac disables the UWP project.

■ **Note**   As for Xamarin.Android and Xamarin.iOS, this chapter cannot fully explain the Xamarin.Forms platform. For a complete reference, make sure you visit the official documentation at www.xamarin.com/forms. Additionally, though this chapter does not require you to be familiar with Xamarin.Forms, I assume you are familiar with some programming concepts such as data binding and asynchronous programming.

Introducing Xamarin.Forms

As you saw in previous chapters, Xamarin.Android and Xamarin.iOS generate solutions in which the user interface is designed using platform-specific objects and tools. Then you access native APIs in C#. With Xamarin.Forms, the development experience takes several steps forward by providing a layer that unifies the way you define the user interface for all platforms using a special flavor of the XAML markup, explained shortly.

The user interface you define in Xamarin.Forms is shared across Android and iOS (and UWP if you work with Visual Studio 2017 on Windows). To accomplish this, Xamarin.Forms maps native controls into a layer made of classes that are responsible for rendering the appropriate visual element depending on the operating system the app is running on. This way, a Xamarin.Forms solution can contain shared code, a Xamarin.Android project and a Xamarin.iOS project. Going in depth, Xamarin.Forms exposes a shared codebase for the user interface and data binding, plus a dependency service that allows invoking native, platform-specific code (as you will see in the next chapter). The code that is shared across platforms, including the user interface, is contained either in a portable class library (PCL) or in a shared project. I already provided explanations about PCLs and shared projects in Chapter 2, but I will review the most important concepts where appropriate in this chapter for your convenience, and I will also show how to use .NET Standard libraries at the end of the chapter. The biggest benefit of Xamarin.Forms is that, whether you choose a PCL or a shared project, the code you write here once will certainly run on all the supported platforms. So, with Xamarin.Forms, you can finally create cross-platform apps by simply sharing code. However, there are two particular situations you must be careful about.

- Xamarin.Forms only maps visual elements that are available to all platforms. For example, both iOS and Android have labels and text boxes, so Xamarin.Forms exposes the Label and Entry controls that certainly will be available on both systems and rendered using the native controls. As a consequence, in Xamarin.Forms, a control exposes only those properties that are available on all platforms.

- Xamarin.Forms is continuously evolving. As an implication, not all the features that we might expect from a XAML-based platform might be available today, but new and updated features become available in every major release.

The full list of controls available in Xamarin.Forms, together with their documentation, can be found at http://developer.xamarin.com/guides/xamarin-forms/controls. Xamarin.Forms actually consists of a NuGet package that Visual Studio for Mac automatically downloads and installs into the shared project. At this writing, the current version of Xamarin.Forms is 2.3.4.247. The best way to get familiar with a development platform is through an example, and the application you will build in this chapter is a simple news reader for Microsoft's Channel9 web site (http://channel9.msdn.com), which will be useful to demonstrate a number of features both in the IDE and in Xamarin.Forms.

■ **Note**   Xamarin.Forms is nothing but a library that you can consume in C#. This library exposes a root namespace called Xamarin.Forms. In this chapter, you will often see type names that are not fully qualified, which assumes they are exposed by the Xamarin.Forms namespace. I will expressly specify if a type is exposed by a different namespace.

Creating and Understanding Xamarin.Forms Solutions

Visual Studio for Mac makes it really easy to create cross-platform apps with Xamarin.Forms via the specific project templates described in Chapter 2. More specifically, when you click New Project on the welcome page or select File ➤ New Solution, in the New Project dialog you will find the Forms App and Blank Forms App project templates under the Multiplatform node.

The Forms App project template generates a Xamarin.Forms solution that also includes an ASP.NET Core back end, whereas the Blank Forms App project template generates an empty Xamarin.Forms solution. Because ASP.NET Core has not been discussed yet, select the Blank Forms App and click Next. Once you discover how to work with ASP.NET Core in Chapters 10 and 11, it will be easy to connect a Xamarin.Forms project to a back end. On the next screen, you have to specify the app name and the organization identifier (see Figure 7-1). Enter **News Reader** as the app name, which must not be confused with the project name.

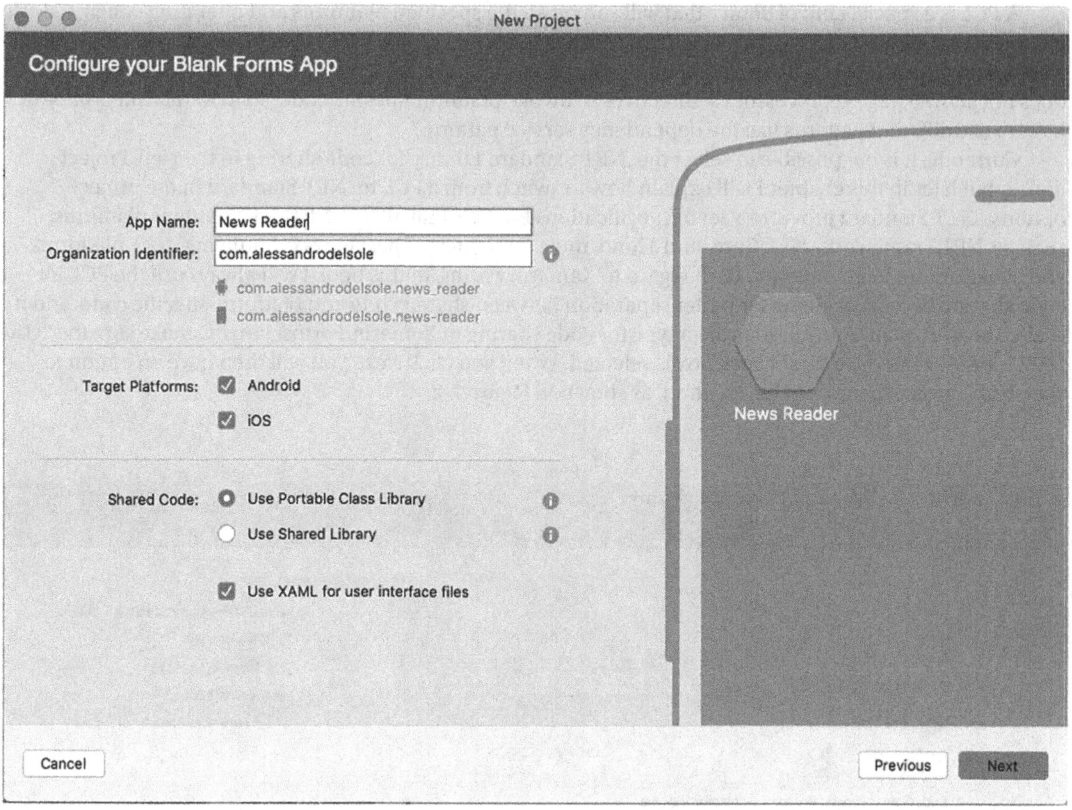

Figure 7-1. *Specifying the app name, organization identifier, target platforms, and code sharing strategy*

When you enter the organization identifier, Visual Studio generates the package identifier for both Android and iOS (for the latter, it is actually the bundle identifier). You can also specify the target platforms: Android and iOS are both selected by default, but you could use Xamarin.Forms just to target one. You might have many reasons to do this instead of using Xamarin.Android and Xamarin.iOS, for example, if you have existing experience with XAML and the PCL project type. In the Shared Code group, you can choose the project type you want to use for shared code between the portable class library and the shared library (that is, a shared project). As you might recall from Chapter 2, a shared library can be thought of as a loose assortment of files, such as code files, images, and XAML files. It does not produce a DLL library, and it can be just referenced from the projects in the solution it belongs to. It allows you to use preprocessor C# directives to invoke platform-specific code easily. For instance, in a shared library, you could write something like the following:

```
#if __ANDROID__
    // Write code invoking the Android APIs
#elseif __IOS__
    // Write code invoking the iOS APIs
#else
    //Write code invoking the Windows APIs
#endif
```

A PCL is a special kind of library that will run on all the specified platforms and operating systems; thus, it offers a common set of APIs that varies and is restricted based on the supported platform. It does generate a compiled library that can be reused in other solutions and that can be distributed to other developers. It does not allow using preprocessor C# directives to invoke platform-specific code, so in Xamarin.Forms you have to use different patterns like the dependency service pattern.

Currently, it is not possible to select the .NET Standard Library for code sharing in the New Project dialog, but later in this chapter I will explain how to switch from a PCL to .NET Standard in the project options. .NET Standard provides a set of specifications for APIs that all the .NET development platforms, such as .NET Framework, .NET Core, and Mono, must implement. This allows for unifying .NET platforms and avoids future fragmentation. With regard to Xamarin.Forms, in this book I will always use the PCL for code sharing because it allows for better separation between shared code and platform-specific code, and it is also the most commonly used project type for code sharing in Xamarin.Forms. Finally, make sure the "Use XAML for user interface files" check box is selected. When you click Next, you will then have an option to specify the project name and the location, as shown in Figure 7-2.

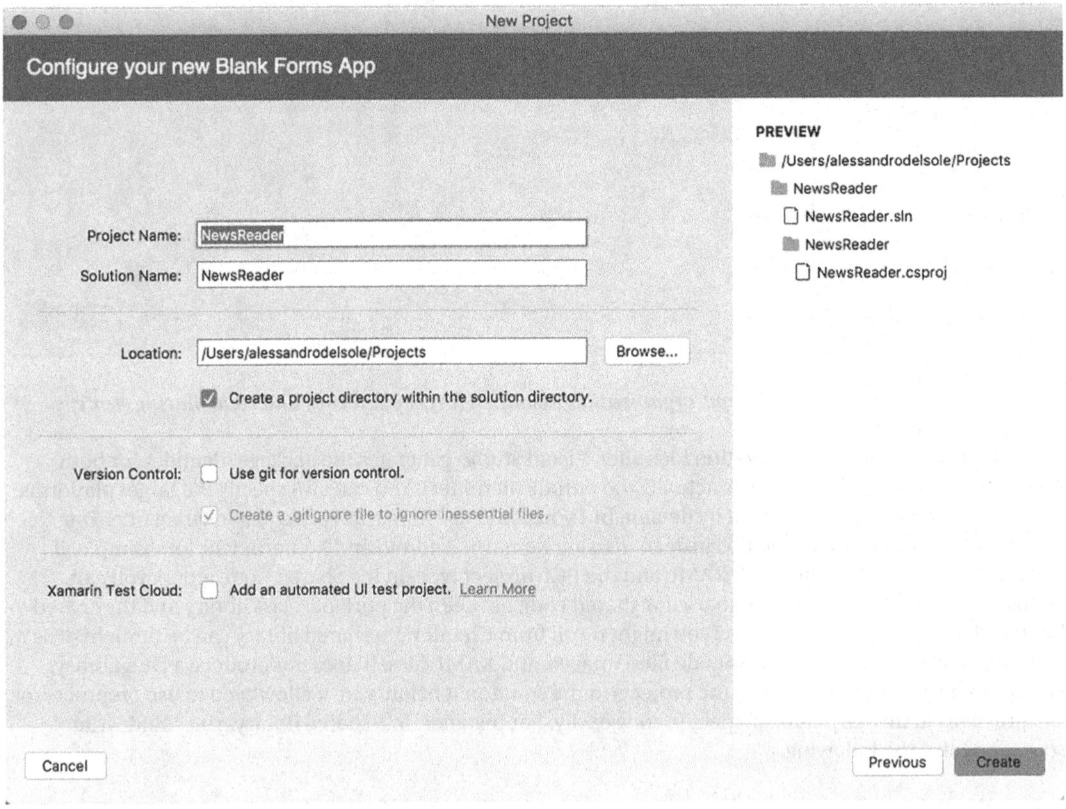

Figure 7-2. *Specifying the project name and location*

You can even enable version control and Xamarin Test Cloud, but these will not be covered in this chapter, so click Create when ready. After a few seconds, the new solution will be ready, and you will be able to browse its structure in the Solution pad.

Understanding the Structure of Xamarin.Forms Solutions

A blank Xamarin.Forms solution that you create with Visual Studio for Mac contains three projects: a project that contains shared code (in this case a PCL), a Xamarin.Android project, and a Xamarin.iOS project. If you were on Windows, the solution would also contain a Universal Windows Platform project. Both the Android and iOS projects have a dependency on the shared project.

All the projects in the solution have their own dependencies on libraries and NuGet packages; the shared project has a dependency on the Xamarin.Forms NuGet package, plus it depends on the so-called .NET Portable Subset (for PCLs), a subset of .NET that fits into the platforms that Xamarin.Forms supports. The Android and iOS projects have exactly the same structure you saw in the previous chapters because they are 100 percent Xamarin.Android and Xamarin.iOS projects. The difference is that with Xamarin. Forms you do not write code in these projects, except when you need to invoke platform-specific code; rather, you write all the code in the PCL project for code sharing. The PCL project can therefore contain XAML files for the user interface, C# files, assets, and resources. By default, the PCL project contains the App.xaml file for resources at the app level, a .xaml file that defines the user interface for the main page of your app, and a packages.config file that contains the list of required NuGet packages. You can also install NuGet packages into your PCL project as you would do with any other project types. In Xamarin.Forms, you must take care of installing NuGet packages at the solution level if the package has libraries that must be consumed by the Android and iOS projects as well as by the PCL. If you need NuGet packages that contain libraries that are only required in your shared code, you can restrict the installation to the PCL project only. In Xamarin.Forms, the most important project is therefore the shared project because here you will write the user interface and the related imperative code. You will then be able to set Android and iOS project properties exactly as you learned in the previous chapters, for example, about icons, compilation options, target devices, and digital signatures for publishing. Before you start designing the user interface and writing the code that reads Channel9's feeds, it is important for you to know how the sample application will be architected; I will discuss designing the user interface before writing models and view models, both for the sake of consistency with previous chapters and to highlight the IDE features first.

Understanding the Architecture of the Sample Application

The sample application created in this chapter will be a news reader that downloads the content of Channel9's RSS feed and displays a list of news. Such a list includes thumbnails for each item and provides an option of browsing the original web page for each item. RSS feeds consist of XML contents and are based on the RSS XML schema. If you are not familiar with RSS feeds, here is a lecture that might help: https://www.w3schools.com/xml/xml:rss.asp.

At a higher level, the architecture of the sample application consists of the following:

- A model class called Item that represents a single item in the RSS feed

- A service class called ItemService that is responsible for downloading the content of the RSS feed, returning strongly typed objects

- A view model class called ItemViewModel, whose purpose is exposing data to the user interface in a way that is suitable for data binding

- A main page that displays the list of news exposed by the view model

- A secondary page that allows viewing the original web page for the selected item in the main page

As you will see in a few paragraphs, the Item class exposes the Title, Author, PublicationDate, and Thumbnail properties; the ItemViewModel class exposes a collection of Item instances called Items, which will be data bound to the user interface leveraging the built-in data-binding engine in Xamarin.Forms. With this information in mind, it will be easier to understand the XAML markup you will write in moments.

Managing the Application Life Cycle

The PCL project contains a file called App.xaml and its code-behind file, App.xaml.cs. The latter defines a singleton instance of the App class, which represents the running instance of the application. In the constructor of the App class, you can write initialization code, but it is important to underline how this file provides a common place to handle application life cycle events.

If you take a look at the code, you will in fact see the following methods:

```
public App()
{
    InitializeComponent();

    MainPage = new NewsReaderPage();
}

protected override void OnStart()
{
    // Handle when your app starts
}

protected override void OnSleep()
{
    // Handle when your app sleeps
}

protected override void OnResume()
{
    // Handle when your app resumes
}
```

The constructor first invokes an infrastructure method called InitializeComponent that initializes required components. It then assigns the MainPage property with an instance of the root page for the app, in this case the page that was automatically generated when creating the project, NewsReaderPage. If you want to change the root page, you can simply change this assignment. Regardless of the operating system, the OnStart, OnSleep, and OnResume methods allow you to write code that the app should execute when it starts, when it goes in background, and when it resumes, respectively. This way, you do not have to deal with platform-specific life cycle events, and you can handle the application behavior in one place. For example, you can store the app's state when the runtime invokes OnSleep, and you can restore the app state when the runtime invokes OnResume.

Designing the User Interface with XAML

Extensible Application Markup Language (XAML) is a markup language derived from XML that was specifically created to write a user interface with a declarative approach.

XAML was created many years ago as a way you could design the user interface in Windows Presentation Foundation (WPF) and then in Silverlight. Microsoft invested so much in XAML that it was adopted to design the user interface in Windows Phone/Windows Store apps, in the Universal Windows Platform (UWP), and in Xamarin.Forms. At this writing, there are several XAML dialects between platforms, which means you have different visual element names in WPF/UWP and Xamarin.Forms. By the way, XAML has an identical structure and common behavior as to WPF and UWP, so if you are familiar with XAML in WPF, UWP, or Silverlight, you will certainly feel at home with Xamarin.Forms' XAML.

■ **Note**   XAML in Xamarin.Forms adheres to Microsoft's XAML 2009 specifications. At this writing, Microsoft is working on the so-called XAML Standard, a specification whose goal is to unify the various XAML dialects into one standard vocabulary. More details are available at http://blogs.windows.com/ buildingapps/2017/05/19/introducing-xaml-standard-net-standard-2-0.

With XAML, an XML node normally represents a layout or control, and XML attributes represent properties. With its hierarchical structure, XAML is a great way to create a complex user interface in a declarative mode. For example, the following XAML markup declares a page with a layout and two controls:

```
<ContentPage>
    <StackLayout>
        <Label Text="Enter your name here..."/>
        <Entry x:Name="NameBox" PlaceHolder="Enter your name..." />
    </StackLayout>
</ContentPage>
```

It is worth mentioning that anything you can do in XAML, you can do in C#, which means that you could completely design the user interface of an application in C#, but using XAML provides many advantages such as the following:

- *Separation*: The logic is clearly separated from the user interface.

- *Patterns*: Because of separation, using XAML makes it easier to implement and use architectural patterns such as Model-View-ViewModel.

- Designers can work on the user interface without interfering with the imperative C# code.

It is worth mentioning that, in the Xamarin.Forms terminology, controls are referred to as *views*. In a typical Xamarin.Forms project, the user interface is made of pages that contain *layouts*. Layouts allow for organizing and arranging visual elements dynamically and act as containers of views. Put succinctly, the hierarchy consists of pages containing layouts containing views. Pages and layouts deserve a more thorough discussion.

Understanding Pages and Layouts

Real-world apps are made of multiple pages. Think of the Facebook app: you see the news feed in the main page; then when you tap a friend's name, a new page is opened and shows the friend's profile. Xamarin. Forms provides a number of pages that satisfy the most common needs of a mobile app, and of course these pages are cross-platform, meaning they are available on Android and iOS (and on the Universal Windows Platform if you work with Visual Studio on Windows).

Every page has a specific layout and purpose and is represented by a class that inherits from a base class called Page. Table 7-1 summarizes the available page types in Xamarin.Forms.

Table 7-1. *Available Page Types in Xamarin.Forms*

Page	Description
ContentPage	Single page that displays a root layout with nested visual elements.
TabbedPage	A page that allows organizing visual elements into tabs. It is assigned with a collection of ContentPage pages, and each ContentPage is placed into a tab.
MasterDetailPage	A page with a flyout on the left side (master) and a detail area. The flyout contains a menu that is represented by the so-called hamburger icon.
CarouselPage	Similar to the TabbedPage as it is assigned with a collection of ContentPage objects, but it can be scrolled horizontally.
NavigationPage	A special page that serves as the support for navigation between pages. It keeps track of the stack of the navigation.
TemplatedPage	An object that you can use to create custom pages.

In this chapter, you will see an example of navigation between two ContentPage objects. Within pages, the user interface is organized through the so-called layouts. The concept of a layout is not new since many other development platforms allow organizing the UI with layouts, such as Android and WPF and UWP. Layouts, also known as *panels* or *containers*, can be considered as containers of views, and their purpose is creating dynamic user interfaces by automatically changing the position and size of the views they contain according to conditions such as the device orientation or the screen size factor. In Xamarin.Forms, there are different kinds of layouts that satisfy the most common requirements for dynamic user interfaces, as summarized in Table 7-2.

Table 7-2. *Available Layouts in Xamarin.Forms*

Layout	Description
Grid	A layout that can be divided into rows and columns
StackLayout	A layout that allows placing controls near one another, horizontally or vertically
AbsoluteLayout	A layout that will be placed at the specified coordinates and that will not change its position
RelativeLayout	A layout whose position depends on some constraints
ScrollView	A container that allows scrolling its content
Frame	A container that draws a colored border around the visual element it contains
ContentView	Allows aggregating layouts and views into a single view that can be reused as if it were a custom control

A page can contain only one visual element, which is normally a layout that contains a hierarchy of nested layouts and views. The code snippet shown at the beginning of the "Designing the User Interface with XAML" section shows the definition of a ContentPage that contains a root StackLayout and two views. Now you will start designing the user interface of the sample application. As you can imagine, the focus here is on understanding how the Visual Studio for Mac IDE provides powerful tools for Xamarin.Forms. I will provide a description for the views that will be used, but for a full reference do not forget to visit the official documentation at https://developer.xamarin.com/guides/xamarin-forms/user-interface/controls/.

Designing the User Interface

Differently from Xamarin.iOS and Xamarin.Android, where you have a real designer and a Toolbox, in Xamarin.Forms you need to design the user interface by writing the XAML markup manually. This is certainly a big difference if you have experience with the other Xamarin platforms or with technologies such as WPF and UWP on Windows, where you have instead a full designer. However, Visual Studio for Mac provides full IntelliSense completion for XAML code and a UI previewer, as you will see shortly.

In the Solution pad, double-click the NewsReaderPage.xaml file, which is also the main page for the application. When the XAML code editor is ready, write the following code, whose only purpose is to demonstrate IntelliSense and other editor features, inside the body of the ContentPage definition:

```
<StackLayout>
    <Label Text="Enter some text:"
        TextColor="Red" FontAttributes="Bold"/>

    <Entry Placeholder="Enter text here..."
    x:Name="Entry1"/>
</StackLayout>
```

While you type, you will immediately notice some amazing features in the code editor. First, you have full IntelliSense. Figure 7-3 shows IntelliSense in action, suggesting the available views in the given layout context.

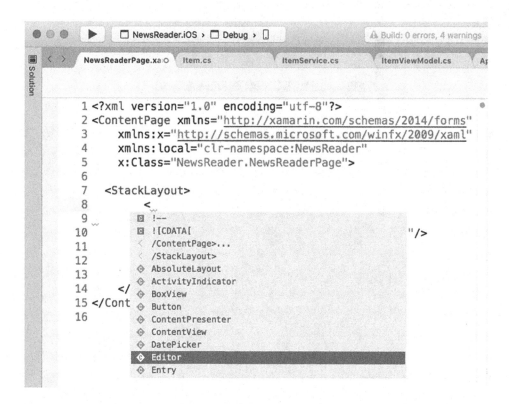

Figure 7-3. *IntelliSense suggests visual elements that can fit into a specific context*

As you get more familiar with XAML in Xamarin.Forms, you will see how IntelliSense only suggests visual elements that can fit into a specific context. For example, if you want to add a child element for a view, IntelliSense will only show visual elements that can be used as a child element for a view. When you scroll the list, a tooltip describes the view or layout. When you assign a property, in some specific cases IntelliSense can provide a preview based on the property type, such as for colors. Figure 7-4 demonstrates this.

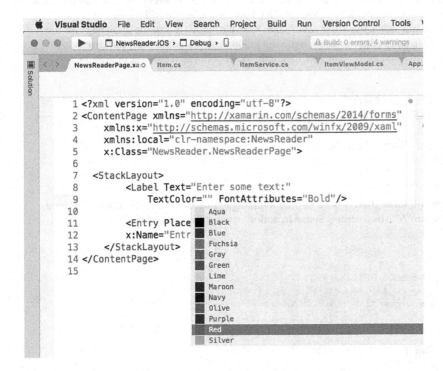

Figure 7-4. *IntelliSense shows a specialized preview based on the property type*

As I mentioned previously, though Visual Studio for Mac does not offer a real design tool, it provides the so-called previewer, which renders visual elements as you type in a preview, as shown in Figure 7-5.

Figure 7-5. *The Xamarin.Forms previewer renders the XAML as you type*

The previewer should be enabled by default, but if you do not see it, click the Preview button at the upper-right corner of the editor window. You can select the platform for the preview (Android or iOS) and the device form factor (Phone and Tablet). You will first need to rebuild the project in order for the preview to render the XAML, and this must be done for both platforms. You can also rotate the preview to simulate a landscape or portrait view. Notice that the previewer will not render the user interface if the XAML contains data-binding expressions; this is why I'm showing how to work with the previewer with a code snippet that will not be part of the sample application, which heavily relies on data binding instead.

■ **Note**   If you create pages with a constructor that takes a parameter, you must also supply a parameterless constructor; otherwise, the previewer will not be able to render your XAML. Of course, this is not mandatory, but it is required if you want to use the previewer on such a page. An example will be provided shortly.

As the user interface becomes more complex, having a visual representation of the hierarchy of visual elements might be important. If you open the Document Outline pad, you will see a visual representation of the hierarchy in the user interface definition, and Figure 7-6 shows an example based on the current XAML markup.

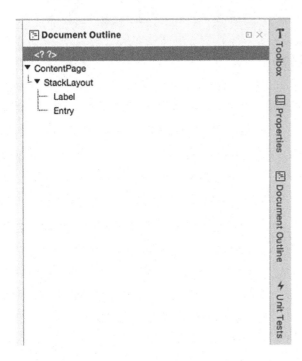

Figure 7-6. *The hierarchical view of the user interface in the Document Outline pad*

Now that you have seen the most important tools for Xamarin.Forms in Visual Studio for Mac, you can write down the markup of the user interface, so delete the StackLayout element and its content. For this example, the user interface is not really complex. The root layout is a StackLayout that contains a ListView. As with other platforms, in Xamarin.Forms a ListView allows you to present a list of data. Each item in the list is actually an instance of the Item class. For each instance, you must specify how the ListView should display its information. The Item class will be defined shortly, but you already know its property names, so you can prepare a so-called data template that defines how the information will be displayed for each Item instance. Let's start with a first, simplified version of the XAML markup for the main page, which looks like the following:

```
<?xml version="1.0" encoding="utf-8"?>
<ContentPage xmlns="http://xamarin.com/schemas/2014/forms"
 xmlns:x="http://schemas.microsoft.com/winfx/2009/xaml" xmlns:local="clr-
namespace:NewsReader"
 x:Class="NewsReader.NewsReaderPage" Title="Channel9 Reader">
  <StackLayout>
    <ActivityIndicator x:Name="NewsActivity" IsVisible="false" IsRunning="false"/>
    <ListView x:Name="RssView" ItemsSource="{Binding Items}"
            IsPullToRefreshEnabled="true" IsRefreshing="{Binding IsBusy}"
            Refreshing="Handle_Refreshing"
            ItemTapped="RssView_ItemTapped" HasUnevenRows="true">
```

```
      <ListView.ItemTemplate>
        <DataTemplate>
          <ViewCell>
            <StackLayout Padding="2" Orientation="Vertical">
              <Image Source="{Binding Thumbnail}" HorizontalOptions="Start" />
              <Label Text="{Binding Title}" FontAttributes="Bold"/>
              <Label Text="{Binding Author}"/>
              <Label Text="{Binding PublicationDate}" />
            </StackLayout>
          </ViewCell>
        </DataTemplate>
      </ListView.ItemTemplate>
    </ListView>
  </StackLayout>
</ContentPage>
```

The ContentPage root element represents a single-view page. Every page definition normally includes a number of so-called XML namespaces, which you can recognize by the xmlns literal. An XML namespace can be considered as the way XAML can reference .NET namespaces. This allows for using objects, such as views, exposed by .NET types also in XAML markup. This requires specifying an identifier for XML namespaces after the xmlns literal. By default, Xamarin.Forms includes the xmlns:local and xmlns:x namespaces, where local points to the current assembly and x refers to the root system namespace. With the same syntax you can include references to other .NET types, such as third-party views. Notice how you can assign a value for the Title property; this will be displayed when the page is in the navigation stack, as demonstrated shortly. ActivityIndicator is a view that is used to display an indicator while an operation is in progress. In this case, the IsVisible and IsRunning propertie are set to false because the indicator will be actually enabled in C# when the application is downloading content. The ListView receives the list of data through the ItemsSource property and via data binding. Data binding is a programming technique that allows for connecting two objects, keeping them in sync. If you are not familiar with data binding, make sure you read the official documentation at http://developer.xamarin.com/guides/xamarin-forms/xaml/xaml-basics/data_binding_basics. ItemsSource is data bound to a collection called Items that will be exposed by the view model. The data-binding syntax requires the {Binding} expression, followed by the name of the object you want to bind. The extended form is {Binding Path = objectName}, but Path is optional. Notice how an event handler is specified for the ItemTapped event, which is raised when the user taps an item in the list. The HasUnevenRows property allows for generating rows whose height is not fixed. Both iOS and Android offer the pull-to-refresh gesture, which allows users to pull and release a list with a finger to update the list content. Xamarin.Forms has support for this gesture through the IsPullRefreshEnabled property, set as true; the IsRefreshing property, which represents the state of the refresh operation and which is data bound to a Boolean property from the view model called IsBusy; and the Refreshing event, whose handler is responsible for refreshing the content. The data template is defined inside the DataTemplate node. When you define a data template in Xamarin.Forms, you actually need to define a *cell*. There are several cells available: EntryCell (label plus text box), TextCell (primary text plus secondary text), SwitchCell (label plus a Switch view), and ImageCell (label plus an image). These are limited to very specific situations, so you can use a ViewCell, a special cell that allows you to write custom data templates. In this case, the ViewCell is made of a StackLayout whose content is aligned vertically and in which the distance between the contained views is set with the Padding property. Padding is different from Margin, because the latter is used to set the distance between a view and other views in the parent layout. In this layout, you see four views. One is the Image view that will display a thumbnail for each item and that is bound to the Thumbnail property of the Item class (it has also the HorizontalOptions property assigned with Start, which aligns an image from left to right; other values are StartToExpand, End, EndToExpand). The others are three Label views that are data bound to corresponding string properties in the Item class. You can specify different appearance settings for each view, such as specifying a different font weight with the FontAttributes property.

Assigning Platform-Specific Property Values

Xamarin.Forms allows you to share the user interface on both Android and iOS, but there is a problem: the two systems manage the user interface differently, so the user interface you designed might be rendered differently on the two systems. To make sure the user interface is consistent, Xamarin.Forms allows you to specify platform-specific properties in both XAML and in C#. In XAML, you can use the OnPlatform tag that allows you to assign properties with specific values depending on the target system. For example, the following markup allows you to distantiate visual elements on iOS. Supplying the proper distance is important, otherwise your page could overlap the iOS tray bar:

```
<ContentPage.Padding>
    <OnPlatform x:TypeArguments="Thickness" iOS="0,20,0,0" Android="0,0,0,0" />
</ContentPage.Padding>
```

OnPlatform requires the data type of the property you are setting, which is System.Thickness for Padding, and the value for each platform. Notice that it is not required to specify platforms for which you are not going to change the default property value, so specifying Android in the previous code is actually redundant but is there to show you the syntax for the full expression. Another example is with the ListView because in iOS it is best practice that you make the item separator transparent.

```
<ListView.SeparatorColor>
  <OnPlatform x:TypeArguments="Color" iOS="Transparent"/>
</ListView.SeparatorColor>
```

The second problem you have with the ListView is the difference in how Android and iOS manage their native counterpart views. In simpler words, Android allows for a dynamic row height, whereas iOS requires you to specify a fixed row height; otherwise, your contents will not be displayed as expected. Consequently, HasUnevenRows can be true on Android and should be false on iOS. With OnPlatform, you can easily satisfy both requirements as follows:

```
<ListView.RowHeight>
  <OnPlatform x:TypeArguments="x:Int32" iOS="200"/>
</ListView.RowHeight>
<ListView.HasUnevenRows>
  <OnPlatform x:TypeArguments="x:Boolean" iOS="false" Android="true"/>
</ListView.HasUnevenRows>
```

In both cases, the type argument is a primitive .NET type (Int32 and Boolean). In such situations, the name of the .NET type must be preceded by the x: prefix, which represents the System namespace in XAML.

■ **Note**   You are not limited to setting platform-specific property values in XAML with OnPlatform. You can certainly do this in C# code as well, and there are situations in which you will prefer setting property values in imperative code. In C#, you can use the RuntimePlatform property from the Device class that can be compared for equality to the iOS and Android string constants. An expression such as if(Device.RuntimePlatform == Device.iOS) is evaluated as true if your app is running on iOS.

For your convenience, the full XAML markup of the root content page is provided here after the modifications shown earlier:

```xml
<?xml version="1.0" encoding="utf-8"?>
<ContentPage xmlns="http://xamarin.com/schemas/2014/forms"
    xmlns:x="http://schemas.microsoft.com/winfx/2009/xaml"
    xmlns:local="clr-namespace:NewsReader" x:Class="NewsReader.NewsReaderPage">
  <StackLayout>
    <ActivityIndicator x:Name="NewsActivity" IsVisible="false" IsRunning="false"/>
    <ListView x:Name="RssView" ItemsSource="{Binding Items}"
            IsPullToRefreshEnabled="True" IsRefreshing="{Binding IsBusy}"
            Refreshing="Handle_Refreshing"
            ItemTapped="RssView_ItemTapped">
      <ListView.SeparatorColor>
        <OnPlatform x:TypeArguments="Color" iOS="Transparent"/>
      </ListView.SeparatorColor>
      <ListView.RowHeight>
        <OnPlatform x:TypeArguments="x:Int32" iOS="200"/>
      </ListView.RowHeight>
      <ListView.HasUnevenRows>
        <OnPlatform x:TypeArguments="x:Boolean" iOS="false" Android="true"/>
      </ListView.HasUnevenRows>
      <ListView.ItemTemplate>
        <DataTemplate>
          <ViewCell>
            <StackLayout Padding="2" Orientation="Vertical">
              <Image Source="{Binding Thumbnail}" HorizontalOptions="Start" />
              <Label Text="{Binding Title}" FontAttributes="Bold"/>
              <Label Text="{Binding Author}"/>
              <Label Text="{Binding PublicationDate}" />
            </StackLayout>
          </ViewCell>
        </DataTemplate>
      </ListView.ItemTemplate>
    </ListView>
  </StackLayout>
  <ContentPage.Padding>
      <OnPlatform x:TypeArguments="Thickness" iOS="0,20,0,0" />
  </ContentPage.Padding>
</ContentPage>
```

The user interface for the first page is ready. Actually, you did not write the C# code that handles the page and its views yet because this requires you to first write the model, the service class, and the view model, which is explained in the next section.

Accessing Shared APIs in C#

Sharing code among platforms is at the core of Xamarin.Forms. In the previous section, you saw how to share the user interface; now in this section you will see how to share C# code that will run on all the supported platforms. Generally speaking, you write your C# code in the PCL project (or shared library if you selected that as the code sharing strategy), and the APIs you will be able to leverage are those summarized in the official documentation (http://bit.ly/2qpwLMC).

APIs that are not included in the portable subset cannot be used from the shared code and therefore require you to write platform-specific code in the iOS and Android projects, as demonstrated in the next chapter. Let's leave this off for now, and let's focus on writing the code required for the model, the service class, and the view model, which will give you a good idea of how you can both access shared APIs and share your code across platforms.

Implementing the Model

In most programming patterns, the model consists of one or more classes that map in code the structure of the data you need to represent. In the case of the sample application that downloads and displays the content of the RSS news feed from the Channel9 web site, you have just one model class that represents a single item in the news feed. RSS feeds consist of XML nodes and elements, so you need a class that represents an XML element in a .NET way.

To accomplish this, in the Solution pad right-click the PCL project name and then select Add ➤ New Folder. A new folder is added to the project, so enter **Model** as the new folder name. Organizing code in folders helps you keep your code well organized. Next, right-click the new folder name and then select Add ➤ New File. When the New File dialog appears (see Figure 7-7), make sure the Empty Class item template is selected, then enter **Item** as the new class name, and finally click New.

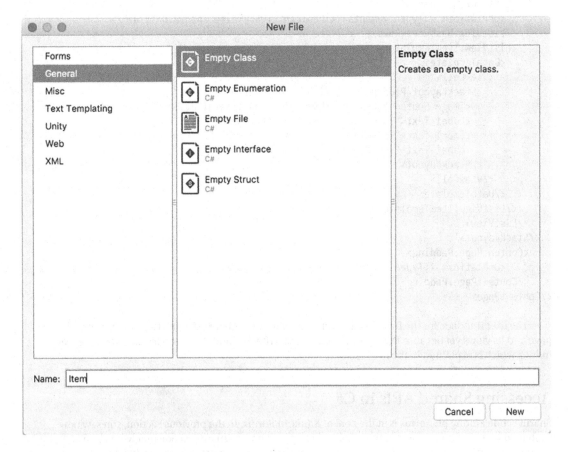

Figure 7-7. *Adding a new empty class*

Visual Studio generates a new C# file called Item.cs. The Item class must expose a number of properties that map XML attributes. In Xamarin.Forms, as well as in other XAML-based platforms such as WPF and UWP, views that are data bound to an object's properties can automatically refresh their content if the bound object raises a change notification. In .NET (and Mono), objects can raise change notifications if they implement the INotifyPropertyChanged interface. With these considerations in mind, write the following code in the Item.cs file:

```
using System;
using System.ComponentModel;
using System.Runtime.CompilerServices;

namespace NewsReader.Model
{
    public class Item : INotifyPropertyChanged
    {
        public event PropertyChangedEventHandler PropertyChanged;
        public void OnPropertyChanged([CallerMemberName]string name = "") =>
                PropertyChanged?.Invoke(this, new PropertyChangedEventArgs(name));

        private string title;
        public string Title
        {
            get
            {
                return title;
            }

            set
            {
                title = value;
                OnPropertyChanged();
            }
        }

        private string link;
        public string Link
        {
            get
            {
                return link;
            }

            set
            {
                link = value;
                OnPropertyChanged();
            }
        }
```

```csharp
        private string author;
        public string Author
        {
            get
            {
                return author;
            }

            set
            {
                author = value;
                OnPropertyChanged();
            }
        }

        private DateTime publicationDate;
        public DateTime PublicationDate
        {
            get
            {
                return publicationDate;
            }

            set
            {
                publicationDate = value;
                OnPropertyChanged();
            }
        }

        private string thumbnail;
        public string Thumbnail
        {
            get { return thumbnail; }
            set
            {
                thumbnail = value;
                OnPropertyChanged();
            }
        }
    }
}
```

Notice how each property setter calls the OnPropertyChanged method to raise a change notification. The method takes advantage of the CallerMemberName attribute, which avoids the need of passing the property name as a parameter because the runtime automatically resolves the name of the caller property.

Accessing the Network with a Service Class

The next step is adding a service class. Its purpose is to download the content of the RSS news feed from the desired web site and generate a collection of Item objects, each per item in the news feed. Generally speaking, in Xamarin.Forms you can work with information on a network through the HttpClient class, from the System.Net.Http namespace. With this class, not only can you download contents, but you can also send HTTP requests through verbs such as GET, POST, PUT, and DELETE, which is the case of invoking web API services.

HttpClient exposes a number of asynchronous methods, which allow the caller client to stay responsive while the operation is in progress. By following the instructions in the previous subsection, add a folder called Services to the project, and add a new empty class file called ItemService.cs to this folder. The first part of the class definition contains using directives and two strings, one that contains the URL of the RSS feed and one that represents the XML namespaces used to specify media files in the feed.

```
using System;
using System.Collections.Generic;
using System.Linq;
using System.Net.Http;
using System.Threading;
using System.Threading.Tasks;
using System.Xml.Linq;
using NewsReader.Model;
using Xamarin.Forms;

namespace NewsReader.Services
{
    public static class ItemService
    {
        public static string FeedUri =
        "https://s.ch9.ms/Feeds/RSS";
        private static XNamespace mediaNS = XNamespace.Get("http://search.yahoo.com/mrss/");
```

The next part consists of a method called QueryRssAsync that uses the HttpClient class and its GetStringAsync method to download the content at the specified URL as a string. A LINQ query then generates a new Item object for each XML element called item and populates its properties with the corresponding XML attribute values.

```
// Query the RSS feed with LINQ and return an IEnumerable of Item
public static async Task<IEnumerable<Item>> QueryRssAsync()
{
    var client = new HttpClient();

    var data = await client.GetStringAsync(FeedUri);

    var doc = XDocument.Parse(data);
    var dcNS = XNamespace.Get("http://purl.org/dc/elements/1.1/");

    var query = (from video in doc.Descendants("item")
                select new Item
```

```
        {
            Title = video.Element("title").Value,
            Author = video.Element(dcNS + "creator").Value,
            Link = video.Element("link").Value,
            Thumbnail = GetThumbnail(video),
            PublicationDate = DateTime.Parse(video.Element("pubDate").Value,
                System.Globalization.CultureInfo.InvariantCulture)
        });

    client.Dispose();
    return query;
}
```

The method returns an IEnumerable<Item> that the view model class will then be able to process in a way that is suitable for data binding. Two additional considerations are that the Channel9 RSS feed also includes links to thumbnail images (.jpg or .png), and the LINQ query invokes a method called GetThumbnail to retrieve the appropriate thumbnail link based on the device factor (the code is provided shortly); the DateTime.Parse method invoked to parse the publication date in the XML uses the invariant culture to avoid errors that might occur if the date format is not supported on the local device culture. The GetThumbnail method analyzes the url attribute of an XML item element and determines how many thumbnails are available, but it takes a step forward. Channel9's RSS feed includes one or more thumbnails with different sizes, from the smaller to bigger, so GetThumbnail returns the smaller thumbnail if the device is a phone. Otherwise, it takes the first thumbnail available with the bigger size. This is the code, which includes closing brackets for the class:

```
private static string GetThumbnail(XElement node)
{
    var images = node.Descendants(mediaNS + "thumbnail");

    string imageUrl;

    switch (Device.Idiom)
    {
        case TargetIdiom.Phone:
            imageUrl = images.FirstOrDefault().Attribute("url").Value;
            break;
        default:
            if (images.Count() > 1)
            {
                imageUrl = images.Skip(1).FirstOrDefault().Attribute("url").Value;
            }
            else
            {
                imageUrl = images.FirstOrDefault().Attribute("url").Value;
            }
            break;
    }
    return imageUrl;
}
}
```

The interesting piece here is the Device.Idiom property, of type TargetIdiom. The latter is an enumeration that allows you to understand if the app is running on a phone, a tablet, or a desktop machine (supported only on Windows 10). Possible values are Phone, Tablet, and Desktop. With this property, you can provide additional UI adjustments based on the device type.

Exposing Data with a View Model

A view model can be considered the place where you write the business logic of your app. It acts like a bridge between the model and the user interface and is responsible for exposing data in a way that XAML knows how to consume.

What the view model in the sample application needs to do is call the QueryRssAsync method from the service class, populate and expose a collection of Item instances that is suitable for data binding, and expose a property called IsBusy that will tell the UI if the view model is busy loading data. With this in mind, add a new folder called ViewModel to the PCL project and add a new file called ItemViewModel.cs to the folder. The code for the class is simple and looks like the following:

```
using System;
using System.Collections.ObjectModel;
using System.ComponentModel;
using System.Runtime.CompilerServices;
using System.Threading.Tasks;
using NewsReader.Model;
using NewsReader.Services;

namespace NewsReader.ViewModel
{
    public class ItemViewModel : INotifyPropertyChanged
    {

        public event PropertyChangedEventHandler PropertyChanged;

        public void OnPropertyChanged([CallerMemberName]string name = "") =>
                PropertyChanged?.Invoke(this, new PropertyChangedEventArgs(name));

        private bool isBusy;
        public bool IsBusy
        {
            get
            {
                return isBusy;
            }
            set
            {
                isBusy = value;
                OnPropertyChanged();
            }
        }
```

```csharp
        private ObservableCollection<Item> items;
        public ObservableCollection<Item> Items
        {
            get
            {
                return items;
            }
            set
            {
                items = value;
                OnPropertyChanged();
            }
        }

        public ItemViewModel()
        {
            this.Items = new ObservableCollection<Item>();
        }

        public async Task InitializeAsync()
        {
            if (IsBusy)
                return;

            IsBusy = true;

            try
            {
                var result = await ItemService.QueryRssAsync();
                if (result != null)
                {
                    this.Items = null;
                    this.Items = new ObservableCollection<Item>(result);
                }
            }
            catch (Exception)
            {

                this.Items = null;
            }
            Finally
            {
                IsBusy = false;
            }
        }
    }
}
```

The class implements the `INotifyPropertyChanged` interface to raise a notification that the user interface can catch to refresh its content, and this will be useful when you see how to implement pull-to-refresh in the UI to reload data. The `InitializeAsync` method invokes the `ItemService.QueryRssAsync` method and generates a new `ObservableCollection` of `Item` objects. This kind of collection should be always preferred in data-binding scenarios with XAML-based platforms. Notice how the code sets the value of `IsBusy` before and after invoking the service method. Now that you have model, service, and view model classes, you are almost ready to write the C# code for the main page. Before we dive into this, it is important to introduce another fundamental concept in Xamarin.Forms projects: navigation between pages.

Navigating Between Pages

More often than not, your apps will be made of multiple pages. Xamarin.Forms provides a built-in mechanism that allows you to navigate between pages easily. Every `Page` object exposes a property called `Navigation`, which represents the context-aware interface for navigating between pages and which is of type `INavigation`. The mechanism of navigation is essentially based on a stack: when the app opens a page, this is pushed to the stack, and when the app navigates back to a previous page, the other page is removed from the stack.

The order in which pages are managed on the stack is platform-specific and is not of interest at this point. The `Navigation` property exposes a number of methods you can call to manage navigation, as summarized in Table 7-3. All methods are asynchronous so that the user interface is always responsive while navigating.

Table 7-3. *Available Methods for Navigation*

Layout	Description
PushAsync	Navigates to a new page
PopAsync	Removes a page from the stack and returns to the previous page
PushModalAsync	Navigates to a new modal page
PopModalAsync	Removes a modal page from the stack and returns to the previous page
PopToRootAsync	Returns to the root page of the app, removing all other pages from the stack
InsertPageBefore	Inserts a page between two existing pages in the stack
RemovePage	Removes a specific page from the stack without navigating back to the previous page

Methods you will use more frequently are `PushAsync` and `PopAsync`. The benefit of using these methods is that Xamarin.Forms enables platform-specific navigation features such as the back button that both iOS and Android draw on the upper-left corner of a page and can understand if the user presses the hardware back button on Android. If you instead want deeper control over navigation, you might want to use `PushModalAsync` and `PopModalAsync`, but implementing the back and forward logic is then up to you.

To use navigation and invoke the aforementioned methods, the root page must be wrapped into a `NavigationPage` object. This means that, inside the `App.xaml.cs` file, you need to replace the assignment of the `MainPage` property as follows:

```
MainPage = new NavigationPage(new NewsReaderPage());
```

When you want to navigate to a different page, you pass an instance of the new page to PushAsync as follows:

```
await Navigation.PushAsync(new CustomPage());
```

If you want to pass data to the target page, you can use a parameterized constructor (an example is coming shortly). If you want to remove the page manually from the stack, you can call PopAsync as follows:

```
await Navigation.PopAsync();
```

This must be invoked manually only if you have custom navigation logic; otherwise, the runtime will automatically remove the page from the stack when you press either the hardware back button on Android or the software back button on both iOS and Android. Now that you have basic knowledge of how navigation works, it is time to write C# code for the root page. Further information about navigation in Xamarin.Forms is available at http://developer.xamarin.com/guides/xamarin-forms/application-fundamentals/navigation/hierarchical.

Writing C# Code for a Page

The user interface in a page can be controlled through the C# code-behind file, which has a .xaml.cs extension. In the code-behind you can handle events, you can interact with visual elements, and you can write any code that is needed to make your user interface work. If you take a look back at the XAML code for the root NewsReaderPage page, you will see that there are two events that need to be handled: an item in the ListView is tapped, and a ListView must refresh its content when pull-to-refresh is invoked.

In addition to this, the page must create an instance of the view model class to load the data it needs to display. Let's start from this last point. In the NewsReaderPage.xaml.cs file, add the following using directives first:

```
using NewsReader.Model;
using NewsReader.Pages;
using NewsReader.ViewModel;
```

Notice that the NewsReader.Pages namespace does not exist yet because a secondary page will be created in the next subsection, so the code will not compile at the moment, but ignore any errors for now. In the body of the class, add the following code:

```
private ItemViewModel viewModel;

public NewsReaderPage()
{
    InitializeComponent();

    this.viewModel = new ItemViewModel();
}

private async Task LoadDataAsync()
{
    this.NewsActivity.IsVisible = true;
    this.NewsActivity.IsRunning = true;
    await this.viewModel.InitializeAsync();
    this.RssView.ItemsSource = this.viewModel.Items;
```

```
    this.NewsActivity.IsVisible = false;
    this.NewsActivity.IsRunning = false;
}

protected override async void OnAppearing()
{
    base.OnAppearing();
    await LoadDataAsync();
}
```

The constructor creates an instance of the view model class, which is represented by a variable of type ItemViewModel. Once you have this instance, you have to invoke the InitializeAsync method that populates the collection of Item objects. This is accomplished in a specific method called LoadDataAsync, which not only loads the data and performs data binding but also sets the visibility for the activity indicator view. Because you cannot call an asynchronous method from the constructor, you can take advantage of the OnAppearing event, which is raised right after a page has been rendered on the screen. This is also the right place to put code that you want to be executed every time a page is displayed, and in this case the code is data binding the collection of Item instances to the ItemsSource property of the ListView. Obviously, in this sample code the data will be downloaded and reloaded every time the page is displayed, but in a real-world app you should implement logic that actually reloads data only when necessary. The next step is handling pull-to-refresh. In the XAML code, the name for the Refreshing event handler is Handle_Refreshing, and the following is the code:

```
private async void Handle_Refreshing(object sender, System.EventArgs e)
{
    await LoadDataAsync();
}
```

There is nothing really difficult in this code: when the event is raised, the collection is simply reloaded and data bound again by calling the LoadDataAsync method defined previously. The next step is handling the selection of an item in the ListView so that a secondary page is opened to display the original web page. This is accomplished by writing a handler for the ItemTapped event, which looks like the following:

```
private async void RssView_ItemTapped(object sender, ItemTappedEventArgs e)
{
    var selected = e.Item as Item;

    if (selected != null)
    {
        WebContentPage webPage = new WebContentPage(selected);
        await Navigation.PushAsync(webPage);
    }
}
```

The ItemTappedEventArgs object has a property called Item, of type Object, that represents the selected item in the list. A cast to the Item type is required because this will be passed to the constructor of a secondary page called WebContentPage. Then, with navigation, the code opens the secondary page. This secondary page is defined in the next paragraph.

Adding Secondary Pages

Visual Studio for Mac allows you to quickly add pages to a Xamarin.Forms project via the New File dialog. In the Solution pad, add a new folder called Pages to the PCL project and then right-click the folder name and select Add ➤ New File. When the New File dialog appears, locate the Forms template folder on the left. As you can see in Figure 7-8, you can select from among a number of item templates that are tailored for Xamarin.Forms, such as Forms ContentPage items and Forms ContentView items.

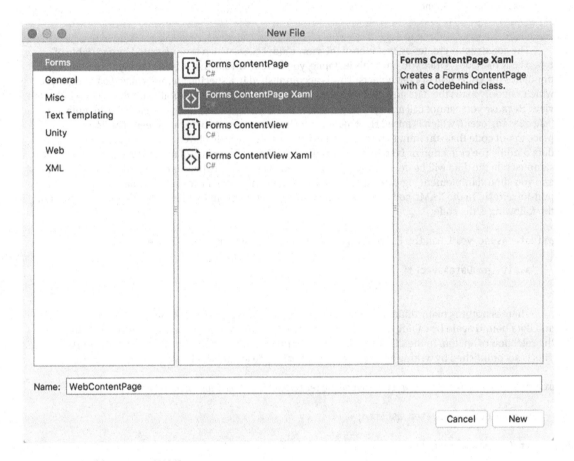

Figure 7-8. *Adding a new XAML page*

When you add a page or content view, make sure you select items whose name ends with Xaml if you want to take advantage of XAML markup to design the UI of a page or content view. In fact, other items are not based on XAML and require you to write the whole UI in C#. In this particular case, select the Forms ContentPage Xaml item and enter **WebContentPage** as the new page name.

After a few seconds, the new page will be visible in the Solution pad. Double-click WebContentPage. xaml so that the XAML editor and the previewer are enabled. As you can see, there is a ContentPage empty definition, whose content for this example will simply be a WebView control that allows for displaying HTML contents. So, the XAML looks like this:

```xml
<?xml version="1.0" encoding="UTF-8"?>
<ContentPage xmlns="http://xamarin.com/schemas/2014/forms"
    xmlns:x="http://schemas.microsoft.com/winfx/2009/xaml"
    x:Class="NewsReader.Pages.WebContentPage">
    <ContentPage.Content>
        <WebView x:Name="ArticleWebView"/>
    </ContentPage.Content>
</ContentPage>
```

Notice the importance of adding a name for the WebView so that you can interact with it in C#. In the code-behind file, you must add code that receives the instance of the Item selected in the previous page. The following is the C# code for the page:

```csharp
public partial class WebContentPage : ContentPage
{
    string link;

    public WebContentPage(Item feedItem)
    {
        InitializeComponent();

        this.link = feedItem.Link;
        this.Title = feedItem.Title;
    }

    public WebContentPage()
    {
        InitializeComponent();
    }

    protected override void OnAppearing()
    {
        base.OnAppearing();
        ArticleWebView.Source = link;
    }
}
```

As you can see, the constructor takes a parameter of type Item. The value of the Link property will be used to provide a source for the WebView control, and the Title property will be assigned to the Title property of the ContentPage so that it displays the title of the feed item.

A parameterless constructor would not be mandatory, but it is required if you want the previewer to be able to render the page. If you do not supply one, the previewer will show an error. Then you can simply assign the WebView.Source property with the URL of the web content. This property, of type WebViewSource, is very versatile because it is able to resolve contents starting from a URL and even from pure HTML passed as a string. After all this work, the sample project is ready for the first build and for debugging.

Building and Debugging Applications

As you saw earlier in this chapter, a Xamarin.Forms solution consists of three projects (in Visual Studio for Mac): a project for sharing code, which can be either a PCL or a shared library; a Xamarin.Android project; and a Xamarin.iOS project.

Both platform-specific projects reference the shared project, but this is not the startup project. Actually you build, debug, and test an app written with Xamarin.Forms exactly as you would do with Xamarin. Android and Xamarin.iOS. The only difference is that you explicitly need to set the startup project, which you can accomplish by right-clicking the Android or iOS project in the Solution pad and then selecting Set As Startup Project. A shortcut is to select the startup project in the Visual Studio's toolbar, in the combo box at the left of the configuration name. Depending on the startup project, you will see the list of available configurations, which are the same as those you already saw in the previous chapters for Xamarin.Android and Xamarin.iOS. Also the same is the way you choose a target device or emulator once you have selected the startup project and configuration.

You can build a project individually by selecting Build ➤ Build ProjectName (where ProjectName is the name of your real project) or the whole solution by selecting Build ➤ Build All. Not surprisingly, all the concepts explained in the previous chapter about configuring Android and iOS app packages certainly apply to a Xamarin.Forms solution: in fact, you still need to edit the Android manifest in the Xamarin.Android project and the Info.plist file in iOS, and you will still configure the build output, including provisioning profiles and signing identities exactly as you already learned. Additionally, creating app archives for publishing has the same behavior, but this time you do not have two separate solutions with separate platform-specific projects. Rather, you have a single solution with both platform-specific projects in one place.

With regard to the sample application, you need to set the Internet permission in the Android manifest (Project ➤ Options ➤ Android Application). You can then supply custom icons and metadata, but this is left to you as an exercise. Once you have configured your build options, manifests, and settings, I recommend you use the Build ➤ Build All command the first time you build your solution. When ready, you can start debugging the sample app on both iOS and Android, and obviously, you will be able to leverage all the debugging tools described in Chapter 3. Figure 7-9 shows the sample app running on both iOS and Android.

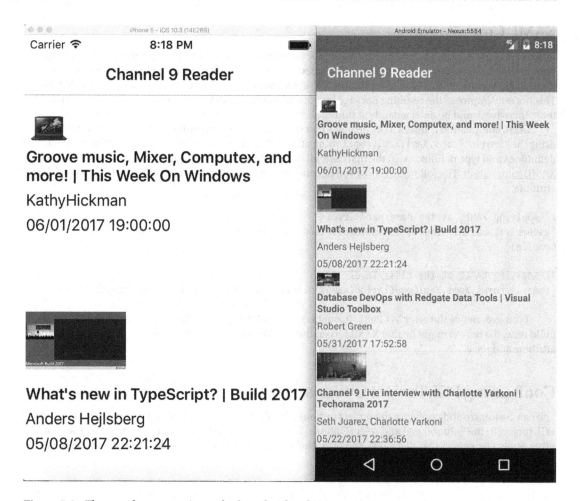

Figure 7-9. *The sample app running on both Android and iOS*

You can also certainly use the Xamarin Live Player app to test your app instead of using an emulator. As I mentioned previously, you can use the same techniques described in Chapters 5 and 6 to publish an app to the Google Play and Apple Store, respectively. With specific regard to iOS, do not forget to follow all the steps required to enable provisioning profiles, signing identities, and certificates.

■ **Note** There is a known issue in Xamarin.Forms that might cause a `TypeLoadException` on Android with the `WebView` control (`https://bugzilla.xamarin.com/show_bug.cgi?id=37499`). If you experience this error, open the Android project options and, in the "Target framework" box on the General tab, make sure that the "Use latest installed platform" option is selected; then rebuild the solution.

XAML Compilation

In Xamarin.Forms, you can optimize the build process with the so-called XAML compilation, or *XAMLC*. Without XAML compilation, XAML files are included in the app package, and then the runtime compiles them at app startup. With XAML compilation, XAML files are compiled into the app package at build time. This not only improves the resulting package but also allows you to discover at compile time errors in XAML that otherwise would be detected only at runtime.

XAML compilation is disabled by default to preserve backward compatibility, but it can be enabled using the Xamarin.Forms.Xaml.XamlCompilation attribute. This attribute can decorate both namespace definitions and type definitions. In the first case, all types belonging to that namespaces are subject to XAML compilation. The following is how you decorate a namespace and a class with the XamlCompilation attribute:

```
// Applying XAMLC at the namespace level
[assembly:Xamarin.Forms.Xaml.XamlCompilation(Xamarin.Forms.Xaml.XamlCompilationOptions.
Compile)]

// Applying XAMLC at the class level
[Xamarin.Forms.Xaml.XamlCompilation(Xamarin.Forms.Xaml.XamlCompilationOptions.Compile)]
```

If you experience the error MT 2001 ("Could not link assemblies. Reason: value cannot be null") at build time, the reason might be that XAMLC is enabled. Should this happen, remove the XamlCompilation attribute and retry.

Configuring PCL Project Options

You can customize and configure the project options for a PCL project. To accomplish this, right-click the PCL project in the Solution pad and select Options. The Main Settings tab is identical to what you saw for other project types, such as .NET Core, Xamarin.Android, and Xamarin.iOS. Under Build, the General tab appears different (see Figure 2-20).

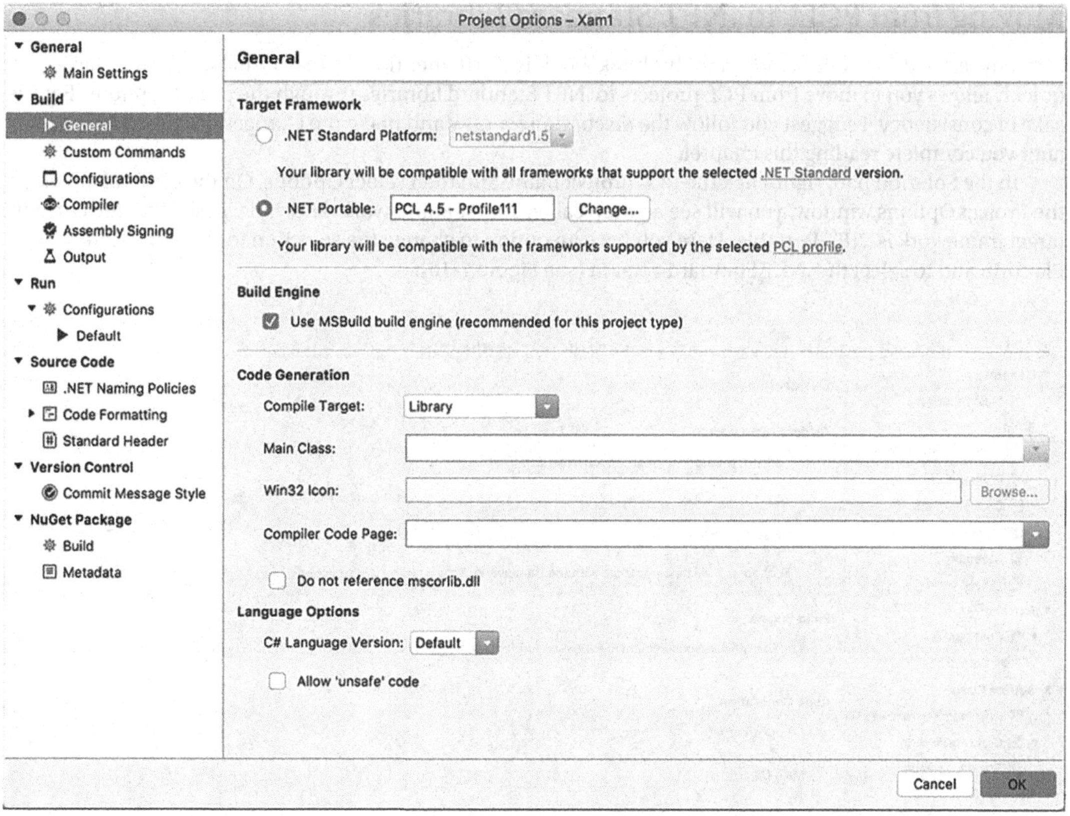

Figure 2-20. *The General tab for a PCL*

■ **Note** These settings are not restricted to the PCL project in Xamarin.Forms. Instead, they are available in any PCL project. Normally, you will not change the PCL profile in Xamarin.Forms, but it is not uncommon in PCL projects outside Xamarin.

In the Target Framework group, you can specify the project target. By default, this is .NET Portable, and the value is PCL 4.5 – Profile111. PCL profiles represent the combination of platforms that the library must target. A full list of available profiles is available at https://portablelibraryprofiles.stephencleary.com. In Xamarin.Forms, it is not recommended at all to change the target. In PCL projects outside a Xamarin. Forms solution, you can click Change, and then you will be able to pick a different profile from a list or to individually select platforms you intend to target. Additionally, you can switch from a PCL to a .NET Standard library by selecting the corresponding item (see the next subsection). At this writing, Visual Studio for Mac only supports up to .NET Standard 1.5 for Xamarin, and this version of the specification does not fully support all the .NET frameworks. For this reason, leave the current selection unchanged. The Build Engine check box is enabled by default and allows Visual Studio to run the MSBuild engine to build the solution, which is certainly the recommended choice. The other options are the same as you already saw previously with regard to .NET Core and Xamarin native projects.

Moving from PCLs to .NET Standard Libraries

I already introduced .NET Standard in this book, but it is worth mentioning that Visual Studio for Mac quickly allows you to move from PCL projects to .NET Standard libraries through the project options. For the sake of consistency, I suggest you follow the discussion for now and make the changes discussed here only after you complete reading this chapter.

In the Solution pad, right-click the PCL project name and then select Options. On the General tab of the Project Options window, you will see a group called Target Framework, and you will see that the current target framework is .NET Portable. Here you have an option to change the selection to .NET Standard Platform and to select the .NET Standard version (see Figure 7-10).

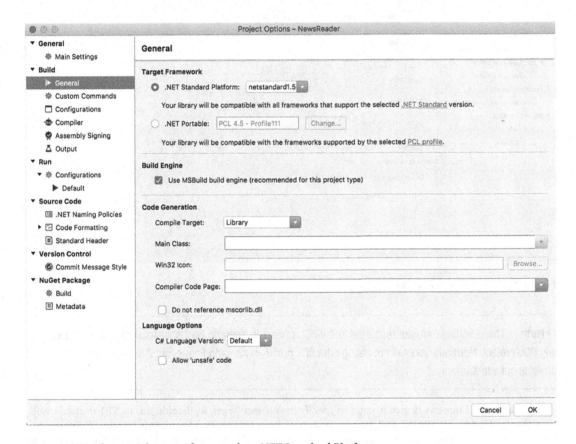

Figure 7-10. *Changing the target framework to .NET Standard Platform*

My recommendation is that you leave the version number proposed by Visual Studio. When you select the .NET Standard Platform target, you will be able to share across platforms all the APIs discussed in the official documentation at `http://docs.microsoft.com/en-us/dotnet/standard/library`. When ready, click OK and rebuild the solution. There is nothing else you have to do at this point.

■ **Note**   In the near future, .NET Standard will be the preferred way to share code across platforms, and this is true not only for Xamarin but also for other development technologies. In addition, the .NET Core runtime already works only with .NET Standard libraries. For these reasons, I suggest you spend some time getting more familiar with .NET Standard and reading the documentation.

Analyzing Applications with Instrumentation

Xamarin ships with some interesting and useful tools that are the perfect companions for the debugger and that allow you to analyze an app to investigate performance issues and to analyze the behavior of the user interface. In this section, you will get started with the Xamarin Profiler and the Xamarin Inspector tools. Notice that their usage is not restricted to Xamarin.Forms, but discussing them in this chapter is a better option now that you have basic knowledge of both XAML and platform-specific UI frameworks.

UI Debugging with the Xamarin Inspector

The Xamarin Inspector is a tool that allows you to analyze the behavior of the user interface while the application is running. Among the others, the Inspector allows you to even see the XAML view definitions and their property values. To start the Inspector, first start your app for debugging, and then in the debug toolbar click the last button on the right. After a few seconds the Xamarin Inspector will start in a separate window.

When it starts, it is in the so-called REPL mode, which allows you to use the tool as an interactive read-eval-print-loop console. This is not what you need, so click the rightmost button at the upper-right corner, which enables Inspector mode. At this point, the Inspector will show the hierarchy of the controls in the user interface, the property values for the selected control, and a live preview of the UI that you can rotate with the mouse in order to see the UI layers. Figure 7-11 demonstrates this.

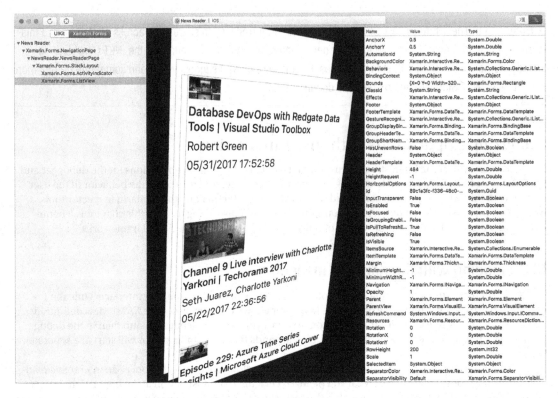

Figure 7-11. *Analyzing the UI behavior with the Xamarin Inspector*

When you select a view in the running app, the Inspector will highlight that view, and it will show its property values. As you can see, the tool shows the property name, its current value, and its .NET type. Not limited to this, you can change a property value in the Value column where allowed, and the new value will be immediately reflected in the running app so that you can have the immediate perception of how the user interface elements appear with different values. The Xamarin Inspector is even more powerful: you can switch to the native view of UI elements by clicking the appropriate button at the upper-left corner, where Xamarin.Forms is the default selection. In Figure 7-11, which is based on the iOS version of the app, you can see the UIKit button. If you switch to the native view, you will not only see the hierarchy of views changing to display native control names, but you will also see the corresponding property names and values on the right. Also, the native view provides more granularity of control over the single UI elements that you will be able to select and highlight directly in the preview and then investigate or change their property values.

Profiling Apps with the Xamarin Profiler

The Xamarin Profiler is a tool that allows you to analyze an app for performance issues, which might involve memory and CPU usage or where the application spends most of its time. The Xamarin Profiler can be launched as a stand-alone application against different kinds of targets, but the simplest way to use it is by selecting Run ➤ Start Profiling in Visual Studio.

When the Profiler starts, it will prompt you with a list of possible investigations you can perform against the app, summarized in Table 7-4.

Table 7-4. *Analysis Tools in the Xamarin Profiler*

Tool	Description
All Instruments	Allows you to execute all the available analysis tools
Allocations	Analyzes memory usage by tracking object allocations
Cycles	Analyzes and detects reference cycles
Memory	Analyzes memory to find problems
Performance	Analyze memory and CPU usage for performance issues
Time Profiler	Profiles a running app at regular intervals

Figure 7-12 shows an example based on the All Instrument tool.

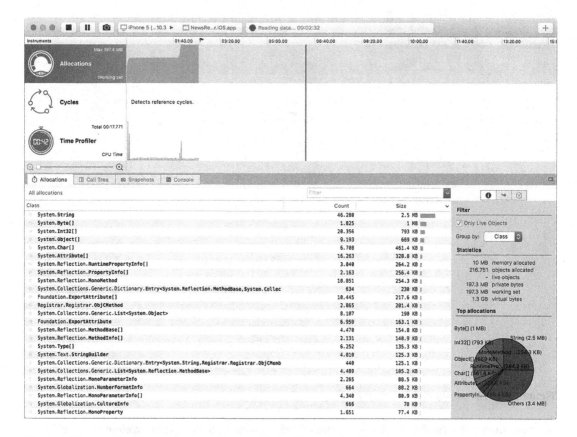

Figure 7-12. *Investigating performance issues with the Xamarin Profiler*

As you can see, the Allocations tool displays the list of object instances and their numbers and size in memory, which can be useful to analyze if the number of instances of an object is reasonable or if there might be a memory leak. The Cycles tool has detected no reference cycles in the sample app, and the Time Profiler tool is showing where and when the app is consuming more CPU resources. In the current example, you can see a peak at the app startup, which is reasonable. On the right side of the window, you can see statistics and a pie chart with top allocations. In the example, only 10MB of memory are allocated by the app, which is pretty good. You can click the Call Tree tab to see the hierarchy of method calls, and a very interesting tool is Snapshots. With this tool, you can take a picture of the memory at a certain point in time, storing the list and number of allocated objects and their types. If you take multiple snapshots, you can then open the Snapshots tab and compare the number of allocate objects between snapshots, as demonstrated in Figure 7-13.

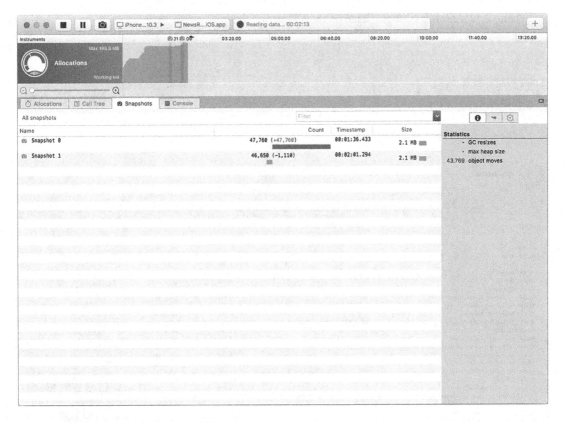

Figure 7-13. *Comparing memory snapshots*

In summary, the Xamarin Profiler is a useful tool when you need to investigate different types of performance issues. You can find more detailed information about this tool at `http://developer.xamarin.com/guides/cross-platform/profiler/`.

Summary

In this chapter, you got started with Xamarin.Forms, Xamarin's framework that allows you to share the user interface and non-platform-specific code across multiple platforms. With Xamarin.Forms, you can create cross-platform solutions by focusing on code sharing and by designing the user interface leveraging XAML, the markup that Microsoft created for declarative user interface definitions.

With Xamarin.Forms, you can share code using a PCL project or a shared library, and in this shared project you can write all the cross-platform code. In the sample application described in this chapter, you saw how you can design a shared user interface and how to tailor it for different platforms and devices, you saw how to access APIs included in the .NET Portable Subset, and you saw how to navigate between pages. Finally, you saw how to build and debug a Xamarin.Forms solution, and you also got started with two interesting Xamarin tools: the Profiler for analyzing performance issues and the Inspector for analyzing the behavior of the user interface. Xamarin.Forms is actually much more powerful than you might think, and therefore it deserves another chapter for further details. In Chapter 8, I will explain how to write and consume platform-specific code in different ways, and, again, you will see how Visual Studio for Mac simplifies the job.

■ ■ ■

Platform-Specific Code in Xamarin.Forms

In Chapter 7 you saw how Xamarin.Forms allows you to quickly build cross-platform apps that run on Android and iOS (and actually Windows 10) by sharing the user interface and a common set of APIs based on portable class libraries, shared libraries, and .NET Standard libraries.

Now the problem is that most apps need to access native iOS and Android features whose APIs are not mapped by Xamarin.Forms, and I'm talking about common tasks such as showing the camera, detecting network connection availability, and reading and writing files. If Xamarin.Forms did not offer a solution to this problem, then it would neither be as useful nor as successful as it is. In fact, it allows you to access native features in several ways, such as leveraging platform-specific APIs with a bridge to Xamarin.Android and Xamarin.iOS libraries and integrating native visual elements that you can use to enrich the user experience. In this chapter, I will walk you through the most common ways you have to add native features to a Xamarin. Forms solution.

■ **Note**   Remember that, in Xamarin.Forms, everything that is available on iOS and Android is also available on Windows 10 through the Universal Windows Platform when you use Visual Studio 2017 on Windows, even though this will not be mentioned in this book.

Using the Dependency Service

More often than not, mobile apps need to access device and operating system features, such as sensors, the camera, files on disk, and network information. iOS and Android have platform-specific APIs that allow you to work with all these features because both the hardware and the operating systems are different from one another. As a consequence, shared code in Xamarin.Forms cannot directly access these APIs.

However, there is a simple feature that allows shared code to access platform-specific APIs based on inversion of control (IoC). In the PCL project (or another shared project type), you create a C# interface that defines the required functionalities; then in the iOS and Android projects, you create classes that implement the interface and that provide a platform-specific implementation of the functionalities. In the PCL project, you then use the DependencyService class and its Get method, which finds the correct implementation of the interface for the platform your app is running on. This enables apps written with Xamarin.Forms to do anything a native app can do. The DependencyService class is a dependency resolver and is able to resolve classes that have been registered as implementations of a given interface. For a clear understanding of how the dependency service works, I will provide an example that extends the News Reader sample app started in the previous chapter. More specifically, I will show how to add local data access support based on SQLite, which not only is a common requirement in most mobile apps but which also requires you to specify a path name for the database. Android and iOS have different APIs to deal with path names and to represent user folders on the device, so constructing the full path for the SQLite database is something that requires the dependency service. The sample app will basically create a table based on the Item class and will store a list of news in the database.

Adding the SQLite NuGet Packages

The first thing you need to do is to add NuGet packages that allow you to work with SQLite databases. SQLite is already bundled in iOS and Android, so it is a convenient choice for local data access. By following the lessons learned in Chapter 2, add the NuGet package called SQLite.Net PCL to all the three projects in the solution. Figure 8-1 shows the appropriate NuGet package in the Add Packages dialog.

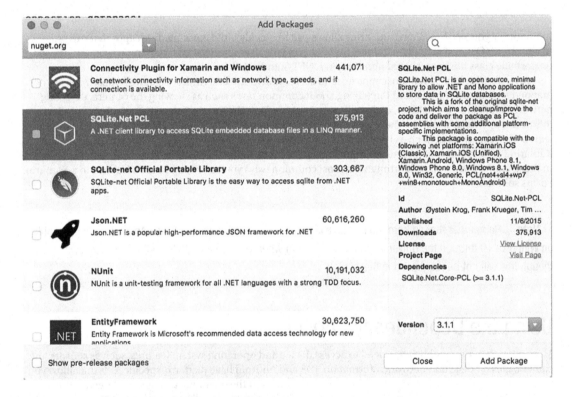

Figure 8-1. Adding the SQLite.Net PCL package

Once you have added the package to the three projects and before you start implementing data access, some minor changes are required to the Item class. In fact, the SQLite library exposes data annotation attributes that you can use to decorate class names and properties to define the table name, column names, identity, required columns, and some basic validation rules such as maximum string length. In Visual Studio, open the Item.cs file and add a using SQLite.Net.Attributes directive first. The next step is to decorate the class name with the Table attribute to specify a table name and define a property called Id that can be used as the identity column. This is the code you need to edit the Item class (the remaining code will be left unchanged):

```
[Table("Items")]
public class Item : INotifyPropertyChanged
{

    private int id;
    [PrimaryKey, AutoIncrement]
    public int Id
    {
        get
        {
            return id;
        }
        set
        {
            id = value;
            OnPropertyChanged();
        }
    }

    // The rest of the code is unchanged...
}
```

Decorating the class name with Table is optional. If not specified, the table will have the same name as the class. In this case, a table called Item would be generated, but a plural name is more consistent, so the Table attribute allows you to specify Items as the table name. The Id property is decorated with the PrimaryKey and AutoIncrement attributes, which set the column as the primary key and as the table identity with auto-increment, respectively. By default, column names reflect property names. You can use the Column attribute to define column names different from property names. Other common attributes are NotNull (marks a property as required), MaxLength (sets the maximum length for a string property), and Ignore (does not include the property as a column in the table).

Implementing the Dependency Service

To access the SQLite database from shared code, you need an instance of an object of type SQLiteConnection that exposes, among the others, the database path name and that allows for creating, querying, and deleting tables. This path name must be constructed in the iOS and Android projects, and both must return a SQLiteConnection object. To accomplish this, in the PCL project add a new interface called IDataAccess.cs. You can follow the same steps you saw to add a class, but in the New File dialog you will find an item called Empty Interface (see Figure 8-2).

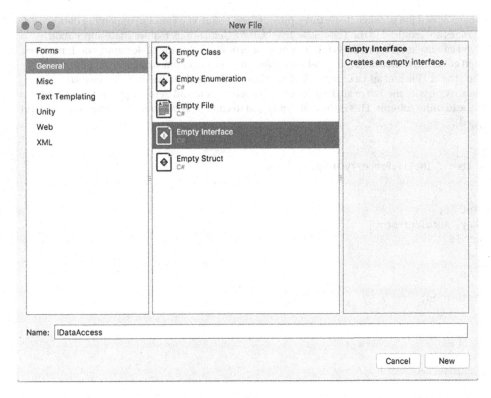

Figure 8-2. *Adding an interface*

The code for the interface is simple and looks like the following:

```
using SQLite.Net;
namespace NewsReader
{
    public interface IDataAccess
    {
        SQLiteConnection DbConnection();
    }
}
```

The interface defines a method called DbConnection that returns an object of type SQLiteConnection. Platform-specific classes will need to expose their own implementation of the method. To accomplish this, add two files called DataAccess.cs, one in the Android project and one in the iOS project. The Android implementation looks like the following:

```
using System;
using System.IO;
using Xamarin.Forms;
using NewsReader.Droid;
using SQLite.Net;
using SQLite.Net.Platform.XamarinAndroid;
```

```
[assembly: Dependency(typeof(DataAccess))]
namespace NewsReader.Droid
{
    public class DataAccess : IDataAccess
    {
        public SQLiteConnection DbConnection()
        {
            string dbName = "newsreader.db3";
            string dbPath =
                Path.Combine(Environment.GetFolderPath(Environment.SpecialFolder.Personal),
                            dbName);

            return
                new SQLiteConnection(new SQLitePlatformAndroid(),
                                    dbPath);
        }
    }
}
```

Platform-specific implementations of an interface that is used with the dependency service must be decorated with the Dependency attribute, which is actually applied at the namespace level with the assembly: enforcement to ensure that only one implementation will be used (and in the case of multiple implementations, the first one is used). As you can see, the class properly implements the interface by exposing the DbConnection method, whose body first retrieves the user's personal folder path on Android and concatenates it (Path.Combine) with the database name, which I have called newsreader.db3 but that you can replace with a name of your choice. Finally, an instance of the SQLiteConnection object is returned, passing the target platform (SQLite.Net.Platform.XamarinAndroid.SQLitePlatformAndroid) and the database path name.

■ **Note**   When concatenating strings that represent folder and file names, do not use the C# string concatenation operator (+) or methods such as String.Concat. Use Path.Combine instead, which ensures that the full path is generated properly and that it does not contain any extra special characters.

Similarly, you need an implementation on the iOS side, which looks as follows:

```
using System;
using System.IO;
using NewsReader;
using NewsReader.iOS;
using SQLite.Net;
using Xamarin.Forms;

[assembly: Dependency(typeof(DataAccess))]
namespace NewsReader.iOS
{
    public class DataAccess: IDataAccess
    {
```

```
public SQLiteConnection DbConnection()
{
    string dbName = "newreader.db3";
    string personalFolder =
            Environment.GetFolderPath(Environment.SpecialFolder.Personal);

    string libraryFolder = Path.Combine(personalFolder, "..", "Library");
    string dbPath = Path.Combine(libraryFolder, dbName);

    return
        new SQLiteConnection(new SQLite.Net.Platform.XamarinIOS.SQLitePlatformIOS(),
                                dbPath);
    }
}
}
```

As you can see, there is a difference in how folders are handled in iOS. Here you have to construct the path of the local library, and then you concatenate it with the database name. The target platform is represented by the SQLitePlatformIOS type. Now you have two platform-specific implementations of a class that generate the path name of the database and that return an instance of SQLiteConnection. The next step is to add some logic to use a database for storing news. The very first time the app starts, it will download the news feed content from the Internet and will store the list of items in the database. This way, the next time the app starts, contents will be retrieved from the local database instead of downloading them again from the Internet, which improves perceived performance and offers offline contents. However, the user must be able to refresh the news list, for example, with the pull-to-refresh gesture. Having that said, open the ItemService.cs file and edit the QueryRssAsync method as follows (explanations will come shortly):

```
public static async Task<IEnumerable<Item>> QueryRssAsync(bool forceReload)
{
    SQLiteConnection database = DependencyService.Get<IDataAccess>().DbConnection();
    database.CreateTable<Item>();

    // if force reload or the table contains no item...
    if (forceReload == true || !database.Table<Item>().Any())
    {
        var client = new HttpClient();

        var data = await client.GetStringAsync(FeedUri);

        var doc = XDocument.Parse(data);
        var dcNS = XNamespace.Get("http://purl.org/dc/elements/1.1/");

        var query = (from video in doc.Descendants("item")
                        select new Item
                        {
                            Title = video.Element("title").Value,
                            Author = video.Element(dcNS + "creator").Value,
                            Link = video.Element("link").Value,
                            Thumbnail = GetThumbnail(video),
                            PublicationDate =
                                DateTime.Parse(video.Element("pubDate").Value,
                                System.Globalization.CultureInfo.InvariantCulture)
                        });
```

```
        client.Dispose();

        database.DropTable<Item>();
        database.CreateTable<Item>();
        database.InsertAll(query);

        return query;
    }
    else
    {
        return database.Table<Item>().AsEnumerable();
    }
}
```

The updated version of the method takes an argument of type bool, called forceUpload. If true, the method will reload contents from the Internet and save them into the database; if false, the method returns the list of Item objects stored in the database. Notice the first line of the method body: it declares a variable of type SQLiteConnection that receives the result of the invocation to the platform-specific implementation of the DbConnection method you saw before. To accomplish this, the code invokes the static DependencyService.Get method, which is a generic method and whose type parameter is the interface that you defined in the PCL project. With this approach based on IoC, you do not need to care about the platform your app is running on. The DependencyService class calls the appropriate platform-specific implementation of the interface and, in this case, of the DbConnection method. The DependencyService class crosses any barriers between Xamarin.Forms and native APIs, and therefore it allows you to do anything you could do with Xamarin.Android and Xamarin.iOS in terms of full API availability. The condition that forces the code to load data from the Internet is either forceUpload = true or that the database contains no items, regardless of the value of forceUpload. The Table generic method from the SQLiteConnection class allows you to interact with the table whose type is represented in the generic type parameter. In this case, Table<Item> allows you to interact with the table of Item objects. This method returns an object of type TableQuery<T>, which implements the IEnumerable<T> interface and therefore supports the LINQ extension method, such as Any, that is used to detect whether the table contains at least one object. So, if either forceUpload is true or Any returns false (which means no items), the code downloads the RSS feed content from the Internet. The code for this is unchanged. When the download completes, the code invokes other methods from the SQLiteConnection instance, such as DropTable (which deletes a table), CreateTable (which creates a table), and InsertAll (that inserts all the items in an IEnumerable collection into the database). Notice that DropTable and CreateTable are generic and require the type parameter that represents the table, the Item class in this case. InsertAll is not generic, and the SQLite library is intelligent enough to automatically resolve the type for the items in the collection, storing them in the proper table. The SQLiteConnection class exposes a large number of methods to work with both individual records and multiple records, such as Insert, InsertAll, Update, UpdateAll, Delete, and DeleteAll, and it also exposes methods to send SQL commands, such as CreateCommand, and methods to work with transactions, such as BeginTransaction and Commit. IntelliSense provides helpful tooltips when calling these methods. If instead forceUpdate is false and there is at least one record in the table, the code returns the collection of Item objects exposed by the Table method, converted into IEnumerable<Item> with AsEnumerable so that callers do not rely on a specialized type such as TableQuery. The next, simple code edit you need to do is in the ItemViewModel.cs class file, more specifically in the InitializeAsync method.

The edit you need to do is to simply accept a parameter of type Boolean that is passed to the invocation of QueryRssAsync and that looks like this:

```
public async Task InitializeAsync(bool forceReload)
{
    if (IsBusy)
        return;

    IsBusy = true;

    try
    {
        var result = await ItemService.QueryRssAsync(forceReload);
        if (result != null)
        {
            this.Items = null;
            this.Items = new ObservableCollection<Item>(result);
        }
    }
    catch (Exception)
    {

        this.Items = null;
    }
    finally
    {
        IsBusy = false;
    }
}
```

Finally, you need to make a couple of edits in the NewsReaderPage.xaml.cs file. In fact, you need to add the same Boolean parameter to the LoadDataAsync method and pass true or false depending on whether the app is starting up or whether pull-to-refresh has been invoked by the user. The following code contains the few edits:

```
private async Task LoadDataAsync(bool forceReload)
{

    this.NewsActivity.IsVisible = true;
    this.NewsActivity.IsRunning = true;
    await this.viewModel.InitializeAsync(forceReload);
    this.RssView.ItemsSource = this.viewModel.Items;
    this.NewsActivity.IsVisible = false;
    this.NewsActivity.IsRunning = false;
}
```

```
protected override async void OnAppearing()
{
    base.OnAppearing();
    await LoadDataAsync(false);
}

private async void Handle_Refreshing(object sender, System.EventArgs e)
{
    await LoadDataAsync(true);
}
```

You have completed the implementation of the required code to store and load data against a SQLite database so that the contents are downloaded from the Internet only when the app is launched for the first time and only if the user pulls to refresh the `ListView` control. You can simply run the sample application and see how it benefits from the steps described in this section.

Using Plug-ins

When you create apps with Xamarin.Forms and you need to access native APIs, most of the time you use features that exist across platforms, with different APIs. Think of the camera. iOS and Android devices have cameras, and their APIs are certainly different from one another, but at least a few of the features are similar, such as launching the camera, taking a picture, and saving a picture on disk.

As another example, think of the GPS sensor. Android and iOS devices mount different hardware for that and expose APIs that are totally different from one another, but in both platforms the GPS sensor can return the current position and can detect whether the position changes. For capabilities that exist cross-platform and that expose common ways of interaction, instead of writing platform-specific code and implementing the dependency service, you can take advantage of *plug-ins*. These consist of an abstract cross-platform implementation for those features that can be shared across platforms and that can be easily consumed in Xamarin.Forms solutions. Plug-ins are available as NuGet packages that you can easily add to your projects, and they are open source. Most of them have been created by Microsoft employees, but developers can create plug-ins that can be shared with other developers as well. A list of plug-ins is maintained on GitHub at `http://github.com/xamarin/XamarinComponents`, and I will shortly teach you how to find plug-ins on NuGet. The sample application described so far lacks an important feature: detecting whether a network connection is available before attempting to download the RSS feed content from the Internet. Detecting the availability of a network connection requires platform-specific code, so you would normally use the dependency service and the iOS and Android libraries. Fortunately, this can be dramatically simplified using the so-called Connectivity Plugin. To understand how it works, in the Solution pad right-click the PCL project name and then select Add ➤ Add NuGet Packages. When the Add Packages dialog appears, search for the Connectivity Plugin for Xamarin and Windows, as shown in Figure 8-3. The identifier of most plug-in packages starts with `Xam.Plugin`, so if you type this search key in the search box, the list of packages will be quickly filtered to show the list of available plug-ins (and remember to only add packages from trustworthy sources).

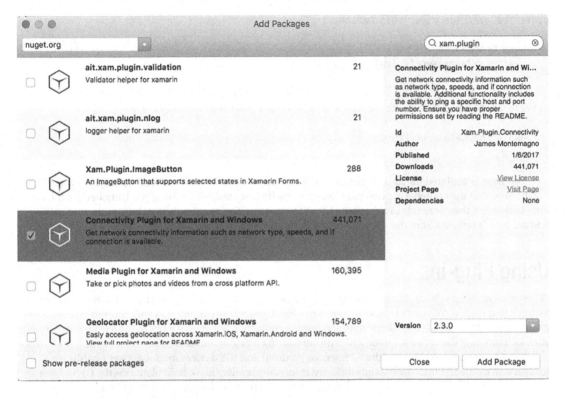

Figure 8-3. *Downloading plug-ins for Xamarin from NuGet*

Click Add Package and repeat the same steps for the iOS and Android projects. Going into depth on the details of a plug-in's infrastructure is beyond the scope of this chapter, so you can refer to the documentation about this topic (http://developer.xamarin.com/guides/xamarin-forms/platform-features/plugins/). By the way, generally speaking, plug-ins provide a singleton class that exposes members, and their purpose is to offer a cross-platform solution to working with platform-specific features. In the case of the Connectivity Plugin, this exposes a singleton class called CrossConnectivity with a Boolean property called IsConnected that returns true or false depending on whether a network connection is available. Using this class is extremely easy. For example, a good idea is to check whether a network connection is available inside the QueryRssAsync method of the ItemService class, before downloading content from the Internet, to prevent app crashes. Open the ItemService.cs file and add a using Plugin.Connectivity directive. This is the namespace that defines the CrossConnectivity class. Next, just before the declaration of the client variable of type HttpClient, add the following line:

```
if (!CrossConnectivity.Current.IsConnected) throw new InvalidOperationException();
```

The Current property represents the actual singleton instance of the class. In this code, if IsConnected returns false, which means no connection, an InvalidOperationException is thrown and will be handled shortly by the caller. Of course, you could decide to implement different logic. With this plug-in and a single line of code, you have called a platform-specific feature without writing all the necessary code yourself. Actually, CrossConnectivity has much more to offer. With the IsReachable and IsRemoteReachable methods, you can ping a host and a remote host, respectively, and with the BandWidths property, you can retrieve a collection of available active network connections. Notice that BandWidths is not supported on iOS and will always return an empty list. On Android, you must make sure that ACCESS_NETWORK_STATE and ACCESS_WIFI_STATE are selected in the application manifest.

■ **Note** When you use plug-ins, I recommend you visit each plug-in's home page for more documentation and to discover potential limitations. Normally, you can find the URL for the plug-in home page on GitHub or when you select a plug-in NuGet package in the App Package dialog.

The next step is to implement error handling in the NewsReaderPage.xaml.cs file. Not only is this a best practice, but in this particular case it is required because an InvalidOperationException is thrown if no connection is available. Let's change the LoadDataAsync method as follows:

```
private async Task LoadDataAsync(bool forceReload)
{
    Try
    {
        this.NewsActivity.IsVisible = true;
        this.NewsActivity.IsRunning = true;
        await this.viewModel.InitializeAsync(forceReload);
        this.RssView.ItemsSource = this.viewModel.Items;
        this.NewsActivity.IsVisible = false;
        this.NewsActivity.IsRunning = false;
    }
    catch (InvalidOperationException)
    {
        await DisplayAlert("Error", "Check your Internet connection", "OK");
        return;
    }
    catch (Exception ex)
    {
        await DisplayAlert("Error", ex.Message, "OK");
        return;
    }
}
```

The code implements specialized error handling for InvalidOperationException and shows a specific error message, and it provides general error handling by catching Exception and showing the exception message. The DisplayAlert method shows a pop-up in the user interface, and the last argument represents the text you want to display in the button that closes the pop-up. There is another method overload that allows you to specify text for both the OK and Cancel buttons and that returns true or false depending on the user choice. If you now try to run the application and attempt to download contents without an Internet connection, you will see an error message, and the app will not crash. By using a plug-in, you have been able to quickly implement a feature that would otherwise require more extensive work on platform-specific projects.

Using Native Visual Elements

In the previous sections, you saw how to call platform-specific APIs in your shared code. Xamarin.Forms offers powerful ways to fully leverage Android and iOS libraries, but sometimes you might have different needs. As you learned in the previous chapter, Xamarin.Forms maps native controls into cross-platform objects that encapsulate everything that is in common between platforms.

However, in some situations you might want to use the native views directly. Reasons for this might be deeper UI customizations or using views for which Xamarin.Forms does not provide a mapping. There are several ways to accomplish this, and this section walks you through all the possible alternatives.

Adding Native Views to XAML

Xamarin.Forms allows developers to add native views directly into the XAML markup. This feature has been available only since a few versions, and it makes it really easy to use native visual elements. To demonstrate this feature, create a new blank Xamarin.Forms project called NativeViews.

In the XAML of the root page, you first need to add the following platform XML namespaces:

```
xmlns:ios="clr-namespace:UIKit;assembly=Xamarin.iOS;targetPlatform=iOS"
xmlns:androidWidget="clr-namespace:Android.Widget;assembly=Mono.Android;targetPlatform=Android"
xmlns:formsandroid=
"clr-namespace:Xamarin.Forms;assembly=Xamarin.Forms.Platform.Android;targetPlatform=Android"
```

Remember that you can choose a different name for the namespace identifier. As you can see, the first two namespaces point to the corresponding C# namespace that exposes native controls. The third namespace points to Xamarin.Forms and is required with Android widgets. Using native views is then really straightforward since you just need to declare the specific view for each platform you want to target, as follows:

```
<StackLayout>
    <ios:UILabel Text="Native Text" View.HorizontalOptions="Start"/>
    <androidWidget:TextView Text="Native Text"
                x:Arguments="{x:Static formsandroid:Forms.Context}" />
</StackLayout>
```

In the previous example, the XAML markup is using a UILabel native label on iOS and a TextView native label on Android. Notice how you can assign properties the way you would with any other view. With Android widgets, you must supply the current Xamarin.Forms UI context, which is done with a special form of data binding that binds the static (x:Static) Forms.Context property to the view. You can interact with views in C# code as you would normally do, such as with event handlers.

Introducing Custom Renderers

Xamarin.Forms renders visual elements by leveraging native views and layouts on each platform, but it is limited to those properties that exist cross-platform. If you need further customizations, you are allowed to use native visual elements directly so that you can make all the customizations you need. Customizations at this level are not limited to layout, but they might also involve changing a view's behavior.

To accomplish this, you use the so-called custom renderers. A custom renderer is a class that inherits from the class that maps the native view (the renderer) in Xamarin.Forms and that must be implemented in each platform project. Here you can edit the layout, override members (where possible), and change the behavior of the native view, which you will then be able to use in XAML. For a better understanding, let's consider the following example, which requires you to create a new blank Xamarin.Forms project called

CustomRenderers. Suppose you have an Entry view in Xamarin.Forms and you want the content of such an Entry to be automatically selected when the user taps the text box. Because the Xamarin.Forms Entry does not support this, you can create a custom renderer that works at the platform level. In the PCL project, add a new class called SelectableEntry, which inherits from Entry as follows:

```
using Xamarin.Forms;

namespace CustomRenderers
{
    public class SelectableEntry: Entry
    {

    }
}
```

Technically speaking, creating a class that inherits from the original view is not mandatory. However, any customizations you provide would affect all the views of the same type (Entry in this case), which is probably not the desired behavior. By creating a derived class, you can customize only this one and decide when to use the customized view or the original view. The next step is creating a class that extends the built-in renderer (called EntryRenderer in this case), and this must be done in both the iOS and Android projects. For example, the following code must be added to a class file in the iOS project (called SelectableEntryRenderer.cs) and demonstrates how to extend the EntryRenderer class by handling the EditingDidBegin event on the UITextField view and calling the PerformSelector method, passing an ObjCRuntime.Selector object that performs the selectAll selection over the text box:

```
using System;
using Xamarin.Forms;
using Xamarin.Forms.Platform.iOS;
using CustomRenderers;
using CustomRenderers.iOS;

[assembly: ExportRenderer(typeof(SelectableEntry), typeof(SelectableEntryRenderer))]
namespace CustomRenderers.iOS
{
    public class SelectableEntryRenderer : EntryRenderer
    {
        protected override void OnElementChanged(ElementChangedEventArgs<Entry> e)
        {
            base.OnElementChanged(e);
            var nativeTextField = Control;
            nativeTextField.EditingDidBegin += (object sender, EventArgs eIos) =>
            {
                nativeTextField.PerformSelector(new ObjCRuntime.Selector("selectAll"),
                null, 0.0f);
            };
        }
    }
}
```

Notice the ExportRenderer attribute: it says that objects of type SelectableEntry will be rendered through objects of type SelectableEntryRenderer. In Android, the logic is pretty similar, so you have to add a SelectableEntryRenderer.cs file to the Android project and write the following code:

```
using System;
using Xamarin.Forms;
using Xamarin.Forms.Platform.Android;
using CustomRenderers;
using CustomRenderers.Droid;

[assembly: ExportRenderer(typeof(SelectableEntry), typeof(SelectableEntryRenderer))]
namespace CustomRenderers.Droid
{
    public class SelectableEntryRenderer: EntryRenderer
    {
        protected override void OnElementChanged(ElementChangedEventArgs<Entry> e)
        {
            base.OnElementChanged(e);
            if (e.OldElement == null)
            {
                var nativeEditText = (global::Android.Widget.EditText)Control;
                nativeEditText.SetSelectAllOnFocus(true);
            }
        }
    }
}
```

In the case of Android, the view is an object of type EditText, and the customization is done by invoking its SetSelectAllOnFocus method. At this point, you can simply add a SelectableEntry view to your XAML as follows:

```
<?xml version="1.0" encoding="utf-8"?>
<ContentPage xmlns="http://xamarin.com/schemas/2014/forms"
    xmlns:x="http://schemas.microsoft.com/winfx/2009/xaml"
    xmlns:local="clr-namespace:CustomRenderers"
    x:Class="CustomRenderers.CustomRenderersPage">

    <StackLayout Orientation="Vertical" Padding="20">
        <Label Text="Enter some text:"/>

        <local:SelectableEntry x:Name="MyEntry"
         HorizontalOptions="FillAndExpand"/>
    </StackLayout>
</ContentPage>
```

The local XML namespace is automatically available in the page declaration. You will see that IntelliSense will help you select the view from the list of objects exposed by the local namespace, and the XAML editor's behavior is the same as with other views. If you now run the application, you will see how the text in the SelectableEntry view will be automatically selected with a tap (see Figure 8-4).

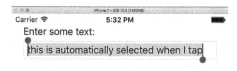

Figure 8-4. *The custom renderer in action*

In summary, with custom renderers you can modify the layout and behavior of a view, and you can then use the view in XAML like any other Xamarin.Forms control.

Introducing Effects

Sometimes you just need to customize some layout properties of a view, without the need to change its behavior. To accomplish this, Xamarin.Forms has the concept of an *effect*. At a higher level, an effect can be thought of as a simplified custom render that is limited to customizing layout properties. An effect is a class that inherits from PlatformEffect and that must be implemented in all the platform projects. For the next example, I will be extending the CustomRenderers project created previously.

Suppose you want to change the background color for some native views. In the iOS project, add a file called BackgroundEffect.cs and the following code:

```
using System;
using CustomRenderers.iOS;
using UIKit;
using Xamarin.Forms;
using Xamarin.Forms.Platform.iOS;

[assembly: ResolutionGroupName("MyEffects")]
[assembly: ExportEffect(typeof(BackgroundEffect), "BackgroundEffect")]
namespace CustomRenderers.iOS
{
    public class BackgroundEffect: PlatformEffect
    {
        private UIColor originalColor;
```

```
        protected override void OnAttached()
        {
            try
            {
                originalColor = Control.BackgroundColor;
                Control.BackgroundColor = UIColor.FromRGB(204, 153, 255);
            }
            catch
            {
                // Cannot set property on attached control
            }
        }

        protected override void OnDetached()
        {
            try
            {
                Control.BackgroundColor = originalColor;
            }
            catch
            {

            }
        }
    }
}
```

An effect definition first requires you to specify a resolution group name. This can be considered as the collection of effects your new class belongs to. Then, with the ExportEffect attribute, you specify the type you are exporting and a name that will be used in shared code for resolving the effect. You then need to override both the OnAttached and OnDetached methods. The first one is called when the effect is assigned to a view, and the second one is called when the effect is removed from the view. In the case of iOS, the background color of a view is an object of type UIColor. For Android, the logic is similar, so you still need a code file called BackgroundEffect.cs in the Android project, with the following code:

```
using System;
using Android.Graphics.Drawables;
using Xamarin.Forms;
using Xamarin.Forms.Platform.Android;
using CustomRenderers.Droid;

[assembly: ResolutionGroupName("MyEffects")]
[assembly: ExportEffect(typeof(BackgroundEffect), "BackgroundEffect")]
namespace CustomRenderers.Droid
{
    public class BackgroundEffect : PlatformEffect
    {
        private Android.Graphics.Color originalColor;

        protected override void OnAttached()
        {
```

```
        try
        {
            originalColor = (Control.Background as ColorDrawable).Color;
            Control.SetBackgroundColor(Android.Graphics.Color.LightGreen);
        }
        catch
        {
            // Cannot set property on attached control
        }
    }

    protected override void OnDetached()
    {
        Control.SetBackgroundColor(originalColor);
    }
  }
}
```

In Android, the background color of a control is an object of type Drawable. At a deeper level of inheritance, it is actually of type ColorDrawable, so a cast is required to access its Color property, whose value is stored for reverting to the original color when OnDetached is called. Then a simple invocation to SetBackgroundColor allows for changing the background color. The next, easy step is to add a class to the PCL project that acts as a bridge between the user interface and the platform-specific effect definitions. Add a class file called BackgroundEffect.cs with the following code:

```
using System;
using Xamarin.Forms;

namespace CustomRenderers
{
    public class BackgroundEffect: RoutingEffect
    {
        public BackgroundEffect(): base("MyEffects.BackgroundEffect")
        {
        }
    }
}
```

This class inherits from RoutingEffect, which provides the infrastructure to expose effects to the user interface. Notice how the constructor of the base class is invoked, passing a string that contains the resource group name and the effect name. The final step is consuming the effect in XAML. For example, you can apply the effect to the SelectableEntry view defined previously, as follows:

```
<local:SelectableEntry x:Name="MyEntry"
 HorizontalOptions="FillAndExpand">
    <local:SelectableEntry.Effects>
        <local:BackgroundEffect/>
    </local:SelectableEntry.Effects>
</local:SelectableEntry>
```

Obviously, you can apply effects to any supported view. Effects must be added to the Effects collection as in the code shown earlier. As you add the effect, the previewer in Visual Studio will automatically render the layout change. You are not limited to using effects in XAML because they also can be added in C# code. In this case, the code you write would look like this:

```
MyEntry.Effects.Add (Effect.Resolve ("MyEffects.BackgroundEffect"));
```

Effects is a .NET collection, and therefore you can invoke the Add method to add an effect. Notice that an effect is not referred to as an object, so you must resolve the effect by calling Effect.Resolve and passing a string that is made of the resource group name and the effect name. With a limited effort, you have been able to change the layout of visual elements without the need to implement a custom renderer, which is instead preferred when you need to change also the behavior of controls.

■ **Note**   In Xamarin.Forms, you can also create custom views. You have two ways to do this. One way to do this is a class that inherits from a view, such as the SelectableEntry shown before, which inherits from Entry. There you can override members and expose other properties. The other way is to create XAML contents of type ContentView. A ContentView appears similar to a ContentPage, with the difference that a ContentView represents an individual, reusable view that consists of the aggregation of multiple visual elements, with its C# code-behind file.

Summary

Being the powerful platform it is, Xamarin.Forms allows you to fully leverage native APIs through several options. The first option is using the dependency service, which requires defining a C# interface; it allows you to implement platform-specific code in the iOS and Android projects for full API access. Then, with an approach based on inversion of control, it automatically resolves the correct implementation through the DependencyService.Get method.

The second way relies on plug-ins, which are shared implementations of code that exist on all platforms. Plug-ins are open source and are offered as NuGet packages, and they expose singleton classes that implement cross-platform APIs that you can call to invoke iOS and Android APIs, including those that allow you to work with hardware capabilities.

Another way is to use native visual elements such as views and layouts. Xamarin.Forms allows you to include native controls directly in XAML markup, but it also allows for further customizations with custom renderers and effects.

This chapter closes the long overview of the Xamarin development platform with Visual Studio for Mac. Starting in the next chapter, you will begin a new journey through one of the most important pieces in the Microsoft vision for cross-platform development: .NET Core.

PART III

Building Cross-platform Applications with .NET Core

CHAPTER 9

■ ■ ■

Introducing .NET Core

Writing code that runs on multiple platforms not only is a dream for many developers, but it is becoming more and more a requirement in the market. In fact, many companies already have (and many others are considering having) platform-specific versions of applications that run on Windows, macOS, and Linux (and its popular distributions). When it comes to web applications and services, the technology you use to build the app or service has an impact on the host you will use. For example, web applications or services built with the .NET Framework can be hosted only on Windows servers (including Azure as the host) but not on Linux servers.

Because server distributions of Linux are extremely popular and you probably have customers that want apps and services to be hosted on Linux servers, you cannot satisfy your customers if your (or your team's) expertise is only in C# and the Microsoft stack. In the last few years, Microsoft has been working hard to bring its most popular development technology and programming language, .NET and C#, to all the most important operating systems. The resulting work is .NET Core, a cross-platform development technology that runs on Windows, macOS, and Linux. Visual Studio for Mac supports .NET Core to build applications in C# and F#, and this chapter provides a high-level overview of the architecture of the platform, before you start writing some code in the next two chapters. It is worth mentioning that all the theoretical concepts discussed in this chapter apply to all .NET Core versions, but the command-line tools and options refer to versions 1.1 and 2.0.

■ **Note**   The purpose of this chapter is to introduce .NET Core, focusing on the concepts you need to build ASP.NET Core MVC applications and ASP.NET Core Web API services, described in Chapter 10 and 11, respectively. The full, official documentation for .NET Core is available at `http://docs.microsoft.com/en-us/dotnet/core/`.

What Is .NET Core?

At a high level, you can think of .NET Core as a subset of the .NET Framework that runs on Windows, macOS, and Linux.

More specifically, .NET Core is a cross-platform, open source, modular, and general-purpose development platform included in the .NET Foundation (`http://dotnetfoundation.org`) that Microsoft supports and maintains, together with the .NET developer community, at `http://github.com/dotnet/core`. .NET Core also runs on devices, which may include mobile devices and IoT devices; therefore, it is not limited to classic desktop and server environments. It is a modular framework in that it ships as NuGet packages, and the idea is that an app built on top of .NET Core will include only the libraries (modules) it actually needs, instead of relying on a full framework like with the .NET Framework. To build applications

---

© Alessandro Del Sole 2017
A. Del Sole, *Beginning Visual Studio for Mac*, https://doi.org/10.1007/978-1-4842-3033-6_9

with .NET Core, you need to download and install the .NET Core SDK, which includes all the tools described in the next subsections and everything you need to build, test, run, and publish your work. As you learned in Chapter 1, Visual Studio for Mac takes care of installing the .NET Core SDK on your behalf. Similarly, if you work on Windows, the Visual Studio Installer for Visual Studio 2017 takes care of installing the .NET Core SDK. If you instead want to use .NET Core on Linux, you must download and install the SDK manually from www.dot.net. Now I will provide you with some information about the architecture of .NET Core, introducing concepts that you must know when building applications and services on top of this framework.

Understanding the Architecture of .NET Core

.NET Core consists of several fundamental parts that work together to bring all the power, flexibility, and compatibility to this amazing technology. The following subsections provide a high-level overview of the parts that comprise .NET Core.

The .NET Core Runtime

The .NET Core runtime, known as the CoreCLR, is a portable, cross-platform component that provides applications with an execution environment. The CoreCLR includes a type system with base .NET data types, a just-in-time (JIT) compiler, a garbage collector, and a base class library called mscorlib. CLR stands for Common Language Runtime, and it basically means that all .NET apps run on the same runtime platform regardless of the programming language they have been written with.

Differently from the full .NET Framework, where applications need .NET to be installed on the target system to take advantage of the Common Language Runtime, with .NET Core the CoreCLR is packaged together with the application and the required libraries. This avoids the need for a pre-installed runtime. The CoreCLR is an open source project available at http://github.com/dotnet/coreclr.

.NET Core Libraries

While the .NET Core runtime includes the base class library, additional types are necessary for serious development. .NET Core provides a large number of libraries that ship as NuGet packages and that expose types for file access, collections, XML, and so on.

Providing the full list of .NET Core libraries is not necessary since Visual Studio for Mac will automatically include the appropriate libraries when creating MVC and Web API projects.

■ **Note** If you are curious, you can open the Nuget.org web site and type **.NET Core** in the search box. The libraries that are considered part of the .NET Core architecture are recognizable by names that start with System.

.NET Core SDK: Tools and Languages

The .NET Core SDK is the set of tools you need to build applications for .NET Core. This includes the .NET command-line interface (CLI) and the programming languages with compilers. The command-line interface is covered in more detail in the next section, so I'll say a few words about programming languages.

Currently, .NET Core 2.0 allows you to write applications using C#, F#, and Visual Basic. The implication is that you can write C#, F#, and Visual Basic code not only on Windows, as you could do in the past, but also on macOS and Linux. This is possible because Microsoft has been working hard to make these popular programming languages cross-platform. In addition, they have been open sourced and offered to the developer community under the name of .NET Compiler Platform, often referred to as Project Roslyn (http://github.com/dotnet/roslyn). With Roslyn, compilers are no longer black boxes that only generate binaries from source code; now they expose the APIs a developer can use to perform code analysis and code generation. Actually, Visual Studio for Mac and Visual Studio 2017 on Windows themselves use the Roslyn APIs to analyze the source code as you type and to report diagnostic information.

Getting Started with the Command-Line Tools

For the sake of platform independence, .NET Core does not need any IDE to create and manage applications, and it allows you to perform all the necessary operations from the command line, including creating, building, running, testing, and publishing applications, plus managing NuGet packages. What you need is just a code editor to write source code.

In .NET Core, the CLI provides the dotnet command-line application that offers a number of built-in options and that can be extended through special NuGet packages (an example of this will be provided in the next two chapters). Table 9-1 summarizes the most common command-line options available with dotnet.exe.

Table 9-1. *Most Common Command-Line Options for dotnet.exe*

Option	Description
new	Generates a new .NET Core project based on the specified template
restore	Restores the NuGet packages for a .NET Core project
build	Builds a .NET Core project
puslish	Packs an application and its dependencies into a folder on the local file system for later publishing to a host
run	Starts a .NET Core application (if a build is not found, it first builds the project)
clean	Cleans the output of a project
pack	Generates a NuGet package from a .NET Core class library project
test	Executes unit tests in a .NET Core project
vstest	Runs UI tests in a file
sln	Allows you to manage MSBuild solution files by adding and removing projects

In most cases, command-line options need further specifications. For example, the new option, which allows you to create a new project, requires you to specify a project template, such as a console or web application, and optionally the programming language between C# and F#. Table 9-2 summarizes the available templates for the dotnet new command.

Table 9-2. *Available Templates for .NET Core Projects*

Name	Description	Language
console	Console application	C#, F#, VB
web	Empty web project	C#, F#
mvc	Web project based on MVC with controllers and views	C#, F#
webapi	Web API project for RESTful services	C#, F#
classlib	.NET Standard class library	C#, F#, VB
mstest	Unit test project	C#, F#, VB
xunit	xUnit test project	C#, F#, VB
nugetconfig	NuGet configuration file	
webconfig	Configuration file	
sln	Solution file	

Creating new projects with the .NET command line is easy. First you create a subfolder that will contain the new project, and then you open a Terminal instance on that folder; you then type the dotnet command followed by the project template, and .NET Core will generate a new project whose name is based on the name of the subfolder you created. For example, the following command line allows you to scaffold a new ASP.NET Core project based on the MVC architecture in the current folder:

```
> dotnet new mvc
```

If no language is specified, the default is C#. With supported templates, you can specify F# with the following command line:

```
> dotnet new mvc -lang f#
```

When you call dotnet.exe to generate a new project, it creates a .csproj file for C# projects (or .fsproj for F#), based on the typical XML structure that Visual Studio projects have always had on Windows, together with all the files that are necessary to the project based on the selected template.

Once you have created a project, you can use your favorite IDE to work with it, such as Visual Studio Code (http://code.visualstudio.com). Obviously, in this book you will see how to use Visual Studio for Mac as the development environment for .NET Core projects. .NET Core projects typically need some NuGet packages, so once a project has been created, you need to first do a package restore with the following command directly in the project directory:

```
> dotnet restore
```

If you want to include additional NuGet packages, with the code editor of your choice you need to edit the .csproj project file and add a line like the following within the ItemGroup node that contains PackageReference elements:

```
<PackageReference Include="PackageName" Version="1.0.0" />
```

PackageName is the fully qualified NuGet package name. Remember to run `dotnet restore` every time you add NuGet packages. Whatever editor or IDE you choose to work with .NET Core, you can then simply build and run your project with the following:

```
> dotnet run
```

This command first builds the project if .NET Core finds no builds. You can also manually launch the build process with the following:

```
> dotnet build
```

As you might understand, except for source code editing, anything you need to create, build, and run a .NET Core project can be done with the `dotnet.exe` tool. This is certainly a powerful application, but doing the whole job from the command line can be painful, especially with large, enterprise projects. Luckily, with Visual Studio for Mac you do not need to interact with .NET Core from the command line since the IDE offers menu commands that make it easy to create, build, debug, and run these kinds of .NET projects via a convenient user interface, invoking the proper `dotnet` commands on your behalf. In the next chapters, you will see how Visual Studio for Mac makes dramatically easy-to-create and manage ASP.NET Core MVC and Web API projects.

Understanding the Relationship Between .NET Core with .NET Standard

In the early chapters, I explained that .NET Standard (`http://docs.microsoft.com/en-us/dotnet/standard/library`) is essentially a formal specification of APIs. Implementations of .NET that implement the .NET Standard specification can be considered as .NET Standard compliant and can support .NET Standard libraries.

.NET Core implements .NET Standard, and it exposes a subset of the APIs that are included in the .NET Framework and Mono.

Summary

In this chapter, you got familiar with .NET Core through a high-level overview of the platform. First you were presented with explanations about its cross-platform architecture built upon a number of pillars such as the .NET Core Runtime (CoreCLR), the .NET Core Libraries, and the .NET Core SDK. The latter includes the `dotnet.exe` command-line tool and the C# and F# compilers, powered by the .NET Compiler Platform (also known as Roslyn).

Except for editing source code, which requires an editor, you can create, build, test, and run .NET Core applications using the `dotnet.exe` tool and passing the proper command-line switches. You can also quickly restore NuGet packages. After some examples of command lines, the chapter provided some interesting considerations about the relationship between .NET Core and the .NET Standard specifications, which you should keep in mind when thinking about libraries you can both consume and build in .NET Core. Now that you know what .NET Core is, it is time to build some cross-platform applications with Visual Studio for Mac, starting with an MVC application in the next chapter, and continuing with a Web API service in Chapter 11.

CHAPTER 10

■ ■ ■

Creating ASP.NET Core Web Applications

With .NET Core, you can create cross-platform ASP.NET web applications based on the Model-View-Controller (MVC) pattern that run on Windows, macOS, and Linux. For the first time, with .NET Core you can create web applications that span platforms using your favorite programming language: C#. Among others, one of the reasons that make this possible is the open source, cross-platform C# compiler offered by the .NET Compiler Platform (also known as Project Roslyn).

This is a tremendous benefit because you are no longer limited to publishing your .NET web apps to Windows hosts (including Azure), and you can easily deploy web applications to Mac and Linux servers reusing your existing C# skills. In this chapter, you will learn how to create an ASP.NET Core web application and how to publish it to Microsoft Azure as the host, directly from Visual Studio for Mac. You will see how the IDE simplifies the whole application life cycle, from development to deployment. For a better understanding, I will provide an example based on a web application that consumes Microsoft Cognitive Services to analyze the content of a picture and that stores the analysis result into a SQLite database, using Entity Framework Core for data access. To complete all the steps described in this chapter, you need a Microsoft Azure subscription. If you do not already have one, you can get a free trial at http://azure. microsoft.com/en-us/free. Make sure you enable the spending limit on your subscription so that you will not be charged if your credit threshold is reached. Being familiar with HTML and concepts such as lambda expressions in C# will be helpful.

■ **Note**   As you can imagine, it is not possible to explain all the APIs in the ASP.NET Core framework, and going into the details of MVC is beyond the scope of this chapter, where the focus is on the Visual Studio for Mac tooling. So, this chapter assumes you are somewhat familiar with the ASP.NET technology and with the MVC framework. I will now provide a brief overview of MVC; I recommend you add the official documentation link to your bookmarks. It is available at http://docs.microsoft.com/en-us/aspnet/core/.

What Is ASP.NET Core?

ASP.NET Core is an open source and cross-platform framework for building modern, cloud-based, connected applications, such as web applications, IoT apps, and mobile back ends. ASP.NET Core provides an optimized development framework for applications that are deployed to the cloud or run on-premises and that consists of modular components. The source code for ASP.NET Core is available on GitHub at http://github.com/aspnet/Home, and Microsoft is accepting contributions from the developer community. At this writing, ASP.NET Core supports the C# and F# programming languages, and support for Visual Basic is planned.

Like .NET Core, ASP.NET Core ships entirely as NuGet packages for improved modularity, and both applications and services can be hosted on Internet Information Services or self-hosted in your own process. As you will see later in this chapter, ASP.NET Core inherits from ASP.NET the so-called model binding, a runtime feature that can map parameters passed with HTTP requests to properties of .NET objects. Put succinctly, ASP.NET Core will be the framework of choice if you want to build web apps and services that run cross-platform, are fully testable, and can be deployed easily regardless of a cloud-based or on-premises host. In a layered architecture, ASP.NET Core is a layer upon the .NET Core architecture described in Chapter 9, so it relies on the CoreCLR, the core libraries and NuGet packages, the C# compiler built upon Roslyn, and .NET Standard.

What Is MVC?

Model-View-Controller (MVC) is the name of a programming pattern built on top of the following elements:

- *Model*: The business objects that represent the data an application needs to work with

- *Controller*: An intermediate object that exposes and manages the model based on the business logic rules

- *View*: The user interface of an application that invokes actions in a controller based on the user input and that displays the result

In ASP.NET and ASP.NET Core, the model is made of C# classes that represent your data. For example, a C# class that maps a table in a database is part of the model; controllers are C# classes that provide methods that execute operations against the model, such as queries or create, read, update, delete (CRUD) operations; and the view is the full user interface made of HTML pages that invoke operations in controllers, such as when the user clicks a button to load or insert data. If you build an application for order management, an Order class might be the model that represents the Orders table in the database; an OrderController could expose methods that allow querying, adding, and updating orders; and an HTML page displays the list of active orders and controls that allow you to add or update orders based on the user input. Notice that model and controllers are not limited to working against databases. In fact, you can map anything you need with a business object, and you can even execute operations from controllers without having a model, such as when you call a web service. Additionally, the ASP.NET Core MVC framework supports identity management and automatically provides plumbing code that configures an app startup. More considerations about MVC will be provided when discussing the sample application in the next sections.

Creating an ASP.NET Core Web Application

You will now build a sample ASP.NET Core web application that allows users to upload an image to the server and that invokes Microsoft Cognitive Services to perform image analysis and recognition. The result of the analysis on each image will be stored in a SQLite database. Microsoft Cognitive Services is part of the artificial intelligence services that Microsoft is offering. Among the available services, which you can discover at http://azure.microsoft.com/en-us/services/cognitive-services, the service you will use is called Computer Vision, and it is extremely powerful in that it can provide a high-fidelity, natural-language description of the content of a picture, and it can also recognize celebrities. Microsoft Cognitive Services supports HTTP requests with HTTP verbs, headers, and contents and returns the result of the analysis in the form of JSON objects. You will see in a few moments how to send HTTP requests to Cognitive Services in C# and how to parse the JSON response.

Cognitive Services is now part of the Microsoft Azure platform, so the first thing you need to do is enable it in the Azure Management Portal. Assuming you already have activated a trial or paid Azure subscription, log into the Azure Management Portal (http://portal.azure.com). Once logged in, click New ➤ AI + Cognitive Services ➤ Computer Vision API. You will be asked to enter some basic information about the new service you are going to create (see Figure 10-1):

- *Service name*: This identifies your app service. For consistency with the figures in this chapter, call the service MyComputerVision.

- *Subscription*: This is Azure subscription that will host the service (if you have more than one subscription).

- *Location*: This represents the data center where your service will be provisioned, so make sure you select the location that is nearest to you (for example, my choice is West Europe because I live in Italy).

- *Pricing tier*: Make sure you select the cheapest option possible (a free option should be available), and also make sure you read the pricing details to avoid any doubts.

- *Resource group*: This allows you to easily and logically group Azure resources you create. You can choose to create a new resource group or select an existing one. For example, create a new resource group called MyResourceGroup.

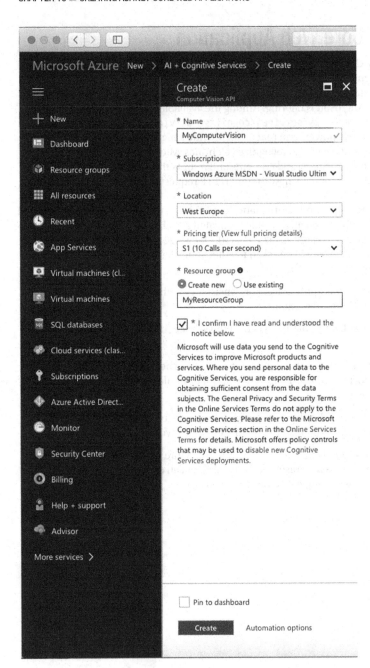

Figure 10-1. *Adding a new Computer Vision service*

Accept the agreement and click Create. After the service has been created, you will be able to access its details from the home page. Figure 10-2 shows the new service details, where you should pay attention to two items: the Computer Vision service's endpoint and the "Show access keys" hyperlink.

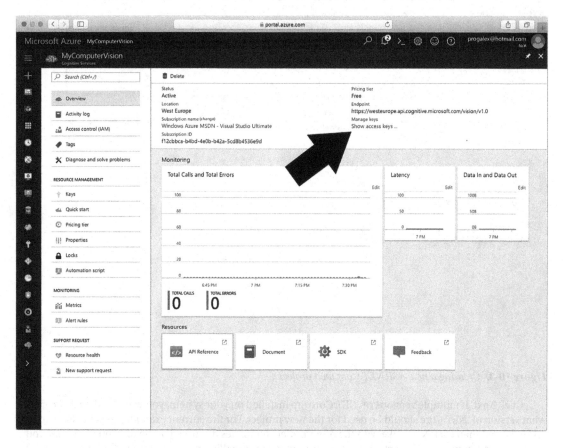

Figure 10-2. *Details of the Computer Vision service*

The endpoint is the service URL you will send HTTP requests to, whereas the "Show access keys" hyperlink allows you to view two secret keys that were generated for you and that you will need to include in your code when sending pictures to the service for analysis. Copy one of the two access keys onto the clipboard or to a text file since it will be used shortly. As you can see, the Azure Portal displays rich monitoring information about the service usage. Now that you have a service enabled, it is time to create a new ASP.NET Core application. In Visual Studio 2017 for Mac, select File ➤ New Solution, and in the New Project dialog, select the ASP.NET Core Web App project template in the .NET Core template folder, as shown in Figure 10-3.

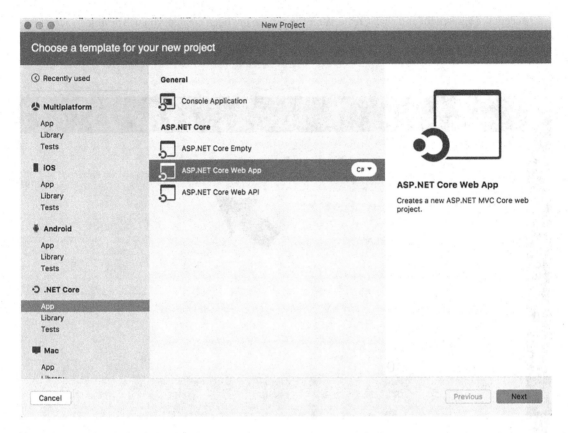

Figure 10-3. *Creating a new ASP.NET Core web project*

Click Next. If multiple versions of .NET Core are installed on your system, you will be asked to specify what version of .NET Core should be used for the new project. For the current example, select either version 1.1 or 2.0 and then click Next. Like with the other project templates discussed in the previous chapters, you will then need to specify a project name, such as **CrossComputerVision** (see Figure 10-4).

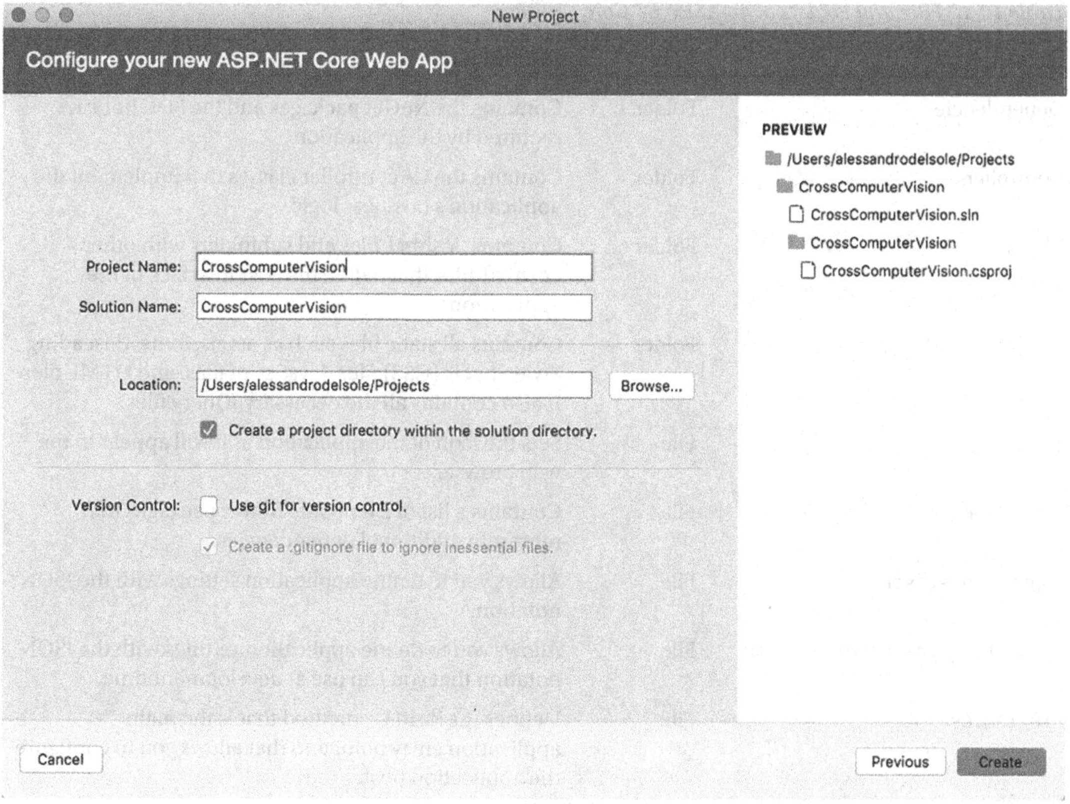

Figure 10-4. *Specifying a project name*

Click Create when ready. Visual Studio for Mac will run the appropriate dotnet command line on your behalf. After a few seconds, your solution will be ready and visible in the Solution pad. I will now provide an explanation of the structure of an ASP.NET Core solution based on MVC.

Understanding ASP.NET Core Solutions

ASP.NET Core solutions are based on the MSBuild solution system (.sln files) and on the C# project system (.csproj). In the Solution pad, you can see a number of files and folders. Table 10-1 summarizes the most important elements that compose an ASP.NET Core solution.

Table 10-1. Files and Folders in an ASP.NET Core Solution

Element Name	Type	Description
Dependencies	Folder	Contains the NuGet packages and the SDK libraries required by the application.
Controllers	Folder	Contains the C# controller classes that implement the application's business logic.
Views	Folder	Contains .cshtml files and subfolders with other .cshtml files that define the user interface of the application.
wwwroot	Folder	Contains all static files such as assets, fonts, Cascading Style Sheets (CSS) files, JavaScript files, and HTML files. It also contains all the necessary JQuery files.
favicon.ico	File	Sets the icon of the application as it will appear in the web browser.
bower.json	File	Contains a list of client-side Bower packages that represent additional dependencies.
appsettings.json	File	Allows you to define application settings with the JSON notation.
appsettings.development.json	File	Allows you to define application settings with the JSON notation that you can use at development time.
Program.cs	File	Defines the Main C# method that is the main application entry point and that allows you to configure the application host.
Startup.cs	File	Defines MVC routing strategies and allows for configuring framework services and host settings.

If you have built ASP.NET MVC applications in the past, you will see that there are many commonalities between ASP.NET MVC solutions and ASP.NET Core MVC solutions. There are certainly important differences, but the structure of a Core solution should at least sound familiar. In the next sections, you will start writing code that interacts with the Computer Vision service by creating an appropriate controller and a convenient user interface that will help users upload an image for analysis. You will also see how to implement data access with Entity Framework Core.

The Model: Working with Entity Framework Core

Entity Framework Core is a lightweight, cross-platform version of the popular and successful object relational mapping (ORM) engine from Microsoft. With Entity Framework Core, you can write C# classes that represent a table in the database (entities) and have properties represent columns in the table. Then, you read, write, and manage a database using a data context C# class.

This way, you work in a strongly type, .NET-oriented approach, and because Entity Framework provides an abstraction layer, it can be used in the same way against several data stores, such as SQL Server and SQLite. In the pure philosophy of .NET Core, Entity Framework Core entirely ships as NuGet packages. In this section, you will see how to include Entity Framework Core in your ASP.NET Core app to store a list of image file names and the result of Computer Vision recognition. If you need more information about Entity Framework, you can visit http://docs.microsoft.com/en-us/ef/.

First, you need a model class that represents the information you want to store in a database. This is called a *code-first* approach. Put succinctly, with the code-first approach, you can start with a simple class definition, and Entity Framework will do the work for you to persist objects to a data store just by using that class.

For instance, you might want to store the image file name, the result of the image analysis returned by the Computer Vision APIs, and a timestamp. To accomplish this, by reusing the knowledge you got in the previous chapters, create a new folder called Models in the project and add a new class file called ImageData.cs. When ready, add the following code:

```
public class ImageData
{
    public int Id { get; set; }
    public string ImageName { get; set; }
    public string AnalysisResult { get; set; }
    public DateTime TimeStamp { get; set; }
}
```

Notice the Id property, which Entity Framework will use as the primary key for the corresponding table. The next step is to add some NuGet packages, but first you have to decide what kind of data store you want to use. In real-world applications, you might want to consider SQL Server or SQL Azure as the data store, but in this chapter I will be showcasing SQLite. The reason is that SQL Server is not available for macOS, and therefore you could not test this option locally; additionally, not all readers might have the opportunity to test Entity Framework against a remote SQL Server. Instead, it is interesting to demonstrate .NET Core's capabilities to work against the serverless, portable SQLite data store that is available on all platforms. You will then be able to use almost the same techniques with a different data store, just choosing the appropriate NuGet packages. In the case of SQLite, the NuGet packages you need are as follows:

- Microsoft.EntityFrameworkCore.SQLite

- Microsoft.EntityFrameworkCore.Design

These provide all the .NET objects required to work against a SQLite database. In the case of SQL Server, you would instead download the Microsoft.EntityFramework.SQLServer and Microsoft. EntityFrameworkCode.SQLServer.Design packages. If you have worked with Entity Framework and .NET Framework in the past, you know that you need a class that inherits from DbContext in order to interact with a database, tables, and columns, and to read and write data. A DbContext class exposes properties of type DbSet<T>, where each property basically represents a table in the database in the form of a C# collection. So, in this case, you need a DbContext class that exposes a property of type DbSet<ImageData>. Having that said, in the Models folder, add a new class file called ImageContext.cs with the following code:

```
using System;
using Microsoft.EntityFrameworkCore;

namespace CrossComputerVision.Models
{
    public class ImageContext : DbContext
    {
        public DbSet<ImageData> ImageList { get; set; }

        protected override void OnConfiguring(DbContextOptionsBuilder optionsBuilder)
        {
            optionsBuilder.UseSqlite("Data Source=ComputerVision.db");
        }
    }
}
```

Notice how the class must override the OnConfiguring method in order to supply a connection string via the DbContextOptionsBuilder.UseSqlite instance method. The connection string contains the name of the local database, which you can replace with a different name of your choice. The next step is to generate the database through Entity Framework Core, which is accomplished via *code migrations*. Put succinctly, code migrations allow you to update the database schema incrementally, every time you make edits to your C# data model. When you apply code migrations, Entity Framework generates some C# code files that are responsible for updating the database schema. At this writing, there is no built-in tool in Visual Studio for Mac that allows you to generate code migrations from within the IDE, so you need to use the dotnet.exe command-line tool. Additionally, command-line tools for Entity Framework are not included by default in the .NET Core SDK, so you need to manually add an additional reference into the .csproj project file. To accomplish this, in the Solution pad, right-click the project name and then select Tools ➤ Edit File. This opens the .csproj file of the sample project in the XML code editor. At this point, add the following XML node:

```
<ItemGroup>
  <DotNetCliToolReference Include="Microsoft.EntityFrameworkCore.Tools.DotNet"
      Version="1.0.1" />
</ItemGroup>
```

This will add command-line tools for Entity Framework Core to the current project. Save the .csproj file, and you will see how Visual Studio for Mac will reload NuGet packages, but this is not enough. With the help of the Finder system application, open a Terminal instance inside the project folder. The project folder is the one that contains the .csproj file, not the solution file. When ready, type the following command:

```
> dotnet restore
```

This command will cause .NET Core to restore NuGet packages for the project and will download and include the tools you specified. The next step is to create a first code migration that you accomplish with the following command:

```
> dotnet ef migrations add FirstMigration
```

When you create a code migration, you need to supply a migration identifier, FirstMigration in this case. You can replace this identifier with another one of your choice, and you are totally free to decide the identifiers you want to use. The final step is to update the database, and because this is the first code migration, the database will also be created. This is accomplished with the following simple line:

```
> dotnet ef database update
```

■ **Note** In the current example, there is only one class that inherits from DbContext. In this case, the Entity Framework tool automatically resolves the class and generates a migration for it. However, it is common to have multiple DbContext classes, such as when you implement authentication. In such situations, you must supply the --context command-line switch and pass the name of the context class that represents the database schema, such as ImageContext in the current example.

You will see in the Terminal a list of SQL commands that Entity Framework Core uses to generate the SQLite database. At this point, you have completed setting up the data context and the data model. You will write code that interacts with the context and the database in a specific controller, as discussed in the next section.

Working with Controllers

Controllers are C# classes that contain the code that executes actions against a data source, such as a database or a web service, according to the required business logic. Any new ASP.NET Core project contains a controller called HomeController.cs that defines methods that invoke the proper pages in the user interface, such as Index, About, and Contact. These methods are also referred to as *actions*. In Visual Studio, there is a page for each action under the Views project folder. This one contains as many subfolders as many controllers you have in your project, and each subfolder contains view pages whose name recalls the name of an action.

For example, the HomeController class has the Index, About, and Contact actions. So, in the Views folder, there is a Home subfolder that contains the Index.cshtml, About.cshtml, and Contact.cshtml pages. Then the ASP.NET Core runtime knows what page it needs to launch according to the action. In the sample application, for a better separation of the logic, you will create a new controller called VisionController.cs, which you add in the Controllers folder. Right-click this folder, then select Add ➤ New File, and in the New File dialog select the MVC Controller Class item, as shown in Figure 10-5.

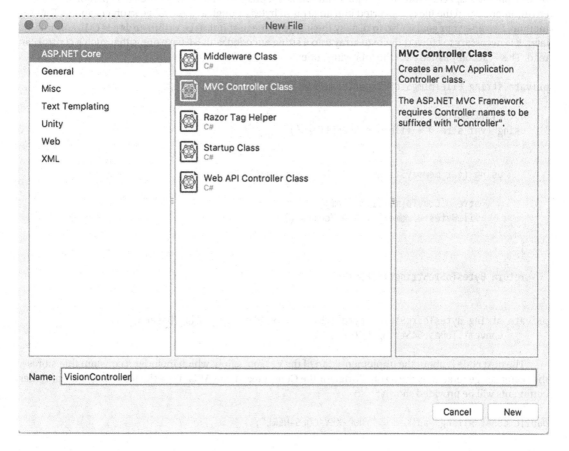

Figure 10-5. *Creating an MVC controller*

The purpose of the new controller is to expose an action called Vision that sends an image file to the Computer Vision API's endpoint and that elaborates the response that the service sends back. In the constructor, you create an instance of the ImageContext class that will be used to persist the image analysis results.

```
ImageContext context;
public VisionController()
{
    context = new ImageContext();
}
```

Before implementing the action, a couple of preliminary considerations are necessary. In ASP.NET Core, a file is represented by an object of type IFormFile. Implementations of this type expose a method called OpenReadStream, which is used to read the content of the file under the form of a Sytem.IO.Stream object. ASP.NET Core uses streams because accessing the file system directly is something that would require platform-specific implementations, but this is not possible in the .NET Core cross-platform environment. Then the file is converted into an array of bytes through a MemoryStream object and its ToArray method. Because your goal is also to display the image in the user interface within an img HTML control later, it is necessary to convert the byte array into a string encoded with 64-base digits that such a control can read. This is accomplished with the following code:

```
private string FileToImgSrcString(IFormFile file)
{
    byte[] fileBytes;
    using (var stream = file.OpenReadStream())
    {

        using (var memoryStream = new MemoryStream())
        {
            stream.CopyTo(memoryStream);
            fileBytes = memoryStream.ToArray();
        }
    }

    return BytesToSrcString(fileBytes);
}

private string BytesToSrcString(byte[] bytes) => "data:image/jpg;base64," +
        Convert.ToBase64String(bytes);
```

The next code is about the implementation of the Vision action, which includes a constant that stores the secret key generated by the Azure Portal for the Computer Vision APIs. Type the following code, and then comments will be provided shortly:

```
public const string _apiKey = "YOUR-KEY-GOES-HERE";

[HttpPost]
[ValidateAntiForgeryToken]
public async Task<IActionResult> Vision(IFormFile file)
{
```

```
    //put the original file in the view data
    ViewData["originalImage"] = FileToImgSrcString(file);
    string result;

    using (var httpClient = new HttpClient())
    {
        // Request parameters
        var baseUri =
            "https://westeurope.api.cognitive.microsoft.com/vision/v1.0/
            analyze?visualFeatures=Description";

        //setup HttpClient
        httpClient.BaseAddress = new Uri(baseUri);
        httpClient.DefaultRequestHeaders.Add("Ocp-Apim-Subscription-Key", _apiKey);

        //setup data object
        HttpContent content = new StreamContent(file.OpenReadStream());
        content.Headers.ContentType =
                new MediaTypeWithQualityHeaderValue("application/octet-stream");

        //make the request
        var response = await httpClient.PostAsync(baseUri, content);

        var responseContent = response.Content as StreamContent;
        // get the string for the JSON response
        var jsonResponse = await responseContent.ReadAsStringAsync();

        // Deserialize the JSON response to retrieve the analysis result
        var jresult = JObject.Parse(jsonResponse);
        result = jresult["description"]["captions"].First.ToString();
    }

    ImageData imageInfo = new ImageData();
    imageInfo.TimeStamp = DateTime.Now;
    imageInfo.ImageName = file.FileName;
    imageInfo.AnalysisResult = result;

    context.ImageList.Add(imageInfo);
    await context.SaveChangesAsync();

    ViewData["result"] = result;
    return View(context.ImageList.ToList());
}
```

ViewData is a property of controllers and is of type ViewDataDictionary. You may think of ViewData as a dictionary that you can populate with key/value pairs dynamically. In practice, in the HTML markup, you will be able to invoke C# code and bind property values directly into the markup. This way, with ViewData you can send to the user interface the information you want to display. In this case, ViewData is used to send to the user interface the image and the analysis result. All of the Cognitive Services receive HTTP POST requests and return a JSON response.

To send a POST request, you use the `HttpClient` class and its `PostAsync` method. You first supply the service URL as the `HttpClient.BaseAddress` value and the secret key in the request headers, by invoking the `HttpClient.DefaultRequestHeaders.Add` method and supplying a key/value pair made of the `Ocp-Apim-Subscription-Key` key and your secret key as the value. The content of the POST request (`HttpContent`) contains the image encapsulated in a `StreamContent` object, populated with the `IFormFile.OpenReadStream` method. `PostAsync` receives a response from the Computer Vision service in the form of a `StreamContent` object that is converted into a string returned by `ReadAsStringAsync`. This conversion is required because the response actually contains JSON, which is an indented string. The following JSON exemplifies the structure of a response you receive by the service:

```
{
    "description":
    {
        "tags":
        [
            "person",
            "man",
            "outdoor",
            "building",
            "smiling",
            "camera",
            "standing",
            "holding",
            "sitting",
        ],
        "captions":
        [
            {
                "text": "a man smiling for the camera",
                "confidence": 0.95715732768096673
            }
        ]
    },
    "requestId": "ddfccd26-96d3-45bf-95c2-c36559d67186",
    "metadata":
    {
        "width": 234,
        "height": 234,
        "format": "Jpeg"
    }
}
```

As you can see, an array of tags contains autogenerated categorization tags for the image, but this is not required for the sample application. The goal is retrieving the text and confidence contained in the `captions` array, so the code must deserialize this JSON string into an object that can be further elaborated.

ASP.NET Core projects already include the popular `Newtonsoft.Json` library that can be quickly used to parse JSON content into .NET types. The `Newtonsoft.Json.Linq.JObject.Parse` method is used to get an array of values, and the result of the image analysis is actually the first value in the array called `captions`, nested in the `description` JSON element. The resulting string contains the type and result of the image analysis. Once you have the image analysis result, you can create an instance of the `ImageData` class and store the result itself, the timestamp, and the file name. Then the new instance is added to the collection of `ImageData` called `ImageList`, and the data is saved using the `SaveChangesAsync` method of the `DbContext` class. This means you are adding a new row to the table in the database, using a completely .NET-oriented approach. Notice the `return` statement: the `View` method will search for a view that is bound to the `Vision` action, passing the `ImageList` collection as the data for the view. This is demonstrated in the next section about views. The last piece of code the controller needs is an action called `Index`, which returns the default view for the controller and which looks like the following method:

```
public IActionResult Index()
{
    return View();
}
```

Now that you have a controller ready, it is time to implement a basic user interface and see how the controller works against the Computer Vision API service.

Working with Views

In the MVC pattern, views represent the user interface. In the case of a web application, views are pages that a web browser can render. In ASP.NET Core, pages are (usually) `.cshtml` files. This kind of file can be considered an evolution of HTML files, in that they fully support the well-known markup language, plus they extend the opportunities by using additional controls and by embedding C# code directly into the HTML code. Visual Studio for Mac provides a great experience when editing HTML files with the usual power. In fact, it provides not only syntax colorization but also word completion based on the context, as you can see in Figure 10-6 and as you will discover while typing the markup code described in this section.

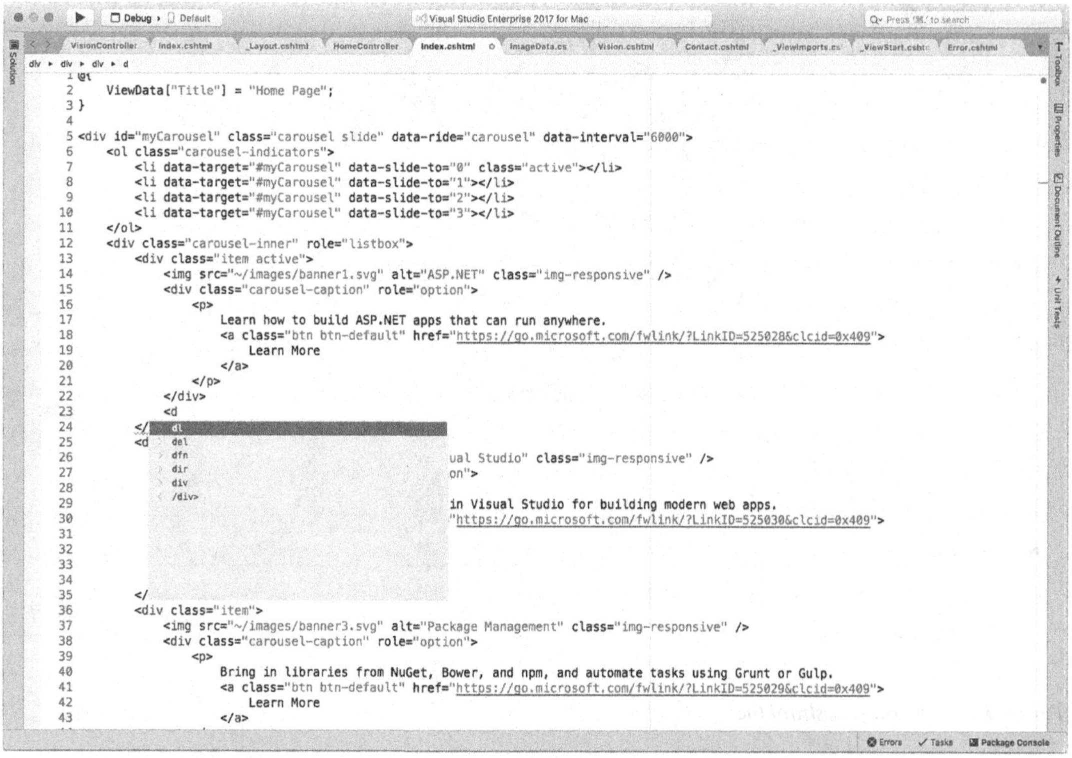

Figure 10-6. *The HTML editor provides syntax colorization and word completion as you type*

When you create a new ASP.NET Core project, a number of pages are already included. In fact, there is a master page, a home page, a contact page, and a page that shows information about the application. Pages are located inside the Views project subfolder and organized within subfolders. The logic for organizing pages is based on which controller a page responds to. For example, the HomeController class has the three actions: Index, About, and Contact. Therefore, the runtime expects to find three pages called Index.cshtml, About.cshtml, and Contact.cshtml inside a folder called Home, whose name is taken from the controller name without the Controller literal. This also affects the URL the application exposes to reach a page. For example, www.myapp.com/home will point to the Home\Index.cshtml page, www.myapp.com/home/contact will point to the Home\Contact.cshtml page, and so on. This is something that you must keep in mind for the next steps and, more generally, every time you work with views and controllers.

Additionally, you can find a Shared subfolder that contains two shared pages: _Layout.cshtml, which you may think of as a master page, and Error.cshtml, a page that displays common error messages. In summary, there should be a page for each action in a controller. The VisionController class has two actions, Vision and Index. As an implication, you must create a subfolder called Vision under the Views folder and add two new pages called Index.cshtml and Vision.cshtml. Visual Studio 2017 for Mac has an item template for .cshtml files, so you must select the MVC View Layout Page template in the ASP.NET Core category, as shown in Figure 10-7.

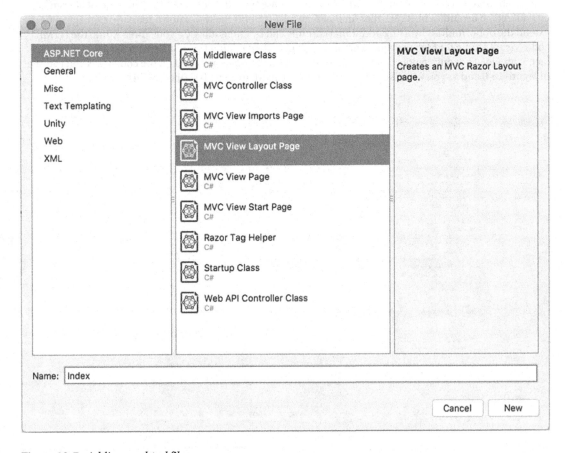

Figure 10-7. *Adding a .cshtml file*

Let's start with the markup code of the Index.cshtml page, which is the main page for image analysis (you will see how to include a shortcut in the master page in a few moments). The code is as follows:

```
@{
    ViewData["Title"] = "Select an image for analysis";
}
<h2>@ViewData["Title"]</h2>
<h3>@ViewData["Message"]</h3>

<div class="row">
    <div class="col-md-12">
        <form asp-action="Vision" enctype="multipart/form-data">
            <div class="form-horizontal">
                <div class="form-group">
                    <label for="file">Image</label>
                    <input type="file" name="file" id="file" class="form-control">
                    <p class="help-block">
                      Images must be up to 4 megabytes and greater than 50x50</p>
                </div>
                <div class="form-group">
                    <input type="submit" value="Upload" class="btn btn-primary" />
                </div>
            </div>
        </form>
    </div>
</div>
```

With .cshtml files, you can embed C# expressions and statements. In the previous code, you can see how the ViewData property from the controller is embedded in the markup. C# expressions must be preceeded by the @ symbol; also, code snippets that contain only C# expressions (and no HTML tags) must be enclosed within curly braces. In the Index page, the Title key in the ViewData dictionary is assigned with a string, and this is pure C# code. In the h2 tag, instead of hard-coding a string, the value of the ViewData["Title"] is displayed by binding such a property value. In the h3 tag, the text that will be displayed instead comes from the value of the ViewData["Message"] property, which is assigned by the controller at runtime. A group of controls is then provided in the form element. Notice how an action in the backing controller is associated with the asp-action attribute. If you are familiar with HTML, the code will be simple to you. In fact, at its core, it contains an input control that allows you to select a file from disk by assigning the type attribute with the file value. The other input control, with type submit, allows you to upload the selected file to the server. The rest of the code is easy. The next page to write is the Vision.cshtml one. This will be displayed once the controller receives a response from the Computer Vision API service and saves the image information into the database. So, this page will display the original image, the result of the Computer Vision analysis, and a table that shows the list of images that were previously analyzed. The following is the code for the page:

```
@model IEnumerable<CrossComputerVision.Models.ImageData>

@{
    ViewData["Title"] = "Image list";
}
```

```
<h2>@ViewData["Title"]</h2>
<div class="row">
    <div class="col-md-12">
        <h4>Original Image</h4>
        <img src="@ViewData["originalImage"]" width="100" height="100"/>
    </div>
</div>

<div class="row">
    <div class="col-md-12">
        <h4>Result</h4>
        <label>@ViewData["result"]</label>
    </div>
</div>

<div class="row">
    <table class="table">
        <tr>
            <th>Image</th>
            <th>Result</th>
            <th>Date</th>
        </tr>
        @foreach (var item in Model)
        {
        <tr>
            <td>
                @Html.DisplayFor(modelItem => item.ImageName)
            </td>
            <td>
                @Html.DisplayFor(modelItem => item.DetectionResult)
            </td>
            <td>
                @Html.DisplayFor(modelItem => item.TimeStamp)
            </td>
        </tr>
        }
    </table>
</div>
```

The @model expression determines the .NET type of the data model bound to this page. This implies that you can bind C# expressions to HTML controls, which provides a lot of flexibility when designing pages.

In this case, controllers can pass to the page any collection that implements the IEnumerable interface and whose type parameter is ImageData such as the List. This data source is referenced in the HTMK markup via the Model property of the bound controller. This allows for iterating the collection with a foreach loop and for using the Html.DisplayFor helper that shows the bound data in the appropriate control depending on the type of the property passed with a lambda expression. This is useful with controls of type table, where you simply define column headers with the th tag, and then you can populate the columns by simply iterating the model with limited effort on your part. Notice how the img control has an explicit size and how the image analysis result will be displayed based on the value of the ViewData["Message"] property assigned at runtime by the controller, once it receives a response from the Computer Vision service. The last step is to add a shortcut to the Vision\Index.cshtml page in the application's master page. To accomplish this, open the Shared_Layout.cshtml file and add the line highlighted in bold:

```
<li><a asp-area="" asp-controller="Home" asp-action="Index">Home</a></li>
<li><a asp-area="" asp-controller="Home" asp-action="About">About</a></li>
<li><a asp-area="" asp-controller="Home" asp-action="Contact">Contact</a></li>
<li><a asp-area="" asp-controller="Vision" asp-action="Index">Computer Vision</a></li>
```

This way, in the application home page there will be a new item called Computer Vision that points to the Index action in the Vision controller and that therefore will launch the Vision\Index.cshtml page. After this much work, you are ready to debug your first ASP.NET Core web application based on MVC.

Running, Debugging, and Testing ASP.NET Core Web Applications

Running, debugging, and testing an ASP.NET Core application in Visual Studio for Mac are tasks similar to what you already saw about Xamarin, which means you can simply select Start Debugging and leverage all the available debugging tools such as breakpoints and debugging pads.

As I mentioned in Chapter 3, .NET Core applications can be debugged using the .NET Debugger, an open source and cross-platform debugger that Visual Studio for Mac attaches to a running .NET application. However, in the case of ASP.NET Core, this is not enough. In fact, a web application needs to be hosted on a web server to be started.

If you have developed ASP.NET applications with .NET on Windows in the past, you had Internet Information Services (IIS) and Internet Information Services Express as available choices to host the application. These are available only on Windows, so .NET Core ships with a special, open source development web server called Kestrel (http://github.com/aspnet/KestrelHttpServer). Kestrel's behavior is similar to IIS Express, with the important difference that it runs across platforms, which means macOS, Linux, and Windows. With Kestrel, you can run, debug, and test your application like it were on a real web server. Having that said, select Run ➤ Start Debugging. After a few seconds, the application will be running inside Safari, as shown in Figure 10-8.

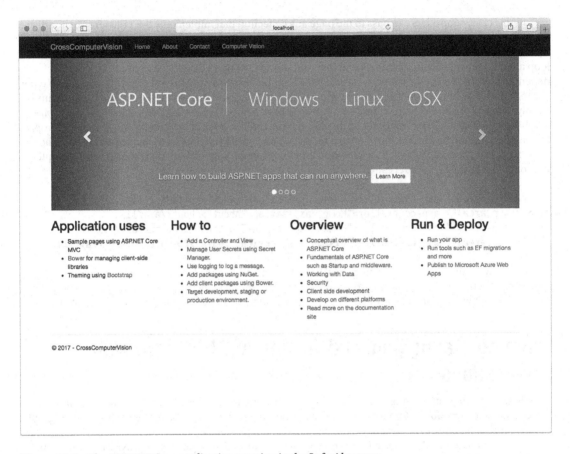

Figure 10-8. *The ASP.NET Core application running in the Safari browser*

As you can see, a shortcut called Computer Vision is available at the top. This is possible because of the addition you made to the _Layout.cshtml file. If you click that shortcut, the Vision/Index page will be shown, as demonstrated in Figure 10-9.

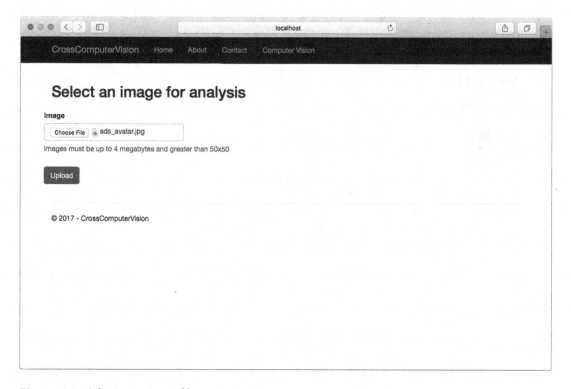

Figure 10-9. *Selecting an image file*

Click Choose File and select an image file. Supported formats are `.jpg`, `.png`, `.gif`, and `.bmp`. Make sure the image is greater than 50 × 50 pixels and that it is no larger than 4MB. When ready, click Upload. After a few seconds, you will see the `Vision/Vision` page displaying the original image, the result of the image analysis, and a table that shows a list of results, as shown in Figure 10-10.

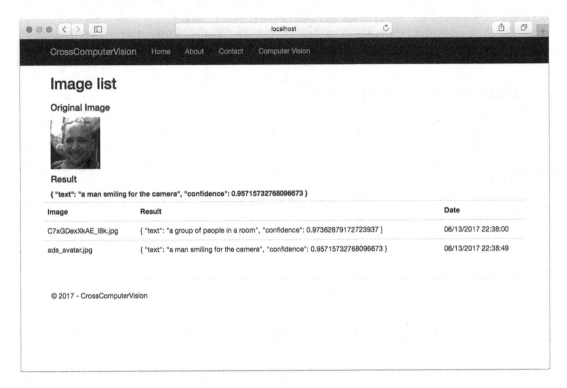

Figure 10-10. *Displaying the result of the image analysis*

The result contains a natural-language description of what has been detected on the image and a confidence level, which is between 0 and 1. The table shows the list of files you uploaded previously with the description, and this data has been stored in a SQLite database with the Entity Framework Core. As you would expect from a development server, the URL for the application always starts with `http://localhost` followed by the port number. You can simply click the address bar to see the current port number. If you want to provide a different port number, you can right-click the project name in the Solution pad, select Options, and see the current value in the Default run configuration under Run ➤ Configurations. The App URL field in the ASP.NET Core tab (see Figure 10-11) contains the current URL, and here you will be able to supply a different port number.

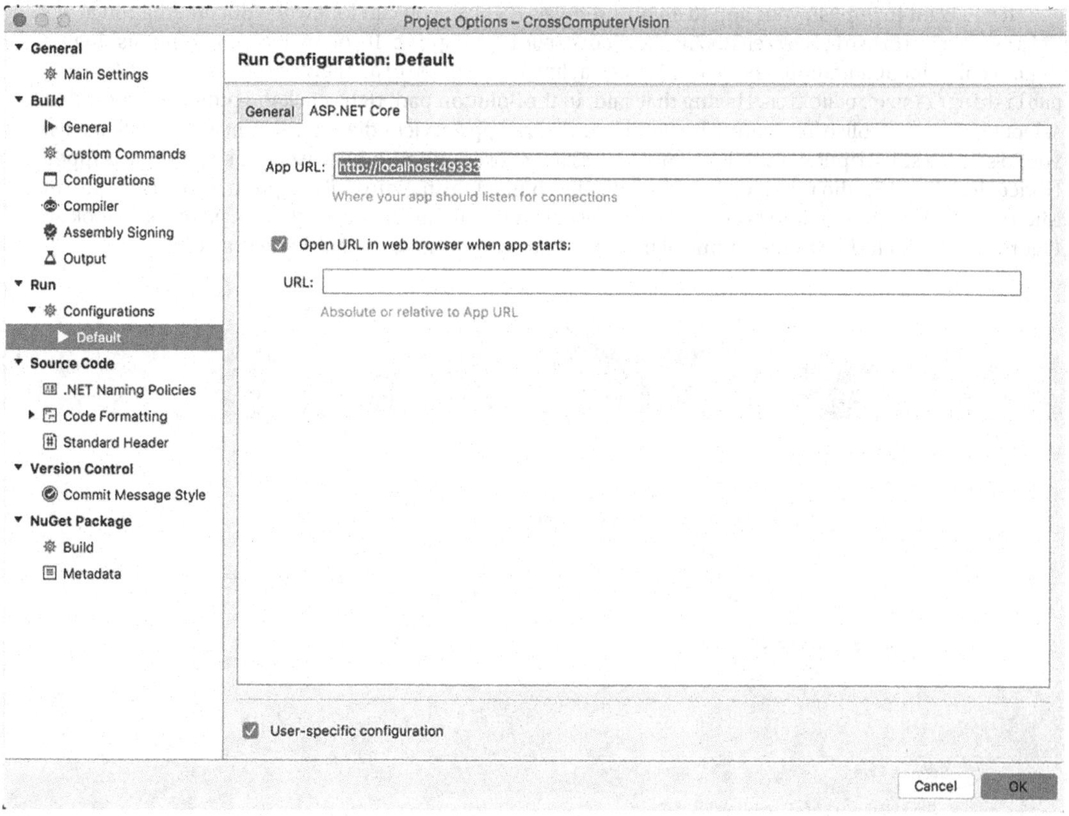

Figure 10-11. *Specifying a port number for Kestrel*

Testing the application locally is certainly fun, but at a certain point you will need to publish the application online so that customers can reach it on the network.

Publishing ASP.NET Core Web Applications

As you would expect, you can publish an ASP.NET Core web application to several hosts, including Linux servers, Internet Information Services on Windows servers, and Microsoft Azure if you opt for a cloud solution. As a general rule, you can generate all the files required for publication on the local file system using the dotnet publish command line, and then you need specific steps depending on the host.

Visual Studio for Mac offers built-in tools that allow you to quickly publish an ASP.NET Core application to Microsoft Azure. Because of the focus on the IDE in this book and because you might not have a Windows PC with IIS installed, in this section I will demonstrate how to take advantage of the built-in tools to quickly publish the sample app to Azure.

If you want to publish your app to an on-premises IIS host, you can follow the documentation at `http://docs.microsoft.com/en-us/aspnet/core/publishing/iis`. If you instead prefer publishing to Linux, the documentation has a specific page at `http://docs.microsoft.com/en-us/aspnet/core/publishing/linuxproduction`. Having that said, in the Solution pad, right-click the project name and then select Publish ➤ Publish To Azure. The Publish to Azure App Services dialog will appear and will first ask you to select a subscription if you have multiple Azure subscriptions; otherwise, this step will be skipped. Notice that Visual Studio for Mac can automatically connect to an Azure subscription if you used the same Microsoft Account to sign into both Azure and Visual Studio. In the dialog, click New. Now take a look at Figure 10-12, which shows an example of how the required information should be provided.

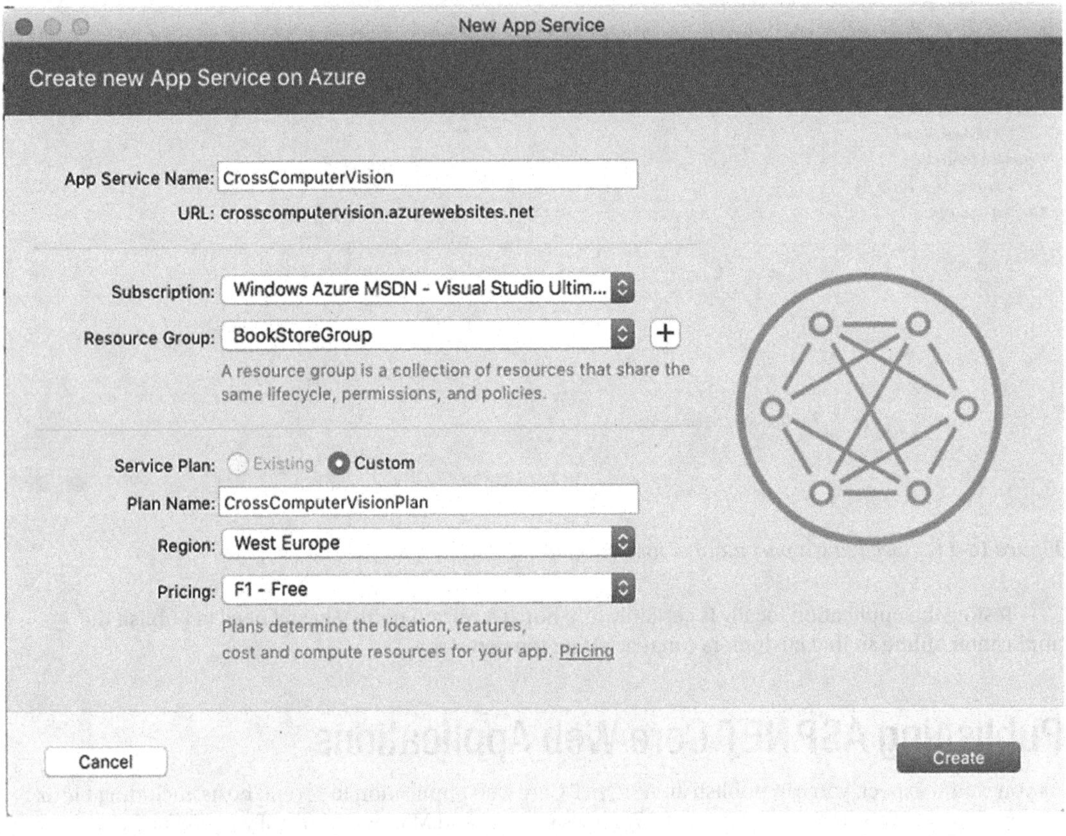

Figure 10-12. Specifying information to publish an app to Azure

App Service Name is the name for your app service on Azure and will also comprise the service URL, which has the following form: *yourservicename.azurewebsites.net*. When you type the service name, Visual Studio automatically checks whether that URL is available. In the Subscription field, you can specify the Azure subscription that will host your app service. The Resource Group setting allows you to specify the Azure resource group that will contain the new app service. You can use the same resource group you used when you created the Computer Vision service. The Service Plan setting allows you to specify the location and pricing for your service. Plan Name is totally up to you, while in the Region field select the location that is nearest to you. In my case, I selected West Europe because it is the closest data center region to where I live. In the Pricing field, select F1 – Free. If you do not see this option, make sure you click the Pricing hyperlink and read the documentation before you select a plan that might result in undesired charges. When ready, click Create. Visual Studio for Mac will show a warning saying that creating the service on Azure will take some time and that you can do other things while waiting. The status bar will show the progress of the operation with messages such as "Provisioning service" and "Publishing to Azure." Additionally, you will be able to follow the publish progress in the Publish pad via the tab that appears at the bottom of the IDE (see Figure 10-13).

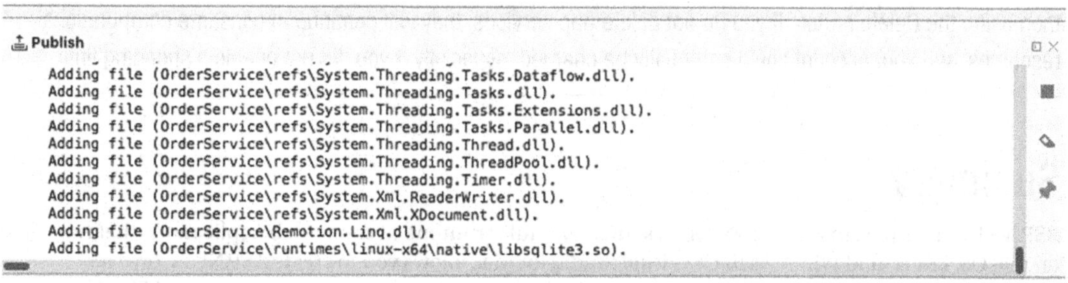
Publish
Adding file (OrderService\refs\System.Threading.Tasks.Dataflow.dll).
Adding file (OrderService\refs\System.Threading.Tasks.dll).
Adding file (OrderService\refs\System.Threading.Tasks.Extensions.dll).
Adding file (OrderService\refs\System.Threading.Tasks.Parallel.dll).
Adding file (OrderService\refs\System.Threading.Thread.dll).
Adding file (OrderService\refs\System.Threading.ThreadPool.dll).
Adding file (OrderService\refs\System.Threading.Timer.dll).
Adding file (OrderService\refs\System.Xml.ReaderWriter.dll).
Adding file (OrderService\refs\System.Xml.XDocument.dll).
Adding file (OrderService\Remotion.Linq.dll).
Adding file (OrderService\runtimes\linux-x64\native\libsqlite3.so).

Figure 10-13. *The Publish pad shows the progress of publishing the app to Azure.*

When finished, Visual Studio will automatically open Safari and launch the application pointing to the publish URL, as demonstrated in Figure 10-14 where you can see the URL in the browser's address bar.

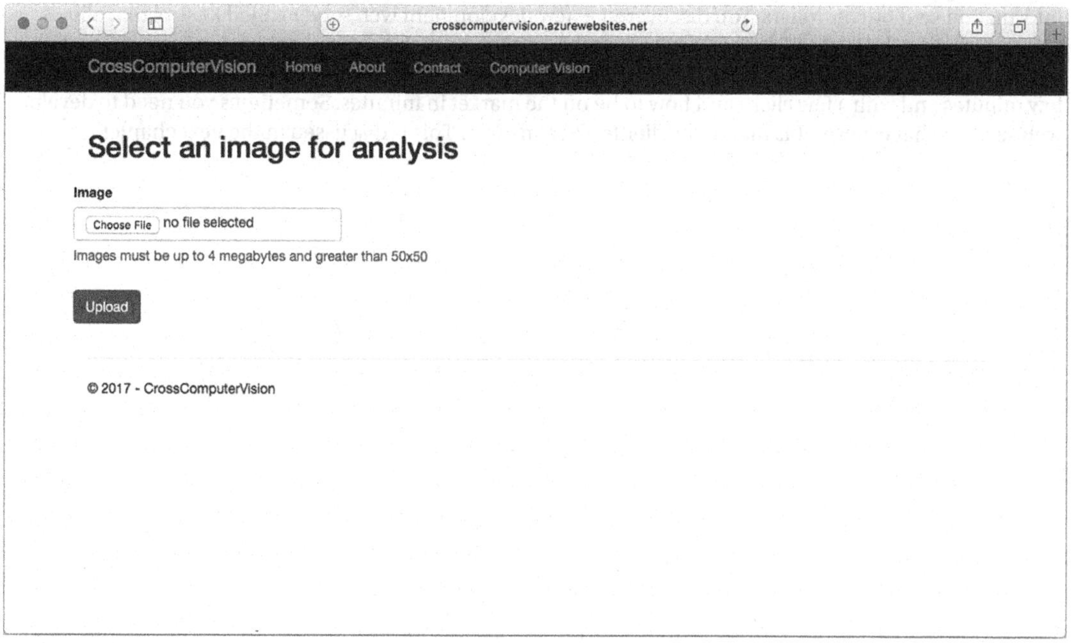
crosscomputervision.azurewebsites.net
CrossComputerVision
Home
About
Contact
Computer Vision
Select an image for analysis
Image
Choose File
no file selected
Images must be up to 4 megabytes and greater than 50x50
Upload
© 2017 - CrossComputerVision

Figure 10-14. *The sample app hosted on Microsoft Azure and available through the Internet*

As you can see, with Visual Studio for Mac and Microsoft Azure you have been able to publish an application online in a few minutes and with a few mouse clicks. Azure is therefore a perfect choice if you do not have your own server infrastructure.

■ **Note**   Remember to completely delete any app services you do not intend to use any longer from your Azure subscription. This can be easily done in the Azure Management Portal by simply selecting a service and then using the Delete button. If you do not delete app services, they will continue to consume computational resources, and your account could potentially be charged, especially if you did not enable a spending limit.

Summary

ASP.NET Core is the cross-platform, open source, modular runtime to create web applications that run on macOS, Linux, and Windows in C#. Visual Studio for Mac allows you to create ASP.NET Core web applications with convenient integrated tools that avoid using the command-line interface. ASP.NET Core web projects rely on the MVC pattern, which involves creating model classes, controllers, and views.

In this chapter, you saw how to use Entity Framework Core to create and access data models against a SQLite database. You saw how to create controllers that expose the business logic and that can execute actions against data sources such as databases and other services. In the sample application, you saw how to interact with Microsoft Cognitive Services to perform Computer Vision recognition over image files managed by a controller. Then you saw how to create pages to allow for user interaction and to display information sent by controllers. You discovered a new development web server called Kestrel that allows you to test and debug ASP.NET Core locally, together with the usual, powerful debugging instrumentation available in Visual Studio for Mac. In the end, you saw how to publish an application to Microsoft Azure in a few minutes and with a few clicks and how to be on the market in minutes. Sometimes you need to develop web services that expose APIs that other clients will consume. This is discussed in the next chapter.

CHAPTER 11

■ ■ ■

Creating RESTful Web API Services

For several years, the ASP.NET Web API has been the framework from Microsoft that developers could use to create RESTful services that a broad range of clients, such as browsers, desktop applications, and mobile apps, can consume via HTTP and HTTPS requests based on the most common verbs such as GET, POST, PUT, PATCH, and DELETE. REST stands for *REpresentational State Transfer* and allows for communication interoperability between clients and servers through standard protocols and data formats, where the service does not retain the exchanged information (so it is *stateless*).

Interoperability of communication between server and client means that the two can communicate via standard protocols regardless of the platform they run on and the programming language they have been written with, and data is typically exchanged in the form of JSON or XML. In the case of the ASP.NET Web API, this framework allows for creating RESTful services in C# with Visual Studio.

Web API services' infrastructure is similar to MVC applications because they also rely on a data model and on controllers that expose methods that can receive HTTP verb requests, but they do not provide a user interface. So, many concepts described in the next sections about models and controllers will already be familiar since they have been discussed in the previous chapter.

Like MVC, .NET Core introduces a cross-platform framework for creating RESTful services called the ASP.NET Core Web API and that you can use to build and publish services to macOS, Linux, and Windows machines writing C#. Because this framework is included in .NET Core, you can certainly use Visual Studio for Mac to create ASP.NET Core Web API services. This chapter provides a high-level overview of the ASP.NET Core Web API, explaining how to create a sample service that can be consumed by any client. Remember that the ASP.NET Core Web API is part of the ASP.NET Core framework, so it has the same base infrastructure as MVC projects described in the previous chapter.

■ **Note**   For all the topics that are not covered by this chapter, you can reference the documentation at
`http://docs.microsoft.com/en-us/aspnet/core/`.

Creating ASP.NET Core Web API Services

Visual Studio for Mac makes it really easy to create an ASP.NET Core Web API service since it provides a convenient user interface that invokes the `dotnet` command-line tool on your behalf. In this chapter, you will create a sample service that allows you to access a remote SQLite database that stores a list of orders. The sample service will expose methods to read, add, and delete items in the list via HTTP. Then you will see how to consume the service from a Xamarin.Forms project. The reason why the example will be offered using SQLite instead of SQL Server is the same as explained in the previous chapter.

To create a service, in Visual Studio for Mac, select File ➤ New Solution. In the New Project dialog, select the ASP.NET Core Web API template under .NET Core ➤ App, as shown in Figure 11-1.

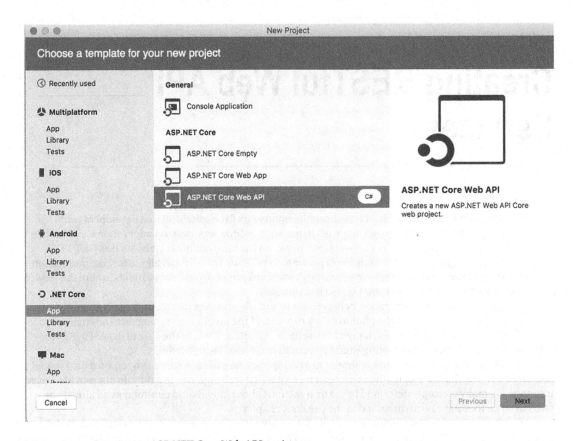

Figure 11-1. *Creating an ASP.NET Core Web API project*

Click Next at this point. Exactly as you did in the previous chapter about a web application, select the .NET Core version (both 1.1 and 2.0 are fine for the current example) if requested, then click Next and specify a project name, and finally click Create. After a few seconds, the new solution will appear in the Solution pad. As you will easily understand, the structure of an ASP.NET Core Web API solution is similar to the MVC projects you saw in the previous chapter, except for the lack of pages, so I will not cover it again. As I mentioned, the sample service will allow clients to call methods that read and write data into a remote SQLite database through HTTP, and JSON will be the data format used to exchange information. The steps are described in the next subsections.

Creating a Model

The first thing you need to add is a data model that represents a single, simplified order. By following the lessons learned in the previous chapter, add a new folder called Models to the project and then add a new code file called Order.cs into the newly created folder. The code for this class models a simplified order entity and looks like this:

```
using System;
namespace OrderService.Models
{
    public class Order
    {
        public int Id { get; set; }
        public DateTime OrderDate { get; set; }
        public string OrderDescription { get; set; }
        public string CustomerName { get; set; }
    }
}
```

The code for this class is simple. It is worth noting the Id property that Entity Framework will use as the primary key.

Adding Entity Framework Core

The next step is to download the Entity Framework Core packages from NuGet and define the DbContext class. Based on what you learned in Chapter 10, download and install the Microsoft.EntityFrameworkCore. SQLite and Microsoft.EntityFrameworkCore.Design NuGet packages.

Once you have downloaded and installed the packages, add a new class file called OrderContext.cs and write the following code:

```
using Microsoft.EntityFrameworkCore;

namespace OrderService.Models
{
    public class OrderContext: DbContext
    {
        public DbSet<Order> Orders { get; set; }

        protected override void OnConfiguring(DbContextOptionsBuilder optionsBuilder)
        {
            optionsBuilder.UseSqlite("Data Source=Orders.db");
        }
    }
}
```

The code you see in this class is essentially the same as you saw in Chapter 10; the only difference is that this time the code works against the Order entity. Because you still need to enable code migrations at the command line, you also need to edit the .csproject file with the following XML node that includes the tools for Entity Framework Core:

```
<ItemGroup>
  <DotNetCliToolReference Include="Microsoft.EntityFrameworkCore.Tools.DotNet"
  Version="1.0.1" />
</ItemGroup>
```

As you might remember from the previous chapter, you now need to open a Terminal at the project folder and type the following command lines to enable code migrations and to generate the database for the first time:

```
> dotnet ef migrations add FirstMigration
> dotnet ef database update
```

Before writing the controller, it is important to make another consideration: the Web API project includes an Inversion of Control container service that avoids the need to create an instance of the OrderContext class in the controller, leaving the job to .NET Core, which will inject an instance via dependency injection. To accomplish this, open the Startup.cs file, locate the ConfigureServices method, and rewrite it as follows:

```
public void ConfigureServices(IServiceCollection services)
{
    // Add framework services.
    services.AddEntityFrameworkSqlite().
            AddDbContext<OrderContext>(options =>
                            options.UseSqlite(
                            Configuration["Data:DefaultConnection:Connection
                            String"]));
    services.AddMvc();
}
```

This method is called by .NET and configures the required services. In this case, the code specifies that Entity Framework Core is required against a SQLite database (AddEntityFrameworkSqlite) and that an instance of the OrderContext class must be injected (AddDbContext) using the SQLite connection string (UseSqlite) stored in the default location, which is the constructor of the OrderContext class in this case. Now that you have all you need to work with data, you can write a controller.

Implementing Controllers

ASP.NET Core Web API projects already include a folder called Controllers and a controller stub called ValueController.cs. Delete this file from the project and then add a new code file to the Controllers folder, called OrderController.cs. Let's start with the first piece of code in the controller, which includes some using directives and a constructor as follows:

```
using System.Collections.Generic;
using System.Linq;
using Microsoft.AspNetCore.Mvc;
using OrderService.Models;
```

```
namespace OrderService.Controllers
{
    [Route("api/[controller]")]
    public class OrderController : Controller
    {
        private OrderContext dataContext;

        public OrderController(OrderContext context)
        {
            this.dataContext = context;
            this.dataContext.Database.Migrate();
        }
}
```

Notice the following:

- The OrderController class inherits from the base Controller, which implements a controller's infrastructure.

- The Route attribute defines the so-called routing strategy, which establishes how a controller can be invoked via HTTP. In this case, the controller will be reachable at http://servername/api/order, where *servername* is the host server, *api* is a prefix, and *order* is the name of the controller without the *controller* literal.

- The constructor of the controller receives an instance of the OrderContext class that is assigned to the dataContext local variable that is used internally by the controller. Such an instance is injected by the .NET Core runtime when instantiating the controller.

- The Database.Migrate method is invoked to ensure migrations are applied. This is particularly useful when publishing your app for the first time, in case migrations are not applied at publish time.

The next step is to implement methods that allow you to work against data via HTTP. By convention, methods have the same name of the HTTP verb they represent (therefore Get, Post, Put, and Delete). You can certainly define multiple actions that respond to those HTTP verbs, such as multiple POST methods, but this is beyond the scope of this section. You can find additional information about multiple actions at www.asp.net/web-api/overview/web-api-routing-and-actions. Let's start with the Get method, which receives HTTP GET requests and which is used to read data from the database. Here are the following two overloads:

```
// GET: api/order
[HttpGet]
public IEnumerable<Order> Get()
{
    return this.dataContext.Orders;
}


// GET api/order/5
[HttpGet("{id}")]
public Order Get(int id)
{
    return this.dataContext.Orders.Where(o => o.Id == id).FirstOrDefault();
}
```

Notice how method overloads are decorated with the HttpGet attribute, which marks them to receive HTTP GET requests. The first method overload returns the full list of orders in the Orders collection as an IEnumerable<Order>. You could also write a LINQ query or use the Where extension method to return only a subset of orders in the collection. The second overload returns a specific Order whose id is passed as a method argument. Notice how comments include the relative URL that the client will need to use, but this will be clearer with a client application later. The next step is to declare methods that accept the POST, PUT, and DELETE verbs and that allow for adding, updating, and deleting an order, respectively. Here's the code, followed by some comments and considerations:

```
// POST api/order
[HttpPost]
public async void Post([FromBody]Order order)
{
    if(order!=null)
    {
        this.dataContext.Orders.Add(order);
        await this.dataContext.SaveChangesAsync();
    }
}

// PUT api/order/5
[HttpPut("{id}")]
public async void Put(int id, [FromBody]Order order)
{
    if(id!=0)
    {
        var oldOrder = this.dataContext.Orders.Where(o => o.Id == id).
        FirstOrDefault();
        if(oldOrder!=null)
        {
            oldOrder.OrderDate = order.OrderDate;
            oldOrder.OrderDescription = order.OrderDescription;
            oldOrder.CustomerName = order.CustomerName;

            await this.dataContext.SaveChangesAsync();
        }
    }
}

// DELETE api/order/5
[HttpDelete("{id}")]
public async void Delete(int id)
{
    var order = this.dataContext.Orders.Where(o => o.Id == id).FirstOrDefault();
    if(order!=null)
    {
        this.dataContext.Orders.Remove(order);
    }

    await this.dataContext.SaveChangesAsync();
}
}
}
```

Like MVC, the ASP.NET Core Web API includes *model binding*, which also allows for mapping parameters passed to the HTTP request to a .NET object, such as the Order type. In other words, if the HTTP request contains JSON or other supported contents that include property values for Id, OrderDate, OrderDescription, and CustomerName, model binding will generate an instance of the type specified as the method parameter, populating properties based on the key-value pairs in JSON. To accomplish this, the Post and Put method signatures require you to supply the [FromBody] attribute before the parameter. Post simply adds the Order instance to the Orders collection if the order is not null; Put retrieves the specified order based on the id and updates property values, if an order with that id is found; and Delete retrieves the specified order based on the id and removes it from the Orders collection. All methods invoke the SaveChangesAsync asynchronous method to save changes to the database. Now you have all you need to expose the service actions through HTTP so that any desktop, web, and mobile client will be able to work against the same data store.

Hints About Identity

Real-world services should be secured to grant data access only to authenticated and authorized users. ASP.NET Core includes an identity service called ASP.NET Core Identity, which is basically a membership system that allows you to add login functionality to an application or service. Users can set up a username and password, or they can use an external login provider such as Facebook or Twitter.

The Web API on the .NET Framework relies on Windows Identity Foundation and simplifies the way you implement identity, but in ASP.NET Core Identity there is no dependency on the operating system. This is an improvement because it allows you to be free to choose your authentication libraries; however, it makes things more difficult to implement. ASP.NET Core Identity stores user information in a SQL Server database, so if you use Visual Studio 2017 on Windows, the IDE will be able to scaffold all the necessary identity objects and to provide the proper debugging support through SQL Server LocalDb or another edition of SQL Server. With Visual Studio for Mac, this is not possible because SQL Server is not available for macOS, and therefore the IDE does not include tools to scaffold all the necessary objects. You could alternatively use an Azure Table Storage service to persist user information, but this would require a thorough discussion about multiple Azure services, and it would be completely out of the scope of this chapter.

However, ASP.NET Core Identity is built in a way that you can use different libraries to implement authentication that can be used in conjunction with its membership system, such as OpenIddict and IdentityServer 4 (other than Azure Active Directory, Facebook, and Twitter). I recommend you read the following articles that were published on the .NET Web Development and Tools Blog: "ASP.NET Core Authentication with IdentityServer 4" (http://blogs.msdn.microsoft.com/webdev/2017/01/23/asp-net-core-authentication-with-identityserver4) and "Bearer Token Authentication in ASP.NET Core" (http://blogs.msdn.microsoft.com/webdev/2016/10/27/bearer-token-authentication-in-asp-net-core). Both articles will help you get started implementing authentication, and the official documentation shows examples based on Visual Studio 2017 on Windows (http://docs.microsoft.com/en-us/aspnet/core/security/authentication/identity).

Debugging and Testing Web API Services

As you would expect, in Visual Studio for Mac you can debug a Web API service by leveraging all the powerful tools offered by the IDE, such as breakpoints, tooltips, and debug pads.

Like an MVC application, a Web API service needs a host web server to run, such as Internet Information Services. For debugging purposes, Visual Studio for Mac invokes the Kestrel development server described in Chapter 10. This means you can simply click Run ➤ Start Debugging and an instance of Kestrel will start to host the service. Additionally, the Safari browser will be launched, even if there is nothing to display. By the way, it is useful to see the full URL with the port number in the browser's address bar. To test the controller, you need a client that is capable of sending HTTP requests that include data. A popular, free, and simple-to-use client tool that many developers use for debugging HTTP requests is Postman (www.getpostman.com). Download and install this tool; then, when ready, type the service URL plus the controller name (on my machine the URL is http://localhost:50096/api/order/). Specify an HTTP verb you want to use, such as GET, and then click Send. Figure 11-2 shows the result of Postman calling the HTTP GET method in the running service.

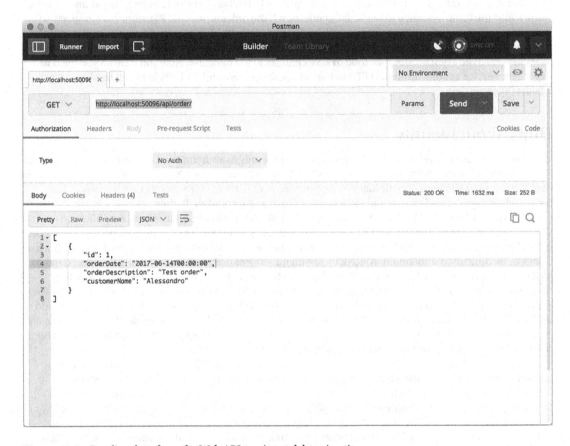

Figure 11-2. Reading data from the Web API service at debugging time

As you can see, the service returns a JSON response if at least an order is available in the database. In Figure 11-3 you can instead see how to send a POST request that writes a new order. Make sure you select the POST verb from the combo box at the left side of the service URL and that you select raw as the data form and JSON (application/json) from the combo box that appears showing Text as the default. Type some JSON code that represents a new order, as shown in Figure 11-2, and then click Send.

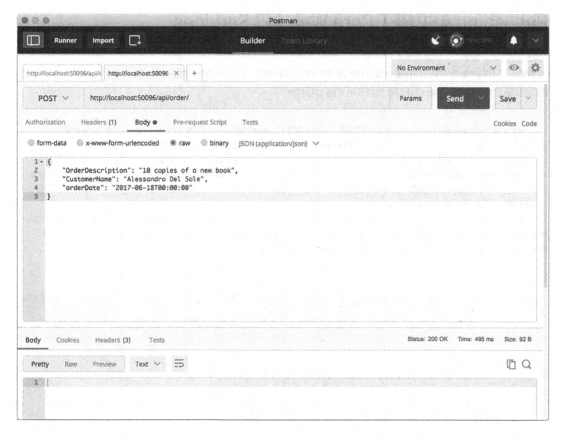

Figure 11-3. *Adding a new order with a POST request at debugging time*

Notice how Postman (as well as other clients) shows a "200 OK" status code, which means that the operation was completed successfully. In a similar way, you could update an order, but this time you should pass the order ID to the PUT request, adding it to the URL like this: `http://localhost:50096/api/order/1`. Then provide the key-value pairs for the `Order`'s properties as you did with the POST request. Now that you have made sure that the service is working as expected, you can deploy it to a host and consume it from real client applications.

■ **Note** The .NET Debugger listens for requests from external clients and is able to intercept such requests and to send messages to any application that is using the debugger. This means that Visual Studio for Mac can receive messages from the debugger listening to HTTP requests and can break the service execution, show breakpoints, and use all the other useful tools it offers even with external clients. Also, Visual Studio for Mac shows messages from the debugger in the Application Output pad, including information about requests sent by clients.

Publishing ASP.NET Core Web API Services

■ **Note**   This section assumes you have an active Microsoft Azure subscription. If you already activated one to complete Chapter 10, you can still use it in this chapter.

Similarly to what you saw with ASP.NET Core MVC applications, Web API services can be easily published to Windows, Linux, and macOS server hosts. Visual Studio for Mac does not include tooling that allows you to publish directly to those hosts out of the box, so you need to use the dotnet publish command line and deploy the service manually. Instead, Visual Studio for Mac has built-in tools that make it dramatically simple to publish a Web API service to Microsoft Azure, in the same way you saw for MVC applications in the previous chapter.

To accomplish this, in the Solution pad, right-click the project name and then select Publish ➤ Publish to Azure. When the Publish to Azure App Services dialog appears, click New. At this point, the New App Service dialog that you already met in Chapter 10 appears and looks like Figure 11-4.

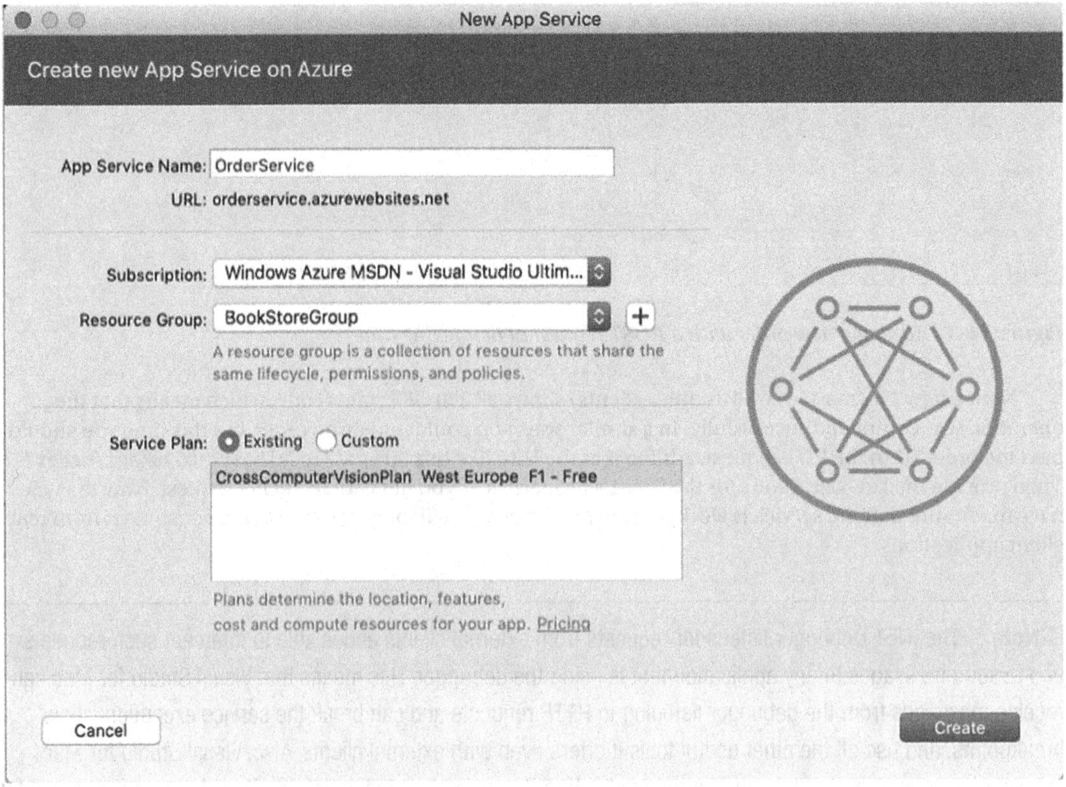

Figure 11-4.   *Creating a new Azure App service*

Enter the service name in the App Service Name box, for example, **OrderService**. Select the subscription and the resource group; you should be able to reuse the same resource group you used in Chapter 10. The same consideration applies to the Service Plan box, where you can select the existing service plan created in the previous chapter. When ready, click Create. Visual Studio for Mac will start publishing your ASP.NET Core Web API service to Azure, and you will be able to work with the IDE while the operation is running. You can see the progress in the status bar at the top of the IDE's window and in the Publish pad. Publishing the service to Azure can take a few minutes. When finished, Visual Studio will open Safari at the service URL, and you will be able to send your requests against the online service instead of Kestrel (see Figure 11-5).

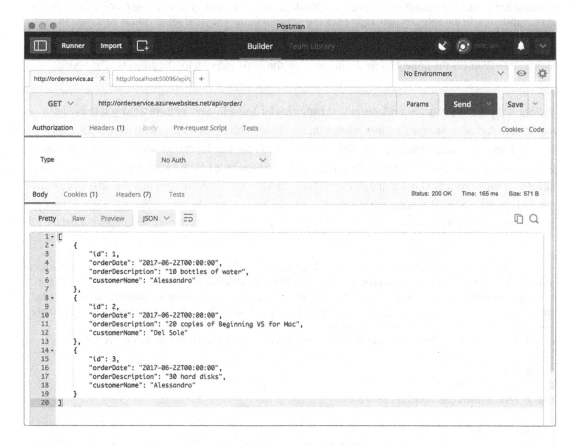

Figure 11-5. *Sending requests against the Web API service published on Azure*

Now that your service is up and running on Azure as the host, it is time to see how you can consume it from a client application. This is the perfect opportunity to see how to combine ASP.NET Core with Xamarin.

Consuming Services: A Xamarin.Forms Client

One of the biggest benefits of Web API projects is that they allow you to generate RESTful services that can be consumed by any client application that can send HTTP requests and receive HTTP responses regardless of the development platform and programming language used to build the application. This implies that you can consume an ASP.NET Core Web API service from a Xamarin project.

The next example is therefore based on creating a Xamarin.Forms client that displays a list of orders and allows for adding, updating, and deleting orders through the service created before. For the sake of convenience and because you cannot open multiple instances of Visual Studio for Mac, you will not create a separate Xamarin.Forms solution. Rather, you will add a Xamarin.Forms project to the current solution. To accomplish this, in the Solution pad, right-click the solution name and then select Add ➤ Add New Project. In the New Project dialog, select the Blank Forms App project template located under Multiplatform ➤ App (and that you already used in Chapter 7). Select the PCL as the code sharing strategy and then go ahead and assign OrderClient as the project name. Then complete the steps and wait for the projects to be added.

■ **Note**   If you remember the available project templates for Xamarin, most of them allow you to include a mobile back end when you create a new solution. In the chapters about Xamarin, you did not include a back end, but if you did, it would simply be an ASP.NET Core Web API service like the one you created in this chapter. So, you are free either to include a back-end project in the solution or to create a back-end project separately. Including a back-end project generated by Visual Studio contains some sample code that you do not have when creating one separately. The client mobile app will consume the service in the same way, regardless of how you create it. You also have an option to create a mobile back end with Azure App Service, discussed in Chapter 13.

I will reuse many techniques and concepts that I already explained in Chapter 7, so I will not cover them again. Just look to Chapter 7 as a reference in case you have any doubts. The first thing you need is a client-side representation of the data you will exchange with the service, which is an implementation of the Order class. This class requires you to implement the INotifyPropertyChanged interface in order to raise a change notification when the value of a property is modified in some way. In the PCL project, add a new folder called Model and then add a new code file called Orders.cs, whose code is as follows (see comments):

```
using System;
using System.ComponentModel;
using System.Runtime.CompilerServices;

namespace OrderClient.Model
{
    public class Order: INotifyPropertyChanged
    {
        int id;
        public int Id
        {
            get
            {
                return id;
            }
```

```
        set
        {
            id = value;
            OnPropertyChanged();
        }
    }

    DateTime orderDate;
    public DateTime OrderDate
    {
        get
        {
            return orderDate;
        }
        set
        {
            orderDate = value;
            OnPropertyChanged();
        }
    }

    string orderDescription;
    public string OrderDescription
    {
        get
        {
            return orderDescription;
        }
        set
        {
            orderDescription = value;
            OnPropertyChanged();
        }
    }

    string customerName;
    public string CustomerName
    {
        get
        {
            return customerName;
        }
        set
        {
            customerName = value;
            OnPropertyChanged();
        }
    }
```

```
        public Order()
        {
            this.OrderDate = DateTime.Now;
        }

        public event PropertyChangedEventHandler PropertyChanged;

        // CallerMemberName supplies the name of the caller member and
        // simplifies the invocation to OnPropertyChanged
        private void OnPropertyChanged([CallerMemberName]string PropertyName="")
        {
            // Use the null conditional operator to execute Invoke only
            // if PropertyChanged is not null
            this.PropertyChanged?.
                Invoke(this,
                new PropertyChangedEventArgs(PropertyName));
        }
    }
}
```

The next step is to add a service class that is responsible for sending HTTP requests to the Web API service. Generally speaking, .NET allows you to easily send HTTP requests and receive responses via the System.Net.Http.HttpClient class. This class exposes methods that represent the most popular HTTP verbs, such as GET, POST, PUT, and DELETE, and it is perfect for Xamarin projects.

■ **Note**   The HttpClient class is offered through a NuGet package called System.Net.Http. This is already included with Xamarin.Forms projects, but you might need to install it manually with other project types.

Having that said, add a new folder called Services to the PCL project and then add a new file called OrderService.cs, whose code looks like the following:

```
using System;
using System.Collections.Generic;
using System.Net.Http;
using System.Text;
using System.Threading.Tasks;
using Newtonsoft.Json;
using OrderClient.Model;

namespace OrderClient.Services
{
    public class OrderService
    {
        public async Task<List<Order>> GetOrdersAsync()
        {
            using(var client = new HttpClient())
            {
```

```csharp
            client.BaseAddress = new Uri(ServiceUrl);
            string jsonResult = await client.GetStringAsync("/api/order");
            var orders = JsonConvert.DeserializeObject<List<Order>>(jsonResult);
            return orders;
        }
    }

    public async Task CreateOrderAsync(Order newOrder)
    {
        using(var client = new HttpClient())
        {
            client.BaseAddress = new Uri(ServiceUrl);
            var content = new StringContent(JsonConvert.SerializeObject(newOrder),
                                        Encoding.UTF8, "application/json");

            await client.PostAsync("/api/order", content);
        }
    }

            public async Task UpdateOrderAsync(Order order)
            {
                    using (var client = new HttpClient())
                    {
            client.BaseAddress = new Uri(ServiceUrl);
            string stringData = JsonConvert.SerializeObject(order);
                        var content = new StringContent(stringData,
                                        Encoding.UTF8, "application/json");

            await client.PutAsync($"/api/order/{order.Id}", content);
                    }
            }
    public async Task DeleteOrderAsync(Order order)
    {
        using (var client = new HttpClient())
        {
            client.BaseAddress = new Uri(ServiceUrl);
            await client.DeleteAsync($"/api/order/{order.Id}");
        }
    }

    public OrderService(string serviceUrl)
    {
        this.ServiceUrl = serviceUrl;
    }

    public string ServiceUrl { get; }
    }
}
```

Notice the following:

- The constructor receives the service URL from the caller and stores this into a field.

- The class exposes methods that map the Get, Post, Put, and Delete methods in the Web API controller. All these methods create an instance of the HttpClient class to send requests to the REST service.

- Because the client and service exchange data as JSON, which is a string, the GetOrdersAsync method invokes HttpClient.GetStringAsync, which directly returns a string and which is deserialized as a List<Order>.

- The other methods invoke PostAsync, UpdateAsync, and DeleteAsync methods from the HttpClient class. PostAsync and PutAsync first serialize an Order into JSON and enclose the resulting string into an encoded object of type StringContent, which is sent to the service. PutAsync also needs the object's ID in the URL, whereas DeleteAsync only needs the object's ID and does not need to perform any JSON serialization.

The next step is implementing a ViewModel class that loads, saves, and deletes orders through the service class and that exposes the list of orders in a way that is suitable for data binding in XAML. Create a new folder called ViewModel in the PCL project and add the following code:

```
using System.Collections.ObjectModel;
using System.Threading.Tasks;
using OrderClient.Model;
using OrderClient.Services;

namespace OrderClient.ViewModel
{
    public class OrderViewModel
    {
        private OrderService service;
        public OrderViewModel()
        {
            this.Orders = new ObservableCollection<Order>();
            this.service = new OrderService("http://orderservice.azurewebsites.net");
        }

        public ObservableCollection<Order> Orders { get; set; }

        public async Task InitAsync()
        {
            var orders = await service.GetOrdersAsync();

            if (orders != null)
                this.Orders = new ObservableCollection<Order>(orders);
        }

        public async Task SaveOrderAsync(Order order)
        {
            if (order.Id == 0)
                await service.CreateOrderAsync(order);
```

```
    else
        await service.UpdateOrderAsync(order);
}

public async Task DeleteOrderAsync(Order order)
{
    if (order.Id == 0)
        this.Orders.Remove(order);
    else
        await service.DeleteOrderAsync(order);
}
}
}
```

Notice how SaveOrderAsync and DeleteOrderAsync check the value of the Id property: if it is zero, it means the order is not in the database yet, so in the case of saving data the service call will be dispatched to CreateOrderAsync, or to UpdateOrderAsync if the order already exists in the database (which means Id is not zero). Similarly, DeleteOrderAsync just removes the order from the in-memory collection if Id is zero; otherwise, it makes a service call to DeleteOrderAsync to completely remove the order from the database.

The last step in the client app is to design the user interface, which will be actually simple: it will show a list of orders and three buttons that allow adding, saving, and deleting orders. The following is the XAML code for the main page:

```xml
<?xml version="1.0" encoding="utf-8"?>
<ContentPage xmlns="http://xamarin.com/schemas/2014/forms"
             xmlns:x="http://schemas.microsoft.com/winfx/2009/xaml"
             xmlns:local="clr-namespace:OrderClient"
             x:Class="OrderClient.OrderClientPage">

    <StackLayout>
        <ListView x:Name="OrdersListView" ItemsSource="{Binding}"
                ItemSelected="OrdersListView_ItemSelected">
            <ListView.HasUnevenRows>
              <OnPlatform iOS="false" Android="true"
                        x:TypeArguments="x:Boolean"/>
            </ListView.HasUnevenRows>
            <ListView.RowHeight>
              <OnPlatform iOS="120" x:TypeArguments="x:Int32"/>
            </ListView.RowHeight>
            <ListView.ItemTemplate>
                <DataTemplate>
                    <ViewCell>
                        <ViewCell.View>
                            <StackLayout Margin="5">
                                <Entry Text="{Binding OrderDescription, Mode=TwoWay}"
                                 Placeholder="Enter description"/>
                                <DatePicker Date="{Binding OrderDate, Mode=TwoWay}"/>
                                <Entry Text="{Binding CustomerName, Mode=TwoWay}"
                                 Placeholder="Enter customer"/>
                            </StackLayout>
                        </ViewCell.View>
                    </ViewCell>
```

```
                    </ViewCell>
                </DataTemplate>
            </ListView.ItemTemplate>
        </ListView>
        <StackLayout Orientation="Horizontal">
          <Button x:Name="AddButton" Clicked="AddButton_Clicked" Text="Add order"/>
          <Button x:Name="SaveButton" Clicked="SaveButton_Clicked" Text="Save"/>
          <Button x:Name="DeleteButton" Clicked="DeleteButton_Clicked" Text="Delete"/>
        </StackLayout>
    </StackLayout>
    <ContentPage.Padding>
        <OnPlatform iOS="0,20,0,0" x:TypeArguments="Thickness"/>
    </ContentPage.Padding>
</ContentPage>
```

The following are a few considerations about the XAML:

- The ListView control has the ItemsSource property assigned with {Binding} because it will receive a collection of Order objects as the data source. It also specifies an event handler for the ItemSelected event, where in the code-behind the selected order will be referenced by a variable that will be used by some of the buttons.

- The ViewCell used as the ListView's data template contains Entry and DatePicker controls that allow users to edit an order directly in-line in order to simplify the user interface.

- There are three buttons that allow for adding, saving, and deleting orders through the proper event handlers.

The C# code-behind for the page has a number of things to do such as loading and binding data through an instance of the view model, adding a new order, deleting the selected order in the list, and saving orders. For the sake of simplicity, saving (that is, creating or updating) is performed against all the items in the collection. The following is the code for the code-behind, which includes comments for better reading:

```csharp
using OrderClient.Model;
using OrderClient.ViewModel;
using Xamarin.Forms;

namespace OrderClient
{
    public partial class OrderClientPage : ContentPage
    {
        private Order currentOrder;
        private OrderViewModel viewModel;

        public OrderClientPage()
        {
            InitializeComponent();
            // Create an instance of the ViewModel
            this.viewModel = new OrderViewModel();
        }
```

```csharp
// Load and bind the collection of orders
protected async override void OnAppearing()
{
    this.IsBusy = true;
    await this.viewModel.InitAsync();
    this.OrdersListView.ItemsSource = this.viewModel.Orders;
    this.IsBusy = false;
}

// Add a new order to the data-bound collection
private void AddButton_Clicked(object sender, System.EventArgs e)
{
    this.viewModel.Orders.Add(new Order());
}

// Save all items in the collection. The SaveOrderAsync in
// the ViewModel knows where to create or update an item
private async void SaveButton_Clicked(object sender, System.EventArgs e)
{
    this.IsBusy = true;
    foreach(Order order in this.viewModel.Orders)
    {
        await this.viewModel.SaveOrderAsync(order);
    }
    this.IsBusy = false;
}

// Remove the current order (if not null)
private async void DeleteButton_Clicked(object sender, System.EventArgs e)
{
    this.IsBusy = true;
    if (this.currentOrder != null)
        await this.viewModel.DeleteOrderAsync(this.currentOrder);
    this.IsBusy = false;
}

// Take note of the selected order
private void OrdersListView_ItemSelected(object sender, SelectedItemChangedEventArgs e)
{
    var order = e.SelectedItem as Order;
    if (order != null) this.currentOrder = order;
}
    }
}
```

Now you can start debugging and testing the client application to consume your ASP.NET Core Web API service. Figure 11-6 shows an example based on the iOS app, but a similar result will be available on Android.

Figure 11-6. *Consuming an ASP.NET Core Web API service from a client app written with Xamarin.Forms*

Of course, you are not limited to Xamarin clients; any kind of client application that supports HTTP requests can consume your RESTful service.

Debugging Multiple Projects

In the previous section, you have been testing your client app against an instance of the Web API service hosted on Azure. However, more often than not, you will need to debug both the client and the service projects concurrently to discover errors and to analyze the flow of requests from the client to the service.

For instance, you might want to use breakpoints in the service controllers to see how requests come from the client. You can also debug multiple projects concurrently by right-clicking the name of a project in the Solution pad and then selecting Start Debugging Item. In this case, you might want to first start debugging the service project and then the client project. If you use this option, remember to change the service URL in the constructor of the OrderViewModel class, passing the localhost URL instead of the service URL on Azure. Finally, you could also consider creating a custom Run configuration in the Configuration Manager tool to set up multiple projects to run in the debugger when you click Start.

Summary

In this chapter, you saw how Visual Studio for Mac is the perfect place to create RESTful services that can be consumed by any client applications and that run on Windows, macOS, and Linux. These services can be therefore published to an incredibly large number of hosts. In the first part, you saw how to create a project and how to implement a data model and a controller to store items in a SQLite remote database.

Then you saw how Visual Studio for Mac has built-in tools to publish a service to Microsoft Azure in a couple of steps. Finally, you saw how to consume a Web API service from a Xamarin.Forms project, using C#. This chapter completes the overview of the applications you can build with Visual Studio for Mac. In the next chapter, you will start learning how to leverage all the powerful tools the IDE has to offer for team collaboration.

PART IV

Collaboration and Productivity

■ ■ ■

CHAPTER 12

Team Collaboration: Version Control with Git

Version control is a way to record changes to one or more files over time. It basically creates a history for each file so that you can recall specific versions later. Version control is not limited to source code files, but this is probably the most common use of it. Using a version control engine is important for many reasons. First, it allows for team collaboration over the same solution; team members can work on different tasks for a solution or project, involving different source code files, or they can make edits to the same code file incrementally, such as in the case of reviewing the work of peers. Second, it allows you to maintain a history of the source code, which is also useful to individual developers; therefore, it is (for example) possible to restore a previous state in the source code.

Many version control systems are available, and the most popular are Git, Team Foundation Server, and Subversion. Team Foundation Server (TFS) is the proprietary, and extremely powerful, version control system from Microsoft that in the last years has been made available through its cloud-based counterpart, Visual Studio Team Services. Visual Studio for Mac supports both Git and Subversion as version control systems, but without a doubt, Git is the most popular version control system in the world. This chapter explains how to work with the Git version control system in Visual Studio for Mac, how to manage changes in your source code, and how to collaborate with peers on the same solution. Apart from a few differences, most of the concepts you will learn in this chapter also apply to Subversion, at least from an IDE point of view.

■ **Note** You will often hear about source control instead of version control. They both refer to the same concept and can be used interchangeably. This chapter uses the version control terminology for consistency with Visual Studio for Mac and its tools and commands.

What Is Git?

Git (http://git-scm.com) is an open source, cross-platform, distributed version control system that makes collaboration easier for small and large projects and perfectly integrates with Agile methodologies. Git relies on the concept of *repository*, which is a container of source code files referring to the same project or solution. Git is based on local and remote repositories. You basically publish your solution to a remote online repository, and then you make a local copy (or the opposite, and then you work on your local repository). When finished your work, you publish your changes to the remote repository so that the version control engine keeps track of your changes with a new version of the file (or files) you changed.

© Alessandro Del Sole 2017
A. Del Sole, *Beginning Visual Studio for Mac*, https://doi.org/10.1007/978-1-4842-3033-6_12

Other people in the team can download the repository locally, work on that, and then submit their changes so that everyone can work on the project concurrently and always have the latest version (or a specific version) of the solution, project, or code. To interact with local and remote repositories, Git provides a command-line interface that integrates with the operating systems, and developers can type a number of commands that allow them to perform all the supported operations against repositories and files. A command-line interface is perfect for cross-platform tools, but dealing with Git commands can be complex. Luckily, Visual Studio for Mac provides convenient dialogs and integrated tools that allow you to interact with Git repositories visually, rather than from the command line. This is also the reason why I will not discuss Git commands in this chapter, which instead highlights the power of Visual Studio. Just remember that the Git engine must be installed on your system before you try to work with repositories. The Visual Studio for Mac installer takes care of installing Git on your system, but in case you have problems, you can download it manually from http://git-scm.com/download/mac.

Git has specific terminology that you will learn as you go through this chapter. To create a remote repository, Git requires a host site. The most popular online host for Git repositories is GitHub (http://github.com). GitHub has become popular over the years as a place for open source projects. However, in the last couple of years, another powerful host for Git repositories has grown in importance: Visual Studio Team Services (www.visualstudio.com/team-services). Visual Studio Team Services (also VSTS for brevity) supports both the TFS and Git version control engines, and it includes a number of incredibly useful tools for teams and for supporting Agile methodologies. For example, it provides continuous integration, test automation, build automation, continuous deployment, a powerful Kanban board for task/bug management, and tools for Agile project management and much more. As well as via GitHub, Visual Studio Team Services is available online, as you would expect from a remote host for solutions and projects, and a benefit of Git is that you can work on local repositories even without a network connection and submit your work once you are back online. Visual Studio for Mac supports any Git repositories, regardless of the remote host. The official documentation for Visual Studio for Mac provides an example based on GitHub as a remote host (http://docs.microsoft.com/en-us/visualstudio/mac/set-up-git-repository). Therefore, in this chapter, you will see how to set up a remote repository on Visual Studio Team Services instead. This requires a Microsoft account, which you certainly have, and it is free for teams up to five members. Therefore, you can try it at no cost. Remember that, from the point of view of the tooling, all the steps you will learn in this chapter apply to any Git repository and remote host.

Preparing an Example

To demonstrate how Visual Studio for Mac integrates with Git, a sample application is necessary. For the sake of simplicity, I will reuse the NewsReader sample app created in Chapters 7 and 8. With the help of the Finder system app, you can create a copy of the project folder and leave unchanged the original project.

■ **Note**   In this chapter, I will use an existing application, and therefore I will show how to enable version control for this scenario. However, remember that Git version control can also be enabled directly when creating a new solution. In that case, a local repository will be created first.

Creating a Remote Repository

Unlike other development environments, where you are free to decide whether you should set up a local or remote repository first, in Visual Studio for Mac you first need a remote repository that will be later registered for local usage. As I mentioned previously, in this chapter I will explain how to set up a remote repository on Visual Studio Team Services.

Having that said, you need to register on the Visual Studio Team Services portal with your Microsoft account by clicking the "Get started for free" hyperlink on the portal home page (`www.visualstudio.com/team-services`). Remember that your subscription is free for up to five team members, and of course you can use it for an individual application management life cycle. Once logged in, follow the instructions to set up your workspace and provide a meaningful third-level domain name (for example, mine is `alessandrodelsole.visualstudio.com`). Completing the registration will provide you with all the management tools you need to create and manage projects, features, and users in the team. You can look at the documentation at any time (`www.visualstudio.com/en-us/docs/overview`) for additional help and for features that are not covered in this chapter. When in the welcome page, click New Project. In the "Project name" text box, enter the name for the new repository, for example **NewsReader**, and optionally provide a description. Make sure Git is selected as the version control engine (see Figure 12-1). Leave Agile selected in the "Work item process" box. In this chapter, the process template has no particular importance, but remember that if you use Visual Studio Team Services for a full application life cycle and project management and not only version control, it is important to select the process template that better represents the management methodology, such as Agile, Scrum, or CMMI, because the management tools that VSTS offers vary depending on this selection.

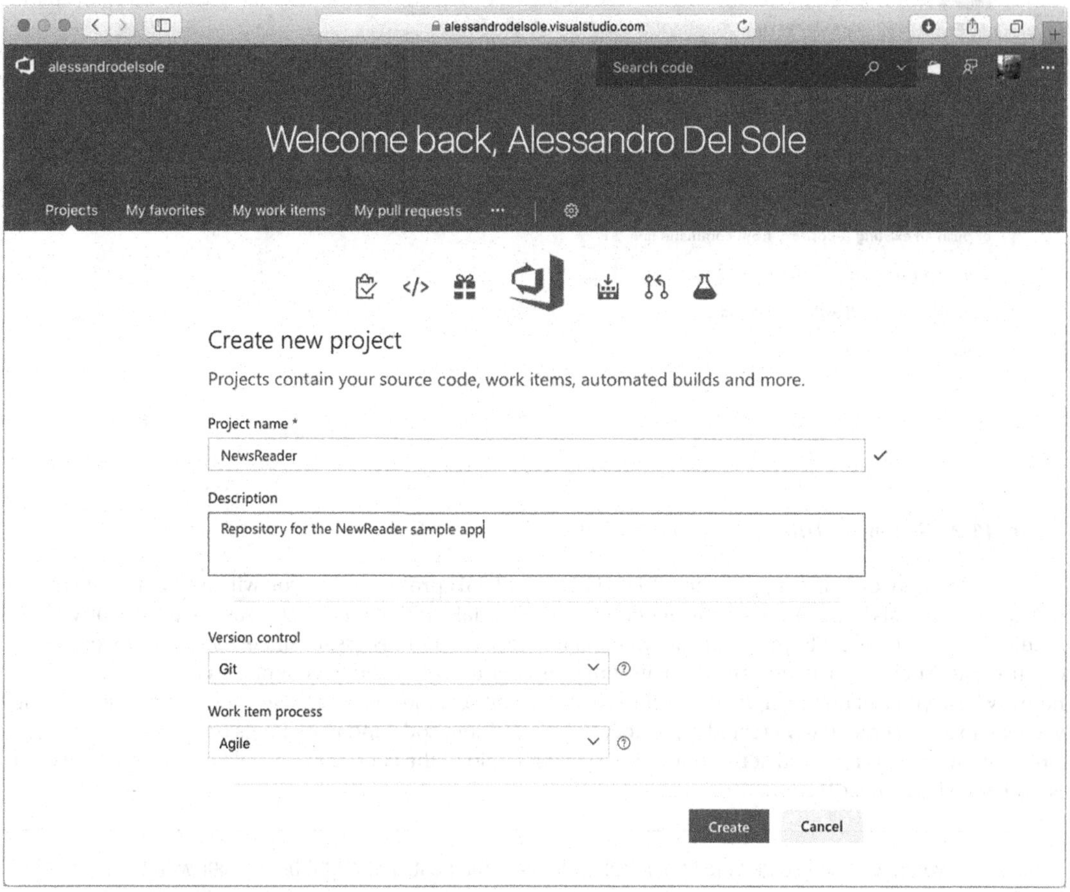

Figure 12-1. *Creating a Git repository on Visual Studio Team Services*

Click Create and wait for the repository to be created. When finished, VSTS shows a summary that includes the remote URL of your repository, as shown in Figure 12-2. Take note of this URL since it will be used in a few moments with Visual Studio for Mac.

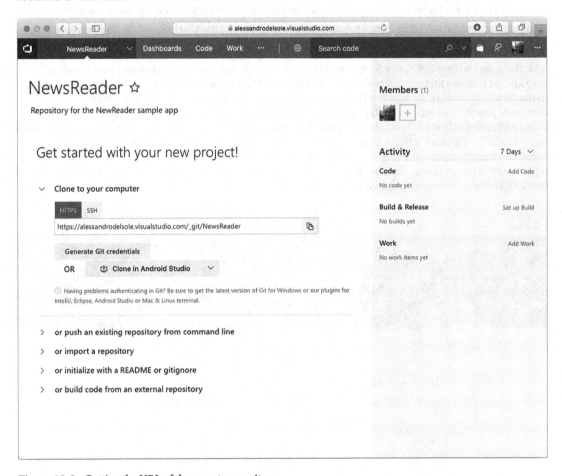

Figure 12-2. *Getting the URL of the remote repository*

Visual Studio for Mac supports the HTTP, HTTPS, and SSH protocols, but you will use the HTTPS one in this chapter. You also have an option to generate Git credentials so that an IDE such as VS for Mac or Visual Studio Code can connect to your repository, but in this case it is not necessary since Visual Studio for Mac can use your Microsoft account. However, in some cases, you might need to generate an access token, and here is where you can do that in the VSTS portal. As you can see, the web page also shows a number of things you can do against the newly created repository, such as adding code and work items or configuring builds. No additional step is required at this point since you will upload the code from Visual Studio for Mac, which is explained in the next section.

■ **Note**   If you have used some version control systems in the past, you might be familiar with the concept of branches. When you create a remote Git repository, a branch called *master* is automatically created. Then you will be able to manage branches from both the portal and Visual Studio. If you are not familiar with the concept of branches, no worries; it will be explained later in this chapter.

Initializing a Local Repository

Now that you have a remote repository, you need to initialize a local repository for your solution. To accomplish this, follow these steps:

1. Select the solution in the Solution pad.

2. Select Version Control ➤ Publish to Version Control or right-click the solution name and select Version Control ➤ Publish to Version Control.

3. In the Select Repository dialog, click the Registered Repositories tab.

4. Click Add to display the Repository Configuration dialog (see Figure 12-3).

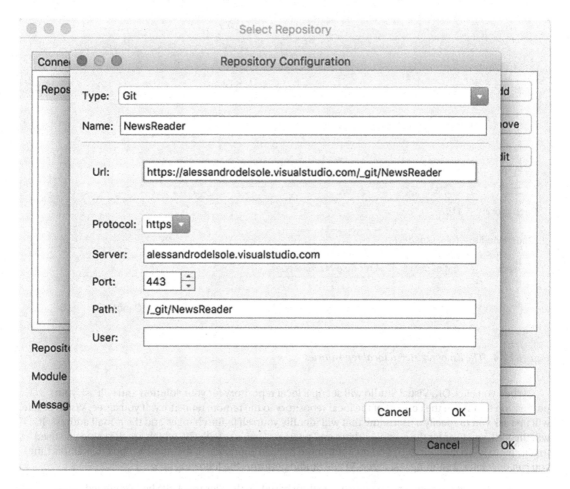

Figure 12-3. *Configuring the local repository*

5. Select Git as the engine, and specify both a repository name and the remote repository URL. Visual Studio will automatically populate the other boxes based on the URL.

6. In the User box, enter the e-mail address you used to log in to the VSTS portal.

289

When you click OK, you will see the new registered repository in the list, as shown in Figure 12-4. You will be able to add new local repositories or to edit properties for the registered repositories.

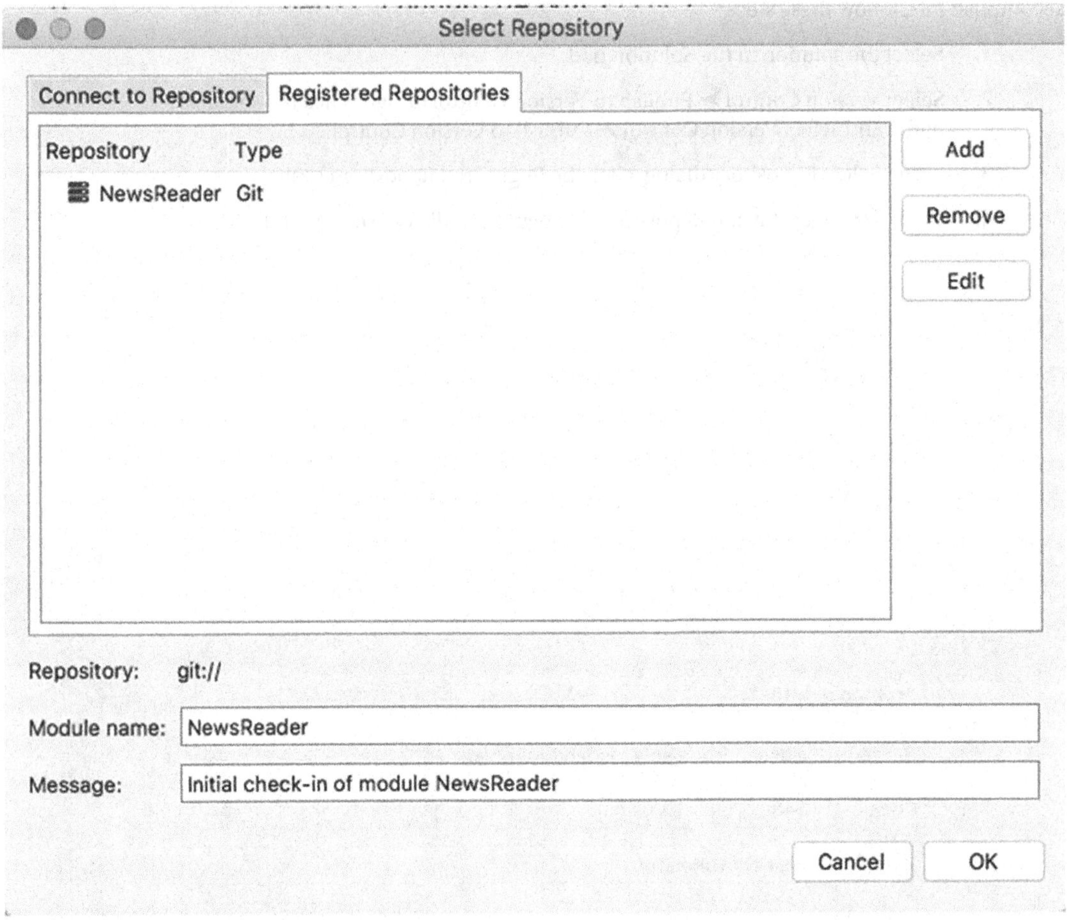

Figure 12-4. *The list of registered local repositories*

When you click OK, Visual Studio will set up a local repository for your solution and will ask your permission to publish the content of the local repository to the remote repository. If you agree, Visual Studio will first ask you to specify a username that will identify yourself in file changes and the e-mail address. It will then ask you to enter the e-mail address and password you use with Git, which are the same you used to register to VSTS in this case. If you do not want to publish your code to the remote repository at this time, you can do it later. Assuming you agree, Visual Studio performs the following tasks:

- It creates a new version of the repository based on the files that have been changed since the last time. Because this is the first time you are updating the repository and therefore this is the first version under control, all the files in the solution become part of it. This operation is referred to as *commit*.

- It marks all the committed files as unchanged.

- It updates the remote repository with all the committed files (in this case all files in the solution), uploading them to your VSTS project. This operation is referred to as *push*.

Generally speaking, with Git you first commit changes to the local repository, and then you push changes to the remote repository. You can easily check whether the source solution has been uploaded to VSTS by clicking Code, as shown in Figure 12-5.

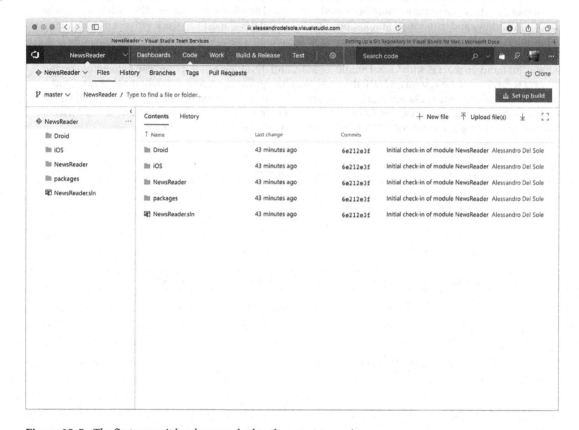

Figure 12-5. *The first commit has been pushed to the remote repository*

Notice that each commit can include a message that can be helpful to identify what changes you made to a specific version. In this case, I left the default message proposed by Visual Studio (see Figure 12-4) for the initial commit. Later you will learn how to include custom comments on new commits. Other options available at this point in Visual Studio Team Services and that are not strictly related to version control are left to your studies and will not be discussed here. Now you have everything you need to start versioning your code and to involve your team in collaborating on a solution.

■ **Note** Every time Visual Studio for Mac calls the Git command-line interface to perform operations against repositories, it will show the output in the Version Control pad. You should be able to automatically see this pad in the IDE, but you can recall it via View ➤ Pads ➤ Version Control.

Cloning Repositories

Other developers in the team will be able to work on the solution by first downloading a remote repository locally. Git will then automatically enable change detection over files. Technically speaking, this is called *cloning a repository* and is the first step to team collaboration.

There is also other good news: because Git is a cross-platform engine that runs on Windows, macOS, and Linux, a repository can be cloned by developers working on different systems. For example, a repository containing a .NET Core solution could be cloned with Visual Studio for Mac on macOS, with Visual Studio 2017 on Windows and with Visual Studio Code on Linux, and developers can work with the development environment of their choice and share their work to the remote repository. As another example, which is also the current case, a repository containing a Xamarin solution could be cloned on Windows with Visual Studio 2017 and on macOS with Visual Studio for Mac, and developers in the team can collaborate on the project regardless of the system and IDE they use. Now imagine you are on a different machine and you want to start working on a solution that is under version control. To accomplish this in Visual Studio for Mac, with no solution open, select Version Control ➤ Checkout. In the Select Repository dialog, select Git as the version control type and enter the URL of the repository you want to clone, as shown in Figure 12-6.

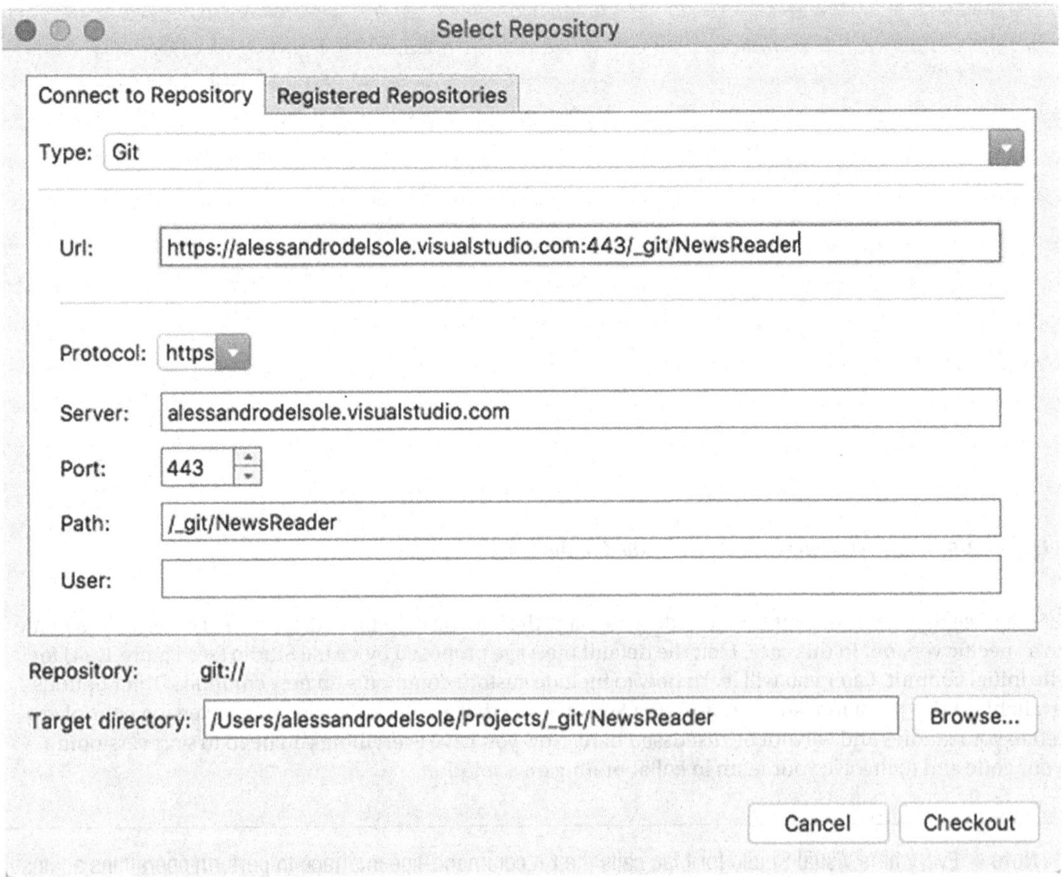

Figure 12-6. Cloning a remote repository

Visual Studio will automatically populate the Protocol, Server, Port, and Path fields, which you must check. Notice that Visual Studio for Mac also proposes a target folder name, which you can see in the "Target directory" text box and that you can change by clicking Browse. When ready, simply click Checkout. Visual Studio for Mac might ask you to enter your credentials like when pushing the repository. When cloning completes, you will get your local copy of the repository in the specified target folder, and version control will be enabled locally. You can then simply open the solution and work on it as you would do normally, also taking advantage of the file change management tools described in the next section. In the section called "Managing Commits," you will learn how to update your local repository with changes made by other developers.

■ **Note**   Obviously, Visual Studio for Mac will only be able to clone the latest version available of the remote repository. Any uncommitted local changes will not be available for cloning.

Managing File Changes

When a solution is under version control, every time you open a source file in the code editor you will see five buttons at the bottom, called Source, Changes, Blame, Log, and Merge. These buttons provide shortcuts to tools that allow you to manage file changes. To understand how they work, let's first make a couple of edits to the source code.

For example, open the ItemService.cs file, locate the QueryRssAsync method, and replace the following comment:

```
// Query the RSS feed with LINQ and return an IEnumerable of Item
```

with the following XML comment that allows IntelliSense to show information about the method:

```
/// <summary>
/// Query the RSS feed and return a list of news
/// </summary>
/// <returns><seealso cref="Item"/></returns>
/// <param name="forceReload">If set to <c>true</c> force reload.</param>
```

Do not forget to save your changes. Now click the Changes tab at the bottom. As you can see in Figure 12-7, the code editor switches to the Diff view, which shows the differences between the latest version on the remote repository (on the left) and the local repository (on the right). This tool is extremely useful to get a quick visual representation of changes in a file.

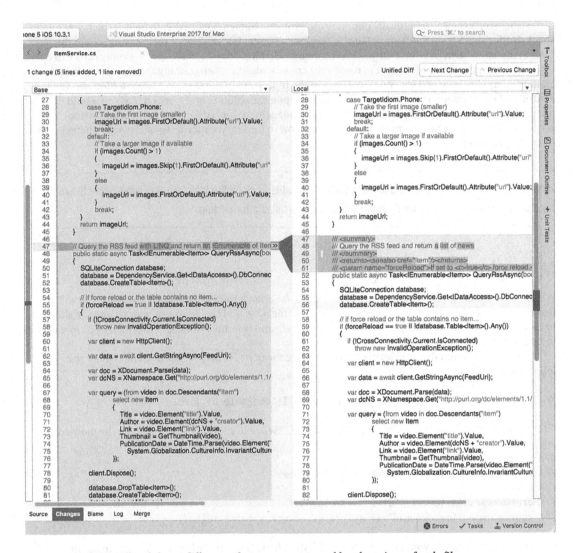

Figure 12-7. *The Diff tool shows differences between remote and local versions of code files*

At the top, you can see summary information such as the number of changes and the number of lines of code added and removed. You can also use the two combo boxes to switch the view between remote (base) and local files, and you can also select a specific version of the file that you can compare to another version. The arrow icon that highlights a difference can be clicked to quickly revert changes. The Blame tool allows you to see who did what in a code file. As you can see in Figure 12-8, Visual Studio shows the name of the developer who made edits to a code block in the last commit, and it also highlights changes that have not been committed yet.

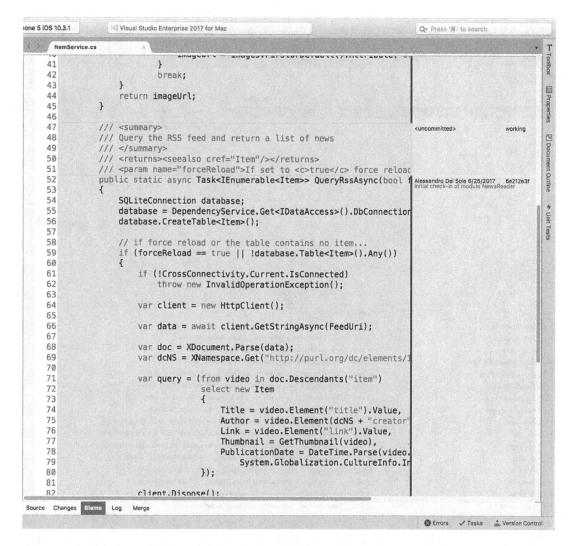

Figure 12-8. *The Blame tool shows information about the authors of changes*

This tool can be useful to project managers who need to see whether the source code was modified as required by the developers who were assigned a task and to other developers in the team who might need to know who implemented a specific part for further clarifications. The Log tool shows a list of the latest operations made against the repository in the last commit; for example, in this case, it shows a list of files that were submitted to version control, as demonstrated in Figure 12-9.

Figure 12-9. *The Log tool shows the list of operations made with the last commit*

The last tool, Merge, is useful if you have a merge conflict on a file when committing your work. It shows the difference between changes made by you and another developer, allowing you to combine both sections of code cleanly.

Managing Commits

Once you have finished working on your changes, you will want to commit the latest version of your code to the repository. With Git, you first commit changes locally, and then you update the remote repository (though Visual Studio for Mac provides a shortcut that allows you to do both things with a single command).

For example, suppose you want to commit changes you made to the `ItemService.cs` file. You have three options: committing changes for the whole solution, committing changes for a single project, or committing changes for an individual code file. Choose the last option only if you made edits to one file or if you do not want to push all the changes you made, for example, because you did not finish your work on all files but other developers might need the latest version of one of them. For the current sample app, I will demonstrate how to commit changes for the whole solution, which is probably the most common scenario. The command and shortcuts you use are then called in the same way. To commit your changes, in the Solution pad right-click the solution name and select Version Control ➤ Review and Commit. As you can see in Figure 12-10, Visual Studio for Mac will show the list of files that will be committed, and you will be able to expand each file to get a visual representation of the edits. In the text box at the bottom, you will be able to provide a comment for this commit. This is optional but strongly recommended because it helps other developers understand what edits you made to a specific version of the solution.

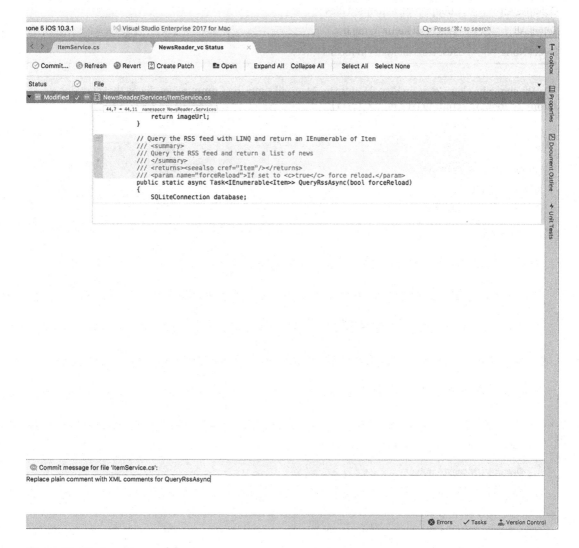

Figure 12-10. *A summary of changes*

The toolbar at the top provides a number of useful commands, summarized in Table 12-1.

Table 12-1. *Commands Available to Manage a Commit*

Command	Description
Commit	Commits your changes locally
Refresh	Refreshes the list of changes in case you made other edits while this window is open
Revert	Reverts changes in the selected file (or files)
Create Patch	Creates a Git patch that allows you to export a commit to file
Open	Opens the selected file in the editor
Expand All	Expands all the files to show changes
Collapse All	Collapses all expanded files
Select All	Selects all items in the list
Select None	Deselects all items in the list

When ready, click Commit. Visual Studio for Mac will show the Commit Files dialog that contains a summary about the commit (see Figure 12-11).

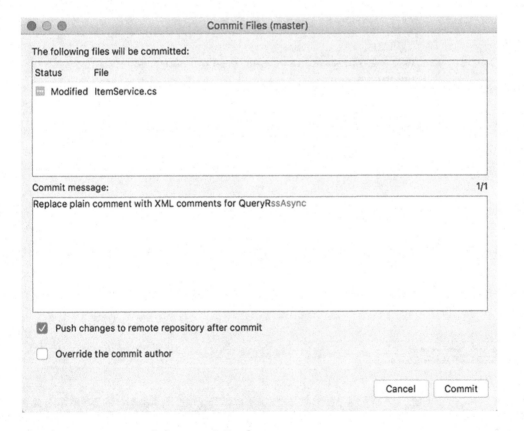

Figure 12-11. *A summary before committing changes*

If you select the "Push changes to remote repository after commit" option, Visual Studio for Mac will also push your changes to the remote repository after the local commit. Click Commit when ready and, in case you opted for remote push, you will see the Push to Repository dialog where you will simply click Push Changes. If you did not select this option, you will be able to manually push your changes to the remote repository with Version Control ➤ Push Changes. Visual Studio for Mac will call the Git command line to create a new version of the code that other developers will be able to use. Once the commit operation has been completed, you will see that Visual Studio for Mac clears the list of changes.

At this point, if other developers want to get the latest version of the repository that contains your changes or if you want to get the latest version of changes made by others, Visual Studio for Mac needs to perform an operation called *pull*. To accomplish this, open the solution and then select Version Control ➤ Update Solution. This operation will update your local repository with the remote changes and will overwrite files that you are currently working on.

■ **Note** Visual Studio for Mac allows you to customize some options about version control tools and interaction with Git. You can select Visual Studio ➤ Preferences ➤ Version Control and use the Commit Message Style options to format the style of commit messages, the Git tab to influence stashes and branches, and the General tab to globally disable version control.

Hints About Stashes

Visual Studio for Mac also supports *stashes*. With stashes, Git allows you to save your edited files on a stack of unfinished changes that you can reapply at any time. This can be useful when you have not finished your work and you want to have a remote copy of your changes without affecting the repository with a commit. If you have experience with TFS, this is similar to the Shelve operation. Stashes will not be discussed in this chapter, but Visual Studio for Mac provides the Stashes, Pop Stash, and Manage Stashes commands in the Version Control menu that help you work with this feature.

Managing Branches

Branches are one of the most important features in any version control system. If you are not familiar with branches, an example will help you understand what they are. Suppose you have a project that, at a certain point, goes to production and you have an updated and tested repository for it.

You need to continue the development of your project, but you do not want to do it over the code you have written so far, keeping your project safe. You can create two separate histories of your project using a branch. When you create a repository, Git automatically creates a default branch called *master*. For example, the master branch could contain the code that has gone to production, and you could create a new branch called *development*, based on master but different from it, where you can continue the development of your project. Visual Studio for Mac includes a number of tools that simplify working with branches. Let's start by creating a new branch. At this writing, Visual Studio for Mac does not allow you to create a remote branch in the IDE, so one must be first created in the Git host you choose, VSTS in this case, but it could be GitHub or Bitbucket. To accomplish this, in the dashboard of Visual Studio Team Services, click Branches and then "New branch." As demonstrated in Figure 12-12, enter the branch name and select the branch on which the new one is based, such as master in this case.

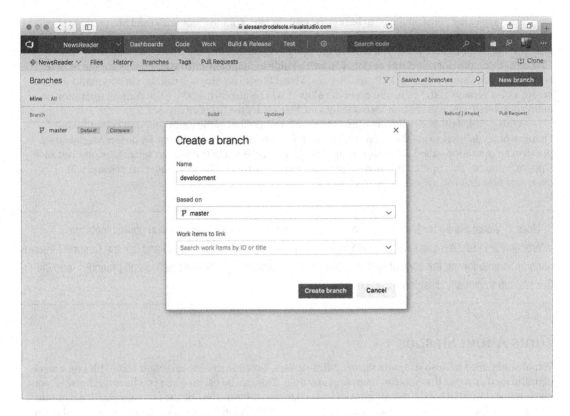

Figure 12-12. *Creating a new remote branch*

Click "Create branch." After a few seconds, this will be available in your repository. The next step is creating a local branch in Visual Studio for Mac and associating this to the remote branch. To accomplish this, select Version Control ➤ Manage Branches and Remotes. The Git Repository Configuration dialog appears and shows the list of branches for the current repository; in this case, only the master branch is available. Click New and in the Branch Properties dialog enter the branch name; then enable the "Track a branch" option and select the origin/development branch (see Figure 12-13).

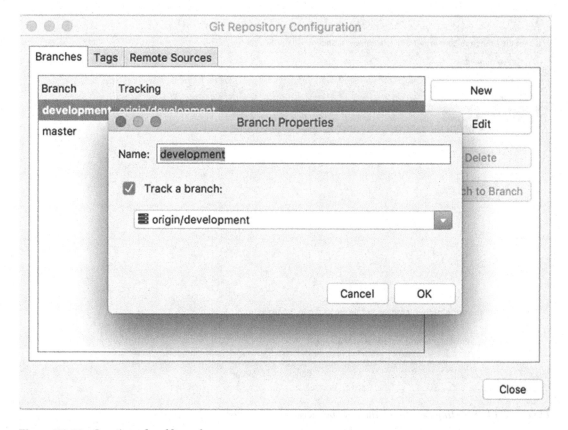

Figure 12-13. *Creating a local branch*

When you click OK, a new local branch will be created and associated to the remote branch so that every time you will make changes, these will be pushed to the new branch. Actually, you must explicitly set the new branch as the target for your changes. This can be easily done by selecting Version Control ➤ Switch to Branch and then selecting the target branch. Once you have switched to the desired branch, you will be able to manage your commits as you learned previously.

Merging Branches

When the development of your project reaches another safe and tested milestone, it is common practice to merge the secondary branch into the main branch. This helps keep branches consistent with the state of the project and helps keep your code organized. In the current example, suppose the NewsReader project reaches another development milestone and therefore you want to merge the content of the development branch into the master branch. Make sure you have pushed any pending changes to the development branch.

First, you have to switch back to the master branch (or to the branch that will receive the content of the secondary branch). You still use Version Control ➤ Switch to Branch. At this point, select Version Control ➤ Merge Branch. Visual Studio will ask you to specify which branch will be merged into master, as demonstrated in Figure 12-14.

Figure 12-14. *Selecting the branch that will be merged into master*

Make sure you select a branch under the origin node in order to merge a remote branch; otherwise, the merge will be performed using a local branch. When ready, click Merge. Merging a branch may take up to a few minutes depending on the number of changes between the two. Remember that you will need again to switch to a different branch for development to keep the master branch clean.

Branching Strategies

You can basically have infinite branches, and the branching strategy is totally dependent on your company's way of working. In my experience, these are the most common branching strategies:

- All the people in the team work on the same development branch, and when the project reaches a milestone, the development branch is merged into the master branch.

- A branch is created for each feature you need to implement in your application and then merged into master when completed. In terms of the Scrum and Agile methodologies, a branch is created for each user story in the sprint backlog. When a story is closed, the branch is merged into the master branch. This model is also known as the GitFlow workflow (http://nvie.com/posts/a-successful-git-branching-model).

- Every team member works on a dedicated branch, and this is merged into a master branch according to the development state of the project.

There is not a perfect branching strategy. For example, the second strategy is okay with a small number of user stories in the sprint backlog; otherwise, managing a large number of branches can be painful. The first option is instead okay if each team member works on specific, separated tasks and source files so that they will seldom have conflicts. Especially when you have many branches that you then merge into a master branch, it is best practice to remove branches you no longer use to keep your repository clean and well organized.

As I said before, the branching strategy is something specific to your way of working, but Visual Studio for Mac has the proper tools to handle all the possible scenarios.

Summary

More often than not, developers work in teams, and they need tools that allow them to work on the same solutions from different workstations and to share their work with other developers. Team collaboration on source code is possible through different version control systems, and Visual Studio for Mac supports Git and Subversion. In this chapter, you learned how to configure Visual Studio to work with Git, as it is the most popular version control engine in the world.

You learned how to configure a remote and local repository, how to clone repositories for team collaboration, and how to take advantage of all the integrated tools that allow for displaying changes over files. You saw how to share your work with commits, and you saw how to work with branches for managing different milestones in the application life cycle. At the end, you saw how to merge branches, and you got hints about possible branching strategies. The Visual Studio for Mac IDE demonstrates, once again, all of its power through a huge number of integrated tools that make your developer life easier. But there is more: in the next and last chapter, you will be guided through a number of additional, integrated tools that will make you even more productive.

CHAPTER 13

■ ■ ■

A Deeper Look at the IDE

As a first-class citizen, Visual Studio for Mac includes many integrated tools for productivity and can be customized in many ways so that you can get the most out of the development environment and organize the workspace in the best way for your needs.

This chapter is totally oriented to the integrated development environment (IDE) and unleashes a large number of useful tools, some related to customizations and others related to productivity. By completing this chapter, you will have in your hands all the incredible power of Visual Studio for Mac, and you will get many tips that will be useful as you start using the IDE on your own.

Customizing Visual Studio

Visual Studio for Mac is a flexible IDE and allows you to customize the appearance, the shortcuts, and the text editor. This section walks through all the available customizations that you will be able to leverage in order to make Visual Studio the perfect workspace for you. Most of these customizations are available in the Preferences dialog, which you open with the Preferences command in the Visual Studio menu.

Customizing Key Bindings

Key bindings are predefined keyboard shortcuts that you can use to invoke commands and tools instead of locating and selecting commands within menus and with the mouse. Key bindings can definitely speed up your activities especially when writing code.

Default key bindings can be overridden with custom shortcuts. To accomplish this, select the Key Bindings tab in the Preferences dialog. In the dialog, you will see a list of commands grouped by category, with their key bindings (if assigned), as shown in Figure 13-1.

© Alessandro Del Sole 2017
A. Del Sole, *Beginning Visual Studio for Mac*, https://doi.org/10.1007/978-1-4842-3033-6_13

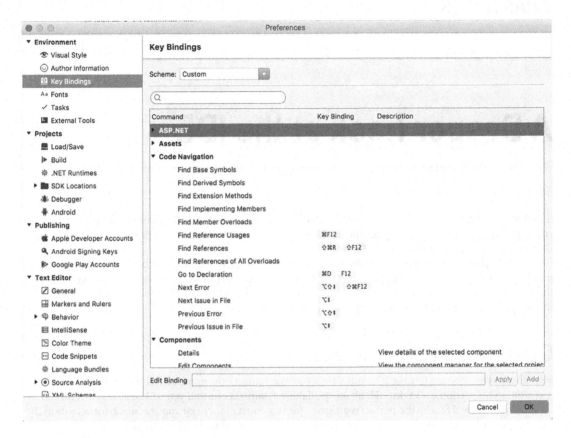

Figure 13-1. *Customizing key bindings*

If you want to customize a key binding, select the command in the list, type the new shortcut in the Edit Binding text box, and then click OK. You can also select a scheme that recalls key bindings available in other development environments, by expanding the Scheme combo box. For example, you can select Xcode, Visual Studio Code, Visual Studio (Windows), Resharper, and a mix of Visual Studio for Mac and Visual Studio on Windows so that you can reuse key bindings that you are already familiar with. The default is Custom, a scheme created for Visual Studio for Mac.

Customizing Fonts

You can change the default fonts in Visual Studio for Mac using the Fonts tab in the Preferences dialog. You can select a different font for the code editor, for all the pads in general, and for the Output pad. Figure 13-2 shows how you can select a font with the font picker.

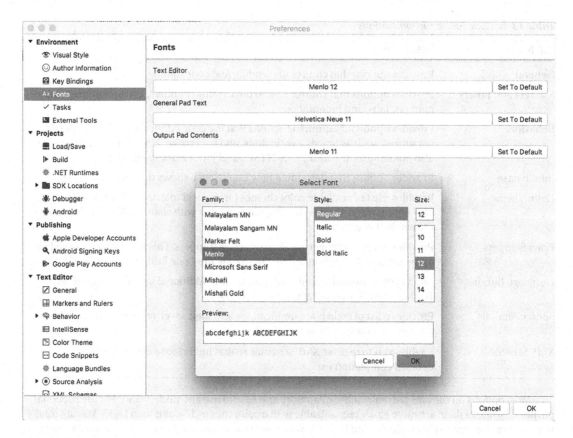

Figure 13-2. *Customizing fonts*

Before you click OK, remember to click Set To Default if you want the selected font to be the new default.

Customizing the Code Editor

Being the place where you spend most of your developer life, the code editor supports a large number of customizations, all available on the Text Editor tab of the Preferences dialog. Table 13-1 summarizes the available tabs and their options.

Table 13-1. *Code Editor Customizations*

Tab Name	Description
General	Provides options that control line ending and code folding.
Markers and Rulers	Provides options that control how to display line numbers, code references, rulers, markers, tabs, and indentation.
Behavior	Provides option for automatic actions that the code editor must take for specific keystrokes, such as braces, semicolons, and backspace. More specific actions are also available for the XML, CSS, HTML, and JSON markup languages.
IntelliSense	Provides options that determine how IntelliSense shows the completion list.
Color Theme	Provides a list of available color themes for the user interface of the code editor. This option was discussed in Chapter 2 together with visual styles, which apply to the whole IDE instead.
Code Snippets	Provides a way to manage IntelliSense code snippets. This feature is discussed in more detail in the section called "Improving the Code Editing Experience."
Language Bundles	Allows you to extend Visual Studio to support additional languages based on the TextMate and Sublime 3 grammar packages.
Source Analysis	Provides a list of code issue notifications and their severity levels that you can change, for example, from warning to error.
XML Schemas	Enables you to register XML schemas so that IntelliSense can display a more detailed completion list.

Most options on the tabs are really self-explanatory and easy to use and understand. For instructional purposes, some of them are more easily recognizable with a color theme different than Light. You are totally free to leave the theme of your choice, but I will now use the Dark theme that better highlights some code editor features in screenshots. By following what you learned in Chapter 2, apply the Dark theme to Visual Studio in the Visual Style tab of the Preferences dialog. Then, in the General tab under Text Editor, select Enable Code Folding, and in the Markers and Rulers tab enable the "Highlight current line" and "Show indentation guides" options. As you can see in Figure 13-3, with code folding enabled, you can now collapse and expand code blocks with a single mouse click and see a preview of the code block in a tooltip; also, you can see the current line highlighted and the so-called indentation guides, which are vertical lines that make it easier to identify the curly braces that delimit a specific code block.

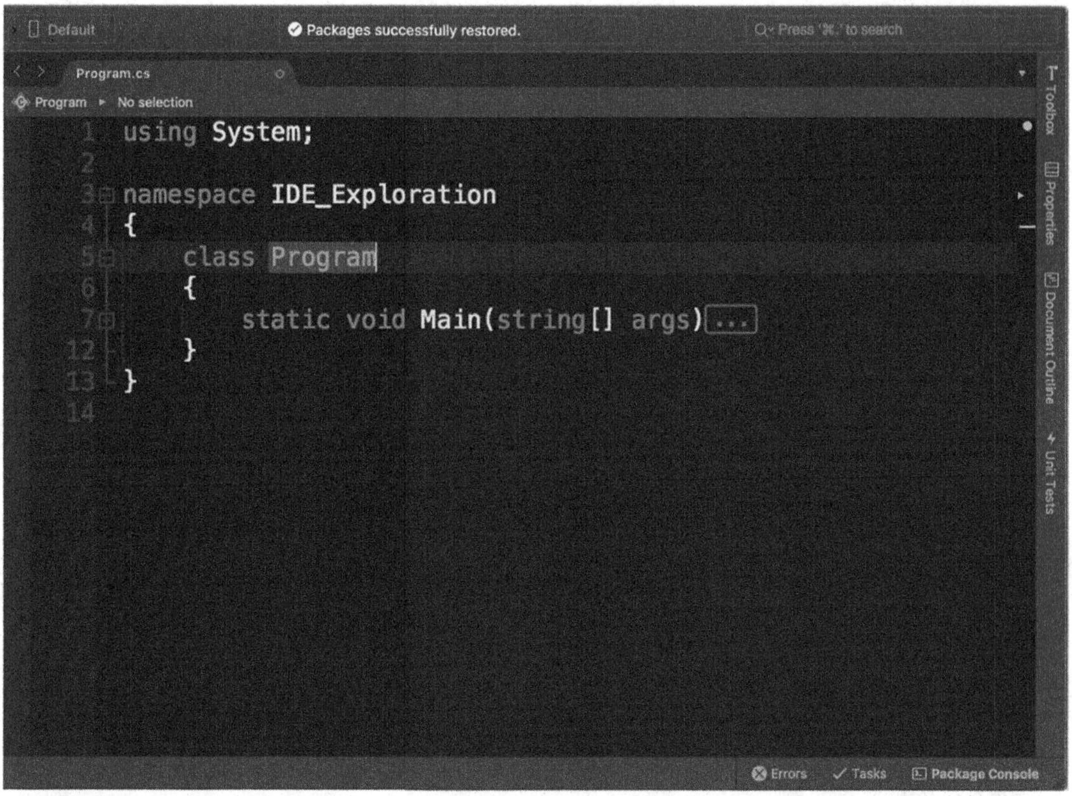

Figure 13-3. *Code editor customizations: code folding, current line highlighting, and indentation guides*

Of course, these are just a few examples of code editor customizations you can set in Visual Studio for Mac, and all the other customizations available are extremely easy to use and set. However, a couple of them deserve more attention and are on the Language Bundles and Source Analysis tabs.

Adding Language Bundles

One of the most amazing features in customizing Visual Studio for Mac is that you can add support for languages that are not included out of the box. In fact, Visual Studio for Mac supports language grammars based on the TextMate and Sublime Text 3 standards.

Both TextMate and Sublime Text 3 are popular cross-platform, enhanced code editors that can work with an infinite number of languages. For each language, they both support language packages, which are archives that include language grammar, syntax colorization, and code snippets. Language packages are also referred to as *language bundles*. Visual Studio for Mac can only work with packages and not with individual files, such as the language grammar definition, so you need an easy way to find the packages you need. For a better understanding of how this feature can enhance your development experience in Visual Studio for Mac, suppose you want to use this IDE to edit Swift code files. Because you are on a Mac, needing to edit

309

Swift source code files is not uncommon. Having that said, I will now provide an example based on Sublime Text 3 because this provides the easiest and fastest way to retrieve language packages. Download the editor at `http://sublimetext.com`, and of course install it and launch it. When ready, follow these steps:

1. Select Tools ➤ Command Palette.

2. Type **Install Package Control**. This will install a package manager that will make it easier to find, download, and install language packages.

3. Open again the Command palette and type **Install Package**; then press Enter. Sublime will show the list of available packages.

4. Pick the Swift package from the list and press Enter.

After a few seconds, the Swift language pack will be installed and available to Sublime. The next step is to export the package so that you can add it to Visual Studio. To accomplish this, in Sublime open the Command palette and type **List Packages**; then press Enter. When the list of installed packages appears, click the Swift package installed previously. This will open a new Finder window pointing to the folder where Sublime stores packages. Copy `Swift.sublime-package` to a reachable directory, such as Desktop, Documents, or Download. Now in Visual Studio, in the Preferences dialog, select the Language Bundles tab under Text Editor. Click Add and locate and select the language package, and this will appear in the list of installed packages (see Figure 13-4).

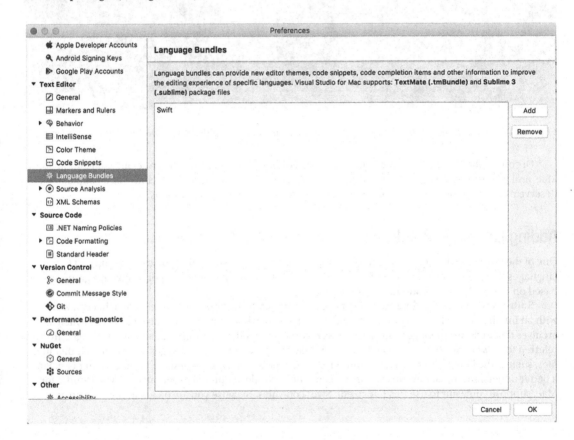

Figure 13-4. *Adding a new language bundle to Visual Studio for Mac*

Now if you open or create a .swift file with Visual Studio, you will not only take advantage of syntax colorization but also of other editor features such as code folding, indentation guides, block delimiters, and much more (see Figure 13-5).

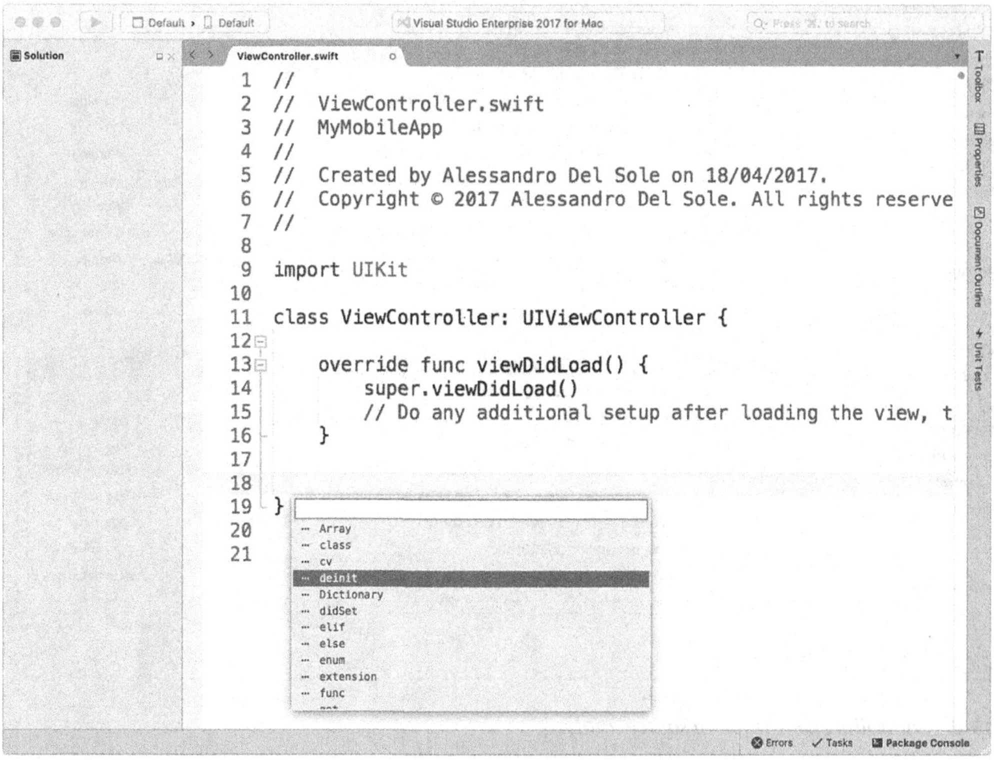

Figure 13-5. *Syntax colorization and other editor features against a language bundle*

Not limited to this, you can add code snippets by right-clicking the code editor and then selecting Insert Template. From the pop-up that appears, you will be able to choose preconfigured code snippets. For languages supported out of the box, such as C#, code snippets are much more powerful, as you will learn later in this chapter.

Setting Options for Source Code Analysis

As you learned in Chapter 2, the code editor in Visual Studio invokes the C# compiler to perform live code analysis and detect code issues as you type, and it also shows error and warning messages at build time in the Errors pad. With live code analysis, the code editor also provides the so-called quick fixes, which are possible solutions to code issues that you can apply while keeping your focus on the code.

In Visual Studio for Mac, you have an opportunity to control how code issues and quick fixes are presented in the code editor. In the Preferences dialog, you can select the Source Analysis tab under Text Editor and enable or disable code analysis, and in the C# tab you can control both code rule violations and fixes. If you take a look at Figure 13-6, you can see the Code Rules tab where a list of code rules appears, organized into categories.

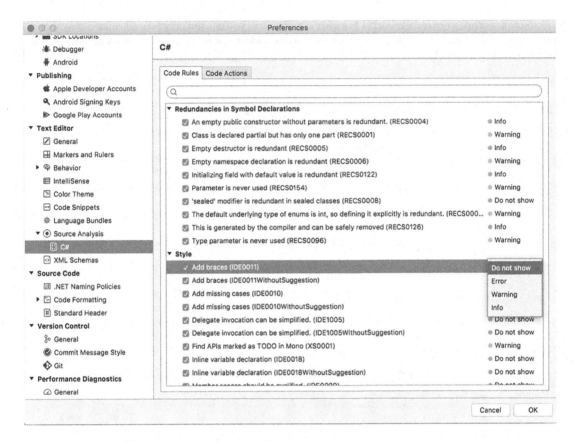

Figure 13-6. *Controlling code rules on source analysis*

You can enable or disable each code rule, and you can specify the severity level among Error, Warning, Info, and Do Not Show by clicking the current severity level. This will present a combo box for selection. This can be useful if you often use some programming patterns that might raise warnings that you want to ignore. It is worth recalling that changing the severity level of a code rule from Warning to Error will cause a build to fail if a violation of that rule is detected; conversely, changing the severity level from Error to Warning will not break a build but might cause runtime errors. The compiler is optimized to raise the most appropriate severity levels, but you need to know that you can change that behavior.

On the Code Actions tab, you can instead enable or disable the most common quick fixes that the code editor provides. Remember that both code rules and code actions are not specific to Visual Studio; instead, they are exposed by the C# compiler's APIs (see Project Roslyn for more details: `http://github.com/dotnet/Roslyn`).

Customizing Options for Projects and Solutions

Visual Studio allows you to customize a number of options related to projects and solutions, available in the Preferences dialog under Projects. I will now provide some information about the available tabs and options.

The Load/Save Tab

The Load/Save tab provides options about the default project location and about loading solutions. Figure 13-7 shows how the tab looks.

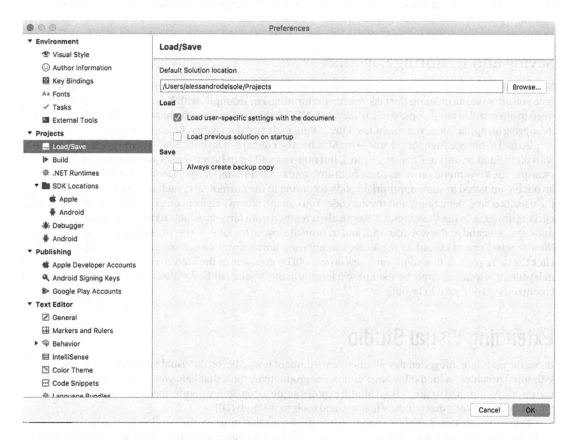

Figure 13-7. *Setting options for projects and solutions*

First, you can change the default folder for new projects. Then you can enable or disable an option that allows Visual Studio to load user-specific preferences when loading a solution. This is enabled by default and can be left unchanged. The "Load previous solution on startup" option will cause Visual Studio to automatically reload the last solution you were working on the last time you closed it. The "Always create backup copy" option will cause Visual Studio to create a backup copy of the solution every time you save it.

The Build Tab

The Build tab contains two tabs, General and Assembly Folders. General includes options that are generally available to all the project types, such as building the project before running, running the build if completed with warnings, saving documents before building, and other self-explanatory options. In Chapter 2, you already saw how to customize options that are specific to .NET Core and Xamarin solutions, so take a look back there for specific customizations.

The Assembly Folders tab allows you to specify additional folders where Visual Studio will look for assemblies.

The .NET Runtimes Tab

By default, Visual Studio 2017 for Mac works with the latest version of the Mono runtime when building and running Xamarin and regular .NET projects. With the .NET Runtimes tab, you can specify additional versions of the Mono framework that you can use to build and run projects. Usually this is not necessary, but it might be useful for backward compatibility with some projects.

Saving and Restoring Layouts

More often than not, the way you organize the layout of your workspace varies depending on the project type you are working on or on the task you are performing. For example, with Xamarin solutions you might need to open and arrange some pads, while in ASP.NET Core projects you might need other pads. Or, when debugging an application, you might need the Debug pads and then, when finished, other pads.

To make things easier, Visual Studio for Mac has the concept of *layouts*. You already saw an example with predefined layouts in Chapters 2 and 3, but now you will learn how to create custom layouts. For example, the View menu provides some built-in layouts called Code, Design, Debug, and Test, and each layout is configured to show appropriate pads according to the current task, such as writing code, designing the user interface, debugging, and testing code. You can quickly switch from one layout to another by simply clicking its name in the View menu. You can also create custom layouts, which allow you to arrange the pads you need and in the way you want and to store the layout for later reuse. To accomplish this, you select View ➤ Save Current Layout. In the dialog that appears, simply specify a custom name for your layout and click Create Layout. At this point, your new layout will be available in the View menu together with built-in layouts, and you will apply it by simply clicking its name. Visual Studio for Mac will also show a Delete command for your custom layouts.

Extending Visual Studio

Being the premiere integrated development environment from Microsoft, Visual Studio (on both Mac and Windows) provides an incredibly large number of productivity tools that help you improve the quality of your work. Not limited to this, Visual Studio exposes some extensibility points; therefore, you can download and install extensions that add new features and tools to this rich IDE.

Extensions are typically of two major types: extensions that improve the development experience and extensions that add new tools to the IDE. A number of integrated tools in Visual Studio are extensions themselves. To extend Visual Studio for Mac and to manage installed extensions, you use the Extension Manager window, which you can open by selecting Visual Studio ➤ Extensions. Figure 13-8 provides a sample view.

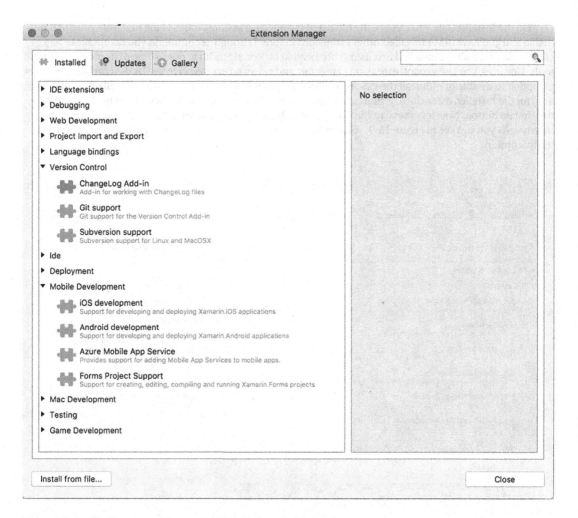

Figure 13-8. *The Extension Manager shows the installed extensions*

On the Installed tab, you can see the full list of installed extensions. If this is the first time you open this dialog and you have never installed other extensions before, I strongly recommend you do not make any changes because all the installed extensions are needed by Visual Studio to offer some of its most important tools. However, you can expand extension categories and select an extension to see its description and to get an option to disable or uninstall the extension. On the Updates tab, you will see a list of available updates (if any) for the installed extensions. When an update is available, you will simply select the extension and click the Update button. Now let's move to the Gallery tab, which allows for downloading extensions from the Internet. As you can see in Figure 13-9, you can browse extension categories and select an extension to see its description.

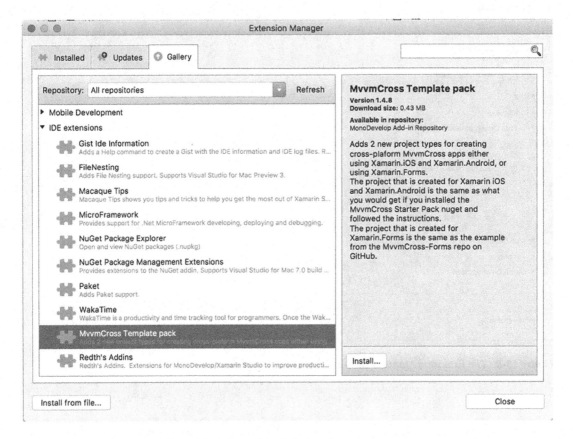

Figure 13-9. Browsing extensions and getting a description

When you have decided to install an extension, simply click Install. For example, in Figure 13-9 you can see the MvvmCross Template Pack extension, which adds new project templates to Visual Studio based on Xamarin and the popular MvvmCross library for Model-View-ViewModel support. If you click Install and close the Extension Manager when finished, you will get new project templates in the Miscellaneous tab of the New Project dialog, as demonstrated in Figure 13-10.

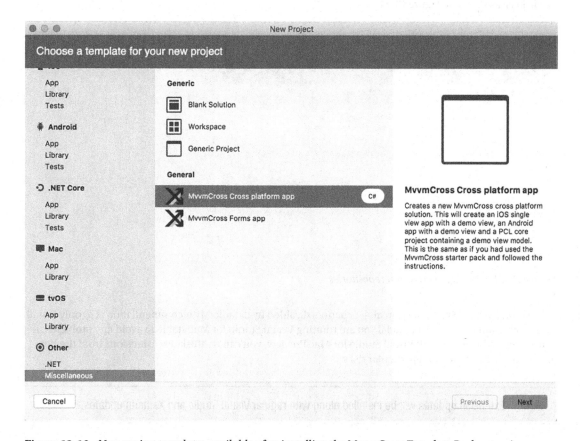

Figure 13-10. *New project templates available after installing the MvvmCross Template Pack extension*

At this point, your extension will be listed on the Installed tab of the Extension Manager, and there you will be able to disable or uninstall it when no longer needed. Notice that, by default, Visual Studio for Mac lists available extensions from both a stable channel and a beta channel. You can change the default by clicking the Repository combo box. Also, from there you will be able to click the Manage Repositories item, which will allow you to select the channels from which the Extension Manager must include available extensions, as shown in Figure 13-11.

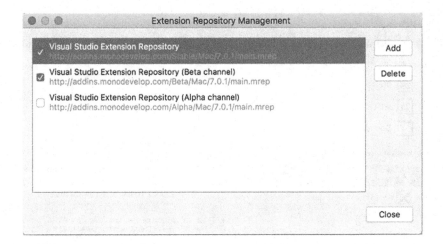

Figure 13-11. *Managing extension repositories*

As you can see, there is also an alpha channel disabled by default. My recommendation is to only install extensions from the stable channel if you are running Visual Studio for Mac stable to avoid any problems. If you are instead working with Visual Studio for Mac Preview, you can try the latest extensions from the Beta and Alpha channels without particular risks.

■ **Note**   Extension updates will be installed along with regular Visual Studio and Xamarin updates.

Hints About Extension Authoring

As you can easily imagine, developers can build extensions for Visual Studio for Mac as they already could do for Visual Studio on Windows. Building extensions for Visual Studio is beyond the scope of this chapter, so it will not be covered. Just as a hint, to build an extension for Visual Studio for Mac, you first need some knowledge of its extension points and APIs, and then you need to install an extension called Add-in Maker.

This extension will add specific project templates tailored for extension authoring. The good news is that you still use C# to develop extensions and XML if the extension has some user interface. Microsoft provides official documentation about extension development in VS for Mac at `http://docs.microsoft.com/en-us/visualstudio/mac/extending-visual-studio-mac`.

Improving the Code Editing Experience

In Chapter 2, you got a deep explanation about the code editor in Visual Studio for Mac and all of its powerful features. In this chapter, you also saw how to customize the code editor and take advantage of other interesting features available as customizations.

By the way, there is more. Visual Studio for Mac makes it simpler to reuse code snippets you use frequently with the help of IntelliSense and can help you write better code based on conventions and styles. In this section, you will learn about IntelliSense code snippets and code-style customization.

Working with Code Snippets

Code snippets are small, reusable pieces of code. Visual Studio for Mac ships with an extensible library of reusable code snippets that you can use to write code faster, with the help of IntelliSense. This is why you will often hear about them as *IntelliSense code snippets*. This will not be new to you if you have experience with Visual Studio on Windows. In fact, IntelliSense code snippets were first introduced in Visual Studio 2005 and have been enhanced over the years to support more languages.

■ **Note**   In this chapter I will explain how to use code snippets with C#, but it is worth mentioning that they are available to a broader set of supported languages, such as F#, HTML, CSS, and XML. The way you use them is the same regardless of the language.

Working with code snippets in Visual Studio for Mac is really straightforward. To see how this feature works, create a new .NET Core console project. You have different options to enable IntelliSense code snippets. In the code editor, right-click and then select Insert Template. This will show a list of keyboard shortcuts, each mapped to a code snippet (see Figure 13-12). You can filter the list by typing in the search box. Adding a code snippet can be done by double-clicking the desired item or by typing its shortcut and then pressing Tab.

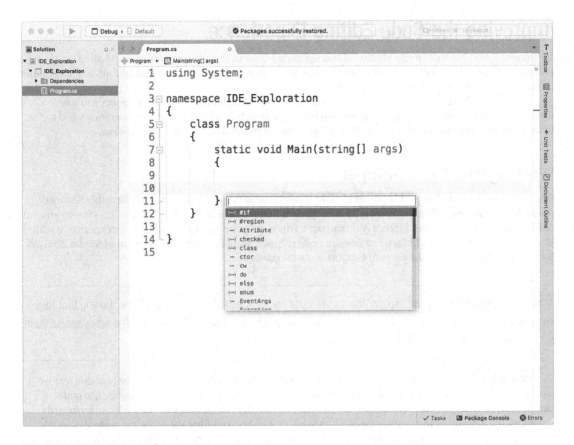

Figure 13-12. *Selecting code snippets*

Shortcuts for code snippets can be recognized by the (...) and ... icons. The first icon represents snippets for container code blocks (such as classes, structures), whereas the second icon represents object members, such as properties and methods, or statements. When you hover over a shortcut, a tooltip will provide a description for the code snippet. For example, if you select the cw shortcut, a tooltip will describe it as a code snippet for the Console.WriteLine statement and will add the following line:

```
Console.WriteLine();
```

Actually, using the Insert Template command is useful if you want to see a list of code snippets and if you want to be able to filter the list, but code snippet shortcuts automatically appear in the IntelliSense completion list, as demonstrated in Figure 13-13.

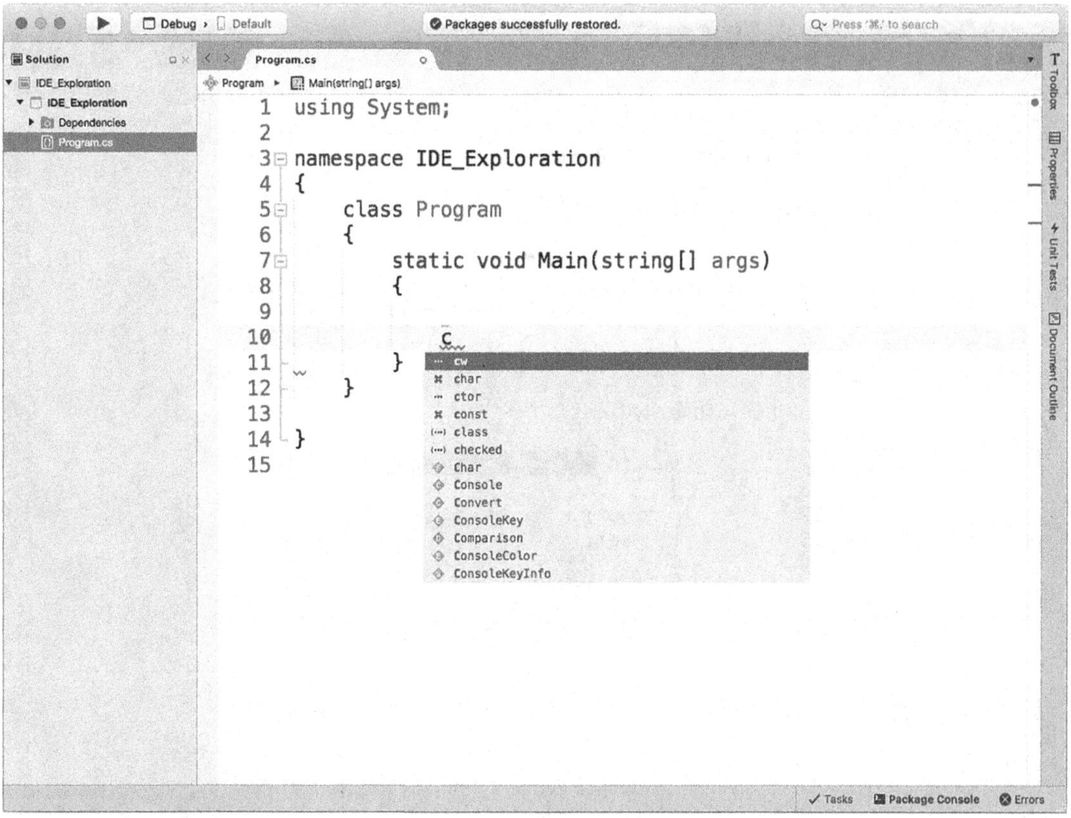

Figure 13-13. *Code snippet shortcuts appear in IntelliSense*

Also, you can simply type the name of the shortcut and then press Tab twice to automatically insert the code snippet. IntelliSense code snippets are more than this; for example, they highlight type names and identifiers that you should replace. After all, a code snippet is a stub, not a ready-to-use code block. To understand how this works, place the cursor before the closing curly brace of the namespace and then type **class** and press Tab twice to insert a class definition code snippet. As you will see, the code snippet will supply MyClass as the class name, and the editor will highlight this because it is a name you will want to replace with a different one. As another example, within the class definition, type **prop** and press Tab twice. This will add a property definition and will highlight both the type name and the property name, as shown in Figure 13-14.

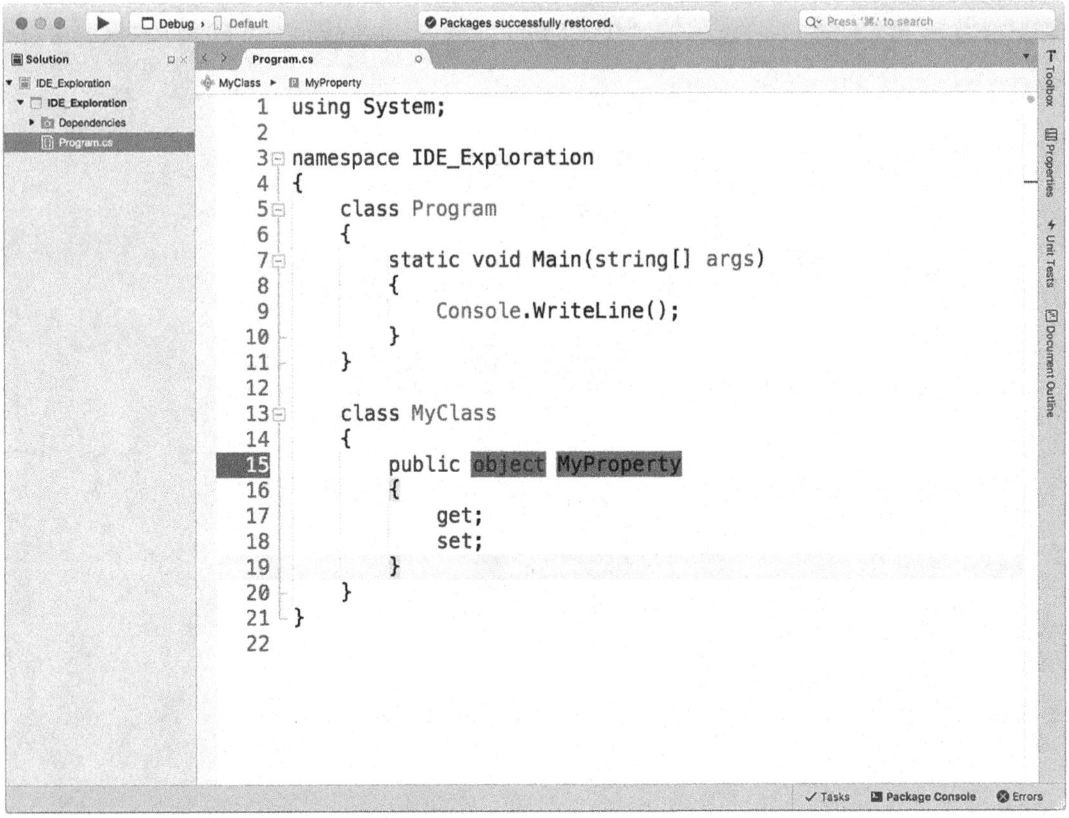

Figure 13-14. Type names and identifiers are highlighted for replacement

Another interesting feature of code snippets is that they can help enclose a code block into another one, without writing the code manually. For example, consider the Console.WriteLine statement you added previously. Now imagine you want to enclose that statement inside a try..catch block for error handling. Instead of writing this block manually and then moving the statement inside it, you can select a code block, right-click, and then click the Surround With item. This command will show a list of code snippets suitable of surrounding the code block you selected, such as if conditional blocks, try..catch blocks, loops, and more. Figure 13-15 demonstrates this.

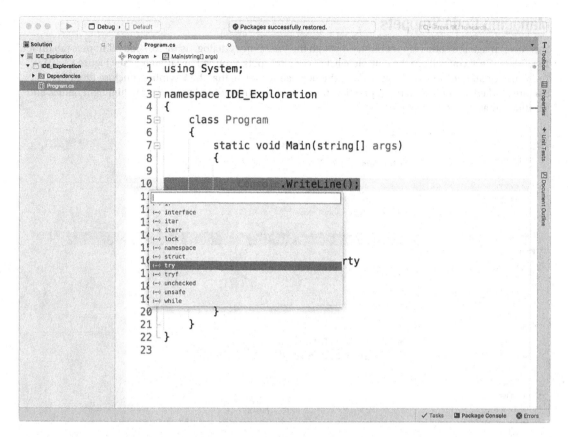

Figure 13-15. *Surrounding a code block with a snippet*

Surrounding the Console.WriteLine statement with a try snippet will produce the following result:

```
try
{
    Console.WriteLine();
}
catch (Exception ex)
{

}
```

As you can see, this approach based on code snippets saved you some time and allowed you to write code more quickly.

Managing Code Snippets

You can manage the code snippet library through the Preferences dialog, using the Code Snippets tab under Text Editor. Here you will see the complete list of code snippets, grouped by language (see Figure 13-16). You can click an item and see its preview in the box below. Notice that the $ symbols enclose identifiers that are marked for replacement; in practice, this is how the code editor knows how to highlight names and identifiers that should be replaced.

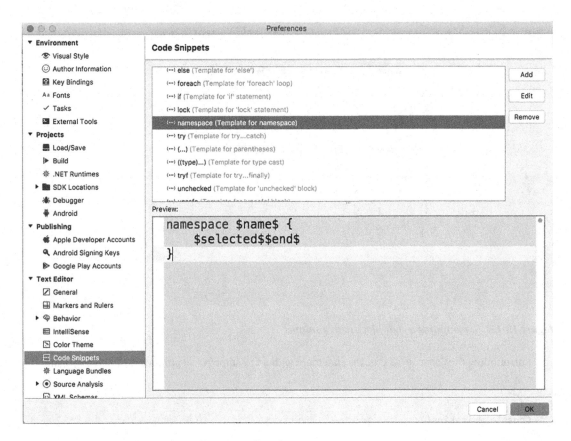

Figure 13-16. *Managing code snippets in Visual Studio*

Notice the $selected$$end$ expression, which delimits the content of the current snippet. You can delete snippets, and you can edit their contents, but the biggest benefit here is that you can create your own code snippets, as explained in the next subsection.

Creating Code Snippets

Visual Studio for Mac allows you to create your own code snippets directly within the IDE. To accomplish this, click Add. Now suppose you want to create a code snippet for an asynchronous method stub. The new template dialog provides some fields that you need to fill in (see Figure 13-17): Shortcut needs you to specify the keyboard shortcut for the snippet (for example, you can enter asf, which stands for asynchronous function); Group allows you to specify the language that the snippet is intended for, so select C#; Description allows you to specify a snippet description, such as Asynchronous method; Mime represents the MIME type for the selected language (in this case, it is text/x-csharp, and additional values can be found in the combo box).

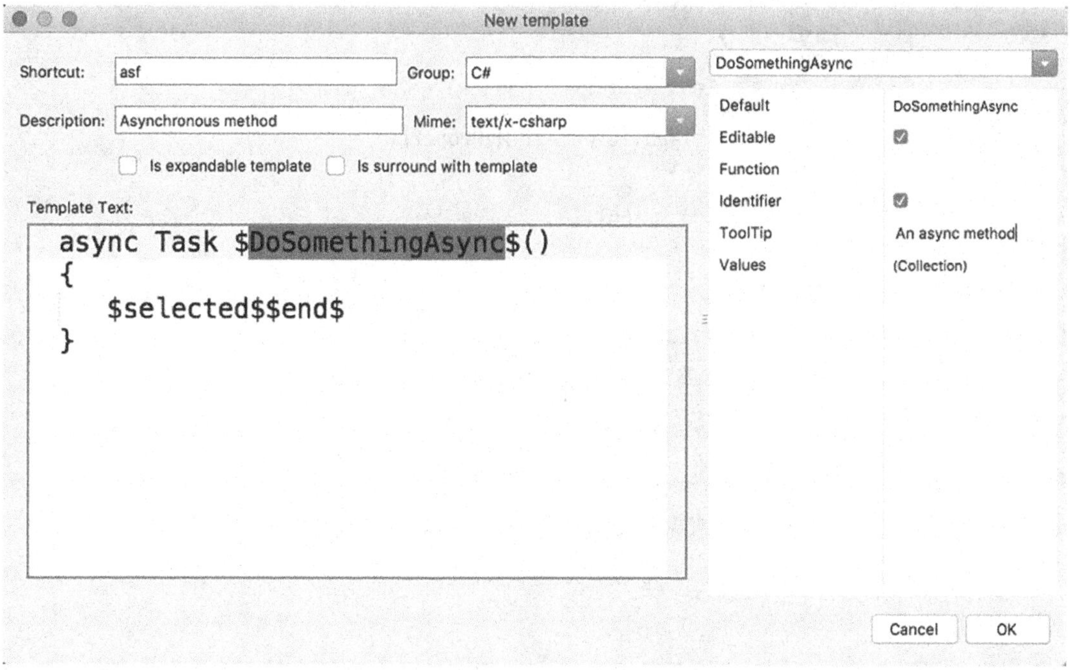

Figure 13-17. *Creating a new code snippet*

If the code snippet contains nested code, you can mark it as "Is expandable template." If the code snippet can act as a container of other blocks, you can mark it with "Is surround with template" and use it as you saw previously. In the text box at the bottom, you simply write the code for the snippet. Notice that you can add the $ symbols to mark the method name for replacement. When you do this, you will be able to select the method identifier in the combo box at the upper-right corner and supply some properties such as the tooltip and the Default property. The latter maps all the occurrences of the identifier that you might have in your snippet to the same replacement. As an implication, the code editor will highlight all the occurrences of the identifier, and the developer using your snippet will simply type a new name to get them all renamed.

■ **Note**   You can hover over each property and see a description inside a tooltip.

When ready, click OK. You will now see your new code snippet in the library. Click OK again to close the window. If you now go to the code editor, right-click, and then Insert Template, you will see your code snippet in the list, as demonstrated in Figure 13-18. When you add the snippet, the method identifier will be highlighted for replacement. In this particular case, the compiler will raise an error if the using System.Threading.Tasks directive is missing because it is required by the method return type (Task).

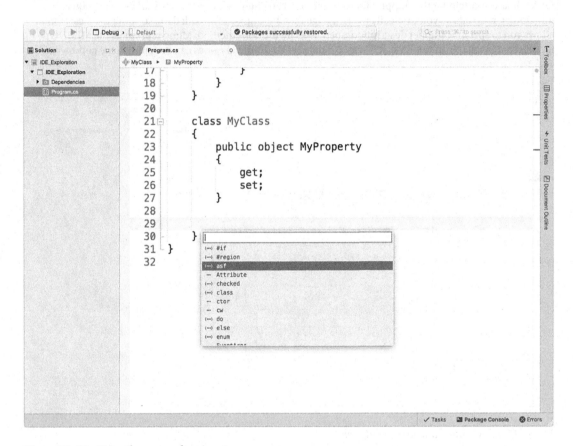

Figure 13-18. *Using the new code snippet*

Code snippets provide a convenient way to create your code library; they definitely help code reuse, and they can take advantage of all the power in Visual Studio's code editor.

Customizing Source Code Styles

The Preferences dialog in Visual Studio also allows you to edit the default styles for source code. If you select the Source Code tab, you will first encounter the .NET Naming Policies node. Here you will be able to edit some options such as associating namespaces with folder names and using the default namespace as root. Figure 13-19 shows the Preferences dialog at this point.

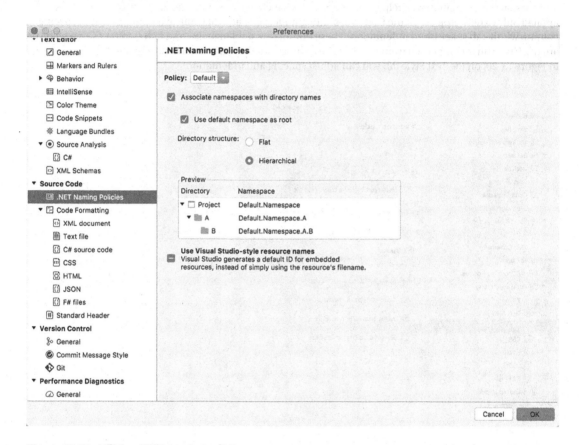

Figure 13-19. *Editing .NET naming policies*

For example, when you add a folder to a C# project and then you add a code file to that folder, the new file is under a namespace whose name is made of the default namespace plus the folder namespace. You can change this behavior by disabling the "Associate namespaces with directory names" option. Additionally, because the default namespace that is defined when you create a new project is also the root namespace by default, if you disable the "Use default namespace as root" option, you will be able to override this default and use a different root namespace. You can also change the directory structure for projects and solutions, and a visual representation will help you understand what changes. Notice that all these options will be applied only to new projects. In the Code Formatting node, you can edit some text options such as spacing, column width, tab spaces, and indentation. These options are per language, and in the case of C# (which you are working with) are inherited from the Text File options, but they can be certainly changed. As you can see in Figure 13-20, on the Text Style tab you can adjust spacing and indentation.

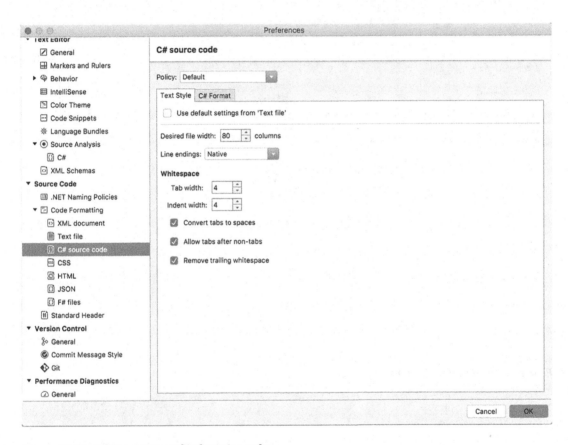

Figure 13-20. *Editing spaces and indentation styles*

In Figure 13-21, you can see a preview of how these settings are applied. Notice that settings are based on the so-called policies. A policy can be thought of as a set of style settings. You will see the Default selection, which is based on the Microsoft Visual Studio policy, but you will be able to choose a different policy and see how the spacing changes, such as when you select the Mono policy.

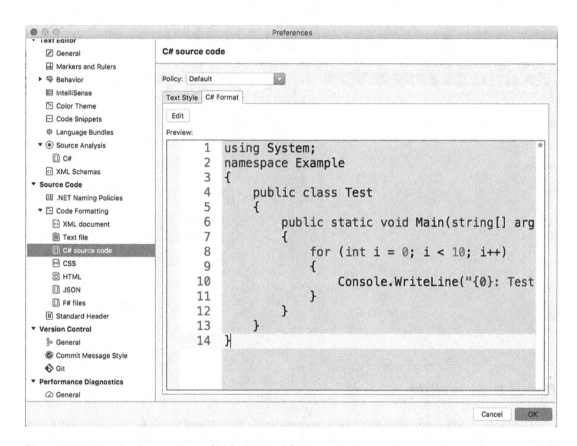

Figure 13-21. *Previewing spacing and indentation policies*

In addition, you can edit default settings for a policy by clicking Edit. This will open the Edit Profile dialog, where you will be able to override the default settings for different categories and see a preview, as shown in Figure 13-22.

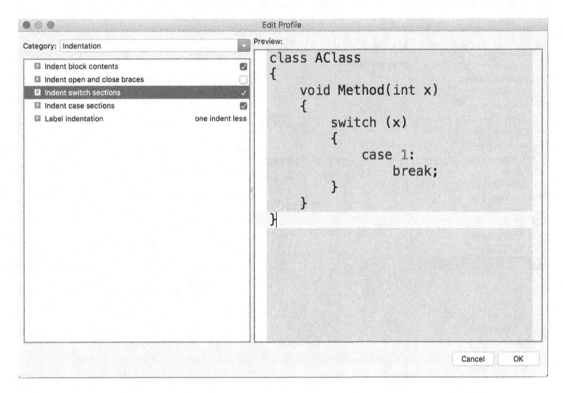

Figure 13-22. *Editing policies*

Code styles can be customized for all the supported languages in Visual Studio for Mac, not just C#, in the same way. The Standard Header tab allows you to view and edit constants that represent items in the solution and that you can use in your text files; you can see how they are applied by selecting templates from the Policy combo box.

■ **Note**   Policies can be set at the global preferences level, at the solution level, or on an individual project. Depending on the level, settings are inherited in that order.

Getting into Advanced NuGet Management

As you have seen through all the previous chapters, NuGet is an important part of development because it is the preferred way to add libraries and their dependencies to projects and solutions. NuGet provides some options that allow for a few customizations and that you will learn about in this section.

Customizing NuGet

The NuGet tab in the Preferences dialog provides the General item, where you can enable and disable automatic package restore and do an update check every time a solution is opened (see Figure 13-23).

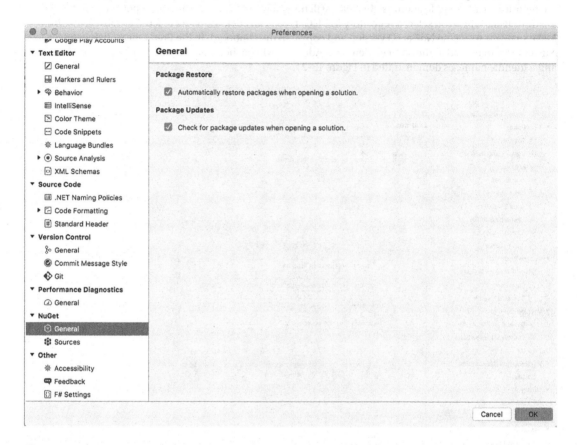

Figure 13-23. *Options to automate NuGet package restore and update check*

I recommend you leave these options unchanged so that you can be sure the required packages are available and updated. In addition, the Sources item allows you to customize the sources where Visual Studio for Mac searches for NuGet packages. In the NuGet terminology, a source is also referred to as a *feed*, and each feed has its own URL that IDEs such as Visual Studio can consume to list the available packages.

Adding and Creating Repositories

One important thing about NuGet is that the NuGet.org web site is not the only source for packages. There are third-party package hosts, and you can create your custom private and public repositories. A popular web site that allows you to create public and private NuGet feeds is MyGet (http://myget.org), which also offers a free plan for personal use.

Not limited to online feeds, NuGet allows you to create local repositories, which means you can store NuGet packages on your local hard drive and have them always available even when an Internet connection is not available. For example, suppose you want to add both an online and a local feed. You can browse the MyGet gallery (http://myget.org/Gallery) for interesting repositories; for the current example, I will use the repository called ApplicationInsightsSdk. I will not really use libraries from this repository, so it is just a sample feed. When you select a repository in MyGet, you can click "Connect to feed" to retrieve its URL. Make sure you select the NuGet V3 version and copy it to the clipboard. In the Preferences dialog, select NuGet ➤ Sources, and in the Sources view click Add. You will be then asked to enter the repository location and a friendly name, as demonstrated in Figure 13-24.

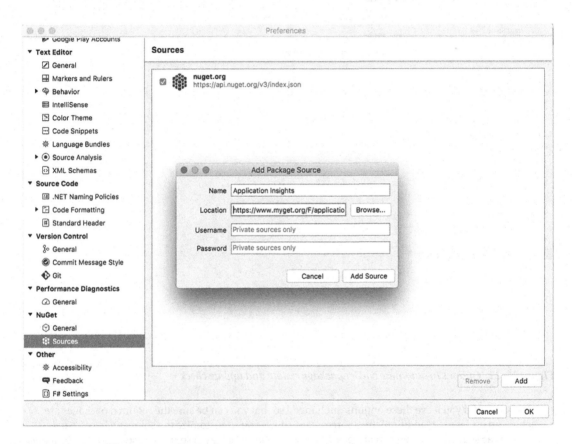

Figure 13-24. *Adding a custom NuGet feed*

As you can see, in the Location text box you can paste the feed URL. Notice that private repositories might require authentication, so you have an option to provide user credentials. When ready, click Add Source. You will see the new feed in the list, but I will come back to this shortly. Now suppose you also want to create a local NuGet repository on your machine or in a shared folder on a server within your network. For example, using Finder, open the Library (or another reachable folder) and add a new folder called NuGetPackages (macOS might require your password to write into certain folders). Then in your browser, visit NuGet.org and search for the Json.NET library; when you are on the library's home page, click Download on the left. Once the download has been completed, use the Finder to copy (or move) the downloaded package to the NuGetPackages folder created previously. Now go back in Visual Studio for Mac and repeat the steps you took to add a new NuGet feed, but this time in the Location box enter the local folder path or click Browse to select the folder more easily. In the Name text box, enter **Local**. At completion, the new local feed will be added to the list, as you can see in Figure 13-25. Notice that you will be also able to enable and disable sources with a simple click on the check box.

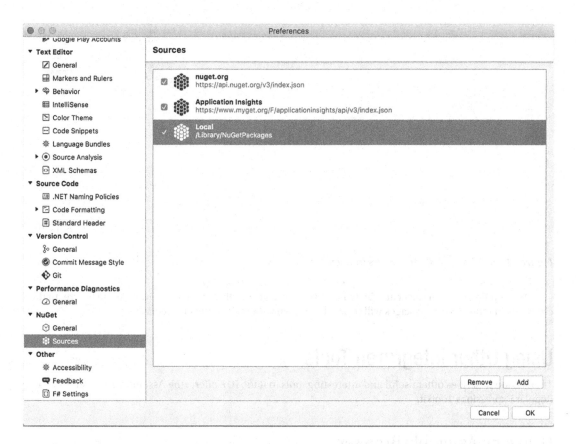

Figure 13-25. *Custom NuGet feeds added to the list of sources*

If you now try to add a NuGet package to any project, you will be able to select the two different feeds as sources in the Add Package dialog, as demonstrated in Figure 13-26 where you can see the Json.NET library available in the Local feed. Simply use the combo box at the upper-left corner to choose a different source.

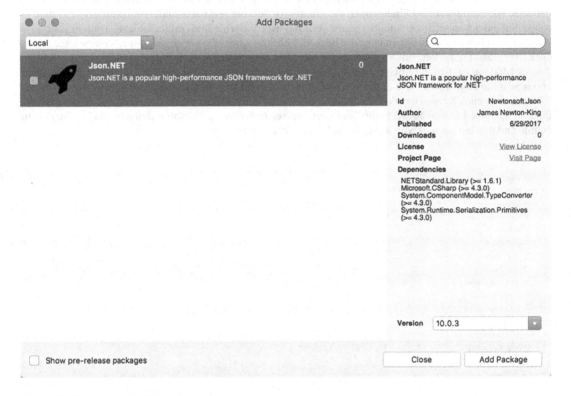

Figure 13-26. *Listing NuGet packages from custom sources*

At this point, you can select and install a NuGet package exactly as you have always done before. In the case of local repositories, packages will be available even with no Internet connection.

Using Other Integrated Tools

This section describes other useful and interesting tools that the IDE offers: the Assembly Browser and the Regular Expressions Toolkit.

Using the Assembly Browser

The Assembly Browser is a convenient tool that displays all the namespaces, types, base types, and members within one or more libraries and that will make it easier to understand how types and members are defined, especially if you do not have the source code available. For each item, the Assembly Browser shows the object's hierarchy and the source code that defines the type or member (thus not the full code). The Assembly Browser can be enabled with the Assembly Browser command in the Tools menu. Figure 13-27 shows the tool in action.

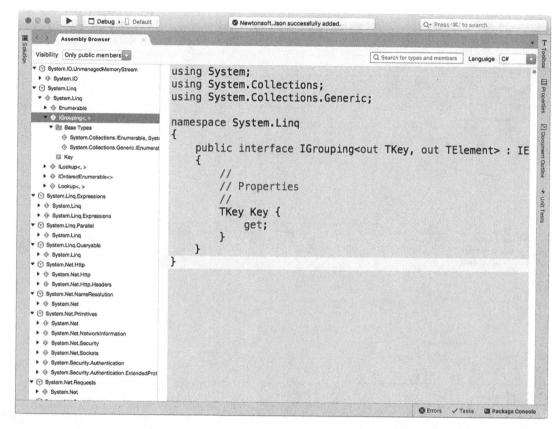

Figure 13-27. *Expanding the object hierarchy and viewing the type definition with the Assembly Browser*

With the combo box at the upper-right corner of the window, you can switch from C# to the Intermediate Language (IL) view. An F# view is not available.

Using the Regular Expressions Toolkit

The Regular Expressions Toolkit is a tool that allows you to test regular expressions against some strings and immediately evaluate the result. Regular expressions can be complex, so for this demonstration I will use a simple regular expression taken from the popular RegExLib.com web site. More specifically, the regular expression used here searches for matches of five-digit ZIP codes within strings and is available at http://regexlib.com/REDetails.aspx?regexp_id=2.

The Regular Expressions Toolkit can be enabled with Tools ➤ Regular Expressions Toolkit. As you can see in Figure 13-28, you write the regular expression at the top and the input strings in the Input text box. Matches are highlighted and grouped in the box below.

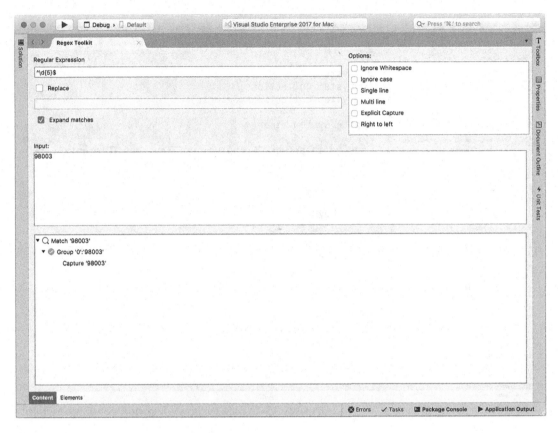

Figure 13-28. *Testing regular expressions*

On the right side of the tool, you also have options that you can use to control the evaluation of an expression, such as ignoring case.

Adding Custom Tools

Visual Studio for Mac allows you to add commands to invoke external tools from within the IDE. For example, you might have analysis tools, compilers, and editors that you want to use against a solution, a project, the build output, or individual files.

To explain how this feature works, I will demonstrate how to add a command that allows you to open a source code file with Visual Studio Code, the popular cross-platform, open source, code-focused development tool from Microsoft available at http://code.visualstudio.com. If you have never tried Visual Studio Code before, this is a good time to do it; you will be impressed by its power and flexibility. Once you have installed and started VS Code for the first time, it is necessary to register its path to the PATH environment variable so that it can be launched from the command line or by other tools regardless of the current directory.

To accomplish this, select View ➤ Command Palette and type the install code command in the PATH environment variable. Now you can close Visual Studio Code and go back to Visual Studio for Mac. Select Tools ➤ Edit Custom Tools, and the Preferences dialog will appear showing the External Tools tab. Here you can specify the name and description of the custom tool you want to invoke and the target of the action. The target can be the solution file, a project file, an individual file, a build output, a directory, or just a part of them.

If you take a look at Figure 13-29, you can see that in the Title text box there is the text for the new command that will be added to Visual Studio, whereas in the Command text box there is the name of the application that the command will launch; in this case, the command starts Visual Studio Code.

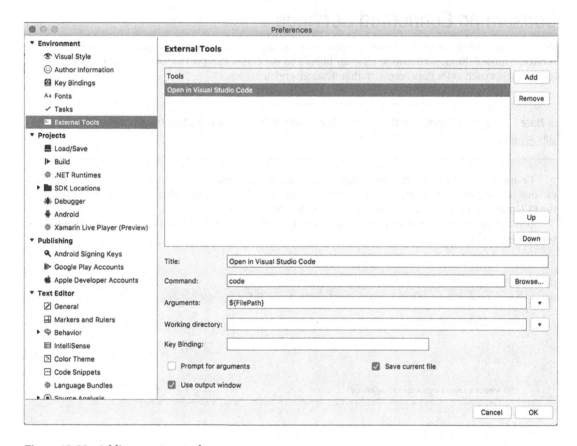

Figure 13-29. *Adding a custom tool*

What you see in the Arguments text box is a constant that represents the full path of the file that is currently opened in the editor. You do not need to learn all the possible constants; you just simply select the target of the action from the combo box at the right, based on the friendly description. Visual Studio will then add the proper constant for you. You can also specify a working directory for the command, and you can specify a key binding. Notice how you have an option to save the file before executing the command and how you can set Visual Studio to ask for other arguments before executing the command. The option "Use output window" is very useful: it will redirect the output of the external tool into the Output pad. When ready, click OK. If you now open the Tools menu, you will find the new command called Open with Visual Studio Code. Open a file in the editor and then select Tools ➤ Open with Visual Studio Code. At this point, VS Code will start, showing the selected file.

■ **Note**   If Visual Studio Code (or another external tool you add) does not start, try to close and restart Visual Studio for Mac. This might be required especially when you make edits to the PATH environment variable.

As you can understand, custom tools provide an easy way to increase your productivity in Visual Studio for Mac.

Consuming Connected Services

Visual Studio for Mac makes it extremely simple for your apps to consume *connected services*. These are services exposed through a network, typically hosted on the cloud, that provide the infrastructure for specific requirements such as for data access, authentication, and analytics.

■ **Note**   Connected services that are currently available in Visual Studio for Mac require a Microsoft Azure subscription.

Connected services are currently available to Xamarin solutions, so for a better understanding, open an existing solution or create a new Xamarin project. When the solution is available in the Solution pad, expand the PCL project, and you will see a node called Connected Services.

If you right-click this node and select Open Service Gallery, you will see a list of available connected services (see Figure 13-30).

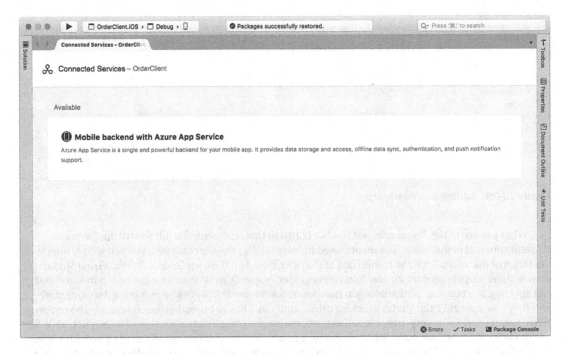

Figure 13-30. *The list of available connected services in Visual Studio for Mac*

At the time of this writing, only the connected service called Mobile backend with Azure App Service is available, but the list might grow in the future. Azure App Service (`http://azure.microsoft.com/en-us/services/app-service`) offers a powerful back end for the iOS, Android, and Windows mobile apps you code with both Xamarin and native technologies and includes data storage with tables and authentication based on several providers. If you click the only service in the list, you will then see a more detailed description, the supported platforms, and a list of dependencies, which includes some NuGet packages that will be downloaded on the client side and some initialization code. Regardless of the service type, you normally install the NuGet packages to the solution following the instructions in Visual Studio; then you can consume the APIs that the service exposes. For Azure App Service, the documentation about both the platform and the APIs is available at `http://docs.microsoft.com/en-us/azure/app-service`.

Summary

In this last chapter, you met a number of interesting features in the Visual Studio for Mac IDE that allow you to have deep control over the workspace. You started with easy customizations, such as key bindings and fonts, and then you moved to more complex customizations in the code editor, with particular attention paid to adding new language bundles and setting options for source analysis. You also saw how to use layouts to save the state of your workspace for quickly restoring your favorite pads.

The discussion moved on to extending Visual Studio for Mac with extensions, both from Microsoft and from a third party. Because you spend a large amount of time in the code editor, you saw how to leverage code snippets, both from the built-in library and from custom ones to write code faster and to have better code reuse.

Visual Studio for Mac also includes tools that allow you to customize NuGet; for example, you can use additional feeds and even create local repositories. In the final part of the chapter, you saw how to take advantage of the Assembly Browser to investigate type and member definitions within libraries; how to use the Regular Expressions Toolkit to evaluate regular expressions; and how to add custom tools that you can execute against a solution, project, folder, individual file, or the build output.

This chapter marks the end of this book. Now you have all the knowledge you need to get the most out of Visual Studio for Mac, and with the help of the official programming reference, you are ready to start building amazing cross-platform mobile and web applications for macOS, Linux, and Windows. Do not forget to frequently visit the Visual Studio blog (`http://blogs.msdn.microsoft.com/visualstudio`) to stay up-to-date on the latest news about Visual Studio for Mac.

Index

A

Android applications, Xamarin
  activity and intent, 116
  APIs in C#
    Activity classes, 123
    Android manifest, 129
    App.cs, 123
    app properties, setting, 128
    CreateDirectoryForPictures methods, 124
    device features (camera), 125–127
    IsThereAnAppToTakePictures methods, 124
    MainActivity class, 123
    sending e-mails, 128
    SetContentView method, 124
  application options, 134
  components, 116–117
  configuration, 113–114
  creation, 112
  debugging
    configuration, 130
    sample app running, emulator, 130
    tools, breakpoints and pads, 131
    Xamarin Live Player, 131
  emulators and SDKs, management, 136–139
  project options
    build options, 133
    default settings, startup activity, 136
    general tab, 132
    package signing options, 135
  references and NuGet packages, 116
  structure, 115
  user interface
    Android design tools, 118
    colors selection, 119
    declarative definition, 122
    Document Outline pad, 121
    material design color shades selection, 120
Android Virtual Device (AVD), 137
Apple ID, 3–4
Apple's software development kits (SDKs), 3, 18

Applications publishing
  archive creation, 140
  archive list, 167
  digital certificate, 141
  iOS distribution channel, 168
ASP.NET Core, 236
ASP.NET Core Web API services
  consuming services, Xamarin.Forms client
    C# code-behind, 278
    debugging and testing, 279
    GetOrdersAsync method, 276
    Get, Post, Put, and Delete methods, 276
    INotifyPropertyChanged interface, 272
    Orders.cs, 272–274
    PostAsync, UpdateAsync, and DeleteAsync methods, 276
    SaveOrderAsync and DeleteOrderAsync, 277
    System.Net.Http.HttpClient class, 274
    ViewModel class, 276–277
    XAML code, 277
  controllers, 264–265, 267
  data model, 263
  debugging and testing, 267–269
  dotnet command-line tool, 261
  entity framework core, 263–264
  identity, 267
  model binding, 267
  OrderContext.cs, 263
  project template, 262
  publishing, 270–271
ASP.NET Core Web applications
  Cognitive Services, 237
  computer vision service, 238–239
  controllers
    HomeController.cs, 245
    ImageContext class, 246
    ImageList, 248
    Index, 249
    JSON, 248
    MVC controller, creation, 245

© Alessandro Del Sole 2017
A. Del Sole, *Beginning Visual Studio for Mac*, https://doi.org/10.1007/978-1-4842-3033-6

Get the eBook for only $5!

Why limit yourself?

With most of our titles available in both PDF and ePUB format, you can access your content wherever and however you wish—on your PC, phone, tablet, or reader.

Since you've purchased this print book, we are happy to offer you the eBook for just $5.

To learn more, go to http://www.apress.com/companion or contact support@apress.com.

Apress®

Printed in the United States
By Bookmasters